Somebody's
CHILDREN

Somebody's
CHILDREN

The Politics of Transracial and Transnational Adoption

LAURA BRIGGS

DUKE UNIVERSITY PRESS
Durham and London
2012

© 2012 Duke University Press
All rights reserved
Printed in the United States of America on acid-free paper ∞
Designed by Kaelin Chappell Broaddus
Typeset in Arno Pro by Keystone Typesetting
Library of Congress Cataloging-in-Publication Data appear
on the last printed page of this book.

For Jennifer

Who tolerated long absences,
believed in this book,
listened to ideas and drafts,
and is the best editor, critic, friend,
and partner anyone could have

Contents

PART III

**EMERGING FIGHTS OVER THE
POLITICS OF ADOPTION**

Acknowledgments

This book is a product of many people, places, and conversations. It has accrued a ridiculous number of debts, and it's my pleasure to acknowledge some of them.

In these hard times in state universities, I am acutely conscious of all those who have contributed to building the material infrastructure that makes scholarly research possible. At the University of Arizona (UA), thanks to the Social and Behavioral Sciences Research Institute, the Center for Latin American Studies, the International Affairs Office, the Southwest Institute for Research on Women, and the donors of the Magellan Circle and the Women's Studies Advisory Committee, who supported my research and conference travel. Thanks too to the many colleagues and friends at UA who supported this project in myriad ways, from discussions over shared meals or when hiking and working out, or by generously reading, listening to, and discussing drafts: Adele Barker, Adela Licona, Mimi Petro, Liz Oglesby, Linda Green, Tsianina Lomawaima, Ruth Dickstein, my colleagues in the Department of Gender and Women's Studies, the Citizenship and Public Cultures reading group, the Department of History, and the Institute for LGBT Studies. Some of my best teachers and colleagues have been, in fact, graduate students—Karin Friedrich, Araceli Masterson, Lucy Lee Blaney, Wendy Vogt, Lauren Carruth, Wendy Sampson, Kate Goldade, Erin Durbin, Mari Galup, and Adrian Flores have all contributed to this project in ways large and small. Thanks, too, to Stephanie Sams and Robert Merideth for hard labor getting the manuscript ready for publication.

I am particularly grateful to the Tepoztlán Institute for Transnational History, a remarkable group of scholars who not only taught me a tremendous amount of Latin American history but also reshaped my understanding of the possibilities of scholarly collaboration. I couldn't hope for sharper readers, more supportive colleagues, or better friends (or more excellent tequila). My thanks especially to Pamela Voekel, Bethany Moreton, Gladys McCormick, David Kazanjian, Josie Saldaña, Ann Rubenstein, Micol Siegel, Elliott Young, Jocelyn Olcott, Nicole Guidotti-Hernández, and Beth Haas.

Some of my most profound intellectual debts are to the remarkable activists and intellectuals in Latin America who have searched for lost children or tried to imagine a world where mothers are less likely to lose them. The Mexico-North Transnationalism Foundation funded a summer's fellowship in Mexico. In Mexico City, I benefited immensely from the lively and incredibly smart feminist intellectual communities: the *Debate Feminista* collective; the Program in Gender Studies at the Universidad Nacional Autónomo de México, in particular Marisa Belausteguigoitia and Lucía Melgar; to Patricia Vega and Gabriela Cano, who opened their homes and libraries to me. Thanks to the many friends and teachers I found in an unforgettable week in the Zapatista community at Oventic, much of it spent in political conversation. In Guatemala, J. T. Way was an invaluable conversation partner and friend. The Centro de Investigaciones Regionales de Mesoamerica (CIRMA) maintains a remarkable archive that has assisted countless researchers; it is one of the sites in Guatemala where people have fought to insist that memory matters. Marco Garavito has been a tireless advocate for the children lost in Guatemala during the civil war through the nongovernmental organization Todos por el Reencuentro. Ila Abernathy and her Guatemala Project at St. Michael's Episcopal Church in Tucson, Arizona, arranged for me to walk through majority-Ixil highland communities forced to flee during the war, from whom numbers of children were disappeared. Thanks to members of the Communidades de Poblaciones en Resistencia, who opened their homes and shared their stories. In El Salvador, Darcy Alexandra helped open doors, and I am particularly grateful to Jon Cortina, S. J., and Zaira Navas at the Asociación Pro-Búsqueda de Niñas y Niños Despaparecidos, who helped me understand the broad political and human stakes in searching for disappeared children.

A fellowship at the Tanner Humanities Center at the University of Utah provided writing time for this book, and the humanities center seminar provided a close reading of chapter 1. Thanks to Susie Porter and Beth Clement for conversation and ideas, and to Kathryn Stockton and Shelley White for excellent adventures. Lisa Duggan, honorary Utahn, and Kathryn read drafts and listened patiently as I tried to figure out how to write them.

The Frances and Kenneth Eisenberg Institute for Historical Studies at the University of Michigan also provided a fellowship and excellent intellectual community. At the University of Michigan, in that visit and others, I benefited from the insights of Ann Stoler, Elizabeth Roberts, Jessaca Leinaweaver, Marcia Inhorn, Geoff Eley, Regina Morantz-Sanchez, Kathleen Canning, Mary Kelley, Phil Deloria, Fernando Coronil, and Alex Stern, most of whom read or listened to drafts, and all of whom did me the tremendous honor and favor of arguing with my ideas and historical accounts.

I have been lucky to find readers, colleagues, and friends among the people who work on adoption in the United States and Canada, including Karen Balcolm, Karen Dubinsky, Ellen Herman, Lisa Cartwright, and Rickie Solinger. I have also been generously and rigorously pushed by adoption scholars in Latin America and Europe, especially Diana Marre and Claudia Fonseca. Margaret Cerullo shared the GLDF files from the "Foster Equality" fight in Massachusetts.

Closer to home, thanks to Ana Ortiz, Maribel Ortiz, and Priscilla Palacios for their invaluable roles in nudging this book into existence. My greatest debt is to Jennifer Nye, who was unstintingly generous about this book, offered support and criticism at just the right times, and sometimes treated the writing of it as a problem akin to the flu, requiring meals and help with basic tasks of daily living. As a civil rights lawyer, she helped me see the way family law and Indian law provide the backbone of these questions. She has listened to every word of this—as ideas, as writing problems, as text—edited it, and finally made it a much better book.

In July 2005 the cover of *People* magazine read, "Angelina Adopts a Baby Girl!" The story was heartwarming. Jolie was adopting an orphan from Ethiopia whose mother had died of AIDS. Someone identified as "a source" by *People* told readers how to understand the event as a particular form of compassion and generosity. Jolie, said the source, "has a hunger about the world and helping people. The whole world is important to Angie, but she's very attached to Africa as a continent. Africa is a country [sic] of survivors. She identifies."[1] The child, subsequently named Zahara, was welcomed by the press with photos of her at the mall, with her newfound family, Brad Pitt tentatively figured as the father, and adopted sibling Maddox, from Cambodia. Although transnational adoption was a half-century old by 2005, and had involved significant numbers of parents and children since the 1980s, Angelina Jolie and other celebrity adoptions in the decade after 2000 marked for many the moment when it become undeniably mainstream, no longer exotic.

However, the sweet and tidy narrative of Jolie saving orphans by adopting them—the early twenty-first century's act of charity par excellence in an era of shrinking government and expanding faith in individual virtue that eschewed a previous generation's confidence in development policy (perhaps especially in a region like Africa, so obscure that it was hard for celebrities or *People*'s editors to remember whether it was a continent or a country)—proved unsustainable. Within months, the celebrity press had found the child's birth mother, Mentwabe Dawit, who turned out to be very much alive. Initial reports suggested that Dawit had been coerced into giving up her child by Wide Horizons for Children, the agency Jolie had worked with. Later reports had it that Dawit became pregnant as a result of rape, but she had, with her mother's help, initially tried to raise the child, whom she named Yemsrach. Poverty made that option impossible, Dawit said, and she watched as the child became too malnourished even to cry. Dawit fled, she said, rather than watch the baby die. Her mother took the baby to an orphanage. When Wide Horizons or maybe the orphanage contacted the baby's grandmother about legal relinquishment, she, not knowing where Dawit was, said that the child's mother had died—putting AIDS as the cause of death—perhaps an oblique reference to the act of sexual violence that had brought them all to this pass.[2]

A year and a half later though, Jolie was in the news again—this time with her image as the "good" adoptive mother repaired, the one who had avoided the pitfalls, illegalities, and unseemliness of transnational adoption that seemed increasingly in the news. Specifically, she was criticizing Madonna's attempt to bring a baby boy, David Banda, from Malawi to the UK in 2007. In an interview with the French magazine *Gala*, Jolie reportedly said, "Madonna knew the situation in Malawi, where [David] was born. It's a country where there is no real legal framework for adoption. Personally, I prefer to stay on the right side of the law. I would never take a child away from a place where adoption is illegal."[3] Madonna's story generated a great deal more hostility from the press than Jolie's adoption of Zahara; *Time* magazine asked, "Did Madonna Save a Life or Buy a Baby?"[4] Initial reports suggested that the baby's father, Yohane Banda, had relinquished the baby for reasons of poverty and his inability to care for the baby after David's birth mother died. (Madonna's subsequent adoption in June 2009 of another child, Chifundo "Mercy" James, reportedly for $12 million, raised more serious questions—about whether the child's father and grandmother even had consented to the adoption.)[5] Some objected that Jolie was in no position to throw stones; in addition to the discovery of Zahara's mother, new investigation had also cast a shadow over her adoption of her other, older child, Maddox. The agency from which Jolie had adopted Maddox, Seattle International Adoptions, was accused of fraud, and adoptions were later halted from Cambodia under a cloud of allegations of corruption and child stealing.[6] The *Time* piece went on to be positively scathing about Madonna adopting a child that had a living parent: "There are surely many millions of children who do not even have what Baby

David had, one loving, living parent close by."[7] But in fact, there surely were *not* many millions of children who have no parents. Full orphans, as many were coming to recognize, were rare, especially babies. In 2008 *Foreign Policy* called the idea that intercountry adoption was dominated by baby orphans "the lie we love."[8]

In the aftermath of the Haitian earthquake in January 2010, these two contrasting kinds of stories both got into play even more quickly, as they had come to represent well-worn pathways—good adopters and bad adopters, child rescuers and child stealers. They performed a kind of containment work: while there might be fraudulent or coercive practices in adoption, these exist only in some (bad) adoptions, preserving a space where adoption is an uncomplicated, good thing. For example, in a story that was extraordinarily well publicized, a group of Baptists from Idaho was imprisoned for picking up children in Port-au-Prince and attempting to take them across the border into the Dominican Republic without papers. And as it turned out, according to the AP newswire, none of the thirty-three children was an orphan; all had close relationships with family before they were packed into the Baptists' van.[9] Commentators were swift in their condemnation: this was child trafficking, and it was wrong.[10]

In contrast, though, the Pittsburgh-based group that airlifted a planeload of orphans out of Haiti from the BRESMA orphanage was understood in the press to be involved in child rescue. Now of course, the key thing that differentiated the Pennsylvania BRESMA group from the much-criticized Baptists is that in those first days after the earthquake, there was virtually no functioning government in Haiti to demand the children's papers, and the BRESMA group included the Pennsylvania governor Ed Rendell, who was brought on the trip because he had friends in the Obama administration who could ease visa problems. While much was made of the fact that the children were "in process" for adoption, it turned out that at least twelve of them actually were not (and were hence unadoptable, because they lacked proper court orders and visas). Furthermore, what it means that children's adoptions were not complete is that there were still supposed to be legal opportunities for their mothers to object, to ask for their children back. And it turned out that all or nearly all of the children *had* mothers, usually single mothers. It was single mothers who were inclined to drop off their children or have them recruited into orphanages—temporarily or permanently—as part of a broader family survival strategy.

When Jamie McMurtie, one of the evangelical women from Pittsburgh who ran the BRESMA orphanage, discussed how she got children, she spoke about persuading impoverished mothers to relinquish them. "Usually that's how we get orphans, the fathers leave," said McMutrrie. "Sometimes parents die or are too sick. But usually it's because the fathers leave and want nothing to do with the kids anymore." She told a story of how the orphanage began, when she traveled for hours into a rural area to find a family she had heard of, a mother with three children, who left her toddlers and young children home alone while she worked all day. The father had left the family and taken up with another woman, and McMurtie walked into this impoverished woman's home and persuaded her to give away her children. She took them back with her to Port-au-Prince where, with the support of her Pittsburgh church, she started an orphanage that housed them and similarly situated children. The children were sent into an adoption with a family in South Dakota.[11] Brutal material circumstances met early twenty-first century evangelical Christian gender politics, and the children of Haitian single mothers became "orphans" available for adoption to the United States. U.S.-based evangelical churches were involved in similar operations around the world, an extension of the Christian Right's intense affection for fetuses and their profound mistrust of the women who carry them. Even after these fetuses were born, the Christian Right did not much trust impoverished mothers to raise their children properly, unless there was a father involved.

The failure of simple, heroic narratives of rescued orphans is telling. The orphans turn out not to be orphans; money, troubling ideologies about single mothers, or the failure to respect legal parental rights corrupt the exchange; relatives' consent seems ambiguous or tempered with loss and tragedy. The dualistic structure separating stories of child stealing (like the Baptists and Madonna) and child rescue (like BRESMA and Angelina Jolie) can't be sustained ultimately, as there is often not much separating the facts to which these narratives are attached.[12] In this book I argue that if we want to understand adoption, especially intercountry and interracial adoption, we need to see that its practices do not resolve neatly into categories of coercive and innocent, good and bad. Adoption may sometimes be the best outcome in a bad situation, but it is always layered with pain, coercion, and lack of access to necessary resources, with relatives (usually single mothers) who are vulnerable. Stranger adoption is a national and international system whereby the children of impoverished or otherwise disenfranchised mothers are transferred to middle-class, wealthy mothers (and fathers). The relative power of these two groups, and the fact that stranger adoption almost never takes place in the opposite direction, sets the inescapable framework in which adoption is inserted. Further, *Somebody's Children* makes an argument that adoption, while a practice that affects a small and shrinking number of people, has been important to national and international politics out of all proportion to its numerical significance. Symbolically and actually, the politics of adoption and what happens to the children of vulnerable populations, usually single mothers, have been critical to Native peoples' sovereignty struggles, civil rights and the backlash against it, human rights, and the Cold War and its political and economic aftermath.

Toward a Different History of Adoption

We have begun to develop a more critical account of adoption, one that asks about it not as a celebrity event or a private, family decision but as one deeply embedded in the politics of race and poverty, gender and sexuality, and international relations and economies. For example, in the arguments of activist groups like Bastard Nation, we have an analysis and feminist account of why young women were sent to unwed mothers' homes in the 1950s and 1960s. They and others argue persuasively that beyond being an effort to help young women who had gotten "in trouble," the social effect of the unwed mothers' homes was a last ditch effort to protect the male-headed nuclear family from being supplanted or rendered as one possibility among many by families composed of unwed mothers and their bastard children—the derogatory language itself suggesting something of how effectively that possibility was being foreclosed.[13] From the distance of a generation and a radical transformation in women's ability to find decently paying work, it is clear that the conditions under which it was in the child's "best interest" to be separated from its mother were historically specific and, well, sexist. Daycare centers, improved (if far from equal) access to wages, and the declining significance of categories like "disgraced" women and "bastard" children have made it entirely possible (if not exactly easy) for single mothers, even young ones, to raise their children in the United States. In the 1970s and 1980s, it is probably true to say that this defense of the heterosexual patriarchal family failed, and the women's liberation movement, expanding employment opportunities for women, the declining stigma of divorce, and a feminist defense of the "nontraditional" family as such made space for single mothers and their children. In the decade after 2000 unwed mothers' homes had hardly disappeared, but they were less mainstream, being championed (and often funded) by Christian Right groups.

We don't, however, have a related account of what happened *after* the 1970s, when young white women stopped losing their children, for the most part, and the adoptable babies and children became disproportionately black, Latino, and Native, or came from overseas. We evade the *politics* of how these mothers came to lose their children and instead tell a demographic and "markets" story. We say that what happened in the late 1970s and 1980s with adoption is that the rise in the availability of abortion, birth control, and mothers' ability to raise their children alone resulted in a shortage of adoptable children, what some came to call, memorably, a "white baby famine."[14] This shortage met with another demographic shift —rising age at first marriage and rising maternal age at first birth—that was producing a structural increase in impaired fertility.[15] More and more women with access to education and careers (or female lovers and partners) were finding themselves involuntarily childless. This fertility gap was met in part through reproductive technology and in part through an expansion of the pool of adoptable children to include children overseas and, even for white parents in the United States, children of color.

I want to suggest that this account is inadequate, a description posing as an explanation. These demographic changes were the effects, not causes, of changes that were politically driven. The concern in the 1970s that there was a shortage of adoptable children was not even new, much less the cause of anything. In fact, every generation in the twentieth century faced a "baby famine." In the 1920s adoptable children were said to be so scarce that in 1929 the *Philadelphia Record* ran a front-page banner headline that read: "Chronicle of a Search for a Homeless Waif in Philadelphia—Where There Aren't Any."[16] In the 1930s Paul Beisser, president of the Child Welfare League of America, testifying unsuccessfully in favor of a bill to allow the entry of German, particularly Jewish, children for transnational adoption, said that on average there were twelve applicants for every adoptable child in the United States.[17] In the 1950s, similarly, when the American Child Welfare League first began placing children with disabilities, the organization justified "special needs" adoptions again because of the shortages in available (nondisabled) infants. In 1955 Estes Kefauver said, in opening the hearings on "black market" adoption: "There has been a tremendous increase over the last 10 years in the demand for children for adoption. As a result, the demand has far exceeded the number of babies available. This disparity has resulted in gross abuses by certain individuals who have exploited the situation commercially."[18]

If the period from 1920 to 1950 saw virtually continuous "crises" of shortages of children for adoption, the 1960s was an exceptional decade in the twentieth century, when increasing numbers of teens were having sex, birth control was hard to get, and a repressive apparatus rained down on the heads of girls who got "in trouble."[19] During that decade, the numbers of children placed in adoptions rose consistently, then the numbers began a steady decline after 1970. Abortion and birth control probably did not have a lot to do with that drop. The greatest single factor seems to have been the growing willingness or ability of single mothers to raise their children. The vast majority of unmarried mothers have always decided to parent their babies; before 1973 about 9 percent of all unmarried mothers relinquished their babies for adoption (this is an intensely racialized story, though; that figure is 19 percent for white women and less than 2 percent for black women). In the period from 1973 to 1981, this percentage declined sharply, to 4 percent for all births to unmarried women; from 1982 to 1988, it fell still further to just over 3 percent. There is still a further reason to think that the decline in adoptable children was a trend independent of abortion. Throughout the 1980s, as abortion rates held steady, relinquishments for adoption continued to decline.[20]

In order to understand the *politics* of the changes in adoption that resulted in the expansion of transracial and transnational adoption, and not just the demographics, we need to widen our lens beyond the largely white and middle-class women who are the subject of that primary narrative and pay attention to how black and Native women in the United States, and those outside the United States, came to give their children up for adoption, or lose them involuntarily, and understand that this story was governed in part by different cultural logics.

This book makes several arguments about the politics of adoption, particularly transracial and transnational adoption. The first is that twice in the twentieth century there was a huge influx of children of color into the child welfare system, where they created a considerable burden on state budgets. The earlier period was quite different for Native and African American families, although both in a broad sense were the result of shifts in the dynamics of race and poverty policy. The first, for Native families, began in the 1950s (when Aid to Dependent Children [ADC] programs for single mothers began to be extended to Native communities, in the aftermath of tribal termination, and when population increase and the loss of historical treaty rights to land, fishing, and water rights made more and more reservation economies unsustainable). Before then, states only rarely had much to do with Native children. The passage of the Indian Child Welfare Act (ICWA) in 1978 was the outcome in a broad sense of a sovereignty movement that recuperated as a politics a fundamental tenet of Indian law stretching back to the beginning of the republic: the United States made treaties with autonomous Indian tribes that never ceded their status as independent nations, a principle repeatedly affirmed by the U.S. Supreme Court. As such, to the extent they might enter into relations of legal protection or dependency (or exploitation, some would say) with the United States, they did so with the federal government, not state governments. ICWA was an important, albeit complex and limited, statement of Native sovereignty, at least over Indian children.

For African Americans, the first time significant numbers of black children entered the child welfare system was during the civil rights movement, when segregationists tried to make an issue of unwed black mothers and their bastard children to counter the image of black dignity and respectability being televised nightly as the peaceful protests of ministers like Martin Luther King Jr. and those often constructed as church folk who marched and sat in were met by the police's apparently out of control violence. The fight to control the behavior of young black mothers mirrored that being waged in the white suburbs, where girls were at this same time being forced into unwed mothers' homes by their parents, but the African American "bastards" in question were considerably less likely to be babies, and it was welfare case workers, not family members, social workers, and psychologists, who were plucking children from their unmarried mothers.

The second struggle over interracial adoption was a moral panic two decades later in relationship to "crack babies" and fetal alcohol syndrome (FAS), which together constituted a moral panic about the health of babies and children that, like fights over segregation and welfare mothers in the 1960s, once again pushed thousands of additional children into foster care. In the 1980s, crack babies became the poster child for the War on Drugs, a tremendously successful effort in Reagan-era America to demonize the poor and push back racial justice claims.

In speaking of these events as a "moral panic," I am deliberately invoking the work of cultural studies scholars in Britain, who have noted how a certain kind of policing gave rise to Thatcherism, close kin to what we in the United States called Reaganomics and Latin Americans and Europeans call neoliberalism. Specifically, this was the public policy initiative in the 1970s and 1980s to shrink government, reduce taxes, redistribute wealth upward, and disinvest in the poor. In the British account of Thatcherism, a particular kind of social crisis, a moral panic about what was taken to be a sudden rise in street crime, specifically mugging (particularly by black youth), spun a whole tale about what was wrong with postimperial Britain and what its remedies might be. What followed was not just harsh sentences for young "muggers" but a whole rhetoric of a return to "tradition" and an expanding, more coercive state role in policing a growing struggle over race, class, international migration, and the economy.[21]

Ruthie Gilmore, Angela Davis, and a collection of scholars, activists, and scholar-activists around a group called Critical Resistance gave voice to a similar set of analyses in the late 1990s and first decade after 2000 in and beyond the United States. What, they asked, are we to make of the steadily growing incarceration rates, particularly of black men? How are we to understand the extent to which this carceral system is run by private, for-profit companies? They suggest that this prison-industrial system is likewise playing a coercive role in regulating the economy and growing class and racial conflict over sanctioned impoverishment and disenfranchisement of racially aggrieved groups, but in the context of a shift from what was at least theoretically a purely state-organized activity—policing and imprisonment—to one that is increasingly about the growth of a private sector that acts in the name of a public sector.[22]

This book sets out to add another layer to these accounts of policing, to notice the pivotal role that the policing of mothers played in the reorganization of race, the state, and economic resources in the last two decades of the twentieth century. It argues that the case for the neoliberal withdrawal of state support for impoverished people, families, and communities was accomplished to a significant extent through a narrative about race and reproduction: specifically, an account of "crack babies" and FAS that sanctified the War on Drugs and other forms of policing and incarceration as protection of the "littlest victims," reinvigorating an old culture of poverty tale in which poverty was caused by bad mothers. The demonization of black and Latino "crack mothers" and Native women perpetrating "genocide" against their children by drinking during their pregnancies sanctioned a massive disinvestment in communities of color and enabled liberals to join the conservative "Contract with America" Congress to shift welfare policy away from providing support to mothers to placing impover-

ished children in (fairly explicitly white) middle-class households as adoptees. The unique characteristic of this new decade's shifting of children of
color from their birth families to white families is that it was done in the
name of *anti*racism: in the context of a reinvigorated argument that black
and Native children were the subject of racism, "languishing" in foster care
because of race-matching policies that preferred placement in black or
Native homes, when so many white families were anxious to adopt.

A second argument of this book is about intercountry adoption. Asking
how mothers outside the United States lost their children is more challenging, because to do it properly (and not just in terms of how we in the
United States or Western Europe view them) requires attending to the
myriad policy and economic changes, to say nothing of wars, that compose
the microclimates and social geographies in which individual mothers
relinquish or lose their children. For this reason, I have narrowed that
question to Latin America, particularly Guatemala. The book does not
consider extensively the histories of adoption from Asia, except to offer a
broad lens through which to view adoption in general. I leave that project
to others, and am grateful that a number of excellent accounts have begun
the work of telling this story in a way that is sensitive to the nuance and
context of local stories in sending countries, particularly Eleana Kim's
Adopted Territory for Korea and Sara Dorow's *Transnational Adoption* for
China.[23] Building on their work, this book takes on the project of narrating
the story of adoption from Latin America.

In fact, there are good reasons to attend to Latin America, both for its
own sake and as a particularly brutal case study of the politics of adoption.
Guatemala in 2006 was the country with the highest per capita rate of
adoption in the world,[24] virtually the only place where gay and lesbian
adopters were welcomed, and a place where adoption was all but unregulated, highly lucrative, and the site of a fair bit of small-scale mob violence.
This story matters immensely because it is one of the possible *futures* of
transnational adoption: very high rates from small groups of tremendously
economically, socially, and linguistically vulnerable groups.[25] Social upheaval on the scale of the attempted genocide in Guatemala is perhaps *the*
essential precursor to any kind of massive intercountry adoption program:
war or economic upheaval that so tears the social fabric that those who
want to raise their children cannot, and those who do not wish to raise
their children cannot find help or friends or family who can take them in.
Where dropping a child off at an orphanage, temporarily or even perma-

nently, becomes one of the reliable strategies mothers use to get food or medical care for their child, transnational adoption thrives.

We also need a history of adoption from Latin America because in the 1970s and into the 1980s, Latin America led the world as a sending region for children in intercountry adoptions (South Korea still had the largest single number for any one nation, but Latin America had the largest combined numbers as a region).[26] Greg Grandin makes the argument that most of the strategies employed by the Bush administration in the war in Iraq—from torture to paramilitaries to relying politically on the strength of the Christian Right—originated in U.S. policy in Latin America in the 1980s.[27] A similar argument can be made for adoption—the dynamics of nations opening and closing to international adoption, struggles over whether it should be the domain of state actors or private ones, the status of gay and lesbian adopters, the question of what happens to children when citizens of the region move to the United States or Europe as immigrants, the question of kidnapping—all of these questions have been vetted by national publics as much or more in relation to Latin America as elsewhere. It was, along with Korea, the place where the legal, visa, and economic relations of international adoption were worked out. It is a region that has a feminist tradition of activism objecting to adoption, most famously in the Asociación Madres de Plaza de Mayo and the Asociación Civil Abuelas de Plaza de Mayo of Argentina who protested against the Cold War, anti-Communist kidnapping of children and their placement, sometimes with the approval of a judge, in adoptions, including adoptions by members of the military or torturers who participated in killing their parents. More recently, too, the Guatemalan feminist group Sobreviventes helped stop adoptions from that country by holding hunger strikes and publicizing the role of kidnapping in providing adoptable children to U.S. agencies and would-be adoptive parents. This tradition among Latin American feminists, of speaking as mothers and grandmothers on behalf of lost and disappeared family members, and against impunity for agents of the state that participated in their disappearance, provides a powerful counternarrative to those who would prefer to start with the assumption that adoptable children are orphans, unwanted, or being separated from abusive or neglectful parents.

In the decades since the 1960s the context in which we might think about questions of reproduction, family, women, and gender in Latin America have changed considerably. Development policy, with its obsessive focus on overpopulation, contraception, and sterilization, has largely faded from view. People who might at least be broadly understood as feminists have come to dominate groups like the Population Council and similar NGOs, advocating women's empowerment over the more coercive terms of contraceptive "acceptors" and "refusers." At the same time, the conservative antiabortion (and anticontraception) strain in the Catholic Church joined forces with the emergent transnational evangelical Christian Right to promote U.S.-style culture wars over contraception, abortion, abstinence, and HIV, with adoption being offered up as an alternative to abortion. The notion of reproductive rights has been transformed almost beyond recognition from a demand on the state by peoples and populations for justice, fairness, and freedom from coercion (articulated alongside human rights). Instead, it has become a struggle between an individual's "right to life" or "right to choose." The problem with framing the questions as the right to choose (abortion, adoption, raising a child), as Rickie Solinger and others have pointed out, is that it only makes sense in the context of consumerism, with individuals picking and choosing between variously enticing but essentially equivalent things (what we might call the *Juno* narrative, after the film released in 2007).[28] I don't know any woman who felt at any point in her life that she could exercise some free choice for a preference between abortion, adoption, or raising a child the way one opts for cheesecake rather than chocolate cake in a cafeteria. These choices, are on the contrary, ferociously constrained by material circumstances or the place women are in their life course or both.

This is the backdrop against which adoption is being debated. Mario Reyes, arrested in Arizona in 1999 for "trafficking" children from Mexico into adoptions in the United States, defended himself by explaining that he was a devout Catholic, and he was trying to prevent abortions.[29] The Central American wars and their complex aftermath are incomprehensible without understanding that Reagan and his right-wing allies in Central America were actively promoting the U.S.-based Christian Right's involvement in the region at the same time that they were calling liberation theology priests and catechists "terrorists" and allowing their murder by death squads.[30] The ideology of overpopulation has largely disappeared, allowing adoption to proceed for the most part from countries with quite low birth rates (Korea, with one of the highest rates of adoption after Guatemala from 2000–2005, has birth rates below replacement levels).[31]

We need to attend to the ways neoliberal globalization has transformed the politics of adoption—and, in fact, how the symbolics of adoption and unwed pregnancy have done ground-clearing work for those who sought freer markets and less government. As Lisa Duggan argues in her essential book, *The Twilight of Equality?*, the "culture wars" over sex and family within the United States did economic policy work—providing good reasons to shrink states and expand the region of the "private" in the service of a neoliberal rationality. States should not be involved in supporting unwed mothers in the United States, since such measures are controversial and offensive to the pious. What we got as a result was not actually a contraction of the state—the federal government in fact became involved in measures to promote abstinence until marriage, marriage classes for the welfare dependent, and the massive expansion of the foster care system. But we did win an agreement that the safety net should be shredded, because, well, the poor were (all) unwed welfare mothers who didn't want to work. With the end of the Cold War we saw something similar happen in places like Guatemala: Latin America did not need development, or access to birth control—which the Christian Right redefined as cultural imperialism—it needed strong markets, relief from the burden of providing social welfare measures, strong families, a network of NGOs and church groups to provide for displaced children, and the ability to send impoverished infants to families in the United States who could care for them. Adoption was indispensable to the neoliberal economic and political order.

By the 1990s virtually the only white, middle-class young women going to unwed mothers' homes were the daughters of the Christian Right, like Billy Graham's granddaughter Windsor, who at the age of sixteen was sent to an unwed mothers' home out of state, where, in her mother's sober and perceptive later assessment, "she felt manipulated and trapped."[32] The Christian Right held on to an earlier generation's resistance to birth control, young women's sexual autonomy, and mother-and-child families. It produced a whole massive (and profitable) network of unwed mothers' homes, largely in Sunbelt states like Arkansas and Texas, that place children in adoptions across the United States. This, though, was no "residual" or "archaic" ideology of family and adoption but a cultural innovation as substantive as the feminist one, a response—akin to the British public's responses to mugging —to the demand for a return to an imagined "tradition" in light of what were construed as the shocking upheavals that rapid social change represented. In the view of the U.S. Christian Right this unraveling of the social fabric was caused by cultural changes in what could be said publicly about family, including homosexuality and abortion. In response, it offered a selective return to tradition, one that interestingly prioritizes resistance to abortion and, somewhat later (as we will see in chapter 7), homosexuality. Thus, it is possible if not necessarily ideal even for such iconic evangelical, Christian Right girls as Windsor Graham (with her second out-of-wedlock teen pregnancy) and Sarah Palin's daughter Bristol actually to raise their children as single mothers, a considerable shift from a half century earlier but consistent with making abortion (not premarital sex, not unwed family making) the cardinal sin.

The third and final argument this book makes is about two groups whose status has risen and fallen in the decades since the Cold War's end: lesbian and gay people and immigrants. In the 1970s, in the context of feminism and an emergent lesbian and gay liberation movement, lesbian mothers (and a few gay dads) began to fight for the right to raise their children when they left marriages, but hysteria about gay sex and its supposed association with child molesting made this struggle sharply contested, along with a parallel one in the 1980s and 1990s for gay adoption. Increasingly, though, as an economist logic that bordered on a free-market fundamentalism rose to dominate political commonsense in the United States, respectable, middle-class gay people came to be seen as less threatening to children and more of a resource to state governments burdened with providing for "hard-to-place" children as the terrain of immorality shifted for all but the Christian Right from the dangers of sex to the dangerous classes of the poor.

Neoliberal globalization had more ambivalent effects on the children of immigrants, as some of the same populations disrupted by Latin America's civil wars were displaced again, this time as a migratory labor force moving to the United States and Europe. While some saw their horizons expanded by this displacement, we have also in recent years seen rising numbers of U.S. citizen children of immigrants taken into foster care as their parents have become more vulnerable to deportation (the United States is not unique in this regard; the same trend is broadly true in the European Union). To the extent that losing children is an index of political or social vulnerability, these two trajectories—of gay people becoming adoptive parents and immigrants losing their children—suggest the rising (but contested) status of queer folk and the declining fortunes of immigrants to the United States.

The Policy Questions

Adoption has been the subject of considerable public policy debate over the half century after 1960. Although these questions have drawn in many hundreds of commentators over the years, in the two decades from 1990 to 2010 one of the most visible and vocal has been Elizabeth Bartholet, an articulate spokesperson for many of the arguments that this book takes issue with. Bartholet has written extensively and been quite active in promoting easier adoption internationally through her Harvard Child Advocacy Program, which has challenged human rights treaties that effectively limit adoption by protecting birth parents' rights,[33] and her advocacy within the United States of policies that make it easier for white families to adopt children of color and, hence, at the same time make it easier for mothers who want them to lose them, which we will see at greater length in chapter 3.

One of the most powerful and compelling moments in Bartholet's writing about adoption is in her autobiographical book, *Family Bonds*. There, Bartholet tells the story of how she left for Lima in the fall of 1985 to adopt the first of two Peruvian infants she would raise. She wrote that she worried about whether her clothes were appropriate; she struggled to prove herself competent as a potential parent to lawyers and officials and was terribly frightened that she would lose "her" children to a legal system she did not understand, communicating in a language she did not speak. She wrote, "I am now engaged in what will be an eight-week process of legalizing our bond, our connection. This process of making him 'my child' as a matter of law will be an agonizing one, in large part because of the threat that this person who already feels like part of me will be taken from me." In the opening pages of the book, she tells the story of her vulnerability with reference to a night in which she fearfully carried "her" two-week-old child down thirteen flights of stairs in the dark, with far too much cash in her pocket to feel safe from petty thieves, with the electricity out as a result of a bombing near her apartment by the Maoist guerilla group Sendero Luminoso, the Shining Path.[34] She tells a vulnerable and moving narrative and returns to argue (uphill, she would say) for the legitimacy of her family by adoption in the face of overwhelming bias for biological bonds.

This move is a characteristic one in constructing narratives about adoption that have the effect of limiting birth parents' rights to their children: the invocation of the vulnerability of the child and the would-be adoptive parent, together with the powerful impulse to protect this child from what

is often construed as a "social nakedness,"[35] an infant alone, without parental protection. Yet there is something troubling about this narrative, something too quick about the scare quotes that designate the legal work of, as
Bartholet says, "making him 'my child' " essentially superfluous to the
emotional bond that has already, after ten days, made the child part of her.
The child whom she calls Michael has birth parents, though she never
refers to them; the legal process is at least theoretically intended to ensure
that their rights are respected and to provide a forum for any grievance or
objection they might raise. And despite Bartholet's sense of vulnerability,
her status as a law professor, from Harvard no less, and a U.S. citizen in
Latin America at the height of U.S. Cold War preoccupation with the
region (and its "terrorists," as the guerillas were consistently named), defines power relations between her and the birth parents that are uneven in a
much different direction than the one she maps. Without minimizing the
real fear that Sendero Luminoso inspired in Peruvian civilians, it is possible
to notice that invoking Latin American Marxists imperiling U.S. mothers
and children is hardly an original story—it reads, rather, as an effort to
incorporate brown children born in Peru into a familiar account of endangered American-ness. And indeed, this sets up the narrative structure of the
book (as it opens onto policy pronouncements): all Peruvian children are
innocent, vulnerable, sick, or crying; all Peruvian adults are threatening,
corrupt, takers of bribes, thieves, or terrorists.

In the one passage where Bartholet does acknowledge the existence of
birth mothers, some are portrayed as "having no good choices," while
others take pleasure in their decision to send their child to the "land of
opportunity." Yet even this marginally sympathetic characterization of
birth mothers is cut short—managing one clause of one sentence in a 276-
page book—and contrasted with young children in Peruvian foster care,
crying alone after being knocked down on a playground, with "birth parents who may never visit and have no apparent ability to function as
parents," and the grief of a would-be adoptive parent whose prospective
child was taken away a few days after she met her, ostensibly because the
birth parent wanted her back but probably, Bartholet thinks (though she
offers no evidence), because some Peruvian official was not given a bribe.[36]
As the historian Rickie Solinger notes, "Americans who have portrayed ICA
[inter-country adoption] as primarily a child rescue mission have tended to
define the situation in ways that insist that the biological mother doesn't
really count," citing Bartholet as a key example.[37] One might add that
adoptive parents are portrayed as vulnerable, endangered, and fearful,

while birth parents are portrayed as cold, indifferent, or (at best) happily sending their children off to a land where they will have more material benefits.

In *Nobody's Children*, Bartholet sets the terms of the discussion most starkly, beginning with the book's title, which ironically uses English common law's name for a bastard child, *filius nullius* (nobody's child, the child of no man), reminding us again how much these are fights rooted in marriage and legitimacy. In it, she discusses domestic U.S. policy, making a polemical case to limit the time that children spend in foster care in favor of adoption, which she suggests is always the best alternative—arguing that mothers with troubles and temporary or permanent foster parents (whether kin, like grandparents, or strangers) leave a child "without what you might call true parents."[38] She supports twelve-month timelines for mothers (or fathers) to reunify with their children, far shorter than was customary in the 1990s, so that these children can stop languishing in foster care and be adopted. She is suspicious of kinship foster care and adoption, suggesting that family members may do it for the money: "When foster and adoptive stipends are paid to abused children's kin, neighbors, and racial look-alikes, these stipends are going disproportionately to the relatively poor and to racial minority group members. The service and stipends may seem far from generous. But they compare well to what exists in the absence. Foster parents are paid stipends that are significantly more generous than typical welfare stipends."[39] In addition to the apparent assumption here that if mothers and children are struggling, their kin must be on welfare, Bartholet argues that kinship foster care is potentially a bad idea because many of the grandparents or aunts who might provide it come from similar backgrounds to the parents themselves —part of a multigenerational cycle of abuse. Group homes she calls "not good places for children to grow up." Foster care, together with parenting judged abusive or neglectful, creates what she calls "modern day orphans," and she argues for adoption as the only good alternative.[40]

Foster care, Bartholet believes, should be a much smaller system than it is, and children should spend less time in it. She argues that there are essentially two reasons why as a matter of public policy we consign children to what she sees as a self-evidently harmful system, often for long periods of their childhood: policies that favor family reunification and "race-matching" policies that, she argues, prevent white families from adopting children of color. Both, she argues, need to be eradicated. Her article published in 1991, "Where Do Black Children Belong," as well as congressional hearings on race-matching policies in the run up to the

Multiethnic Placement Act of 1994 and the Interethnic Provisions of 1996 (MEPA-IEP), reactivated a vigorous public debate about race and adoption that had receded in the decades since the National Association of Black Social Workers' Statement in 1972 and the debate from 1968 to 1978 about whether jurisdiction over Native children should reside in tribal courts or state courts that culminated in ICWA.

In the Alternative

This book makes a different kind of argument. If we open up the historical record, it suggests, we find that the conditions under which black and Native women in the United States and Latin American mothers lost their children into adoptions are rather more troubling and, indeed, violent than Bartholet's and similar accounts would lead us to believe. One of its broadest goals, then, is to narrate a history of adoption that pays as much attention to the position of those who *lose* children in adoption as to those who receive them.

My own interest in transnational and transracial adoption began in 1999, when I and my then-partner became foster parents of an eleven-year-old Mexican American girl, the child of immigrants (who may or may not have had indigenous, Yaqui-Mexican ancestry). I am Anglo, my partner, Puerto Rican. In 2000 my partner adopted her. I was prevented from adopting her, not because of race, but because the state in which we lived prohibited (and prohibits) a child from legally having two mothers. The state of the national debate about race matching in adoption seemed significantly at odds with our "on the ground" perception of it, which encouraged me, as a historian and analyst of race and reproduction, to pursue the subject further.

Furthermore, as a lesbian with no legal right to my child, I was particularly sensitive to the fear of losing one's children and sometimes identified more with parents who had lost their kids to foster care than with my class peers, the caseworkers and lawyers in the child welfare system. As our social circle expanded to include more and more people with kids with a history of abuse, people who had, or were threatened with, losing their children, sometimes I was horrified at the reasons Child Protective Services (CPS) took kids: irregular school attendance by the child, seemingly manageable parental mental illness like bipolar disorder, and homelessness. In addition, as a gender and women's studies professor for more than a

decade, I've known CPS workers, too, former students with no more training than a bachelor's degree in women's studies or psychology, sometimes
sheltered young women or men who have admitted to me their complete
sense of inadequacy in the face of even understanding what is going on in
the families they investigate.

It also seemed apparent to us from our experience with social workers,
from attending foster- and adoptive-parent trainings and support groups,
and developing an extensive local network of friends and acquaintances
involved in fostering and foster adoption that strikingly little attention was
being paid by anyone to race matching for the black and Latino children
whom we knew in foster care and public adoption services, and this had
been true for at least the past decade. When I attended parties and picnics
first for foster children and then for adoptive children, nothing about the
hundreds of families I saw indicated to me that anyone had sought racial
matching. Furthermore, my daughter had spoken only Spanish when first
removed from her birth family in 1990; she was not then or ever, until she
came to our house, placed with anybody who spoke Spanish. When we met
her in 1998 she was attending a school where the only nonwhite kids were
foster children from a particular group home, and they were cruelly teased
in racist ways. It is hard to find an all-white school in the urban Southwest,
but the foster care system, in its wisdom, had found a white and wealthy
enclave in which to isolate these kids from the majority Latino and Native
school systems nearby. All her foster parents had been white, except for
one, who was African American. In apparent ignorance of ICWA, we were
also invited to think about adopting a Native child. When we responded
skeptically about the legal framework for such an adoption, the social
worker responded: "What's ICWA?"

I was also struck by the strangeness of the assumption that what was
happening in foster care was "languishing," and that adoption was always a
preferable alternative. While "languishing" evokes an image of children
sitting on suitcases, in the circles I moved in children in foster care seemed
busy—going to school, going to therapy, visiting parents, playing with their
foster siblings and friends. Adoption did not seem like the best alternative
for all of them, nor did foster care always represent a bad alternative—and
certainly not an alternative in which they were unloved or bereft of support
or guidance. The foster parents I knew were generous, compassionate
people with terrific skills with kids; not at all what I had expected from the
public conversation. I met plenty of grandparents raising grandchildren
whom they adored (and to my knowledge, none were on welfare). While

they were universally furious at their children for the ways they had messed up their own lives and those of the grandchildren, they never said adoption was their first choice. They knew how their grandchildren never stopped missing their parents and hoped that leaving open a route to being with their children again might provide a path toward sanity and healing for their own sons and daughters.

For my daughter, legal adoption was a disaster. It created a painful sense of divided loyalties, for no matter how we tried to offer her an alternative narrative, she believed (and not without reason) that adoption creates an exclusive relationship with one family that terminated all relatedness to the other family (and it certainly did not improve her relationship to adoption that only one of the two people raising her could legally adopt her). Foster care does not disrupt the possibility of a continuum of kinds of family relationships the way adoption does. Ironically, while the adoption community in general is moving toward greater openness, and maintaining ties with birth parents, in foster care policy we are trying to shut down the one legal mechanism that really does allow children to have two sets of parents. Furthermore, as increasing numbers of children in the United States are raised in stepparent and blended families, a broad cross-section of the population has experience with nonexclusive relationships where children belong to more than one family. Arguments that foster care represents inferior parenting relationships because they are not exclusive rest, at least in part, on an outmoded nuclear family ideal.

Adoption also creates material challenges not faced in foster care. For us, it terminated many health-related benefits my daughter had received as a foster child. Since there is virtually no private health insurance plan that provides very much in the way of mental health benefits, this was no small loss.[41] Indeed, it was not long after her adoption that I came to realize that from the point of view of most of the state mental health workers whom we encountered, adoption had terminated not only her entitlement to some services but also her need for any (since family cures everything), which was, not incidentally, tremendously helpful for their budgets.

Our daughter came to us from a painful past, and prior to federal-level changes that provided bonuses to states and agencies for adoptive placement, she had been identified as a child who ought not be adopted—the exact sort of assessment to which Bartholet has so strenuously objected. Yet while she, at the age of thirteen, and we were compelled by the narrative that the agency therapist told us, that most of her struggles would abate when she was adopted, on the contrary, they turned into a full-fledged nightmare. Although she felt close to us, she spoke often about how family triggered her, setting off cascades of painful memories and feelings, and how group homes were easier.

For my daughter, there was considerable pain and trauma in her young life, and one of those traumas was being removed from her birth family. If there is a glimmer of hopefulness in her story, it is that when she turned twenty, she decided she wanted to have a relationship with her birth family—although that is full of its own complications; they are hardly the relatives I would choose for her. Nevertheless, that decision seems to have opened up some new possibilities for her life. For me, she obviously became "my daughter" without legal adoption or exclusivity; for her and my then partner, legal adoption created new problems without adding anything to their existing relationship. Had we not adopted her but continued as her foster parents, she would not have been any less our child, but she would have had access to additional resources and maintained the legal form, at least, of her relationship to her birth family, which I suspect would have spared her a good deal of pain.

While this experience does not make me antiadoption, for older children or anyone else, I *am* struck by the fact that smart social workers with twenty and more years of experience working in child welfare were correct in their judgment that adoption was a bad idea for my daughter—and were overruled by funding-starved local agencies who, in response to federal incentives made available in the 1990s (in response to Bartholet and others), pushed adoption as the correct course for all children. If our experience does not point in any one, singular direction as the right or wrong way to negotiate foster or adoptive relationships, federal policy does, requiring that a "permanency" plan—either family reunification or adoption—be made within strict time limits, usually a year.

For a scholar like me, there is a tremendous advantage to actually having raised a foster child. Although many scholars make pronouncements about the foster care system, it is actually surprisingly difficult for scholars to get empirical data about children in care or even to accurately describe child policy. Generalizations about foster care are ridiculously hard to make because there is not *a* foster care system in the United States but diverse systems in fifty states, eight U.S. territories and possessions, 562 federally recognized Indian tribes, and the District of Columbia. Institutional review boards at universities put up considerable—and perhaps appropriate— obstacles to studying "vulnerable" populations like foster children; the adoption placement agencies I contacted guarded the privacy of adoptees and birth parents jealously, even from inquiries about things that took place decades ago. Until recently there was no national reporting system that even tracked something as basic as the number of children in these diverse foster care systems. Even in 2010, state-level tracking systems were sufficiently different that getting relevant data was extremely challenging. Caseworkers often have considerable latitude in determining what happens to children, so the kinds of things that may be recorded as policy (like "we don't take children for reasons of poverty") may or may not be enacted when an individual caseworker walks into somebody's house. Transparency is not a virtue embraced by child welfare systems, and the confidentiality promised to foster children can equally cloak malfeasance by the adults in the system, who include a complex mix of mental health providers, group home staff and administrators, lawyers, judges, foster parents, social workers, and welfare and child protective service caseworkers. While this book is not in any sense autobiographical, my nine years of experience with the child welfare system in a particular state do shape my questions and intuitions.

Outline of the Book

This book is composed of seven chapters and three parts. The first part is about adoption within the United States. Chapter 1 tells the story of some of the first feminists to defend unmarried welfare mothers from losing their children: the National Association of Black Social Workers, who argued that "black children belong in black families," not in white and wealthier counterparts. Chapter 2 explores the resistance to the Christian missionary assimilationism that sought the termination of American Indian tribes and the adoption and conversion of Native children. The American Association of Indian Affairs, born out of the land and cultural autonomy politics of the 1920s, fought for tribal sovereignty in child welfare issues, ultimately winning ICWA in 1978. Chapter 3 tells the story of "crack babies," FAS, and the reinvigoration of what we might call the Moynihan Report story: the problem with the poor is their disorganized, pathological families. However, Moynihan at least thought their families ought to be supported. Newt Gingrich promised to take the children of the poor and put them in orphanages. In a surprising alliance with feminists and liberals like Bartholet, this goal was transformed into moving those children into group homes and foster families and then out again, into adoptions.

The second part explores transnational adoption to the United States, beginning with chapter 4 on the birth of transnational adoption in the refugee crises and political conflicts of the 1930s, 1940s, and 1950s in the constitutive conflicts of the twentieth century: Communism and Fascism, first, and then Communism and "democracy" (or perhaps more accurately, U.S. and NATO anti-Communism). It argues that two crucial ideologies of adoption were born in these moments—solidarity and rescue. Participants in anti-Fascist solidarity movements began fostering child refugees from Franco's Spain and Hitler's Europe. An anti-Communist U.S. State Department promoted programs to foster children from behind the "Iron Curtain" after the Second World War and from Castro's Cuba after 1959, and evangelical Christians promoted adoption programs to save children from Communism and starvation after the U.S. wars in Korea and Viet Nam. Chapter 5 takes us to Guatemala and elsewhere in Latin America for the *guerras sucias*, the dirty wars, that composed the Cold War and follows a story that we don't much tell but should: the birth of transnational adoption from Guatemala in the kidnapping and disappearances of children from the families and communities of supposed leftists. Chapter 6 explores how the end of the war marked a turn to a hypercapitalism and the transformation of the problem of reproduction and reproductive governance from a concern about ideology—whether children would become Communists—to one about markets, on the one hand (whether enough children could be found to feed a vigorous market to the north in adoptable children), to, on the other, individualizing solutions to poverty and replacing community development with adoption.

Finally, the last part turns to the hottest parts of the culture wars in the United States in the first decade of the twenty-first century: struggles around the status of queers and immigrants. Chapter 7 notices how the position of lesbian, gay, bisexual, and transgender (LGBT) families has shifted: at first, lesbians were people who lost their children as a result of an account of the moral contamination caused by homosexuality. Now, there is a fight between the Christian Right, which actually has intensified its account in recent years of the moral danger to children of queer parents and queer adoption, and some states, which have found the privatization of dependency, specifically by allowing LGBT people to raise children, to be a positive good in a neoliberal state and thus have endorsed gay marriage as a way to ensure that children not become wards of the state. To end in this contradictory place is to mark the most recent site of contestation, over queers and over the state: whether laissez-faire will trump moralism or not.

The book closes with a brief epilogue about the increasing role of foster care and adoption as a placement for the U.S. citizen children of deported immigrants, often from Latin America. In a chilling reenactment of Latin America's dirty wars, parents are being disappeared off the streets by agents of Immigration and Customs Enforcement (ICE), leaving children at daycare, at school, and at home, from whence they sometimes make their way to U.S. foster care and adoption.

In studying adoption we also follow the traces of all the big stories of the last seventy or eighty years, because people lost their children in circumstances of exceptional vulnerability and powerlessness and because adoption was implicated in them. Civil rights and the struggles over race, indigeneity and the fight for self-determination, the rise of the Christian Right, struggles over socialism and neoliberalism—all took place surprisingly often with reference to adoption. A history of adoption tells us about the political shift from development and anti-Communism to individuals, rights, and markets in the relationship between "First" and "Third" Worlds. It tracks the rise of new transnationalisms and new forms of government and governance. It reveals the trajectory of the rise of the Christian Right in U.S. politics and international politics. It shows us some of the ways feminist and queer politics have given rise to new family forms. It tells us a great deal about race and the contradictory effects of neoliberalism. It may even, ultimately, reveal the emerging shape of repression against immigrants. Families are where we live our economic and social relations, and in families formed by law the fiction that families are "private," constituted in opposition to the "public," is laid bare as the fairy tale that it is.

PART I

Transracial Adoption
in the United States

ONE

African American Children and Adoption, 1950–1975

When we talk about "transracial" adoption, what we usually turn to is the controversy over "where black children belong," which followed on the National Association of Black Social Workers' (NABSW) statement of 1972. For example, in his book *Interracial Intimacies*, published in 2003, Randall Kennedy makes the NABSW statement the origin point and the site of continued resistance to placing black children with white families in order to set up a positive argument about the capacity of white parents to raise black children: "The late 1960s witnessed a small but significant upturn in the number of whites adopting blacks. . . . Then the NABSW announced its opposition and mobilized resistance. It got results, and almost immediately: in 1973 the number of black children adopted by whites declined, to 1,091 [from a high of 2,284]. In 1974 the total fell to 747." In the present, he writes, "although the NABSW statement condemning virtually all transracial adoptions has never been formally embraced by any jurisdiction in the post–Jim Crow United States, it has been and remains influential."[1] As the reference to Jim Crow would suggest, Kennedy goes on to argue that racial separatism in how we think about families does not lead to racial justice and that white parents can make outstanding and loving parents for black children. As an aside, though, it bears noting that the numbers alone might cast doubt on the continuing power of the NABSW statement: in 2003, when Kennedy wrote this, more than 3,310 black children were adopted by white families—a higher number than before the NABSW statement.[2] Similarly, Margaret

Howard argued in an article published in 1984 that the NABSW in 1972 had "condemned transracial adoption in terms so militant that transracial adoption fell by 39 percent in a single year."[3] These moves are characteristic of most scholarship on transracial adoption in the post–civil rights era: the NABSW was aggressively unreasonable and attacked well-meaning white parents as incapable of raising black children, and that move was detrimental to black children who were therefore denied loving homes with white families.

In contrast, Leora Neal, executive director of the NABSW chapter in New York City wrote in 1996 that

> The resolution was not based on racial hatred or bigotry, nor was it an attack on White parents. The resolution was not based on any belief that White families could not love Black children, nor did we want African-American children to languish in foster care rather than be placed in White adoptive homes. Our resolution, and the position paper that followed, was directed at the child welfare system that has systematically separated Black children from their birth families. Child welfare workers have historically undertaken little effort to rehabilitate African-American parents, to work with extended families, or to reunite children in foster care with their families.[4]

In a position paper in 1994 titled *Preserving Families of African Ancestry*, the NABSW suggested that the statement of 1972 had been widely misread, "Many thought that the organization's position focused exclusively on transracial adoption. Yet, this was one component of the position statement, which instead emphasized the importance of and barriers to preserving families of African ancestry." In these NABSW accounts, questions related to white families were effectively an afterthought, and references to Jim Crow are misplaced; the goal of the statement was to keep black families together.

Who is right? Should we understand the NABSW statement as primarily an attack on white parents' skills or an effort to keep black families together in the context of coercive separation of black children from their families dating back to slavery? The plainest reading of the statement is that it is a set of criticisms of white families. It reads, in part

> The National Association of Black Social Workers has taken a vehement stand against the placement of black children in white homes for any reason. . . . In our society, the developmental needs of Black

children are significantly different from those of white children. Black children [in Black families] are taught, from an early age, highly sophisticated coping techniques to deal with racist practices perpetrated by individuals and institutions. . . . Only a black family can transmit the emotional and sensitive subtleties of perception and reaction essential for a black child's survival in a racist society. . . . We fully recognize the phenomenon of transracial adoption as an expedient for white folk, not as an altruistic humane concern for black children. The supply of white children for adoption has all but vanished and adoption agencies, having always catered to middle class whites developed an answer to their desire for parenthood by motivating them to consider black children.[5]

This is strong language, and white parents raising children of color could surely be forgiven for believing that they were being criticized in harsh terms.

Yet if that point seems obvious, this chapter lays out a counterargument. Social workers had good reason to believe that a statement like this one—and perhaps only a statement like this one—could keep black families together. It also reads: "*We affirm the inviolable position of black children in black families where they belong.*" In 1972 black parents—single mothers, really—were losing their children in ways that were political. My contention here is that it was so self-evident to most observers that black or mixed-race children would be better off away from their unwed mothers and with white parents—for reasons of economic advantage, schools, housing, and the supposed "tangle of pathology" that the Moynihan Report and even President Johnson had identified as haunting the black family[6]—that in order to get any traction in an uphill argument that supported black single mothers, the NABSW *had* to identify defects in white families. It was not enough for the NABSW to show that African American mothers were entitled—legally and morally—to raise their own children. Just as twenty years earlier the NAACP had successfully argued that black children were psychologically and educationally harmed by segregated schools—in *Brown v. Board of Education*—the NABSW had to show a psychological benefit to black children to being raised in their own communities.

Although we rarely remember it this way, one of the crucial battlegrounds of the civil rights movement (and the black freedom movement in general) in the 1950s, 1960s, and 1970s was found in issues of single motherhood and reproduction. Sterilization—and laws mandating sterilization particularly of "unwed" black mothers, as well as taking black single mothers' children away—were tactics in the fight against rebellious black folk in the South. Southern white officials got a lot of traction for their opposition to the civil rights movement out of criticizing and even breaking up fatherless black families. In fact, as we will see, this is how the contemporary foster care system was born. The NABSW and other activist groups (including the Southern Nonviolent Coordinating Committee, SNCC) fought to uphold the "legitimacy," as it were, of single mothers and their families and to defend them against the myriad attacks that began to rain down on their heads: threats of jail and sterilization, and efforts to take the children of single black mothers who sought public assistance but maintained an "unsuitable home" for their children—which could mean exposed wires, lack of groceries, and all the failures to which impoverished mothers renting substandard housing and making do on woefully inadequate income are subject—but it mostly meant allowing a lover to stay the night.

Groups like the NABSW, SNCC, and the National Welfare Rights Organization may not have always used the word "feminist" to describe their politics, but on the key issues of sexual autonomy, illegitimacy, and the role of the state in paying wages for motherhood so women could raise the next generation, they were very much engaged in a battle on the same terrain as self-described feminists. Yet if feminists were largely successful in the 1960s and 1970s in taking much of the sting out of "illegitimacy," the notion of a "broken home," and making divorce easier and less stigmatized, these victories had the most force with respect to white and middle-class women. The broad cultural resistance to feminism in the United States landed most forcefully on the fertile, sexualized bodies of women of color, expressed in the lexicon of the unsuitable home and materialized as taking mothers' children and threatening them with sterilization.

This chapter argues that much of our scholarship has missed the point and the force of the NABSW statement and its astute diagnosis of the state of national politics and black mothers' grief.[7] Race, reproduction, and the politics of unwed mothers were *the* shoals on which the progress of the civil rights movement foundered. The failure of the feminism of the NABSW to carve out respect for the public citizenship of black and Latina women and their mothering provided opponents of both civil rights and feminism the tool to limit the gains of civil rights to the respectable and the middle class, ensuring that the guarantees of formal racial equality won by the movement did not change the race or gender of poverty. As we know now in hindsight, the politics of disgust for (always implicitly black, and by definition, unmarried) "welfare mothers" (who also bred crime, it bears remembering) became a crucial battleground for both the Democratic and Republican Parties nationally. It also, as we will see in chapter 3, became the grounding for the twin projects of neoliberalism, which were begun in this era of the 1970s: shrinking the state and defeating a vision of the state as a guarantor of equality.

But before we pursue that story, we need to look at other, countervailing forces that served at the same time to make black children adoptable and desirable—to see why so many thoughtful and well-informed people, white and black, were distressed by the NABSW statement. The civil rights movement unleashed powerful desires to build a "beloved community" in which black children had brighter futures than those promised by the Jim Crow South and ghettoes in the North (dreams symbolized memorably in the international media in the tears running down Jesse Jackson's face the night Barack Obama was elected president). At the same time, the extent to which out-of-wedlock births and "broken homes" were stigmatized—white and black, but especially black—gave rise to a climate in which many black professionals and church folk were deeply embarrassed by the apparent epidemic of single motherhood in black communities. Just as white suburban parents were horrified by their teen daughters' pregnancies and packed them off hastily to unwed mothers' homes, many black social workers sought to make the adoption system more available to black single mothers. That it was difficult to find placements for black and mixed-race children was an obstacle they sought to overcome, to make it possible for black women and girls to engage in the same strategies available to white girls who got "in trouble" to redeem and reform themselves and have respectable families.[8] These efforts sometimes included placing black children with white families (especially mixed-race children). Above all, though, these efforts proceeded by trying to remove obstacles for black families to adopt. Some programs, like Adopt-a-Child in New York City, redefined what constituted an acceptable adoptive family—from age to income to neighborhood—and sought to show that it was possible to do adoptions differently.

It is hard to overstate how much the 1950s and 1960s in the United States were saturated with Freudian anxieties about gender in general and mothers in particular, on the one hand, and adoption as a symbol of the new, postwar, antieugenic American order of things, on the other. In 1955 Philip Wylie's *A Generation of Vipers* gave U.S. culture the term "momism" to describe a smothering, overprotective mothering that bred men who were weak willed, tied to the apron strings, sniveling cowards overwhelmed by an Oedipus complex. Mothers were powerful people indeed, and as Leontine Young explained in her influential *Out of Wedlock* (1954), girls and women who became pregnant out of wedlock were deeply disturbed people who "may seek to use the baby to fill neurotic purposes of their own, and unless protected the child may become no more for them than a pawn in their . . . struggle."[9] Harsh as this judgment was, it turned out to be only about white unmarried mathers; Young identified black single mothers as in even worse psychological condition, for theirs was not an individual pathology but was rather part of a "social pathology." As Young wrote, "where poverty is combined with any considerable degree of social disorganization such as may be found in some of the overcrowded slum areas of large cities . . . the rate of illegitimacy is unquestionably higher. In these circumstances it becomes only one of a series of social ills." Lest there be any confusion about whether she was referring to African Americans in all but name, Young goes on to clarify by reference to the broadly antiblack attacks on Aid to Dependent Children (ADC): "Some of the attacks made upon . . . Aid to Dependent Children have focused upon unmarried mothers belonging to these socially disorganized groups. Unfortunately the attacks have failed to take into account the . . . fact that illegitimacy here is only one symptom of general social breakdown. . . . Any solution to the problem of illegitimacy here must begin with the basic social and economic evils which have caused this degree of group disintegration." Elsewhere, Young refers to a "cultural pattern" that "accepts as normal an out-of-wedlock pregnancy."[10] In this context, the insistence by those who sought to place black and mixed-race babies in adoptions that black mothers with out-of-wedlock pregnancies were pathological and in need of adoption was also, in a way, an antiracist act, a kind of affirmation that African American communities were not "socially disorganized groups" facing "social breakdown" and "group disintegration."

Black and Transracial Adoptions, 1950–1970

In the 1950s two major initiatives in the black community attempted to make adoption available to black children. The first, organized by the National Urban League, was a nationwide project on Foster Care and Adoptions for Negro Children, and it ran from 1953–1959, starting even earlier in some localities.[11] The project took a form typical for the Urban League: first, it launched a social study to demonstrate the existence and nature of the problem, then the group worked with local agencies to establish services to address the problem. Although the project was active across the country, the results in one locality, Kansas City, Missouri, were closely examined in the 1970s by Andrew Billingsley, a scholar of black families and children. There, the Urban League began by organizing a study-action committee. The study found that in 1952 only 3.9 percent of children adopted were black, although 12.3 percent of the population was black. The Kansas City Adoptions Department responded with what was by then already the classic rationale—there was no need for or interest in adoptions among African Americans; illegitimacy did not carry stigma, and black families would always make room for one more.[12] At a time when rural black children were suffering from malnutrition-related diseases like rickets and pellagra in notable numbers (and within a decade, some would be diagnosed with malnutrition by activist doctors who would write prescriptions for food[13]), the idea that there in fact *was* room for one more— and that neither the state nor private agencies had any responsibility for black children—was presumptuous indeed. And, unsurprisingly, the Urban League study found that these platitudes vastly misstated the nature of what was happening. There was a need for placements of children besides the birth mother and informal care; many African American children were already in out-of-home care—one in five of the children in out-of-home care in Kansas City was black, but only one in twenty-five adopted children was black. When black babies were not being placed in adoptive homes shortly after birth, they were being sent to foster care and other institutions as they grew older (and less adoptable). In Kansas City, most hospital-born black babies were born in General Hospital No. 2 (which accepted maternity cases without regard to marital status; others would not deliver the baby if the mother was unmarried), but no caseworkers from the adoptions department ever went to General Hospital No. 2. Inquiries to hospital staff revealed that about fifteen black mothers had asked about adoption at the hospital in 1952, but none had been referred to the adoptions department. It turned out that the Kansas City Adoptions Department had a strong financial incentive not to take black babies. Although officially a city service, the city paid only the department's utilities; for salaries and other expenses, the department had to rely on adoption fees. Since white babies were easily and quickly adopted, for fees, that is whom the department accepted. The study-action committee also found that while many black couples inquired about adoption at the adoptions department, few followed up, and interviews with twenty couples who had not completed their applications found that they had been discouraged by their contact with the (all-white) agency staff—that they were too poor, too old, had other children, or were simply judged unsuitable on sight.[14]

After the Urban League submitted its report to city government, the adoptions department, and the city's family court judges, the study-action group wanted to move forward with a demonstration project to show that there was need and there were adoptive families available. What happened next was a case study in bureaucratic stasis or the persistence of racist practices, depending on one's point of view: the leadership in Kansas City's city government stalled, launched yet another study of the problem, and, two years later, launched a small demonstration project that excluded all the members of the study-action committee and with no black people involved. The new demonstration project redefined the problem and sought adoptive homes for a broad category called "hard-to-place" children —older children, children with disabilities, and black children. Most of the children the group ultimately placed were white. So the net effect of six years of work by activists, sociologists, and social workers seeking adoptive homes for African American children was more adoptive homes for white children.[15]

The second major effort, also begun in 1953, was the Adopt-a-Child initiative launched by black social workers in New York City to place black and Puerto Rican children in adoptions. It was a major interagency effort, in which the workers in Adopt-a-Child recruited families through public forums, radio, community meetings, did intakes, and referred them to member agencies. In 1954 during the last year of the administrative organization of the project and before they began their recruitment work, the total number of black, Puerto Rican, Asian, and "other" children placed in adoptions in New York City was 115. In 1959, the last year of the project's existence, that number increased to 237, more than a 100 percent increase. Still, that number seems a good deal smaller than it might have been, considering the number of black and Puerto Rican families that the Adopt-a-Child project had screened and found eligible to adopt—1,134. Constituted as an interagency group, the black social workers could recruit and screen families, but for the actual placement of children they had to refer the families to the member agencies. The agencies rejected these families in massive numbers. The major reasons the agencies offered for these families' ineligibility were housing density (certain neighborhoods were deemed ill-suited to raising children by virtue of being overcrowded), age, absence of birth, marriage, or sterility certificates; mothers that worked;

income too low; and one or both members of the couple being unable to keep appointments during the day. For the social workers in Adopt-a-Child, these were unreasonable standards; it was almost as if being black by definition excluded one from adoption eligibility requirements. (Certainly, the housing guidelines reeked of redlining). Finally, although these criteria were gospel to many social workers, it wasn't really true that they actually made sense—there were children being happily raised by mothers who gave birth to them in all these neighborhoods, income levels, and employment situations—the guidelines were primarily a way of excluding white adoptive parents at a time when there were 182 inquiries by white families for every 100 white babies, according to one study.[16] (Another, from 1969, found 116 approved homes for every white child, but it acknowledged that many agencies simply stopped accepting inquiries when they had too many. Even more revealing, many agencies also admitted that even at that late date, they were still refusing to accept black infants because their budgets depended on adoption fees, and they believed black children to be unadoptable.)[17] Stiff exclusion criteria for prospective adoptive parents were profoundly unfair to black would-be adoptive parents and children when there were so few inquiries for black babies that agencies were doing everything in their power to keep black babies out of their service.

In the 1960s, however, efforts by black social workers, church people, and others (mostly women) finally began to bear fruit. Although the numbers were still not very large, a few big city agencies—in Los Angeles, Chicago, and New York—finally began placing black children for adoption. In 1967 the Los Angeles County Department of Adoptions, for example, placed 222 black children for adoption (albeit out of a total of 2,483 total adoption placements, which is to say that 8.9 percent of its placements were of black children).[18] A number of agencies in New York and Chicago also began making significant numbers of placements of black children in adoptive homes, including the Louise Wise Agency, a Jewish agency in New York City (which, even more remarkably, began allowing black women admission into its maternity homes). Still, the numbers remained small; in New York in 1967 Louise Wise placed 31 black children (out of 278 placements); Spence-Chapin, 54 black children (out of 465 placements); New York Foundling, 35 black children (out of 366 placements); and New York Department of Social Services, 67 black children (out of 130 placements); in Chicago, Cook County placed 52 black children (out of 92 placements) and Chicago Child Care, 53 black children (out of 107 placements).[19] By 1969 there were forty-seven organizations around the country designed to place black, Puerto

Rican, Asian, and Mexican American children, including Parents to Adopt Minority Youngsters (PAMY), founded in cooperation with the Minnesota Department of Public Welfare in 1961, and Minority Adoption Recruitment of Children's Homes (MARCH) in San Francisco.[20] Some agencies participated in setting up satellite agencies in black neighborhoods staffed entirely by African American social workers, creating essentially a parallel adoption system for black children and families. In New York, Louise Wise set up Harlem Dowling Children's Services, the most famous of these; they drew mixed responses from African American social workers, some of whom saw these agencies as much-needed compensatory practices, being in conspicuous contrast to the "insensitive" and discriminatory treatment black people received in the majority white agencies; others reportedly called Harlem Dowling "the plantation" and regarded working there as career suicide. In other places, black social workers and philanthropists set up autonomous agencies, including in Philadelphia, the Women's Christian Alliance, and in Detroit, Homes for Black Children.

No longer able with the same clear conscience to refuse to accept black and other nonwhite children for adoption, but largely unsuccessful at recruiting and approving black adoptive parents, agencies began to turn to the obvious alternative: social workers began placing black children in their "excess" white homes. By 1968 the Los Angeles County Department of Adoptions had placed more than one hundred children in transracial adoptions; Louise Wise, fifteen; and other agencies, a few.[21] Some of the earliest longitudinal studies suggest something about how agencies began placing these kids and how the families in which they placed them responded. On the one hand, much of their data found that children were happy, healthy, and well-adjusted; one major study put the percentage of "successful" adoptions at 77 percent.[22] At the same time the data also suggest that some agencies and social workers, in their enthusiasm to promote what they undoubtedly saw as politically progressive measures, sent black and mixed-race children into what had to have been difficult situations, just as some of the children in the highly publicized school desegregation struggles went into unwelcoming schools and communities. Lucille Grow, reinterviewing 34 families who had, in 1972, adopted a mixed-race (black and white) child three years later, found that 12 of these families still said that adopting a child of color had been "second choice" and would have preferred a white child if one were available.[23] Another, more extensive study of 125 families from all the cities except New York where significant numbers of transracial adoptions had taken place—Boston, Chicago, Los Angeles, Minneapolis-

St. Paul, Montreal, and Seattle—found children in sometimes questionable situations. Less than a third attended a school that employed any black teachers.[24] Nearly half were in all-white neighborhoods; another 45 percent were in predominantly white neighborhoods.[25] A third reported that all of their relatives were, at least in the beginning, opposed to their family adopting a mixed-race child.[26] Fourteen percent of the parents had not even told their adopted children that they had African ancestry, including a few whom the interviewers identified as having a "clearly Negroid appearance."[27] About 20 percent of parents were rated by interviewers as "not accepting" of their child's racial background, and an equal number identified their children as appearing more white than the interviewers did.[28] Sometimes, communities reacted with tremendous hostility to the adoption of black children by white families; in one much-publicized case, the family of a minister in an all-white community in Orange County, California, had a cross burned on their lawn and were subject to such unrelenting daily hostility that they gave the five-year-old mixed-race adoptive son back to the agency.[29]

This experiment in the 1960s with white families adopting nonwhite children was, then, of mixed success. It never represented very many children—one estimate has it at 5,383 in the entire period from 1968 to 1974, another at 12,000 for all the years before 1975 (by way of comparison: an estimated 4,200 black-white transracial adoptions took place in 2006 alone)[30]—and to some extent, agencies sent these children as emissaries of a utopian vision of a different, integrated world, which it was not always clear their families or communities wanted. On the other hand, one could argue that these adoptions were as or more successful than adoptions of older white children into white families, and whatever challenges awaited them in their adoptive families and communities, it was better than foster care or institutions. Then again, as we shall see, it is not always clear that those were the alternatives—to some extent, at least, the alternative may have been growing up with birth mothers who wanted them. And, as will be discussed below, rates of transracial adoptions apparently dipped in the mid-1970s (although the last year for which we have any good data at all is 1975, and some suggest that even these numbers underestimate the numbers of transracial adoptions), but the practice did not stop. Black infants and children had gotten on to the radar screens of private and religious agencies, and, for better or for worse, at least some black women and girls had the option of relinquishing babies and children.

Welfare, Illegitimacy, and the
Sterilization of Black Women, 1950–1975

At the same time that social workers and activists were debating whether (disproportionately middle-class, or at least "respectable") black women and girls could relinquish their children, and whether white couples should adopt those children, something much harsher was afoot for those unwed mothers of "bastard" children or those in "broken homes" who wanted to raise their children. "Illegitimacy," sterilization, and putting the children of black single mothers in foster care became a volatile site of struggle in the civil rights movement.

In the 1950s the mechanization of cotton picking meant the end of a way of life for African Americans—work in agriculture and the concentration of black Americans in Southern rural counties. At the same time, work in the Second World War defense industries—which had drawn many black people, including women, into cities or northward—disappeared as the country demobilized. As a result, the battle between South and North over access to black labor changed abruptly. In the 1940s some towns in the Mississippi delta had made it illegal for bus companies to sell black people a one-way ticket north or west, but entrepreneurs with cars and defense labor recruiters responded by running their own transportation services.[31] By the late 1950s rising black unemployment—in shantytowns and other segregated, substandard housing built up around now-quiet defense plants in the North and West and on the "wrong side of the tracks" in small Southern towns—meant that states, towns, and municipalities began competing with each other over who could come down most harshly on impoverished black people in an effort to drive this migratory labor force out of town. Adding heat to the debate was the fact that in 1954 Congress had eliminated the historic exclusion of those who worked in agriculture and domestic labor from eligibility for ADC, and for the first time there was some scrutiny of arbitrary denials of ADC benefits, especially in the South—which is to say, black women and children were receiving welfare in real numbers for the first time.[32]

When black women began getting welfare in Mississippi the state responded with rules that banned "immoral" and "unsuitable" homes—and expelled thousands of "illegitimate" children from the ADC rolls. Several years later, in 1959, Florida followed suit, expelling 14,000 "illegitimate" children and their siblings.[33] From 1958 to 1964 the Mississippi state legislature debated bills on sterilizing mothers and illegitimacy each year. In its final form in the 1964 session the bill made bearing or begetting an illegitimate child a felony, punishable by sterilization or three years in the state penitentiary. The rationale for this legislation was explicitly racist. The sponsor of the bill in 1958 claimed that "during the calendar year 1957, there were born out of wedlock in Mississippi, more than 7,000 negro children, and about 200 white children. The negro woman, because of child welfare assistance, [is] making . . . a business . . . of giving birth to illegitimate children. . . . The purpose of my bill was to try to stop, or slow down, such traffic at its source."[34] Some said the legislation was the work of the White Citizens' Councils, those civil rights-era groups organized to uphold white supremacy.[35] In a floor debate in the state legislature on the bill in 1964, one state legislator argued that "when the cutting starts, [the Negroes will] head for Chicago."[36]

These bills (and attacks on reproductive rights in general) were read, quite correctly, as an attack on the civil rights movement.[37] Our histories of the civil rights movement, too often wrapped up in narratives of heroic men, have often failed to notice the extent to which the movement and the resistance to it were also deeply involved in fights over reproduction and single motherhood.[38] The Student Nonviolent Coordinating Committee (SNCC), one of the key organizations coordinating civil rights activity in the South, issued a pamphlet entitled "Genocide in Mississippi" that argued that the intent of these bills that would have criminalized illegitimacy and sterilized black single mothers was to eliminate African Americans from the state by preventing their reproduction.[39] One of the civil rights movement's most visible female leaders, Fannie Lou Hamer, spoke repeatedly on national stages against the sterilization of African American women in Mississippi, telling audiences that 60 percent of black women in Sunflower County—the mostly rural area in Mississippi where Hamer had been a sharecropper—had been subject to unwanted sterilization.[40] Hamer was best known for founding the Mississippi Freedom Democratic Party, which staged a very-televised standoff with the all-white "official" Mississippi delegation to the Democratic Convention in 1964. On this occasion Hamer argued against a compromise that the national Democratic Party was trying to force between her delegates and the all-white delegation, saying she was disgusted "with a Democratic Party [that] would even consider seating people who had helped participate in the sterilization of women in Mississippi."[41] On another occasion, in 1969, Hamer was credited with stopping

a National Institutes of Health proposal floated at a White House conference for federal legislation requiring the sterilization of any minor who
had a second illegitimate child.[42]

As feminist scholars have noted, the 1970s was arguably even more
alarming than previous decades for black women's reproductive rights,
because the War on Poverty (decried by its opponents as the War against the
Poor[43]) provided federal funding for sterilization through the Department
of Health, Education, and Welfare (HEW) and the Office of Economic
Opportunity (OEO). Between 1970 and 1979, HEW provided funding for
sterilization operations for between 192,000 and 548,000 women a year who
received public housing, welfare, food stamps, and/or Medicaid assistance
—which represented a one-hundred fold increase over even the busiest years
of eugenic sterilization.[44] There were many documented cases of abuse, and
most involved black, Latina, and Native American women who were seen as
a drain on public coffers, irresponsible for having children while poor, and
became vulnerable subjects on whom medical residents trained.

In 1973 the Southern Poverty Law Center and the National Welfare
Rights Organization (NWRO)—derived from civil rights and a working-
class feminism, respectively—took up the cause of two sisters in Alabama,
Minnie and Mary Alice Relf, who were twelve and fourteen years old at the
time they were sterilized. In Senate hearings, the girls' parents testified that
ever since the family moved into public housing, a local agency had sought
out their daughters and administered Depo Provera shots to them. While
the parents were out one day, a nurse from the clinic had come and taken
Minnie and Mary Alice to the hospital. It wasn't until after they returned
home that their parents learned that they had been sterilized.[45] In the
subsequent court cases of *Relf v. Weinberger* and *NWRO v. Weinberger*, the
organizations sued the secretary of HEW, Caspar Weinberger (yes, that
Caspar Weinberger, Ronald Reagan's secretary of defense, notorious for his
role in the illegal government activities known as the Iran-Contra scandal).
Gerhart Gesell, the district judge who presided over the combined cases,
summarized what had been revealed, "There is uncontroverted evidence in
the record that minors and other incompetents have been sterilized with
federal funds and that an indefinite number of poor people have been
improperly coerced into accepting a sterilization operation under the belief
that various federally supported welfare benefits would be withdrawn unless they submitted to irreversible sterilization." That same year, Joseph
Levin of the Southern Poverty Law Center brought another case, this one
involving the apparent requirement by every obstetrician in Aiken County,

South Carolina, that if a woman's delivery was paid for by Medicaid, she had to submit to sterilization following the birth of her third child. Otherwise, the obstetricians would refuse to deliver her third baby.[46]

Taking the Children of Black Single Mothers

In 1960, in what became known as the "Louisiana incident," Governor Jimmie Davis responded to a federal order to desegregate the schools in New Orleans by cutting 2,300 black children from the ADC rolls—presumably in hopes he could force their families to move elsewhere—claiming that the children were "illegitimate" or their siblings were, and their mothers were therefore keeping an "unsuitable home." By invoking this moral claim, legislators (especially Southern ones) were turning "illegitimate" children into a political issue in two ways; first, by suggesting that women were having babies *in order* to get ADC benefits (as if—the benefits amounted to $24 a month for each additional child in Mississippi as late as 1992[47]); second, by suggesting that if a woman got pregnant while receiving public benefits, it amounted to evidence in itself that she was committing welfare fraud, since it indicated that her children had a "substitute father" who was responsible for their support, and she was no longer eligible for benefits. The more African Americans in the South fought for civil rights, the more officials cut benefits to working-class women and children; in the period between 1957 and 1967, the city of Birmingham decreased its total expenditures on welfare from $31,000 to a mere $12,000 a year.[48]

The federal government was resistant to these shenanigans by Southern states, at least when they were enacted in open defiance of federal initiatives, and recognized them for what they were: punishment aimed at African Americans to try to break the black freedom movement. "Suitable home" or "main-in-the-house" rules rested on humiliating and degrading enforcement—a caseworker would walk in recipients' front door, unannounced, while another guarded the back, trying to catch a man escaping; or they would show up at midnight or weekend raids, hoping to catch black men in bed with women receiving benefits.[49] So when Jimmie Davis cut children from the welfare rolls in retaliation for the efforts to desegregate the New Orleans schools, citing illegitimacy and suitable home rules, the federal government responded with the Flemming rule: the secretary of HEW, Arthur Flemming, issued a rule that states could not deny aid to (black) needy children with rules restricting eligibility to suitable homes—

unless state officials and social workers removed the children from these
supposedly unsuitable homes and made benefits available to them elsewhere, in foster homes.

In trying to stop Southern states from evading their responsibility to
provide eligible black families with ADC, however, HEW inadvertently gave
them license to engage in wholesale terrorizing of single black mothers.
Although the Flemming rule is often remembered as a *victory* for welfare
rights, it has fallen to scholars of child welfare to notice its corollary effect:
tens of thousands of women lost their children to a punitive welfare system.[50] The following year, when the Flemming rule was made into law,
Congress authorized funding for the program known as ADC-foster care,
which provided matching funds to states to place children in out-of-home
care. The cost of supporting a child in Southern states in the early 1960s
was around $27.50 a month on ADC, in foster care, about $50, and in an
orphanage or boarding schools, about $95. Because ADC was so much
cheaper to states than foster care or orphanages, Washington policymakers
had trouble believing that officials would maliciously pull children when
the economic costs were so high and the very slight state coffers in the
South made it so difficult to do, even if the federal government's matching
funds made foster care more affordable to states.[51] Federal officials under-
estimated two things: the effectiveness of even a few mothers losing their
children in deterring other women from applying for benefits, and the
depth of the belief that black welfare recipients were contemptible. In the
first year after the promulgation of the Flemming rule, in 1961 alone,
150,000 Southern children were placed in out-of-home care.[52] In subsequent years, as states first evaded and then were finally compelled to
respect the Flemming rule (enacted as Public Law 87–31 and the Public
Service Amendments of 1962), it transformed ADC and foster care from a
system that ignored black children to one that acted vigorously to take
them.[53] In a place and time where it was and is repeated as a truism that the
one thing a person never recovers from is the loss of a child—and this
means death, because it is almost outside the (white, middle-class) social
imaginary that one could lose a child to the state—these numbers reflect a
willingness to inflict an incredible depth and breadth of pain. Justifying
these actions required a dehumanization of those whose children were
taken or an extensive sense that these children were in danger (when they
had not been in danger before). For the most part, social workers did not
resist; rather, they took refuge in the notion that their role was to produce
"objective" standards for determining when to take children from (almost

always black) mothers.[54] So many black children subsequently entered the child welfare system in the next decade that "some observers began to describe this decade as the 'browning' of child welfare in America."[55]

It is worth noting that this was really the beginning of an extensive, coercive state child welfare system; the current system, in which parents can lose their children to a state child welfare system was born in this moment. This Southern discovery of what we might retrospectively term something like "neglect" was followed by what some have also called the "discovery" of child "abuse."[56] While an earlier generation *had* discovered child abuse in the 1870s, following the wide publicity in New York City of a heinous case of a child being beaten and left in a basement, the "Mary Ellen" case, as it was known, gave rise really only to a generation or two of intervention in families accused of abusing their children. Outside of New York City, most of these philanthropic efforts to provide foster boarding care foundered on the shoals of the sheer amount of money required to support children in out-of-home care, usually well before but certainly by the Depression. (In New York City, city officials' willingness to pay a stipend to support these efforts kept them alive.) From the 1920s through the 1960s, concerns about the treatment of children by their parents were, on the one hand, sporadic, local affairs, typically involving the police; on the other hand, the broader social issue of abused children tended to be expressed as concerns about juvenile delinquency.[57] In 1962, however, C. Henry Kempe and his collaborators published a paper in the *Journal of the American Medical Association* entitled "Battered Child Syndrome."[58] Building on the work of radiologists in the 1940s and 1950s, who were using newly developed X-ray technology and finding evidence of repeated, healed fractures even in very small children seen in emergency rooms, physicians began reluctantly to conclude that some parents inflicted serious, repeated, and hidden injuries on their children.

Kempe and his collaborators' paper is widely described in the histories of child abuse and family violence as the event that set off a new wave of child protective services—which was true, for white children. Between 1963 and 1967, all fifty states passed laws mandating that anyone who suspected child abuse report it. In the late 1960s and early 1970s, states began to authorize social workers to remove children from what they *suspected* to be abusive or neglectful families—without substantiation, without the intervention of police or having to present evidence before a judge. In the context of the social movements of the period and the War on Poverty, state and federal governments became progressively more interventionist to protect children from harm in their homes.[59] By creating a system that favored the protection of children over the due process rights of the family, and operating in a context where civil rights struggles were being fought out over the terrain of pregnancy and children, officials created a dangerous situation—with predictable results. There were widespread reports of abuse of this power by social workers and of cultural misunderstanding.

Issues of the black family, single mothers, and their children subsequently reached beyond Southern states, up to the federal government. In 1965 the uneasy relationship between the civil rights movement and the federal government reached a crossroads. It was the year after Fannie Lou Hamer had called out the "Dixiecrats" on the national evening news, preventing Lyndon Baines Johnson from using the Democratic National Convention as a platform to celebrate the passage of the Civil Rights Act of 1964 (which had outlawed legal segregation in public accommodations). It forced the Democratic Party to take a stand on the white primary and the systematic exclusion of black voters in the South since Reconstruction— threatening the "Solid [Democratic] South," and thus the Democrats' grip on national power, by opening up to the Republicans the possibility of being the party of segregation, a position it had ceded with Lincoln and Reconstruction. With the passage of the Voting Rights Act of 1965, there was a credible position to some that the goals of the civil rights movement had been met—formal legal equality had been accomplished. Others, of course, looked at the concentration of African Americans in substandard housing and ghettoes, without access to a living wage or often even work, and communities that still didn't have streetlights, sidewalks, reliable trash collection, medical care, or even high schools, never mind a route to higher education, and said that the work—of, say, building an interracial movement to end poverty and degradation—had only just begun.[60] In this context, the White House and the Department of Labor attempted to get out ahead of this issue, turning, as Southern officials had, to the question of black single mothers. First in a speech at Howard University, then in the Department of Labor Report, *The Negro Family: The Case for National Action* (subsequently known as the Moynihan Report, for its author, labor secretary, sociologist, and later Senator Daniel Patrick Moynihan), the Johnson administration laid out an argument that the source of black poverty and unemployment was single mothers. In its much-protested formulation, the Moynihan Report characterized the black family as a "tangle of pathology," characterized by a "Black Matriarchy" that emasculated sons, making them unfitted for the competition for jobs.[61]

Some of the people best positioned to protest—the experts on the black family, on welfare, illegitimacy, sterilization, and birth control—were social workers. The 1950s, 1960s, and 1970s may well have been the high point of the power of social workers. Their long fight for professional legitimacy (as a largely female profession concerned with the relatively unimportant concerns of the "private sphere"[62]) met the technocratic middle of the twentieth century, with the growing importance of social science, social problems, and practical solutions—all of which were the arenas in which social workers excelled. While social workers as a group tended to be more progressive than the United States as a whole, they were also more conscious than the rest of the country of a sociology literature—in which their training was steeped—that was often relentless in its pathologization of black single mothers.[63] Indeed, Moynihan's defenders argued that *The Negro Family* merely repeated the conclusions of sociological scholarship, which was true enough. Since the white psychologist John Dollard's *Caste and Class in a Southern Town* of 1937 and the black sociologist E. Franklin Frazier's *The Negro Family in the United States* of 1939 the sociological literature had argued that slavery and cropping produced disturbed forms of the black family, characterized by promiscuous single mothers—abandoning the willingness to discuss the role of coercion, violence, and rape in the sexual and reproductive lives of black women that had characterized the abolitionist literature and black women's narratives.[64] Social workers were positioned to be both the most ruthlessly critical *and* the most sympathetic to working-class black families, and questions of public policy related to race, family, sexuality, and single mothers became painfully contentious issues in social work forums. In 1968 black social workers walked out of the annual meeting of the National Conference on Social Welfare over their lack of access to policy groups, among other things, and pledged to strengthen the loose-knit, regionally based Association of Black Social Workers into a national organization that could offer an antiracist perspective on the issues of the day.[65]

It was on this highly contested and fraught landscape—in which everyone, from Southern white supremacists to an emergent racist wing of the Republican Party that was poised to become the force that would enable Republicans to win presidential elections to the Johnson administration to "respectable" civil rights leaders, was lambasting black single mothers—that black social workers found a voice to defend these unwed, despised mothers and their "bastard" children. The National Conference of Black Social Workers (later, the NABSW) held its first national meeting the next year, in 1969 at Bright Hope Baptist Church (a location characterized by the *New York Times* as "the heart of North Philadelphia's slums").[66] The group that became the NABSW fought on this terrain of reproduction and family. Speakers at that first conference, themed "The Black Family" ("in all its variety of structures and forms"),[67] called for a "Black Renaissance"— black community development (which was contrasted with self-centered black capitalism, which was what was being advocated by the Nixon administration) and antiracist education that would combat "anti-blackism" within the African American community—and celebrate blackness and the unique culture of African Americans rather than value the ways black Americans were like white people. It was an opening commitment to renounce the politics of respectability and to stand with working-class African Americans, to respect the cultural forms that emerged out of this community. From the outset, the group was willing to say unpopular things, even or especially things that offended the sensibility of respectable, church-going, middle-class black people. At that first conference, Drs. Alvin Puissant and Andrew Billingsley decried the Moynihan Report (a version of which, it should be noted, was vetted by Dr. Martin Luther King Jr.; civil rights leaders from Bayard Rustin to James Farmer had condemned unmarried black mothers),[68] punitive welfare measures that condemned the immorality of single mothers who had a male companion (because receiving welfare benefits did not mean that one had given up the right to have a sexual life), and called for an end to the categorization of some children as "illegitimate."[69] In subsequent years conference participants joined with the NWRO to call for an end to social workers' condescension toward black mothers receiving AFDC, marched with the group for increased benefits and credit in department stores, and argued against the policing of welfare recipients' sexual lives.[70] The organization also expressed disgust with the practice of paying foster parents nearly twice what it paid welfare recipients to raise the same children. It called for increasing housing options for single mothers.[71] At its fourth annual conference, it issued a statement calling for the right of grandparents to foster their grandchildren, and it issued another denouncing both coercive use of birth control and barriers to birth control use.[72] It was, in short, an organization that was not embarrassed to defend black families that were in straits, which some felt made African Americans as a group look bad, and was willing to speak forthrightly about sexuality.

In 1972, at its fourth national meeting, the NABSW also issued the statement for which the group is best remembered, calling transracial adoption a "form of genocide." It argued that ethnic pride had long been denied to black people, and it was principally through the family that this kind of social self-esteem could be built. As a result, it suggested, "Black children belong physically, psychologically, and culturally in Black families," because black families could better meet the different developmental needs of black children, including primarily "highly sophisticated coping techniques to deal with racist practices perpetrated by individuals and institutions." They denounced the process by which black families were rendered ineligible to adopt, contending that it was a myth that blacks wouldn't adopt. It was, in short, a civil rights manifesto about the right of black communities and black unwed mothers to make their own rules about what constituted a "legitimate" family and a good and loving place to raise black children.

The statement was not kind to white adopters, although not without reason; as we have seen from Grow and Shapiro's study, it was a context where some white parents were trying to deny that their children had any black heritage and others were still openly admitting that their adopted black child was second choice. The statement argued that it was primarily the shortage of white children that made black or mixed-race children of interest to white adopters. The statement denounced as disingenuous the redefinition of children with one white parent as "biracial," "black-white," or "interracial," when for the previous two centuries such children had always been understood "by law and immutable social custom" as African American; in doing so, the statement argued, agencies were "emphasizing the whiteness as the adoptable quality." The group also expressed uneasiness about the ways black children became a project in white families rather than a family member like others. In this profoundly segregated time and place, they noted, white parents had to seek assistance to figure out how to deal with black children's hair, to learn black culture, to "try to become Black." Authors of the statement noted with concern the frequency with which white families had to sever all ties with their own parents in order to parent a black or mixed-race child, suggesting that it weakened the family and left scars on the parents that affected the child. Finally, the statement commented on the crisis of black male adolescence in an all-white community and school—given the prevalence of a "but would you want your daughter to marry one" sentiment in white communities, who was he supposed to date?[73]

By insisting that African American families were not the "tangle of pathology" of the Moynihan Report but a good and healthy resource for black children—and, indeed, that they offered certain nonreplicable resources for black children in learning to cope with white racism—the NABSW followed the architects of the *Brown* legal arguments to produce a "best interests of the child rationale" to insist that child welfare workers should place children there. As we have seen, despite what were presumably good intentions by majority white agencies, and sometimes heroic efforts by black and Puerto Rican social workers, black families seeking to adopt *were* being rejected in overwhelming numbers for their supposed deficiencies—neighborhood, age, and income prime among them. In this context the NABSW sought to make arguments for the affirmative virtues that black families brought to the practice of rearing black children. The NABSW had challenged the growing practice of interracial adoption and foster placement.

One of the founding members of the NABSW, Andrew Billingsly, observed acerbically in 1972 that slavery was the only comprehensive child welfare system the United States ever had for black children—a child in the slave South could always be dropped off at the nearest plantation to be raised.[74] There *was* a certain bitter irony in the fact that over the long century after the end of slavery few white people took any interest in the fate of black children on their own—at best, sponsoring a few segregated orphanage slots for them, at worst, consigning them to labor on the chain gang—but when, through the concerted efforts of organized racial justice groups, black babies began being available for adoption, there was an unseemly scramble to make them available to white families rather than black families, notwithstanding the sometimes heroic efforts by black communities to support black orphans with few resources in the previous century. The heart of the NABSW's position was a broadly historical argument, that until one recognized the economic, political, and historical forces separating black children from their families, until one recognized what it meant that for most of U.S. history black families could not possess their children because someone else owned them, one could not produce a coherent black child welfare system, never mind argue that an essential component of it ought to be white adoption of black children. In order to make sense of their argument, it is worth briefly considering the previous century of black child welfare.

Black Children on Their Own before 1950

One of the "essential features," of slavery, as the black sociologist W. E. B. Du Bois argued in 1908, was that unfree people had no control over their children.[75] Indeed, harrowing accounts of mothers separated from their children were a staple of abolitionist writings; take, for example, this scene witnessed by Silas Stone in Charleston, South Carolina, in 1807:

> On the left side of the steps as you leave the main hall of [the Exchange Building] was a stage built, on which a mother with eight children were placed, and sold at auction. . . . The sale began with the oldest child, who, being struck off to the highest bidder, was taken from stage or platform by the purchaser, and led to his wagon and stowed away, to be carried into the country; the second and third were also sold, and so on until seven of the children were torn from their mother, while her discernment told her they were to be separated probably forever, causing in that mother the most agonizing sobs and cries, in which the children seemed to share. The scene beggars description.[76]

In 1851 Sojourner Truth famously made the same point with more anger and less sentiment: "I have borne thirteen chilern and seen most all sold off into slavery, and when I cried out with a mother's grief, none but Jesus heard."[77] An exception makes the point most poignantly that the law made no provision to protect the relationship of an African or African-descended mother and her child; on the contrary, it ensured precisely that black or mulatto children could not be protected if their mother was a slave—except in Louisiana. "Louisiana, least American of the Southern States," wrote Frederic Bancroft in 1931, "was least inhuman. In becoming Americanized it lost many a liberal feature of the old French *code noir*, but it forbade the sale of mothers from the children less than ten years of age (and vice versa) and bringing into the state any slave child under ten years of age without its mother, if living. The penalty for violating either prohibition was from $1000 to $2000 and the forfeiture of the slave. That would have meant much if it had been strictly enforced."[78] Yet if black mothers' relationships to their children were not valued in the slave-holding South, this is not to say that black children were treated as priceless by the communities of the free North. On at least two occasions, in 1838 in Philadelphia and 1863 in New York City, white mobs burned "colored" orphanages, the latter as part of the famous draft riot protesting recruitment into the Union forces in the Civil War.[79]

More than just being the targets of violence, though, the greatest problem for black children after the end of slavery was that there often simply were no provisions for children who, through whatever legal or extralegal violence, illness, or other catastrophe, were not under the care of their mother or another relative. Former slave owners quickly saw that "the dreaded abolition has a bright side," specifically the opportunity to "rid themselves at once of the care of all superfluous negroes, including the young children," whether under the care of their mothers or not.[80] The Freedman's Bureau saw black children as potential dependents on the bureau or the military and, anticipating every argument about black children, welfare, and foster care in the mid-twentieth century, were a priori skeptical of black parents' and relatives' willingness or ability to support them. When black men had, under slavery, contracted more than one marriage, the Freedmen's Bureau compelled him to take the mother of his children as his wife, regardless of the preferences of anyone involved. Some whites insisted that freedwomen would rather murder their infants than work hard to support them. Others accused black parents of being cruel, compelling their children to labor hard "without encouraging words of hope and cheerfulness." When grandparents of orphaned black children sought to take them in, the bureau's primary consideration was not sentiment but to challenge them to show that they could support the children without recourse to charity; others suspected relatives of intending to exploit the children's labor rather than to care for them.[81]

Numerous small efforts for black orphans were supported through the efforts of philanthropists, white and black, and African American communities. Before the Civil War, there were a number of such institutions supported by white patrons in New York and Philadelphia (including those targeted by mob violence). Some seemed to see their primary function as the training of servants, as for example the one whose annual report noted, "It is always interesting to watch the development of the children, and we are often surprised to see how useful and dependable they become. There is an old saying: "Good mistress—good maid," and it is often so with these children, when they have conscientious, painstaking caretakers the children grow naturally into good habits."[82] In the South, there were many smaller efforts, kept functioning with the support of a black church, day school, or Sunday school. In the sometimes extraordinarily impoverished situations of small or rural African American communities, any black institution was the center of whatever social support work it could manage, as the state frequently did nothing. Sometimes orphanages were combined with old folks' homes. Most often, they were supported through the scrap and ceaseless efforts of an individual founder, who told stories of how their fortunes were turned around by the donation of, say, a goat, or a cup and plate. The woman who started the Reed Home and School in Covington, Georgia, marks its beginnings from a time when she was at Atlanta University, where she was one day crossing above a chain gang working on the road. She reports that she "heard a pitiful scream down below":

> I looked down and there stood a poor little boy of about nine or ten years old, with the lash being applied to his back. There was no one to say a word of comfort to the dear little fellow. . . . I pleaded with the Lord and asked him for strength to complete my course, that I might go out to save one boy from the chain gang. . . . In June, 1884, I set up housekeeping for the purpose of caring for one little girl. I made most of my furniture of dry goods boxes, and now and then a friend gave me a plate, a cup and saucer or some little piece necessary for housekeeping, and we did our cooking in ovens and frying pans on the fireplace, as I had no stove. I set up housekeeping in one room, and lived in this room until there were five little ones in the family.[83]

These efforts often did not survive beyond the lifetimes of their founders, who often kept such institutions together through sheer force of will. In addition, black families who never saw themselves as institutions also performed social welfare functions for their neighbors, kin, and strangers, taking in boarders—paying and not—of many ages, including children.[84]

For many African Americans in the South, labor systems changed little from the era of slavery to the 1950s. Children went to work very young, usually between the ages of five and eight. Immediately after emancipation some former slave owners apprenticed male youths, usually from twelve to fourteen years old, but some as young as six, insisting that their parents could not support them (thus leaving the parents with the economic responsibility for their younger children and often destroying the economic viability of the family as a whole by removing wage earners).[85] Apprenticeship differed from slavery in that it was a fixed, time-limited contract, but the promise of future freedom many years hence must have been cold comfort indeed to boys who thought that emancipation meant, well, being free. Even the Freedmen's Bureau often apprenticed black children whom they denominated as orphans, indenturing them rather than placing them with their free, extended family.[86] Some African Americans moved out of the

South, and others bought their own land or shops. Most, though, when Reconstruction drew to a close, found themselves in a significantly similar situation to that of slavery: working in agriculture, often on the same plantations, with the police patrolling for "vagrants" who could be arrested for idleness and put on a chain gang—even children. Black workers—"free" and prisoners alike—often picked cotton under the shadow of supervisors with guns. Just as slavery had formed a sort of child welfare system, so too did the chain gang.[87] Under such a system, black children need not be adopted—they could work. As late as 1923 there were only fifty-two orphanages of whatever size in the seventeen Southern states that served black children—about three per state.[88]

In this context we can understand efforts to produce a freer labor system for black children (although even the woman who ran Covington house needed the orphanage children to work in fields to support the orphanage), and to combine it with some education, to be an act of resistance to the draconian labor systems of the South. In a similar sense the historian Jacqueline Jones has argued that the effort to produce a "private space" in sharecropper cabins where women and children did not work, or not as much as men—roundly condemned by white Southerners as black women "playing the lady"—was a kind of resistance. Farm owners would ration out groceries, not for the number of children in the family but for the number of "hands" working. At harvest few escaped the pressure to go out into the fields, even mothers of very young children; if she was the only available caregiver, she sacrificed the kind of nurture she could give her child, like the mother who put her baby to sleep on a fence and then returned to find "a great snake crawling over the child."[89] Disease, malnutrition, and accidents claimed huge numbers of infant lives.[90]

In the 1930s women in the New Deal coalition pressed for and won ADC—also known as "welfare"—which, built on the Mother's Pension programs of the 1920s, allowed single mothers (presumed to be widows) to stay home and care for their children. This represented a huge shift in the care of "orphans"—their mothers themselves could raise them rather than farm them out to apprenticeship, work, relatives, or orphanages. However, white Southerners—no fans of the New Deal under the best of circumstances (and the reason why African Americans and agricultural workers in general were excluded from New Deal programs)—were adamantly opposed to ADC taking black women out of the work force, where they were needed not only in the fields and mills but to clean homes and care for children in white households. Some states made it a crime for black women to refuse such jobs. Nowhere did black women receive ADC in any numbers worth counting before the 1950s.[91] As birth control activists and federal programs pressed to make birth control minimally available in the rural South, they encountered vehement opposition by those who saw it as depriving them of potential workers, black and white. Indeed, birth control —especially subsidized birth control that farm workers who were largely paid in scrip, not cash, could afford—was sufficiently rare that the historian Johanna Schoen has argued that in North Carolina women sought steriliza-tion under the auspices of the eugenics board in order to control their fertility.[92] For the most part, in the agrarian and semifeudal South, black children were needed, and they were needed to work.

Two transitions marked child welfare before 1960, at least from the point of view of black children: the Progressive era and the New Deal saw the availability of public money for child welfare, meaning that there were real public services (besides jail and the chain gang) for black children. This was at least in one sense a considerable improvement over religiously funded and private philanthropic institutions, which overwhelmingly ex-cluded African American children. In the 1920s and 1930s, increasing num-bers of public child welfare institutions were founded, and, while they did not total more than one-third of child welfare institutions in the country (and in some places, like New York City, there weren't any), by 1933 the majority of public institutions accepted black children, at least officially (although further investigation sometimes revealed that in practice, they simply never did accept any black children).[93]

One of the most significant innovations of the public system in the 1920s was the creation of the paid foster boarding home, where parents were given a stipend for the maintenance of the child, in contrast to the free boarding home, which provided no stipend and usually carried the as-sumption that the child would work for his or her keep.[94] (Public agencies also began setting up adoption services in the 1920s, although they did not place black children.) The foster boarding home was a success in the black community for a number of reasons. First, as we can see, it was an institu-tional form in significant continuity with the ways orphanages were orga-nized in the nineteenth century. An individual or a couple with more or less strong ties to a church supported as many children in their homes as their own resources and donations were able to maintain. Second, given the pervasive impecuniousness of even middle-class black households, simply offering money did a great deal to support an already functioning system. For white institutions, too, foster homes for black children relieved the burden of trying to find spaces for them in the still often-segregated private orphanages (and the sometimes de facto segregation of public ones).

A snapshot from 1963 suggests the cumulative effects of a century of segregated orphanages, a preference for incarcerating black children (even when their crime was simply being homeless and black—"vagrants") and the relatively well-functioning foster boarding home system. Black children were significantly more likely to be in foster care than in orphanages. According to one study by the sociologist Helen Jeter, among children being served by public agencies 31 percent of white and 41 percent of black children were in foster care; private institutions were supporting 27 percent of white and 50 percent of black children in foster boarding homes. Jeter also noted that black children tended to stay in foster care much longer; she attributed this to the much higher likelihood that white children would be adopted. Of those children receiving care from public dependency services, 8 percent of white and 5 percent of black children were receiving adoption services; in private dependency services, 24 percent of white and 17 percent of black children were in adoptive homes.[95] These statistics, though, can misstate the situation of black children; overall, even in 1960, they were mostly not getting services; only about 20 percent of black children in care were served by dependency institutions at all, and 54 percent of black children in out-of-home care were in correctional facilities, this in contrast to 20 percent of white children in correctional facilities.[96]

Why Was *Adoption* the Problem?
The NABSW Statement and the Importance of Scarcity

The NABSW statement on transnational adoption was promulgated at workshops on the black family, where a participant expressed the concern that transracial adoption was "a growing threat to the preservation of the Black family."[97] That statement merits some unpacking. As we have seen, after the promulgation of the Flemming rule, the subsequent provision of federal funding for foster care, and then the elaboration of child neglect and abuse as national issues, black families started getting broken up by social workers on a regular basis. The NABSW statement, by resisting the placement of black children in white families, attempted to introduce some scarcity back into a system that seemed to be expanding limitlessly in the seventies in its capacity to absorb black children. If one believed that black children really were being harmed in their families, expanding capacity would be a good thing, but many suspected that the politics of loathing of black mothers in general and fighting against racial justice claims on the terrain of the black family were contributing to the sudden and extensive entry of black children into foster care and adoption. Black social workers, trained and steeped in the case report literature, would be aware of case reports like the following from the late 1950s. It suggested a pre-Flemming, pre-transracial adoption status quo that provided good reason to oppose black children being adopted and fostered in white homes:

> Mary E. had three illegitimate children before she came north to live with her mother and stepfather. When she had two more, her step-father threw her out of the house. The one room she could afford was crowded enough for an adult and five children; it was also cluttered with unwashed clothes, soiled dishes, and hills of dirt. The neighbors reported that her children roamed the streets while she entertained a man at late drinking parties. When Mary applied for ADC, the agency worker thought the home situation was almost hopeless. But she knew the difficulty of finding foster homes for Negroes. She began helping the mother to clean up her room, and to exercise more adequate control over her children. At first, progress was slow—the family didn't even see the dirt. But the mother and her teenage daughter were unusually eager to learn, and to improve their condi-tion. The worker made weekly assignments for housecleaning, laun-dry, and similar chores, and Mary met the challenge. The oldest son, living in the next town, was contacted. He checked on the children almost daily and eventually, they were always in the house after dark. They got to school on time, with faces washed, hair combed, and clothing clean. If "suitable home" policies had been strictly applied, the family would have been broken up. With ADC money and ser-vices, they stayed together and actually moved toward becoming a responsible family.[98]

There are many things to notice in this narrative and the genre to which it belongs. Its elements include the helpless, hopeless subject of casework and the heroic caseworker, who, applying principles of good social work, firmness, and compassion, completely transforms the situation by acting upon the apparently unpromising raw material of her client. It has the sound of a Protestant conversion narrative, and, indeed, the milieu from which professional social work emerged in the early twentieth century had strong missionary elements. But this story also reveals some of the institutional parameters that both defined and limited social work in the 1950s. First, Mary E. brought this institutional apparatus down on her head—the social worker who contemplated taking her children away, who began visiting her home on a regular basis to evaluate her housekeeping and her dating and drinking habits—by applying for ADC. Whether or not Mary E. and her daughter were "unusually eager to learn," Mary, her neighbors, her family, and her children's school teachers had not identified a problem, at least not one they wanted a social worker's help with. The caseworkers associated with ADC did that. The only thing that saved Mary from having her children taken away by the state was "the difficulty of finding foster homes for Negroes."

Adoption, then, played a critical role in expanding the foster care system. Not only did it simplify the economics—keeping children in foster care was expensive for states and the federal government, while adoption cost them nothing and in fact generated fees—but since a study in 1959 had identified a pattern of "foster care drift," of multiple placements for children in care, foster care had been characterized as damaging to children's well-being, and social workers were under pressure to try to move children out of care and into adoptions.[99] The NABSW's position in 1972 on interracial adoption worked to restore some of the difficulty of pulling black children—to try to nudge social workers in general back in the direction of the problem of the lack of foster (and adoptive) placements for black children—in hopes of encouraging caseworkers to stop separating black children from their mothers. In an article published in 1987 in Ebony, the president of the NABSW explained the statement in exactly that way, "Our position is that the African-American family should be maintained and its integrity preserved. We see the lateral transfer of black children to white families as contradictory to our preservation efforts."[100] For all of the post–civil rights era scholarship on the NABSW statement that imagines the group as almost supernaturally powerful in its ability to stop the adoption of black children, it merits noting that the group failed; by 1970 the number of black children in out-of-home care had skyrocketed.[101]

The NABSW statement was effective, however, in persuading agencies to slow down the rate of interracial placements. Always a controversial program, the number of children placed interracially was reduced by 1974 in numerous states, including the states that had placed the largest number of children for transracial adoption, New York, California, and Illinois. The Child Welfare League of America revised its guidelines for adoptive placement twice in the years between 1968 and 1973, first to displace an ideology that children should physically "match" their adoptive parents and second to clarify that inracial placement was a preferable first choice to transracial placement, but not to the point where it should unreasonably delay an adoptive or foster placement.[102] Although in later years much pundit ink was shed in the belief (or at least the position) that the NABSW statement had something equivalent to the force of law and halted transracial adoption— neither is true. (Because, seriously, when in the history of the United States did a small group of black women overpower what everyone else wanted?) The year 1970 was the high point in this early period of transracial adoptions, with 1,743 transracial adoptions. By 1974, when the NABSW statement was promulgated, that number had already dropped to 591.

It is in the question of transracial adoption that we find the clearest separation between the two strands of racial justice activism around child welfare, just as an interracialist civil rights movement split from a separatist black nationalist movement over questions of class (although historians and political commentators may well have made far too much of the differences and not enough of the similarities and alliances in these tendencies). Those who sought access to placing a child for adoption for black girls and women who got "in trouble," who saw white families as a resource for black children with no place to go, had a different set of concerns than those who sought to halt the sterilization of black single mothers, who fought for increased benefits and freedom from harassment for unmarried black mothers who had lost their jobs but wanted to keep their children in order to stem the hemorrhage of black children from their working-class families.

The NABSW statement was criticized first and hardest in the black community. No less fierce an advocate of racial justice than the *Chicago Defender*, for example, was sharply critical of the NABSW position on transracial adoption. An editorial called the position that black children couldn't find a secure identity as black in a white adoptive home an excessively "emotional assessment" that was unconcerned with the "ultimate welfare of the adopted black child."[103] The *Chicago Defender* columnist Audrey Weaver wrote not one but two biting columns denouncing this position as heartless, quoting an adopted black youngster responding to the claim that it was better for black children to be raised in institutions than in white homes, saying, "Nobody wants to stay in a place like that."[104] *Ebony* ran an article that was deeply sympathetic to white adoptive parents of black children, pointing out that it was only in the North and a result of federal court decisions that black children had begun to be placed with white parents, arguing that transracial placement was a victory for integration along the same lines that participants in the civil rights movement had long sought. In addition to stories of black children who loved their white foster parents and now risked losing them, the article concluded with a quote from black social service administration professor Leon Chestang, saying, "It's possible this kind of adoption might produce new leaders. This kid will have had a novel relationship with a white family. At the same time he will have been exposed to the plight of the black person. It's a potentially liberating kind of combination."[105] James L. Curtis, a black psychiatrist at Cornell University Medical Center with twenty years of experience in child welfare termed the position "the most destructive that could be taken."[106] For those like Weaver for whom the struggle was unequivocally about racial democracy, the NABSW position was anathema: "At this point we have black social workers condemning the practice which allows white families to adopt black youngsters if they wish. Strange, but for decades we have been condemning the U.S. for saying it is a democracy while practicing so many undemocratic actions."[107]

On the other hand, for those whose sympathies lay with demonized working-class black mothers, white fostering and adoption of their children was just one in a long series of attacks on their families that began with slavery, when mothers literally did not own their children. And although the psychological literature had by this time started favoring adoption decisively over foster care, it bears remembering that foster care had a long and admirable tradition in the black community as the alternative to orphanages with few places for black children and worse opportunities on the street or the chain gang. In a context where would-be black adoptive parents were being turned away from adoption agencies in droves, it might also be true to say that foster care was what we might call "black adoption," the arena where being older or poorer or widowed was not a bar to taking in children.

In sum, then, in our relentless focus on the earnestness and sensitivity of white families, and the emotional well-being of black children, we have missed the point of the NABSW statement. Single black mothers lost their children as part of the fight over civil rights, an event made more likely by the long history of slavery that normalized taking black mothers' children. The NABSW's real and substantial contribution to our understanding of the history of black child welfare is that it tried to call attention to the ways black single mothers were targeted by child protection systems, and it tried to defend those mothers.

TWO

The Making of the Indian Child
Welfare Act, 1922–1978

While much of the debate about transracial adoption has centered around black children, they were not the only—or even the first—subjects of debate about "transracial" adoption. From the Indian Adoption Project (IAP) in the 1950s to the long political fight over the Indian Child Welfare Act (ICWA) from 1968 to its final passage in 1978, Native children, too, have been the subject of almost continuous questions about where they "belong." Indeed, one could point to compulsory boarding school—where for decades, between the 1890s and 1960s, many Native families had to send their children far away from home, to the care of mostly Anglo, English-speaking strangers—as a form of involuntary "transracial" placement that has defined life in Native communities for most of the twentieth century.

The first question we need to ask, though, is whether "transracial" is actually the right word, whether members of Native nations belong to a "race." Much writing by ICWA's opponents in the post–civil rights era identified the law as being about race and hence illegitimate or even unconstitutional. For its supporters, though, the debate over ICWA was about sovereignty—about the self-government of tribes or Indian nations as such, distinct legally from the larger United States and the states that envelop them. In this argument, ICWA was founded on a tribal definition of Native peoples' rights—hence defined by the nature of their political and legal, not "racial," status.

Particularly in the 1990s, this chapter will argue, opponents of ICWA

rewrote its history, locating it in relation to the black freedom struggle and
the National Association of Black Social Workers' (NABSW) statement. The
historian Barbara Melosh, for example, writes in *Strangers and Kin* that
"transracial adoptions of African Americans and American Indians occupied the same historical niche, and both groups challenged the practice
with similar nationalist arguments. . . . The ICWA . . . openly uses racial
preference" in placement.[1] Similarly, in a law review article published in
1991 about African American children and adoption, Elizabeth Bartholet
writes:

> A parallel development [to what happened with black children] oc-
> curred with respect to the adoptive placement of Native American
> children. Indian children were first placed in significant numbers in
> non-Indian homes in the period from the late 1950s through the 1960s.
> Certain Native American leaders took a public position against these
> placements in 1972, the same year the NABSW issued its historic state-
> ment against trans-racial adoption. Several years later Congress
> passed the Indian Child Welfare Act of 1978 which mandates a power-
> ful preference for placing Indian children with Indians as opposed to
> non-Indians. In recent years several states have passed laws modeled
> on the Indian Child Welfare Act, mandating a same-race preference in
> adoptive placement.[2]

Or, in *Nobody's Children*, a policy book written to change adoption law,
Bartholet suggests:

> In 1972 certain black and Native American leaders stepped forward to
> challenge transracial placement within the United States. The Na-
> tional Association of Black Social Workers (NABSW) denounced
> transracial adoption as racial genocide and issued a manifesto de-
> manding that all black children be kept within the black community,
> whether in foster or adoptive homes. Native American leaders simul-
> taneously attacked the practices which had resulted in the placement
> of many Indian children in white homes and called on Congress for
> legislation giving tribes the power to control the destiny of these
> children. These appeals found a receptive audience. The establish-
> ment forces readily conceded that the black and the Native American
> communities had a right to hold onto "their own" and that black and
> Native American children truly "belonged" with their groups of
> origin.[3]

These claims, that the historical roots of ICWA lay in the NABSW statement and race-based separatism, derive from the work of the psychologist Rita Simon,[4] and they have been widely repeated elsewhere.[5]

However, this intertwined historical and legal argument is wrong on both counts. As we will see, the struggle for ICWA was begun by the American Association of Indian Affairs (AAIA) with a press conference in 1968—a year before the founding of the NABSW and four years before that group's statement on black children and foster and adoptive placement. In fact, we might ask if the lines of influence ran the other way. It might have been the increasingly visible resistance of tribal peoples in the 1960s and 1970s to losing children to adoption by Anglo families—rooted in the long tradition of Native survivance that had, for more than a century, built fierce responses to the taking of children—that influenced the NABSW's statement on the adoption of black children by white families.[6] Furthermore, the historical argument is wrong in another way: this was not exclusively a group of "Native American leaders" as Bartholet says; still less a "national-ist" or separatist group as Melosh writes. The AAIA—born in the 1920s out of the group of Anglo writers and artists that organized around Mabel Dodge Luhan in New Mexico and began a romantic but successful cam-paign to defend Indian culture and land[7]—coordinated Native resistance to the taking of children, usually of unmarried mothers, in the most effective ways it could find, including advocacy by white lawyers, Washington lobby-ists, and political organizers.

This inaccurate historical claim about ICWA's relationship to the NABSW sought to locate Native child policy within a story about the unconstitu-tional use of race in law.[8] Carole Goldberg, in her article "Descent into Race," suggests something of the irony of this legal claim. She argues there have been two different eras in which legal scholars and judges have de-fined Native people as belonging to a separate "race." In the nineteenth and early twentieth century it was deployed to deny them rights and entitle-ments as a result of the "backward" or "primitive" state of their race, which was said to limit the use they could make of things promised to tribes by treaty (like land). In the post (African American) civil rights era, the racialization of Native Americans in legal contexts, Goldberg argues, was deployed to ensure strict scrutiny that could deny Indians benefits that might derive from tribal membership.[9]

Whatever the degree to which the federal government does or does not recognize the sovereignty of Indian tribes, communities, and nations, try-ing to turn tribal peoples into a "race" as a matter of law is to try to fit the square peg of Native governance questions into the round hole of a black-white racial paradigm. The Supreme Court has ruled repeatedly on the question of whether tribal peoples are racial groups under the law. In 1974, in *Morton v. Mancari*,[10] the Supreme Court held that Native peoples in the United States should be treated as members of political rather than racial groups and, specifically, that the equal protection clause that prohibited *racial* preferences—in this case in federal employment—did not apply in Indian matters, allowing the Bureau of Indian Affairs (BIA) to maintain its preference for employing qualified Native people. Preferences were not being given to Native Americans "as a discrete racial group, but rather as members of quasi-sovereign tribal entities."[11] Further, the Court found in *Washington v. Confederated Bands and Tribes of Yakima Nation* (1979) that this "unique legal status" permits policy initiatives "that might otherwise be constitutionally offensive" because they would appear to enact racial preferences.[12] The Court has consistently found that the federal government made treaties with tribes as sovereign nations, exchanging Native lands for certain concessions by the U.S. government, made in perpetuity. A century or two after many of these treaties, in 1831, *Cherokee Nation v. Georgia* upheld the right of tribes to be treated as nations, "distinct, independent political communities, retaining their original natural rights, as undisputed possessors of the soil" (albeit "domestic dependent nations").[13] Or, as Felix Cohen affirmed in 1942 in his important treatise for the Department of the Interior, *Federal Indian Law*:

> Perhaps the most basic principles of all Indian law supported by a host of decisions . . . is the principle that *those powers which are lawfully vested in an Indian tribe are not, in general delegated powers granted by express acts of Congress, but rather inherent powers of a limited sovereignty which has never been extinguished.* Each Indian tribe begins its relationship with the Federal Government as a sovereign power, recognized as such in treaty and legislation. The powers of sovereignty have been limited from time to time by special treaties and laws designed to take from the Indian tribes control of matters which, in the judgment of Congress, then, must be examined to determine the limitations of tribal sovereignty rather than to determine its sources or its positive content. What is not expressly limited remains within the domain of tribal sovereignty.[14]

These legal questions were in fact vetted in the context of the debate over ICWA in the 1970s. When the U.S. Justice Department questioned whether the proposed version of ICWA then under consideration by the legislature constituted an illegal use of race in determining jurisdiction (as ICWA moved some cases involving Indian children to tribal courts), lawyers for the AAIA responded that the bill was not about race but political status, a position ultimately accepted by the Justice Department and Congress.[15] The appropriate analogy then would not be to black children or questions about the NABSW but to a relinquishing parent of whatever race who crossed state lines for an adoption. (Indeed, state jurisdiction questions arise frequently, and adoptions are complicated immensely by them—birth mothers might be trying to thwart a biological father who opposed an adoption or travel to a state that allows adopters to be generous in their reimbursement of expenses for a mother, which another state might con- sider "buying" a baby.[16]) Just as an adoption involving a child whose residence was Florida should not be heard in Louisiana, a child who was an enrolled member of a Lakota tribe (or eligible for enrollment) should have a hearing in a Lakota court, not a North Dakota court.

In fact, the way ICWA was written—over the objection of many tribes, whose representatives felt it excluded many children who were self- evidently Indian—ensured that it was not about race. Many children who might be readily identified as "racially" Indian are not covered by ICWA. For example, Native children from Canada or Mexico are not covered by ICWA. Native Hawaiians are not covered by it because Hawaii was essentially seized by the U.S. government—there were no treaties with indigenous people in the archipelago, and hence no tribal or national status was ac- corded them. In the United States there are 562 federally recognized Indian tribes, but, by one researcher's count, nearly 200 nonrecognized or termi- nated tribes.[17] Children from these groups, who might be descended "ra- cially" only from Indian ancestors, are not covered by ICWA. Another com- mentator offered the following example to suggest the weakness of the law: a woman living on a reservation, an enrolled member of federally recognized tribe, with one-quarter Indian "blood" marries a man who is also enrolled and also has a one-quarter blood quantum. They have a child, who would be covered by ICWA. She then remarries another man with one-eighth Indian "blood," and her second child is unenrollable and not covered by ICWA.[18]

Finally, ICWA not insignificantly covers a considerable group of people who have no form of indigenous ancestry: the non-Indian birth parents of children who are members, or eligible for membership, in American Indian tribes. ICWA provides enhanced notice requirements from courts to parents in the event that they are at risk of having their parental rights terminated; it indicates a preference for placement in extended family, which is often preferable for parents who are losing rights to their children; it requires that child welfare workers demonstrate efforts to keep the family together; and most significantly, it provides a higher standard of proof—"clear and convincing evidence" that continued custody of the child by the parent is likely to result in serious emotional or physical damage to the child rather than a "preponderance of the evidence." If courts wish to go beyond removing the child from the parent's custody and terminate parental rights, again there is a higher burden of proof, "beyond a reasonable doubt" rather than "clear and convincing evidence" that the parent will harm the child.[19] ICWA strictly limits itself to status (enrollment or eligibility for enrollment), not ("racial") Indian-ness. Native politics, issues, and child welfare are then (not surprisingly) quite different from black child welfare questions.

Finally, ICWA clarified, rather than fundamentally changed, a confused set of questions about jurisdiction. Because child welfare, like all family law, is usually a state issue, jurisdiction has to revert to tribes as a simple matter of logic—federal courts have no jurisdiction with respect to child welfare, and states have no authority in Indian matters. Even before ICWA this is how federal courts held: in *Fisher* (1976), for example, the federal district court of Montana found that adoptions had to go through tribal courts.[20] The oldest recorded case is from 1899, *In re Lelah-Puc-Ka-Chee*,[21] which held that tribes had to consent to the removal of a child to a boarding school (a legal holding more notable in the breach than the observance, but nevertheless, one that upheld the *principle* of tribal sovereignty over child welfare).

Vine Deloria, in his widely read book, *Custer Died for Your Sins*, published in 1969, theorized the differences in the ways Native people and black people had been disenfranchised, dwelling on the ways they had been dispossessed of their children or what children had been denied, albeit in language that now sounds slightly archaic:

> The white world has responded to the non-white groups in a number of ways. Negroes were considered draft animals, Indians, wild animals. When liberals equate the two they are overlooking obvious historical facts. Never did the white man systematically exclude Indians from his schools and meeting places. Nor did the white man ever kidnap black children from their homes and take them off to a government boarding school to be educated as whites. The white man forbade the black to enter his own social and economic system

and at the same time force-fed the Indian what he was denying the black . . . The white is after Indian lands and resources. For Indians to continue to think of their basic conflict with the white man as cultural is the height of folly. The problem is and always has been the adjustment of the legal relationship between the Indian tribes and the federal government. . . . [For Black people, the] problem is social, and economic, and cultural, not one of adjusting the legal relationship between the two groups. . . . A socio-economic, rather than legal adjustment must consequently be the goal.[22]

Deloria's largest point here is that the forms of racialization, the forms of inclusion and exclusion of African American and Native people, was quite different. He argues that the history of the enslavement of African Americans meant that the forms of participation and oppression of African Americans had to do with labor, markets, and (self-) ownership. For African Americans, the guarantees of legal citizenship and self-possession in, for example, the Fourteenth, Fifteenth, and Sixteenth Amendments to the Constitution were only partially successful, because law in the sense of citizenship (as opposed to law in the sense of ownership) was not the medium of African American oppression. In contrast, the U.S. federal government was never particularly interested in Native people's labor, only their land—and citizenship and civilization, through education and individual rights, were the measure of indigenous people's dispossession. Treaty rights, not civil rights, were the struggle.

Boarding Schools

From Helen Hunt Jackson's *A Century of Dishonor* to Dee Brown's *Bury My Heart at Wounded Knee*, the broken treaties and genocidal slaughter of Native peoples in the United States periodically erupted into the nation's consciousness. But this national engagement with Native history often stops in 1890, with the Wounded Knee Massacre marking the end of the Indian Wars, the courageous but doomed resistance of Crazy Horse, Geronimo, and Chief Joseph; confinement on reservations; terrible epidemic disease; and population decline. The questions and controversies of the twentieth century—significant population rebound (and hence the increasing unsustainability of life on the paltry reservation land base), continued major land loss, fights over access to natural resources (water rights, mineral rights, and fishing rights), and questions of whether tribalism and resources held in common are "communism"—often fall by the wayside in some confused mixture of images of vanishing Indians and wealthy casino owners. But the basic question of Indian country in the twentieth century was sovereignty, and the most fundamental question about sovereignty was whether Native nations had control over their children.

Beginning in the 1890s separating Native kids from their families and communities was foundational to federal policy to "civilize" the savage, to teach children English, and to extinguish traditional religions and ways of life. Where the wars and reservation policy of the nineteenth century were the essential components of the struggle over the land base of Indian country, boarding schools were liberal or progressive measures established at the suggestion of the Indian Peace Commission and various "friends of the Indian" groups. The commission was created by Congress to seek the source of warfare on the plains in the 1860s. To their credit, members identified racism by settlers and railroads, charging that employees of the railroad were shooting down Indians "in wonton cruelty." But they also said that the problem was "the tribal or clannish organization" of Native people and their failure to speak English. "Now, by educating the children of these tribes in the English language, these differences would have disappeared, and civilization would have followed at once. Nothing then would have been left but the antipathy of race, and that too is always softened in the beams of a higher civilization."[23] The possibility that the problem really was that Native people were fighting railroads and settlers for land seems not to have been entertained.[24] Missionaries in particular urged the "civilization" of indigenous peoples rather than their massacre; in the next several years, three different (white) "friends of the Indian" groups were formed, and in 1883 the Lake Mohonk conferences began, which also urged boarding schools as a way (in the immortal words of the founder of Carlisle Indian School, Richard Pratt) to "kill the Indian to save the man"—eliminate children's cultural "Indian-ness" as an alternative to extermination.

In 1881 Congress declared school attendance for Indian children compulsory and authorized the BIA to deny benefits guaranteed by treaty right; they were to "withhold rations, clothing, and other articles from those parents who resisted sending their children to school."[25] Indian boarding schools spread rapidly through the West and Midwest. Few Native children attended day schools, in some places until the late 1970s.[26] Off-reservation boarding schools were popular among advocates of assimilation, Native and non-Native. As the American Indian studies scholar K. Tsianina Lomawaima writes, "The famous 'before and after' pictures of Carlisle students are as much a part of American iconography as the images of Custer's Last Stand. 'Savages' shed buckskin, feathers, robes, and moccasins; long black hair was shorn or bobbed or twisted into identical, "manageable" styles; pinafores, stiff starched collars, stockings, and black oxfords signified the 'new woman.' "[27] The regimes of Indian schools combined changes in fashion with transformations in language—children were punished, often harshly, for speaking indigenous languages; dress was carefully monitored and checked by staff. De-tribalizing Native children was the goal, and children were trained in domestic and farm work to encourage adult life among white people (albeit as their menial laborers).[28] Native children would often return home having forgotten their mother tongue—sometimes with no language in common with their parents; often, they could not do the basic work of subsistence, being not even able to herd sheep as children can. Andrea Smith has argued that sexual abuse of girls and boys was rife in boarding schools; an investigation into sexual abuse in boarding schools in Canada in the 1970s resulted in 3,400 complaints of sexual abuse. (No similar investigation has taken place in the United States, although some have argued that any full inquiry into the crimes in U.S. Indian boarding schools would find starvation, medical experimentation, involuntary sterilization of girls, and physical punishment that amounted to torture.)[29]

Activist groups, including the American Indian Defense Association (AIDA)—grandmother of the AAIA—began in the 1920s to mount successful campaigns for Native peoples to hold onto their land, religion, and lifeways, and one of their greatest successes was the reform of boarding schools. These groups became a thorn in the side of congressional and BIA efforts to allow non-Indians to develop the natural resources of Native lands—oil, water power, mineral resources, tourism—consistently testifying about violations of treaty rights, the failure of the United States to consider Native best interest in its role as trustee, and the conflict of interest inherent in locating the BIA in the Department of the Interior, with its role in managing natural resources. The AIDA's greatest victory in this period was an indirect one: prompted by what he called "harmful attacks and propaganda" (by the AIDA), Secretary of the Interior Hubert Work commissioned an "impartial" survey of conditions in Indian country from the Institute for Government Research (subsequently known as the Brookings Institute).[30] The result was the Meriam Report, published in 1928, which harshly criticized U.S. policy for its effects on the state of health and nutrition among Native people, the effects of allotment on indigenous landholding, and the consequence of the BIA's management of Indian resources with respect to their wealth (this being the first era of the image of the rich Indian, an image offered as a rerun when states fought to secure a portion of casino earnings).[31] Some of its harshest words were reserved for boarding schools. "The continued policy of removing Indian children from the home and placing them for years in boarding schools," the report's authors wrote, "largely disintegrates the family and interferes with developing normal family life."[32] It described children living in overcrowded dormitories, without even adequate toilet facilities at times, subsisting on a vastly inadequate diet and subject to terrible health conditions. Children were engaged in day labor half of the day—probably in violation of child labor laws—to support the school, with the other half of the day spent studying a curriculum of little value to them, the report suggested. They had virtually no leisure time and students were subject to extraordinarily harsh discipline. It was a grim picture indeed, worthy of Dickens.

The Meriam Report put pressure on the Hoover administration to close boarding schools, and it also discredited allotment—the Dawes Severality Act of 1887, or Dawes General Allotment Act, which had legally eviscerated many Native nations, eliminating the basis for holding land in common or for tribal jurisdiction over indigenous affairs. It and related legislation had led to the legal breakup of reservations, the allotting of tribal lands to individual households, and federal and state citizenship for those indigenous people who became "successful" farmers and ranchers. Its enactment was helped along considerably by a group with an interest in reducing Native land holdings: white homesteaders, who saw in this reform the opportunity to remove all that "unproductive" reservation land and give it to "productive" white settlers. Native peoples were redefined en bloc as farmers, even or especially those who got their livelihood from hunting, fishing, or forest products. This resulted in two particularly useful outcomes for those who sought white control of reservation land: American Indians needed a smaller land base, and there was leftover land to sell to white homesteaders and the railroads at bargain prices. Oil was discovered in Oklahoma, and the so-called Five Civilized Tribes—having suffered the Trail of Tears and Jackson's policy of removal from Georgia on the promise that in Oklahoma, at least, they would be undisturbed by Anglo settlers— were beset with hosts of oilmen, shady business dealers, and even the members of organized crime syndicates, who robbed and cheated them out of their land, people who made their living "grafting off the Indians," as the practice was popularly known. From the Southeast to Kansas to the Southwest, it is estimated that the land base of Indian country was depleted from 138 million acres of treaty land in 1887 to a mere 48 million acres when allotment was finally halted in 1934, of which 20 million of the remaining land was desert or semidesert.[33]

The Meriam Report sparked reform of the BIA and, ultimately, with the election of Franklin Delano Roosevelt, catapulted the AIDA's John Collier into the leadership of the BIA, as commissioner of Indian affairs. While much might be said about Collier's tenure, two things are important for our story here. First, he set out to replace boarding schools with day schools, allowing some Native children to be raised by their parents—for the first time in generations on many reservations. In both the remaining boarding schools and the day schools, he curtailed missionary and religious activity, forbidding compulsory attendance at religious services. He and his director of education got rid of menial labor in boarding schools and transformed the curriculum from teaching "civilization" to vocational education and rural development.[34] The second thing Collier accomplished in his tenure was the passage of the Indian Reorganization Act (IRA). Sometimes called the Indian New Deal, it contained provisions to restore communal (tribal) land ownership, an attempt to restore the integrity of reservations that had become "checkerboards" of Indian and non-Indian land through land sales to homesteaders, miners, and others. Finally and most controversially, he attempted to establish a framework through which tribal sovereignty—political and legal—could be established on a more substantial basis. To this end he consulted with tribes and organized votes on a political framework that included a constitution, tribal councils, a tribal chairman, and tribal courts. The majority of enrolled tribal members voted for it, but the measure was controversial. One complaint was that Collier strong-armed Native peoples, giving them one chance to vote for or against the political provisions—and accepting these provisions came with economic benefits. Another controversy was that it imported alien political traditions (essentially presidential and parliamentary) and brought competitive 50 percent plus one elections to peoples who had previously made decisions by consensus or through other corporate decision-making structures—essentially inflaming painful divisions within tribes already torn between "traditional" and "progressive" groups. For the most part, though, the IRA was seen as the best thing that had happened, politically, to Native people since the 1830s, when killing Indians became official U.S. policy (not exactly a high standard, admittedly). The basic concepts of restoring land and sovereignty were overwhelmingly popular.[35]

The New Deal also saw the passage of the Social Security Act of 1935, including Title IV, the Aid to Dependent Children (ADC) program, which had contradictory effects on the abilities of Native communities to maintain sovereignty over their children and of "unwed" Native mothers to raise them. Although the program was federal, it was implemented by state governments (which also contributed some of the funds), and states set the eligibility rules and the stipend amounts (to the detriment of black single mothers in the South—unmarried mothers, as pundits in the period would have it—but also Native mothers in the West). In the end its effect was to open up the conflict over the relationship of tribes to states, and the relationship of both to children, that culminated in the fights over massive numbers of Indian children in foster and adoptive care and hence over what became ICWA.

During the congressional debate on the original Social Security Act, Senator Norbeck of South Dakota proposed an amendment to make ADC for Indians a $30 a month *federal* stipend; this and subsequent efforts to get states out of the business of delivering benefits to reservations, however, failed.[36] As one state commissioner of public welfare put it in 1949, "Until Social Security benefits came into being, it was understood by the states that Reservation Indians were wards and under the control of the United States Government."[37] Some Western states, like Nevada, Arizona, and New Mexico, fiercely resisted assuming any responsibility for the support of Native children and their unmarried mothers—Arizona in fact evaded paying any benefits until 1960. In the 1940s and 1950s, Nevada had no ADC program for anyone in order to avoid paying benefits to Native mothers.[38] Although the Social Security Board prohibited denying ADC to any citizen based on race (which Southern states dealt with by claiming to exclude black mothers based on *morality*), Arizona claimed that unmarried Native mothers on reservations were not citizens because they did not pay taxes and few spoke English.[39] In 1947 the National Congress of American Indians (ADC) urged Native mothers on their own who were being systematically denied ADC in Arizona and elsewhere to demand a fair hearing for each denial, presaging a major tactic of the welfare rights movement of the 1960s. By forcing welfare officials into administrative hearings, the NCAI hoped to raise the visibility of Indian single mothers' issues and raise the cost to states of these wholesale denials.

Yet if this systematic denial of ADC to unmarried Native mothers was a problem, so too were the effects of winning benefits. Advocates saw the expansion of ADC—state administered welfare programs—to reservations as a logical extension of bargains made in treaties, which ceded land in exchange for resources and support for Indian people in perpetuity. Yet ADC also brought state welfare workers onto the reservations, and they saw their responsibility as including the supervision of children, unwed mothers, and foster mothers. What they found, as described by Arnold Lyslo, director of the IAP, was what many believed they saw whenever they were talking about unmarried mothers: "many of these children were left unsupervised on the reservation without proper care."[40] Others disputed this claim, saying what they were seeing was the absence of the traditional nuclear family, and instead, it was childrearing by extended families and communities.[41] Regardless, by the 1950s and 1960s the extension of ADC to reservations provided the warrant for state welfare workers to remove children from unmarried Indian mothers at massive rates—and, one could observe cynically, once the children were removed, the mothers were no longer eligible for state benefits.

Termination and the IAP

With the end of the New Deal, Collier and those sympathetic to his politics were once again on the outside of federal Indian policy. The 1950s brought the return to the BIA and to Indian policy missionaries who sought a program of assimilation for Native people and inaugurated the policy of "termination." Like allotment before, termination (initially called "liquidation," until policymakers concluded that carried unfortunate echoes of Nazi policies) was offered up as a policy that would bring justice and equality to indigenous peoples. It promised "to end the wardship status of the Indians and to grant them all the rights and prerogatives pertaining to American citizenship."[42] Congress was correct, of course, that wardship or trusteeship treated indigenous people as children. But termination envisioned the evisceration of all tribal government and federal infrastructure (like roads and hospitals), something trusteeship protected. Further, the law ended the ability of tribes to hold land in common or enjoy other collective rights that other corporate enterprises in the United States were acknowledged to have—companies, municipalities, and states, for example. When these rights were held or sought by Indians, it was pejoratively called "Communism."[43]

The other thing that came with termination—even for tribes that were not terminated—was new forms of involvement of states in tribal affairs, including child welfare. Public Law (PL) 280, passed in 1953, gave some states jurisdiction over civil and criminal matters on reservations (California, Minnesota, Nebraska, Oregon, and Wisconsin; and then Alaska upon statehood) and allowed other states to acquire jurisdiction at will. This caused all sorts of confusion about which courts (tribal, federal, state) were responsible for what kinds of legal issues, but, most importantly for our purposes, it brought Native children into state child welfare systems. Another termination-era policy complicated Indian child welfare questions even further. Having abandoned the framework of self-sufficiency on a communal land base, the federal government determined that Native people were both poor and far from cities where jobs could be found. Thus was born a federal policy that Wilma Mankiller called the second Trail of Tears: the BIA Indian Relocation Program paid some expenses and urged Native people to migrate to cities and take jobs (in an echo of development policy, as in Puerto Rico for example where policymakers urged working-class people there to migrate to cities like New York). This created, in a sense, the opposite jurisdictional question that PL 280 did with child welfare questions: if Native children or families were in trouble, they were coming into the state child welfare system from the cities, for the first time in significant numbers—with concomitant questions of jurisdiction, should urban Indians be referred to reservation-based tribal courts? Within a decade or two, these two kinds of encounters with the child welfare system—through states' reaching into reservations and tribal members moving to cities—had resulted in a startlingly extensive transfer of children from the households of tribal members to non-Native families. By 1968 more than one tribe had *all* of its children in out-of-home placement, living with non-Indians.[44]

In the 1940s and 1950s sufficient numbers of Native children were in state custody as to constitute a concern—and a potential new source of adoptable children, as there were about twice as many would-be white adoptive parents as there were white adoptable children. The IAP, a joint project of the (termination-era) BIA and the Child Welfare League of America (CWLA), sought specifically to place Native children with white families "far from the reservation," in the title of the famous outcome study.[45] In addition, beginning in 1957, social workers employed directly by the BIA won the authority—through contracts with state agencies—to seek voluntary relinquishment of children from their parents. Between 1958 and 1967 the IAP placed nearly four hundred children with white families, mostly on the East Coast. Intended as a demonstration project, it also sparked many agencies outside of the immediate program to place Indian children with white families.

Assimilation, Sovereignty, and Gender

The most explicit defense of the placement of Native children in Anglo families took place in the context of the IAP, even though the project was arguably its least important form, since compared to boarding schools or even the Mormon foster placement program the scant four hundred children it adopted out were hardly significant. Still, its symbolic value is considerable, since it was run by the most important players in federal Indian policy and child welfare matters—the BIA and the CWLA, respectively. It was the first and still the only federal government program that was designed specifically to promote (what it called) "transracial" adoption. Arnold Lyslo, the project's director, told the story of how it came into being this way:

> It had been apparent for some time, from the reports of the Area and Agency Welfare Staff of the Bureau of Indian Affairs, that many children who might have been firmly established in secure homes at an early age through adoption had been passed from family to family on a reservation or that they spent years at public expense in federal boarding schools or in foster care. They had never had the security of family life to promote their development and assure their future. Bureau of Indian Affairs social workers had reported that planning for the adoption of Indian children been difficult, largely due to a lack of facilities for finding families who were interested in adopting these children, and therefore the adoption of homeless Indian children had not been widespread. The Indian unwed mother seldom receives the assistance from social agencies usually available to the non-Indian. Isolation and a general sense that her situation is "natural" have precluded the counseling indicated to give her any choice in planning for herself and her child. From the experience of the Bureau of Indian Affairs, many of these children were left unsupervised on the reservation without proper care, and no permanent plan was made for them . . . very few unmarried mothers were ever given any choice but to keep their children.[46]

In Lyslo's account some Native American children needed adoption because they were, essentially, barely cared for, fed, or clothed. Native unwed mothers were being denied the opportunity to relinquish their children into adoption because of a lack of infrastructure to move their children from the reservation to white, would-be adoptive families, and unmarried mothers were denied "assistance from social agencies." The solution, as Lyslo, the BIA, and the CWLA framed it, was a program that could place them "far from the reservation," where there were proper resources for them.

In contrast, four years earlier in 1968, William Byler, executive director of the AAIA, had characterized the situation much differently. Speaking at a news conference at the Overseas Press Club in New York City with a delegation from the Devil's Lake Sioux (now the Spirit Lake Dakota Nation), Byler said:

> As sad and as terrible as the conditions are that Indian children must face as they grow up, nothing exceeds the cruelty of being unjustly and unnecessarily removed from their families. . . . Today in this Indian community a welfare worker is looked on as a symbol of fear rather than of hope. . . . The Devil's Lake Sioux people and American Indian tribes have been unjustly deprived of their lands and their livelihood . . . and now they are being dispossessed of their children. Indian leaders and parents charge . . . that county welfare workers frequently evaluate the suitability of an Indian child's home on the basis of economic or social standards unrelated to the child's physical or emotional well-being and that Indian children are removed from the custody of their parents or Indian foster family for placement in non-Indian homes without sufficient cause and without due process of law.[47]

Byler went on to say that 25 percent of the children of the Devil's Lake Sioux had been taken from their families to live in boarding schools, foster, or adoptive homes by state welfare agencies. Even a ruling by the North Dakota Supreme Court in 1963 that held that tribal courts had jurisdiction over child placement had not stopped welfare workers and others from removing children, nor had protests by those who were raising the children.[48] Mrs. Alex Fournier, a Devil's Lake Sioux foster parent that spoke at the same press conference as Byler, said "I told them they would take that child over my dead body," as she presented the story of a county welfare worker whom she said had tried to drag her three-year-old foster child out of her arms. She said that a Fargo adoption agency wanted to place the boy in a white adoptive home and were demanding his removal from the reservation. Similarly, Elsie Greywind told of being sent to jail for refusing to relinquish her grandchildren, whom welfare workers wanted to place in a white foster home.

These two statements could be taken as emblematic of the two positions on "transracial" placement of Indian children after 1950. The IAP was the last gasp of termination policy. Byler's claims about "due process" derived from an anti-termination politics, rooted in the activism of the AAIA throughout the 1950s, which insisted that termination policy was an illegal violation of treaty rights and an assault on the communal land base of Native peoples. In this view, treaties still carried force, and Native peoples had legal rights as members of separate nations that had formal legal relationships with the federal government.

Both Lyslo and Byler in fact saw these as the issues. Each located Native child welfare policy as another front in a larger struggle over U.S. Indian policy. Lyslo linked the difficulty of Native unwed mothers finding the infrastructure to place their children for adoption to President Lyndon Johnson's policy speech on Native issues, calling the problems of Indian country the problem of the "forgotten American." Native people, in Lyslo's account, were insufficiently integrated into the larger society, relegated to rural reservations, and denied access to the social services offered by the states, including adoption agencies and social workers. In contrast, Byler identified the question of child removal within a long genealogy in which Native people were deprived of lands and livelihood—part of a broader struggle for sovereignty and treaty rights, a set of relationships formed through law, in which tribes are political entities with rights to self-government and whose political relations are with the U.S. federal government, not with states. The broad question, then, was whether Native people were to be enclosed in a protective welfare state or left alone.

Seeing ICWA as critical to sovereignty politics (as the AAIA did) also helps locate Native mothers (biological, foster, de facto, or otherwise) at the center of this fight over sovereignty. From their testimony at court hearings and in congressional testimony, we get a sense of how tenaciously these caregivers fought to get their children back and the sometimes really difficult financial straits and other troubles they were negotiating. We can also see how thoroughly disregarded and powerless they were. Social workers and missionaries took children without any color of law; congressional representatives disregarded their testimony. It is revealing of the state of gender and Native politics in the early 1970s that ICWA was passed only when the AAIA abandoned the strategy of having mothers and sympathetic (mostly Native) social workers testify, replacing their testimony with statistics. It is striking to note that even in the context of fighting to defend unmarried mothers and other (mostly female) people raising children, mothers were still strikingly powerless to speak for themselves and to be heard.

In *Far from the Reservation* researcher David Fanshel interviewed white families who adopted children under the IAP and the children themselves, who were all eleven years old or younger at the time. From these interviews Fanshel determined that most of the children were doing well (only three-quarters, though—hardly a ringing endorsement), that they were largely able to make the adjustment to white families, and the families seemed happy with their decisions to adopt an Indian child—that they had not suffered overmuch from racial discrimination within their communities.[49] This and other outcome studies have for the most part defined the terms of debate about interracial adoption: are the kids all right? Some critics have raised questions about Fanshel's methodology, suggesting that the children were not old enough for him to make determinations about whether they were all right or not, and in fact, subsequent studies of rates of alcoholism, depression, and suicide among adoptees as adolescents and adults suggested tremendous pain.[50] Further, these critics point to the existence of the Lost Bird Society (named for a child found at the breast of her dead, frozen mother and taken by soldiers at the Wounded Knee Massacre), of adoptees seeking their lost Native communities and families, to suggest that all was not well at all.[51] Defenders of interracial adoption have argued, on the contrary, that there is essentially nothing to debate—that the outcome studies all point in the same direction, and the kids are fine.

But there is also a sense in which these questions are a red herring—not for the individuals involved, certainly, but from the perspective of the policy question Fanshel's book was supposed to answer: was the placing of Native children in white families a bad thing, an ethical good or not? The issue is not so much whether the four hundred children in the IAP thrived or did not—although certainly we should be concerned if they suffered life-long emotional harm—but why mothers, families, tribes and Native communities were losing their children in such numbers. Outcome studies tell us nothing about whether justice was done, why or how Native children became available for adoption.

Although federal policy has followed Byler in seeing ICWA and the adoption of Native children as a question of jurisdiction and sovereignty, welfare, and foster care, scholars and pundits, as we have seen, have largely followed Lyslo and Fanshel in seeing the issue as a question of race, adoption, and the problem of exclusion from social work and formal adoption. Like Lyslo and Fanshel, historians and commentators on adoption have most often started with the fact of the adoptable child and the quality of his or her relationship to white adoptive parents rather than inquiring

after the circumstances that separated that child from kin and community.[52] This view is deserving of a corrective. As with the NABSW and black
children, the crucial question about Native children was not whether white
families *could* raise them but, rather, why Indian mothers, families, and
communities were losing them in the first place.

The Campaign for ICWA

In 1968 the AAIA received a call from Louis Goodhouse, tribal chairman of
the Devil's Lake Sioux. The tribe had been struggling for years with child
welfare issues, insisting that adoption and other matters had to go through
tribal courts, not state courts. North Dakota's welfare bureaucracy, since it
controlled ADC, insisted that as a matter of policy it was entitled to take
children and place them in foster or adoptive care as its officials saw fit. As
we have seen the tribe had already taken them to court, all the way to the
North Dakota Supreme Court in fact, on this question—and won.[53] When
Goodhouse contacted the AAIA, county welfare officials, apparently imper-
vious even to state Supreme Court rulings, had struck again. Ivan Brown, a
six-year-old boy, had been living on the reservation with his grandmother
or, rather, with someone whom tribal tradition recognized as his grandmother. She was sixty-three. County welfare officials had decided that
Ivan's grandmother was too old to care for him and had placed him off the
reservation with a white foster family. The AAIA sent a young, long-haired
lawyer, Bertram Hirsch, to North Dakota to pursue the association's first
child welfare case. In the course of trying to get Ivan Brown back into the
custody of his grandmother (which they did, although it took months),
Hirsch and the tribe found that a quarter of the tribe's children had been
placed off the reservation—either in boarding schools, in white foster
homes, or in adoptions—and that while Native people comprised only 2–3
percent of the populations of North and South Dakota, their children
represented 50 percent of the young people in foster care in the states.[54]
The Tribal Council continued to take the position that state and county
welfare officials had no right to place their children at all and passed a
resolution forbidding county officials from removing children from the
reservation at all. County officials retaliated by halting welfare payments
(from the BIA, hence they were federally funded) to the tribe.[55] As we saw
above, a delegation from the Devil's Lake Sioux that included Tribal Chairman Lewis Goodhouse and five women who became activists through their

involvement with children—Alvina Alberts, Elsie Greywind, Mrs. Alex Fournier, Annie Jane DeMarce Leftbear, and Genevive Hunt Longie Goodhouse—went to New York for a press conference, then to Washington to negotiate with the BIA. Greywind had been to jail for refusing to give up her grandchildren. Mrs. Fournier was a foster parent who was fighting the county to retain custody of her foster child on the reservation rather than have him adopted by a white couple in Fargo. Another mother had lost five children to foster care. "They want to make white people out of the Indians," said Alberts. "They're starting with the kids because they couldn't do it to us." Alberts continued: "They use their own standards to judge us. What is the difference if an Indian home is poor but there is plenty of love?" Genevive Hunt Longie Goodhouse spoke of unemployment on the Fort Totten reservation, which exceeded 90 percent most of the year. Under North Dakota state law, "chronic dependency"—that is, long-term use of ADC entitlements—was a reason to remove a child from the home, meaning that, given the employment rate on the reservation, somewhere above 90 percent of the children at Fort Totten were at risk of being removed by welfare officials.[56]

The press conference got attention in the international media, which embarrassed President Lyndon Johnson. He apparently called Secretary of the Interior Stewart Udall and Department of Health, Education, and Welfare (HEW) Secretary Wilbur Cohen and told them, "You have got to do something about what is going on in Devil's Lake."[57] Although this story seems incredible in the context of how little scrutiny most Indian child welfare matters received, it is important to remember that this was the Cold War. Johnson, in particular, was sensitive to charges that the United States was abusing poor and minoritized populations. With the pressure generated from the press conference and their own lobbying, the group was wildly, even startlingly, successful. They got the BIA food stamp program rerouted through the tribal government rather than the county. In 1971 the Devil's Lake Sioux began to receive HEW funding for a Family Development Center—run by a Child Welfare Board appointed by the Tribal Council—that provided counseling and other services for families at risk of losing their children. They also finally succeeded in having child welfare cases go through the Tribal Court rather than the bureaucracy of the county welfare department, which, after a federal-level HEW investigation and "staff shakeups," developed "cordial relations" with the tribe.[58]

Hirsch's preliminary research into the high rates of out-of-home placement on this one reservation led the AAIA to conclude that the organization needed a child welfare program. "It was not conceivable that the Devil's Lake Sioux could stand alone" in this high placement rate, Hirsch said later. In 1968 and 1969 the group conducted a survey of child-placing agencies, correctional institutions, and the BIA's statistics in sixteen states and found that 25 to 35 percent of Native children were in out-of-home placements in states with a large Native population; 85 percent were with non-Indian families, with little concern for whether the children even spoke English. In some states, where the overwhelming majority of non-Indian children were white, the magnitude of the difference between placement rates for Native and non-Native children was astonishingly large: in Washington, Indian children were 19 times more likely to be adopted than their non-Indian counterparts and almost 10 times as likely to be in foster care; in Wisconsin, the rates were nearly 18 times higher for adoption, 14 times higher for foster care. In South Dakota, adoptive placements were 7.5 times more likely to occur with Native children, and foster care was 15.7 times more likely.[59]

In early October of 1968 the AAIA also participated in an effort to address another component of the separation of Native children from their families—boarding schools, which, while enrolling a smaller percentage of youngsters than in the 1920s and 1930s, were nevertheless very much still in existence. The Senate Subcommittee on Indian Education collected four volumes of testimony on Indian boarding schools, and psychiatrists, tribes, and activists testified to the harm they caused. Dr. Daniel O'Connell of the AAIA testified to the necessity of the federal government building day schools that would enable Native children to live with their families. In this and subsequent testimony, the AAIA pointed to the youngest children in boarding schools—nine thousand children under the age of nine years old, comprising, at the high end, 90 percent of Navajo children. In his statement, O'Connell included the following, "Whatever may have been the official governmental attitude, education for the Indian in the past has proceeded largely on the theory that it is necessary to remove the Indian child as far as possible from his home environment; whereas the modern point of view in education and social work lays stress on upbringing in the natural setting of home and family life." Then he added, "The source from which I am quoting is the Merriam Report," written forty years earlier. Since Collier's resignation as commissioner of the BIA in 1945, little progress had been made in closing boarding schools. In fact, in some ways they had become worse; increasing numbers of Native children, particularly teens, were being sent to boarding schools as a "social placement"—as an alternative to foster care or to deal with disruptive behavior at school, alcohol abuse problems, or mental health issues. Concentrating kids in pain and in trouble, coupled with very little adult supervision (ratios were eighty children to one adult and even worse), made boarding schools difficult and even frightening environments for many of the children in them, perhaps especially those there in "social" placements.[60]

In 1972 the publication of *Far from the Reservation*, increasing activism in Canada, and the AAIA's ongoing efforts brought attention to child welfare issues from a wider number of groups. The influential Mohawk newspaper *Akwesasne Notes* of upstate New York publicized activism by Native, Inuit, and métis people in Canada to try to halt what researcher Patrick Johnson called Canada's "Sixties Scoop" of indigenous children.[61] Since the Adoption Resource Exchange of North America (ARENA) program was placing Native Canadian children in the United States, and American Indian children in Canada, the efforts in the two countries were necessarily tied to each other.[62] *Akwesasne Notes* (AN) began to publish regular, large articles decrying the "social genocide" of the adoption of Indian children by white families, stressing that while the paper did not want to see existing adoptions undone (although the AAIA did and had to be reeled back by activists and social workers from proposing a sixteen-year retrospective review of adoptions in their draft of the bill that became ICWA),[63] they did want Native readers to seek licenses to become foster and adoptive parents and white readers not to apply to adopt Native children. AN also offered to work with ARENA officials to publicize the need for adoptive homes for Native children—an offer that ARENA personnel declined. The National Indian Youth Council ("the SNCC [Southern Nonviolent Coordinating Committee] of Indian Affairs")[64] likewise sharply questioned ARENA efforts.[65] Also that year three more Lakota tribes—the Sisseton-Wahpeton Sioux, the Standing Rock Sioux, and the Oglala Sioux—joined the Devil's Lake Sioux (1968) and the Three Affiliated Tribes of the Fort Berthold Reservation (1971) in passing Tribal Council resolutions denouncing the manner and the rate at which children from their nations were being placed in off-reservation foster homes.

Meanwhile, the AAIA—meaning primarily Hirsch—became involved in a steadily increasing number of child welfare and custody cases, primarily in the Midwest and West. The AAIA litigated more than twenty such cases, including that of four-year-old John, who was taken from his mother, Cheryl Spider de Coteau (Sisseton-Wahpeton Sioux), on the grounds that she sometimes left him with his sixty-nine-year-old great-grandmother, Melinda

Spider, whom the welfare caseworker believed was too old to care for him. The welfare department, after obtaining a court order for John (which a judge granted without even holding a hearing), followed up by taking Spider de Coteau's other child—this time without bothering with the court order. Although the mother got her two children back after a long court battle (and a long period in strangers' homes for the young children), it was a mixed victory to bring children lost as preschoolers home years later.

In the month of June of 1972 alone welfare officials took twenty-two other children from Sisseton-Wahpeton Sioux families on grounds that included poverty, poor housing, lack of indoor plumbing, and overcrowding. Blossom Lavone, a three-year-old Rosebud Sioux child, was taken by California social workers when her aunt brought her to that state, anticipating that the mother would follow in a month. Although they had no evidence of her mother's unfitness, social workers made a blanket argument that a reservation was no place to rear a child.[66] In 1973 Delphine Shaving Bear (Standing Rock Sioux) gave the South Dakota State Department of Public Welfare temporary custody of her one-year-old son, Christopher, so she could hitchhike several hundred miles in a successful, week-long quest to recover custody of her other two children. When she returned, the welfare department refused to return the baby because his foster parents wanted to adopt him, despite the statement at the bottom of the form that Shaving Bear had signed: "I understand that this does not give the Division of Child Welfare the right to place my child for adoption." Child welfare officials argued that her relinquishment of Christopher in itself constituted evidence of neglect, authorizing them in fact to place Christopher for adoption—in clear contradiction of the form's assurances to the contrary. A year and a half later, when Christopher was nearly three, a circuit court decided that since Christopher had been living on the reservation, the state court had no jurisdiction and returned the boy to his mother.[67] In 1974 Vivian Shomin (Ottawa) left her six children in the care of a close friend in Peshawbestown, Michigan, to look for a place to live. When the friend applied for welfare benefits to help support the children temporarily, a caseworker obtained an emergency court order for the children, saying that the friend was not a licensed foster parent. Shomin arrived at the friend's house half an hour after the welfare department had put the children in foster care. At a hearing, welfare workers then changed tack, saying that Shomin's home was inadequate as it lacked indoor plumbing (according to the census, as late as 1990, 20 percent of Indian homes lacked indoor plumbing;[68] this argument was tantamount to saying that being poor, or occupying the particular sociological niche of poverty which Native mothers were offered, was reason in itself to lose your children). The children ranged in age from four to fifteen when they were taken; it took nearly a year and the involvement of the AAIA before the children were returned.[69]

In another case Benita Rowland, a three-year-old Oglala Lakota child from the Pine Ridge reservation in South Dakota, was taken from the reservation on January 1, 1972, and "adopted" by two women from Wisconsin, including the University of Wisconsin-Whitewater history professor Janette Bohi and her former student Judy Athas with the blessing of a local missionary group—but not a court.[70] As the lawyer for Rowland's father, Frederick van Hencke, put it, "there was not only no adoption, their was no *pretense* of adoption, no color of law. These people had absolutely no legal right to take that little girl."[71] In a letter to Rowland's mother, the pair wrote of the religious basis for the adoption, "We have not taken Benita from you; you gave her physical birth, which we could not give, and we can give her opportunities which you could not give—so she belongs to both of us. But far more, she belongs to the Lord."[72] When the AAIA got involved on behalf of Rowland's father, the group found that the pair also had another child from the reservation, Vina Bear Eagle, an infant from Wounded Knee. Ten months later Rowland's father went to court in Milwaukee and got their child back, and the couple also returned Vina Bear Eagle.[73]

This was a disturbing but not all that unusual scenario, in which families could lose children without any pretense of legality. For those who are accustomed to being fully citizens, in the sense of being the subject of law, this is hard to understand; a few years later, the Native social worker Evelyn Blanchard was testifying to a panel of lawyers and judges about how (even after the passage of ICWA) a child could be taken from his or her family and placed in a boarding school or foster placement against the family's wishes. Startled, the panel asked how this could be done, legally, and even reading the transcript one can sense their incomprehension as she tried to explain that it is done *without* any legal mechanism.

> JUDGE JAMES DELANEY: How do the kids get there? Who puts them there?
>
> MS. EVELYN BLANCHARD: Either Bureau of Indian Affairs social workers place them there or state social workers place them there. Tribal social workers will even place them.
>
> JUDGE JAMES DELANEY: Are they placed without a court hearing or a court order?

MS. EVELYN BLANCHARD: At times, yes.

JUDGE JAMES DELANEY: And who gives the placement agent the right to take a child from the home and place him? How does he get that authority?

MS. EVELYN BLANCHARD: Sometimes there is no authority . . . some children are removed without any authority except the decision of the caseworker. That's what the Association survey revealed, and it continues as a practice in communities.[74]

That there really was no necessary connection between a court order and losing your child—the caseworker just comes and puts the child in her or his car and drives away, with more or less fighting and crying, either way—seems almost incomprehensible to the judge. But the fact that this was frequently the case is also evidenced by the fact that the AAIA won every child custody case in which it intervened—no one on the other side had even tried to act within the law. It was just Indian kids.

The Benita Rowland case suggests another dimension of the problem of Native child custody—religious groups, Protestant, Mormon, and Catholic, had long operated without much oversight on reservations. The extent of their customary authority can be felt in their outrage in having it challenged —and in the fact that it was religious groups and the federal government (the BIA, HEW) that opposed ICWA. The Church of Jesus Christ of Latter-day Saints (LDS, or Mormons), for example, testified against ICWA, saying it would jeopardize their placement program, which had 2,700 Native children in foster care with Mormon families—often for most of their childhoods, according to the affidavits of adults who had participated as children—to allow them to attend schools and churches outside the reservation. Harold Brown, testifying for LDS Social Services (a state agency), said that while in general his agency had no opposition to ICWA, they wished for the LDS Placement Program to be exempt. Notifying the tribe would be an undue burden because, as he began his testimony, "Some do not have tribal councils; they would not know what to do with the information if it came. Some small bands may not be well organized, we find some difficulty," but he was then cut off by backers of the bill who protested from the audience.[75]

The LDS Church had a long and rather complex history with Native children, dating back to their first days in Utah, when it was still part of Mexico, and they would purchase Native children sold in a slave trade to "redeem" and convert them. The Mormons also had a theologically complicated relationship to Native peoples, believing them to be a lost and fallen tribe of Israel, and felt a special entitlement—even a duty—to convert them. And for all that Mormons denounced Indian slavery as cruel, and certainly believed that Native children were entitled to an upbringing akin to that of their own children, LDS leader Brigham Young also urged them to buy Indian slave children—to prevent their sale to heathen Mexican Catholics and because bondage was, well, convenient to the project of conversion. To this end, when Utah became part of the United States the state legislature outlawed slavery (of Indians, not of African descendents) but legalized another form of bondage—the indenturing of Native children. (Territorial New Mexico, in contrast, outlawed all forms of bondage, of indigenous people and of Africans—although by all reports it continued anyway.[76]) Although the LDS Church was quite successful in conversions among the Navajo (in 1981 an estimated 20 percent of Navajos were Mormons), the placement program drew the ire of the Navajo Tribal Council long before the campaign for ICWA. The LDS Placement Program was begun in 1954, and already by 1956, and again in 1960, the Tribal Council had passed resolutions saying that while the nation neither favored nor disfavored adoption of Navajos by people who were not Navajo, the *only* legitimate reasons for a non-Navajo to remove a minor child from the reservation was either pursuant to an adoption or other custody order issued by the Navajo Tribal Council or to attend a nonsectarian program approved by the BIA. The 1960 resolution continued, eloquent in its fury and frustration: "The Chairman of the Navajo Tribal Council is hereby directed to cause an investigation to be made of missionaries and other non-Navajo persons who may have been violating [the 1956 resolution], and where there is ground to believe that such missionaries or other persons propose to continue violating said [resolution], to cause them to be excluded from the Navajo Reservation. In case such missionaries or other persons operate from islands of fee-patent land on the Navajo Indian Reservation, the Chairman is nevertheless authorized . . . to have said persons physically removed from Navajo Tribal land."[77] It is noteworthy that in 1978 the LDS program was far larger than the IAP ever was, although the criticism of it was far more muted—limited to a Children's Bureau study in 1975–76, which found little benefit to Native children's participation in the Mormon foster home placement program.[78] Marshalling testimony from Native people who had participated in the program as children and parents, however, LDS representatives succeeded in carving out an exception for themselves in ICWA.

Catholic Social Services, in contrast, was less successful. In her testimony on ICWA, Sister Mary Clare Ciulla of Anchorage said that the National

Conference on Catholic Charities opposed the bill. She argued that the requirement to notify the tribe (and offer tribal judges the right to request that jurisdiction be transferred to tribal court or that tribal officials have standing in state court as interested parties) was tantamount to telling a girl's parents, relatives, and whole community about an unwed pregnancy that she might seek to keep secret. Further, Sister Ciulla argued against a provision then in the bill allowing a mother a long period of time to revoke consent to an adoption, saying that it needlessly jeopardized adoptions by leaving would-be adoptive parents in a position of risk for an awkward and untenable period. She also questioned the need to bring adoptions before a judge at all, saying without apparent embarrassment that it was not customary practice for her agency or others in Alaska to seek court approval when dealing with Inuit or Alaskan Native children (the AAIA child custody cases suggest this may well have been true in a great many places, although only Sister Mary Clare apparently was bold enough—or entitled enough—to admit it before Congress). She suggested that as long as there was a "trained social worker" involved, it was overly formal and bureaucratic to have a court involved in a mother's relinquishment.[79]

The testimony of both the LDS representatives and Sister Mary Clare was answered directly by Faye La Pointe (Puyallup), coordinator of the Tacoma Indian Center, a supporter of ICWA who took serious exception to both. She argued that their concerns about whether tribal governing agencies could handle confidential information appropriately—information regularly exchanged among social workers and agencies, not to mention within state governments—was in itself evidence of anti-Indian racism. She described the LDS program as one aimed at removing Indian children from their homes "disguised" as an educational program. Calling Christianity a "foreign influence" on indigenous ways of life, she suggested that unwed pregnancy was only a source of shame to a woman or girl who had been alienated from traditional beliefs—that the Christianity that offered itself as the answer to unmarried pregnancy was in fact the problem. "An Indian person who has been trained in Christianity will feel the stigma of *sin*. This is the reason unwed mothers must seek outside help and feel the need to relinquish their rights to the child." But, she added, that was not a traditional Native belief, in which it would be understood that "a child is a gift from the Creator."[80]

It was not an accident that resistance to child removal blossomed among the Lakota or at Pine Ridge—the Benita Rowland case was litigated at a time and place where the American Indian Movement (AIM) received a great deal of support there, and just a few months before the beginning of the three-year FBI occupation of the Pine Ridge reservation that culminated in the armed standoff at Wounded Knee, where two FBI agents were killed and, many charge, Leonard Peltier was framed for their murder. He is serving a life sentence at this writing.[81] Initially, Peltier fled to Canada to avoid being arrested by the FBI and fought extradition, proclaiming his innocence of the charges and saying he could not get a fair trial in the United States (not without reason; in Senate hearings on AIM a few years later the testimony of FBI agents who had infiltrated the group were replete with references to "Moscow" and "AK-47s," suggesting that AIM members were on the wrong side of the Cold War, allied with the Soviet Union, and, similar to decolonization movements like that in North Vietnam that had armed themselves with the Soviet-made AK-47, they were perhaps aiming to overthrow the U.S. government).[82] Myrtle Poor Bear was the author of an affidavit against Leonard Peltier that said she was his girlfriend and that she saw him kill the agents. While she later disavowed the affidavit, saying she was not even at Wounded Knee, it secured his extradition from Canada, his trial—although it was not entered into evidence at the trial—and in a sense his sentence. Poor Bear later said that she wrote it because she was threatened by the FBI: "They started threatening me about my daughter, that's Marty. They said that they were going to take her away from me and I wasn't ever going to see her again, and that I had to cooperate with them. They said, you're going to say this, we're going to make you say it, and if you don't say it, then you aren't going to see Marty no more."[83] After Benita Rowland, after Ivan Brown, Vina Bear Eagle, Blossom Lavone, Christopher Shaving Bear, and all the other incidents where courts said that children had been improperly taken from their families among the Lakota—to say nothing of the Tribal Council resolutions of the Sisseton-Wahpeton, Devil's Lake, and Standing Rock Sioux—it was completely credible (whether as a threat by the FBI or even a confused or dishonest story) that Myrtle Poor Bear was afraid of losing her daughter.

In 1972 the AAIA attempted to duplicate its earlier study of placement rates, to understand if placement rates were continuing at the same high rate, but without success: the BIA—no doubt feeling burned by the AAIA's use of the data the first time to criticize the bureau's placement practices— told its area offices and agencies not to cooperate. Only after the AAIA threatened legal action on its Freedom of Information Act request did the BIA finally comply with their request, releasing data on foster, adoptive, and institutional care for Native children. This time, the AAIA was able to gather wider data, producing the number that dominated the debate in the years to follow: 25 percent of Native children were, or would be, in out-of-home care. This number was based on Minnesota, where over the course of the 1960s the average number of Native children adopted had more than doubled, and the group's estimates of the number of Native children under a year old adopted was one in four. Based on the rate of increase, the AAIA expected that within a decade 25 percent of Native children would be adopted. This number, perhaps more than anything else, enabled the AAIA to win a wide public hearing.

In 1973 Joseph Goldstein, Anna Freud, and Albert Solnit published *Beyond the Best Interests of the Child*, a controversial book even in the child welfare community, and one that subsequently merited the AAIA's lone published book review. The book distinguishes between "biological parents" and "psychological parents," arguing that above all what children need is continuity in their relationships with a significant adult or adults, who may or may not be the biological parents. While this might seem straightforward, it had all sorts of ramifications that had a disproportionate impact on Native, black, and impoverished communities. First, they argue that foster care, because it represents a family status always subject to change at the whim of the state, is a much less desirable alternative than adoption, which provides permanence. Second, it provides a rationale for preferring continuity to fairness. At the extreme, it argues that even if a parent has unjustly lost custody of a child, a court or social worker should prefer a continuation of that situation (particularly if it has continued for a considerable period of time, as measured in the *child's* perception, which could actually be quite short if the child were unfairly placed from birth) to returning the child to a parent who is, in effect, a "stranger" to that child. This argument separates the interests of children and biological parents, suggesting, basically, that adults should bear even extreme injustice for the good of the child: "Whatever the court decides, inevitably there will be hardship. It may be the biological parents, already victimized by poverty, poor education, ill health, [racial] prejudice, their own ambivalence, or other circumstances, who are denied their child." It provided a logic by which courts and social workers could do what they often preferred to do anyway: award custody to middle-class white adopters as opposed to impoverished or racially minoritized parents, and all in the best interests of the child, breaking the cycle of poverty by placing the child with the wealthier family: "only in the implementation of this policy does there lie a real opportunity for beginning to break the cycle of sickness and hardship bequeathed from one generation to the next by adults who as children were denied the least detrimental alternative." Within a generation, this argument would become commonsense, but the AAIA recognized it for what it was: a serious attack on the legitimacy of even thinking that impoverished parents had a "right" to their children and a post facto legitimation that even an unjust placement was the "best" because the foster or adoptive parents represented the "psychological" parents.[84]

In the context of the emergence of these "commonsense" arguments for child removal, in the 1970s the AAIA began working more consciously to build popular awareness of questions of justice in Indian child welfare issues, starting a quarterly newsletter, *Indian Family Defense*, that it distributed free of charge to between three and five thousand groups and individuals, including tribes, urban Indian groups, and public libraries all over the country. The National Congress of American Indians, not the first nor the only but surely one of the most significant pan-indigenous (rather than tribally based) organizations, passed a resolution that year calling for change. The *American Journal of Psychiatry* published an influential editorial, written by the chairman of the American Psychiatric Association's Task Force on Indian Affairs, that called Indian boarding schools "a hazard to mental health."[85] AN published another set of ever-more critical articles, calling now not only for more Native foster and adoptive parents but for an end to "abusive practices" that were bringing children into the system, which the paper now began to identify as the root of the problem.[86] A small group of Native mothers out of New Mexico organized a conference and formed an organization, Native American Children's Advocates, calling for measures to make it easier for Native people to become foster and adoptive parents—charging that agencies were discriminating against them—and urging social workers to place foster children with grandparents, instead of strangers, when families were in crisis. They also called for services to make it possible to care for and educate children with disabilities at home— instead of special boarding schools—and to create mobile health units that could provide medical care for children with disabilities, as well as prenatal care, on reservations.[87]

After years of calling for a national investigation of Indian child welfare practices, in 1974 the AAIA finally got one when James Abourezk, junior senator from South Dakota (and the first Arab-American senator) held hearings. These hearings, as Evelyn Blanchard (Laguna and Yaqui) of the Association of Indian Social Workers and a BIA employee argued a few years later, were really the beginning of widespread grassroots organizing against abusive child welfare practices.[88] The hearings themselves could be heartbreaking: "Margaret Townsend, a Paiute of Fallon, Nevada, described how her children were forcibly taken from her home without her consent and placed in foster care by county welfare workers after she had been arrested—for the first time in her life—for driving while intoxicated. Her daughter, Anna, was also a witness. She was planning to describe to the subcommittee the treatment she and her brother had in their foster home. Instead, after a brave start, she broke down and cried, a testimony more effective than her words could have been."[89] Many of the families that the AAIA had previously helped win (or get) child welfare hearings testified about their experiences—Ben Rowland, Cheryl Spider DeCoteau, and Mrs. Alex Fournier of Devil's Lake. Betty Jack (Chippewa) testified about sterilization on the Lac du Flambeau Reservation in Wisconsin, telling the story of an unmarried mother who was told by a welfare worker that she could keep her four children only if she consented to sterilization; she agreed, under duress, and they took her children anyway. Another unmarried mother, she said, was sent to the Keshena Women's Prison when she became pregnant for the third time; at delivery, she was sterilized and the baby placed for adoption. Others testified about the problems of Native adolescents who had grown up in foster, adoptive, institutional, or boarding school care, who ran away (or back) to the reservation, who were lost, who had chronic behavior problems. Still others talked about the problems with providing subsidies to Native foster homes that non-Native foster parents received as a matter of course—because the funding stream for foster care came from the federal government to the states through the Social Security Act, but tribes were ineligible—and many states believed they lacked the jurisdiction (or, perhaps, the desire, given the poverty and poor housing of the population) to license foster homes on reservations.[90] The University of Minnesota psychiatrist Joseph Westermeyer talked powerfully about what happens to mothers, families, and communities that systematically lose their children: for the adults as much as the children, it is a trauma that exacerbates any problems that might exist—unemployment, say, or alcoholism—by adding layers of despair, humiliation, and grief. He chronicled what happened in eight families after children were taken and placed in (white) foster homes—binge drinking became alcoholism, there were suicide attempts, divorces, mental health treatment, behavior problems in the older children, people left the community. For communities as a whole, he called the process "ethnocide" and a "modern Trail of Tears."[91]

At the request of Senator Abourezk, in 1976 the AAIA drafted the first version of the Indian Child Welfare Bill. It, and the hearings that followed, are a study in the transformation of a subaltern, incoherent, unnarratable tale of children lost into an official story of statistics. Wrong was done that could be undone through law. Indeed, legal scholars often still narrate it this way. For example, the following comes from a legal manual published in 2001: "A 1974 study by the Association of American Indian Affairs showed that 25 to 35 percent of all Indian children had been removed from their families and placed in foster, adoptive, or institutional care . . . In an attempt to correct this problem, Congress passed the Indian Child Welfare Act in 1978."[92] No activism, lobbying, newsletters, court cases, national organizations, messy, incoherent stories by weeping mothers, no barely believable tales of welfare workers forcing children into cars or missionaries talking shamed, unmarried mothers into giving up their children without court orders—there was a problem embodied in a number, and Congress acted. It is a structure of explanation replicated by law review articles, commentary, and even a Supreme Court case on ICWA, elegant in its simplicity, its assumption that injustices are self-correcting—and its funda- mental wrongness.[93] The AAIA, coordinating with Abourezk and his staff, drafted the bill, coordinated the witness list, sent copies of the bill to tribes and urban Indian groups for comment. It was a masterful political cam- paign, born of fifty years of experience doing similar work, in delivering an "Indian" point of view to Washington, and ten years of figuring out how to present child welfare and custody as an issue. Alcoholism, lack of indoor plumbing, old cars that break down, communities without schools, moth- ers who leave their children with "relatives" who are only relatives through complex tribal traditions, people who don't speak English, dirty, ill-clothed, and runaway children, an incoherent system where no one could say with certainty how many Native children were in it, except that there are a lot of them—all made for difficult, complicated stories that are hard to present sympathetically to outsiders. Even more, the stories themselves so often seemed barely rational, hard to credit: a social worker just walked up to your child when you were in court about the other one, took him by the hand, and walked out? And there was never a dependency hearing, never a finding of parental unfitness?[94] These things made no sense in Congress.

One of the ways the hearings of 1974, 1976, and 1977 transformed these narratives from impossible or incoherent to an official story was by re- gendering them. While there are plenty of exceptions, the narrative about Indian children being "scooped" was mostly a story about conflicts and problems between and among women and girls—mostly female (and mostly Anglo) social and welfare workers, missionaries, and adoptive and foster mothers and (usually Native) mothers and grandmothers on the reservation, and pregnant, unwed girls. The AAIA masculinized it. It introduced male lawyers, invited (mostly male) tribal chairmen to testify, offered up social science to develop statistics, and called on male psychiatrists, academics, and executive directors of urban Indian groups. This is not a reproach to the AAIA—their witness list probably had more women on it than any comparable list for congressional hearings, and it is very clear that this was a group that *did* listen sympathetically and carefully to dispossessed women on reservations who were distraught about their children, even to those who might appear at first glance to be less-than-perfect mothers, or only informally mothers at all. (The AAIA also did have an internal history of female leadership.) As advocates, the AAIA did what was necessary to win: offer witnesses who would give credence to the testimony of distraught mothers. The group built powerful alliances with tribal authorities and sought and found witnesses like Joseph Westermeyer, a psychiatrist and academic, to testify to the harmful effects of separating children from their families. However, it is a commentary about the gender of authoritative discourse. Between the hearings of 1974 and the hearings of 1977 the distraught mothers, unwed girls, weeping children, and incoherent stories—so powerful and prominent in 1974—disappeared, replaced instead with the social science treatise that makes innumerable guesses and leaps but arrives at singular, distilled numbers: Indian children are disproportionately in out-of-home care.[95]

As part of the hearings in 1976 the AAIA finally presented a written version of its data on Native children in foster, boarding school, and adoptive care. The first—and in many ways most interesting—thing that emerges from the data is how hard it was to find out how many Native kids were in foster or adoptive care. Most states kept no statistics on the percentage of their foster care population that was Indian—and of course, the broader experience of the AAIA in advocating for families was that many Native kids passed into foster, institutional, or even adoptive care outside the legal system and hence would not have turned up in the statistical picture anyway. Private foster and adoptive agencies—including the massive LDS Placement Program—often declined to participate in the AAIA survey. County-by-county surveys yielded tremendously various pictures, suggesting certainly a harshness about the treatment of Native families—even where Native populations were tiny there were still often high rates of foster and adoptive placements—but above all a system where authority is vested very locally, in individual social workers and administrators. Michel Foucault tells us about governmentalities and statistics, of the control of population. Yet the interesting thing here is that the absence of central control, the absence of statistics, the creation of a vast, unpredictable, poorly regulated system with little oversight is equally capable of producing regular, predictable results— Native children were tremendously likely to be separated from their parents.[96] The absence of statistics, like the absence of legal regulation in how children were taken, speaks to another kind of dispossession by the state that we have barely begun to name, a kind of a-lawfulness and official indifference that speaks volumes about the varieties of forms of fraught inclusion.

There was, still, one vast and centralized administrative apparatus in relation to Native children—the BIA boarding school. In the nineteen states the AAIA surveyed, there were an estimated 330,000 Native children, of whom more than 29,000 lived away from home in BIA boarding schools or dormitories—nearly 10 percent. However, this, too, was deeply uneven— most Inuit and Alaskan Native children who attended high school were in boarding school; Arizona, with the largest Native population of any state in which they gathered statistics, had nearly 11,000 (of 54,000) Native children in boarding schools or more than 20 percent.[97] Boarding schools were still a vast "civilizing" machine: converting Diné speakers into English speakers, estranging them from non-English speaking grandparents; the purveyors, too, of a curriculum that bred failure as much as knowledge, alcoholism, violence, and loneliness as often or more often than empowerment or poetry or the ability to participate effectively in communities and public spheres. The boarding school system did explicitly what the disproportionate rates of foster care and adoption did implicitly: participate in the larger policy of termination, of the systematic extinction of tribes, communal lifeways, and communal landholding.

There were two major policy proposals in the testimony for the bill and the behind-the-scenes negotiations about it that failed, and these are quite as interesting as what the bill did do. The first was funding. There were various proposals, including that funding for Indian child welfare programs in tribes should be routed through HEW rather than the BIA, as the BIA was seen as part of the problem, and that Title XX of the Social Security Act be amended so that federal funds for foster care could be routed directly to tribes rather than only to states.[98] There were also a variety of proposals for crisis intervention services that would keep families together.[99] All were killed in the final version of the bill, at the behest of the Carter administration—the BIA, HEW, and Justice Department all indicated that the act seemed to signal an entitlement of tribes to federal funds for foster care that, they suggested, merely duplicated state services.[100] The second was to expand the definition of "Indian" or "Indian tribe" to include those not eligible for enrollment for varieties of reasons, to include terminated tribes and state-recognized tribes, to encompass those who lacked sufficient "blood quantum" to be enrolled.[101] The blood quantum rules, the product of Dawes Act-era allotment rolls and negotiations between tribes and the federal government (which sought to count as few people as possible as Indians) over tribal enrollment rules, were an unfortunate by-product of the effort to ground ICWA in the notion of tribal sovereignty rather than some other notion of Indian-ness. Although fighting for broader inclusionary rules about the nature of tribal "citizenship" would not preclude an argument that the bill was grounded in questions of political status rather than race, the AAIA sought to politically position tribes as already existing entities with polities, structures, courts, and constitutions and preferred not to open up those questions for debate. So while the AAIA fought hard to support tribes on the funding questions, they were unresponsive to the broad problems of which children could be enrolled.

When ICWA did pass in 1978 what remained were procedural requirements that enshrined the notion of tribal sovereignty. Indian child welfare cases were to be considered in tribal courts when children resided on the reservation. When children did not reside on the reservation state courts may, if there is good reason, exercise jurisdiction. There is a preference in the bill for keeping Indian children with their own extended family, first, other tribal members, second, other Native people, third. The act sets the evidentiary standards higher than for non-Native children in dependency hearings (in which parents might lose custody of their children to, say, foster care) or termination of parental rights. There is a requirement that the family be offered crisis intervention services before a child can be taken. Unfortunately, it all had to be done on no money. As we will see, it seemed to work for a while. The number of Native children in out-of-home care declined until 1988, when it jumped to rates higher than before.[102] But that is the story of the next chapter.

THREE

"Crack Babies," Race, and Adoption Reform, 1975–2000

The post–civil rights era saw a formidable backlash against the National Association of Black Social Workers' (NABSW) statement and the Indian Child Welfare Act (ICWA), one that has dominated the way we have written their histories, as we have seen, and that used the antifeminist politics of the condemnation of unmarried motherhood as a key issue in a broader conservative movement. Two wings of this movement, one neoconservative and the other neoliberal, dominated conservative politics in the postwar United States. Neoconservatives, following Moynihan, emerged largely out of the Democratic Party in the mid-1960s and were concerned with questions of family and morality—particularly the supposed immorality of unmarried black mothers.[1] Neoliberals, in contrast, were free market fundamentalists who wanted to shrink government, relegating many things that had been public services and benefits to the private sector.[2] For both, the politics of unwed motherhood and child welfare mattered a great deal, as they picked up the thread from the Southern "Dixiecrats" in treating unmarried black mothers' supposed immorality as a singularly important issue. After the presidency of Richard Nixon both the neoliberal and neoconservative tendencies, together with great numbers of formerly Democratic Southern whites, were represented in the Republican Party. (Nixon was the transitional figure; the Democrat Moynihan followed him into his administration, and Nixon also sponsored a proposal for a national guaranteed minimum income that would have vastly expanded welfare benefits in the South and on reservations by making welfare a federal—not state—benefit.)[3] Initially under Reagan and then under Newt Gringrich's leadership of congressional Republicans in 1994, neoliberal and neoconservative child welfare projects came together. First, there was Reagan's presidential campaign promise to punish welfare cheats and chislers, the welfare mother with the pink Cadillac (shrinking government while punishing unmarried impoverished women), and then there was Gingrich's promise to put the children of welfare mothers in orphanages, subsequently enacted as a split bill, half eliminating Aid to Families with Dependent Children (AFDC), the other half providing incentives to *adopt* the children whose mothers could not raise them as a result of its elimination—tax breaks for the adoption of "special needs" children (a category that included all children of color).

The third group that increasingly dominated the Republican Party and conservative politics was the Christian Right, rising to national prominence with the founding of the Moral Majority Foundation in 1979, born of disparate antigay, anti–Equal Rights Amendment, and "pro-family" elements, from white evangelical churches, Mormons, and, later, conservative Catholics. Although adoption was never as central an issue for Christian Right conservatives as abortion, adoption was nevertheless an important part of their politics of family. As we have seen, the rates at which women voluntarily put their children up for adoption declined after 1970.[4] In secular politics and in mainline Protestant churches, "legitimacy" was remade during the 1960s and 1970s, becoming increasingly about whiteness and economics and less about sex and morality. Or rather, immorality became increasingly rooted in popular imagination in the United States in the fertile bodies of women of color, and single motherhood among white and middle-class women no longer signaled the certainty that they were bad mothers. While it was possible for a Child Welfare League of America researcher to claim in 1970 that "since illegitimate births are the main source of supply for non-relative adoptive applicants, any changes in the number or rate of illegitimate births should have some effect on adoptive agencies," by 1975, with feminism and changing forms of labor participation for women, the fact of an unwed pregnancy no longer meant an adoption. This phenomenon—of white single mothers keeping their children—infuriated conservatives almost as much as black single mothers getting a welfare check. One of the game-changing events in the political battle to end AFDC was a *Wall Street Journal* editorial by Charles Murray on "The Coming White Underclass" that argued that white women were starting to act just like black women—having children out of wedlock, which would

make their offspring poor, unemployed, and criminal.[5] A related development, of adoptee groups like Bastard Nation calling for open records laws,
likewise generated considerable opposition, as it, too, marked a turn away
from the 1950s model in which good girls who got in trouble could, through
institutions of secrets and even lies, get a second chance at virtue and a
proper nuclear family.[6]

Finally, broad labor market and demographic changes in the lives of
middle-class women (and men), mostly but not exclusively white, created a
"class" of adopters, sometimes a consumer market, sometimes a political
bloc, and in recent years, always on the Internet. Declining real wages after
1972 sent middle-class, married, heterosexual women into the work force in
droves,[7] and feminist victories opened career advancement paths for some.
But this produced a conundrum. A long period of education and early
career uncertainty produced a kind of crisis in the middle class (one faced
for centuries by working-class, poor, and unfree laborers): if everyone in
the heterosexual family had to work, who would care for the children and
do other domestic labor? As Arlie Hothschild recorded in *The Second Shift*
in 1989, this was a gendered question: the way it was getting resolved in
families was that women were coming home and doing a "second shift" of
care work at home.[8] There was not much momentum to make it a shared,
society-wide problem that government should help solve: despite gestures
in that direction—feminist campaigns for wages for housework in the 1970s
or stipends for single mothers (mothers' pensions in the 1920s, Aid to
Dependent Children [ADC] and AFDC from the 1930s to the 1990s). The
social welfare tradition of Europe or the collectivized childrearing of Cuba
and Israeli kibbutzim never got much traction in the United States. Indeed,
as we will see, there was an active conservative campaign in the 1980s and
1990s to make care work *more* privatized. As a partial resolution to these
problems, middle-class women delayed childbearing to their late twenties
and even thirties, despite the fact that fertility declines for both sexes as
they age, particularly for women beyond the age of thirty.[9] While the
"epidemic of infertility" reported in the press in the 1980s was a myth,
rising ages at first birth meant a growing incidence of structural, impaired
fertility.[10] This was not what a previous generation meant by infertility but
was rather a phenomenon resulting from the ways labor markets and
economies of caring labor made it increasingly difficult for women in
particular to be middle class and have children in their early twenties. This
changed the nature of adoption as a political issue; increasingly, its public
face was what the anthropologist Sarah Franklin called the media image of

the "desperate infertile couple."[11] In broad strokes adoption shifted from being significantly a practice of "making room for one more" to being framed as an issue of reproduction, even reproductive rights—including for lesbian and gay people. Raising the question of whether some people had a "right to adopt" increased the political stakes over separating children from "unfit" parents in the United States and abroad as well.

The Rise of Conservatism in the United States and the Politics of Race and Adoption

Many scholars in recent years have tried to pinpoint when and how a conservative movement gathered the force to defeat the vision of a democratic, socialist, redistributive state that had seemed so near to realization in the civil rights era. The roots of conservative movements were multiple. In the United States grassroots white suburbanites organized networks in the aftermath of the defeat of Barry Goldwater as a presidential candidate.[12] The recession of 1974 mobilized business against decreasing profit rates, contributing to their support for shrinking taxes and hence the size of governments; in California this was joined to white and middle-class objections to a welfare state and influentially expressed as a homeowner "tax revolt" embodied in Proposition 13.[13] There was also the reduction of federal aid to cities, geographies that had previously been seen as the engines of national economic growth, a policy shift that was debated most significantly in the bankruptcy of New York City in the 1970s—resulting from the withdrawal of federal grants to municipalities, white flight, and disinvestment in the growing number of "chocolate cities" (as the Parliament song had it) in the East and the deindustrializing Midwest.[14] There was also the rise of a transnational, evangelical Christian capitalism and cultural values sedimented in Wal-Mart and Sunbelt megachurches.[15] Internationally, Keynesian economics as an idea, alongside Marxian and "dependency theory" ideas about the causes of poverty, was defeated by ideological movements associated with Karl Polanyi and Milton Freedman and militarily through anti-Communist wars.[16]

This chapter narrates another key episode in that story: the exceptional resonance and political work accomplished in the Ronald Reagan era by blaming unmarried mothers (again) for all that ailed U.S. America, followed by a moral panic that demonized black and Latino "crack mothers" and Native American women who were committing "genocide" by giving birth to fetal alcohol syndrome (FAS) babies. These events, centered around 1989, were a crucial episode in shutting down the welfare state—albeit a much smaller and more punitive welfare state than those who dreamed of a genuinely redistributive possibility longed for—and inaugurating an era that at least imagined small government, even if the reality (under Reagan and George W. Bush in particular) was a steadily expanding national security state.

This period also saw a defeat of feminist visions of transformations in domestic and intimate labor, in which it could be shared equally within heterosexual couples on the one hand and supported by federally funded daycare centers or mothers' pensions and AFDC on the other. What replaced this hope, instead, was delayed childbearing (supplemented by adoption and reproductive technology) and, for those who could afford it, paid domestic labor from Latin America. Finally, the 1990s culminated in a failed effort to overturn ICWA and a successful campaign to reject the vision of the NABSW of black children in black families: the end of AFDC and the victory of the Multiethnic Placement Act of 1994 (MEPA) and the Interethnic Provisions of 1996 (IEP) (the MEPA was amended by the IEP, hence it became known as MEPA-IEP), which guaranteed white families access to adoption of non-white children.

As governor of California, Reagan had been unusually explicit about the politics of race, taxes, sexuality, and gender in which AFDC was embedded. On the one hand, he articulated a "small government, low taxes" mantra that justified limiting income supports for unmarried mothers. He also frequently said "You play, you pay," while governor, meaning that women who had heterosexual sex while unmarried should suffer—a punitive and humiliating politics with respect to black and Native women's sexual autonomy and an ideology of blame that white women were allowed to escape at the price of losing their ("bastard") children through adoption.[17] From his focus on "welfare cheats," in his presidential campaign of 1980, it was obvious from the outset that it was high on the agenda of the Reagan and then the George H. W. Bush presidential administrations to shut down any space that had been opened up by feminists, the welfare rights movement, and others who thought that single mothers ought to be able to raise their children. How they did this was a textbook case for neoliberalism: they began by demonizing working-class black, Latino, and indigenous women and children as unworthy of help—plagued by personal irresponsibility, moral and intellectual inferiority, and other unattractive personal characteristics—and then moved on to white and middle-class families, particularly mothers and children, as potentially *just like* the demonic working-class Latino, black, and Indian families. White and middle-class families, this argument contended, would be like working-class Latino, black, and Indian families if they got government assistance: irresponsible, with damaged children. In place of this, neoliberals offered risk, personal responsibility and security, "crack babies," FAS, and anxieties about child death and disability that erupted as legislation requiring child car seats and bike helmets.

By 1979–80 those who opposed Reagan in his presidential bid might be forgiven for thinking there was something almost nostalgic about the invocation of this 1960s-era formula of blame, as "bastard" and "unwed mother" had been dropped from the public policy vocabulary, and the increasing availability of decent jobs for women of all races—nondomestic, nonagricultural jobs for black women, and for white women a handful of jobs outside the "pink collar ghetto"—meant that increasing numbers of single mothers of all classes and races were able to keep their children. As we have seen, just as soon as women's income began rising, they started keeping their children.[18] However, this did not make them or their children not poor, and nothing, it seemed, could still the anger that single mothers inspired in conservatives. By 1992 these politics of blame had been reinvigorated to the point where it was possible for Bush's vice president, Dan Quayle, to make a major policy speech about Murphy Brown, a fictional white, middle-class single mother portrayed on television, blaming the Los Angeles riots on (white?) unwed mothers like her (and a whole imagined trail of black single mothers after her) causing a "poverty of values."[19]

At about the same time, in 1989, "crack babies" were the news story of the year. Major newspapers ran huge, multipage features,[20] and network news shows bombarded their audiences with images of women using crack cocaine during their pregnancies, characterizing their offspring as likely to be born early, to experience exceptionally high rates of perinatal mortality, to be born addicted and quivering, to experience a host of neurological, digestive, respiratory, and cardiac problems, and to be headed toward a childhood of learning difficulties, hyperactivity, and, ultimately, delinquency and jail.[21] It was an intensely racialized moral panic. Although the typical user of cocaine was a young white male, by 1985 television and print media were portraying crack as a drug used primarily by African Americans and, to a lesser extent, Latinos. From 1988–1990 the nightly news was engaged in a war against crack mothers—who were almost by definition black. In that period 55 percent of the women portrayed in network TV news stories as using crack were black; in later years, from 1991–1994, it was 84 percent.[22] The newspapers were, if anything, worse.[23]

The bitter irony of all of this rhetoric is that it was vastly exaggerated. In March 2001 the medical researchers Deborah Frank and colleagues did a meta-analysis of *all* the research on the effects of prenatal cocaine exposure published in English between 1984 and 2000 that met certain minimum criteria: they had a control group, subjects were prospectively recruited, examiners were masked as to which children had been exposed to cocaine, and children with exposure to more than one risk factor in utero (opiates, amphetamines, phencyclodine, or HIV) were excluded. Their conclusions, published in the prestigious *Journal of the American Medical Association* (*JAMA*) are worth quoting at length; the researchers wrote:

> Public expectations of "blighted" children fuel controversial punitive policies directed toward addicted mothers. Since 1985, more than 200 women in 30 states have faced criminal prosecution for using cocaine and other psychoactive substances during pregnancy. Scholars and professional organizations have condemned efforts to sterilize or criminally prosecute addicted mothers as ethically and legally flawed, racially discriminatory, and an impediment to providing appropriate medical care to these women and their children. Recent reviews and articles show that most initial predictions of catastrophic effects of prenatal cocaine exposure upon newborns were exaggerated. After controlling for confounders, the most consistent effects of prenatal cocaine exposure are small but statistically significant decrements in . . . fetal growth for gestational age and less optimal neonatal state regulation and motor performance.[24]

Further, Frank et al. wrote: "The literature on prenatal exposure to cocaine has not shown consistent effects on cognitive or psychomotor development . . . Prenatal cocaine exposure, independent of exposure to alcohol, has not been found to be associated with levels of behavioral disturbances detectable by standard scoring of epidemiologic and clinical report measures by parents and teachers . . . However, 7 studies show that environmental factors such as caregiver (biological mothers vs kinship care or foster parents) . . . were statistically significant correlates of test scores." Or, as another commentator in *JAMA* described the group's conclusions, "the data are not persuasive that in utero exposure to cocaine has major adverse developmental consequences in early childhood—and certainly not ones separable from those associated with other exposures and environmental risks . . . the modest and inconsistent nature of the findings to date suggest that these harms are unlikely to be of the magnitude of those associated with in utero exposure to the legal drugs tobacco and alcohol."[25] Despite predictions of devastating effects on fetuses and children, neither IQ nor behavior problems seemed to be reliably correlated with prenatal cocaine exposure— but they were reliably correlated with being put in foster care.

Most of the effects once attributed to cocaine turn out to be the effect of things like alcohol, tobacco, marijuana, heroine use, or environmental factors—including homelessness, domestic violence, and even the effects of placing chidren in foster care. Other researchers and analysts have largely confirmed this account in the medical literature—peer-reviewed, adequately controlled, large-scale prospective longitudinal studies have shown modest and inconsistent effects of in utero cocaine exposure.[26] But this assessment has still had little effect on popular culture or policymaking. As suggested in Wendy Chavkin's commentary on the research by Frank and her colleagues in the same issue of *JAMA*, the entire "hullabaloo" about crack babies seems to have had much more to do with politics than it ever did with the medical effects of cocaine on fetuses.[27]

Neoconservative commentators were among the most vociferous in promoting the notion that there was a "crack baby" crisis. Douglas Besharov of the conservative American Enterprise Institute referred to the birth of a "bio-underclass" that Head Start could not help. This analysis was quoted by the syndicated columnist Charles Krauthammer, who, in high eugenicist mode, referred to a "generation of physically damaged cocaine babies whose biological inferiority is stamped at birth," claiming this problem affected between 5 and 15 percent of all black children.[28] Even liberal African American commentators like Derrick Z. Jackson of the *Boston Globe* and William Raspberry of the *Washington Post* joined in, arguing that high rates of black infant mortality were caused by crack and that efforts to decriminalize drugs should be opposed because of the effects of cocaine on babies.[29]

While in one sense the hysteria *was* about politics, medical researchers were among those who had led the charge against "crack mothers." It was their work that provided the foundation for the media, child welfare, and public policy assault on cocaine-using pregnant women. There was a strong bias within the peer-review system among researchers on this issue for work that confirmed that cocaine had terrible effects on pregnancy; plenty of articles (that we now know were wrong) were published that insisted on links between crack exposure and elevated rates of premature labor, placenta previa, neural and digestive system abnormalities, kidney malformations, attentiveness problems, and hyperactivity. At the height of the anticrack campaign in the media in 1989, one researcher noted that the likelihood that a study of cocaine effects on pregnancy outcomes would be accepted for the annual meeting of the Society of Pediatric Research was significantly affected by whether or not it found adverse effects. Studies that showed no effect on a pregnancy had an 11 percent acceptance rate, while those that found undesirable effects on fetuses had a 57 percent acceptance rate, despite the fact that negative studies tended to be better designed, more likely to have a control group, and more likely to compare polydrug exposure with and without cocaine.[30]

The effect of this media, medical, and policy discourse was to produce a new punitive regime for black women. At the urging of the federal drug czar William Bennett, many hospitals—especially those serving mostly black patients—introduced routine screening for cocaine into delivery rooms, and mothers who tested positive lost their newborns on the spot; a number went to jail still bleeding from labor.[31] Although a Supreme Court case ultimately found the practice illegal (and, their lawyers argued, racially discriminatory), the decision came too late for many women and their children.[32] Between 1985 and 2000 more than two hundred women faced criminal prosecution for using cocaine and other drugs during pregnancy, and tens of thousands lost their children to foster care.[33] Black women, in particular, went to jail for cocaine use out of any proportion to their representation among drug-using pregnant women.[34]

Like the Flemming rule, the "crack baby" epidemic resulted in a vast expansion of the foster care and child welfare system—the number of children in it nearly doubled—and most of those who entered it were black children.[35] Between 1985 and 1988 the number of children in out-of-home placement—foster care, psychiatric institutions, and the juvenile justice system—increased by 25 percent.[36] In the emerging neoliberal social service landscape, these policies initially taxed foster care systems to the breaking point, but "crack babies" quickly became a rallying point for agencies to lobby for—and get—massive new funding. Congressional reports, hearings, and funding appropriations reflected the new urgency about caring for the "littlest victims" of crack and built a much larger institutional capacity. Foster parents of these so-called crack babies were canonized in rescue narratives in the popular press; they were caring for "babies in pain," who disrupted families and would never be normal.[37]

There is a haunting question about how the most vulnerable, most impoverished people in the United States—pregnant women, often sex workers, sometimes using multiple drugs (prominently alcohol and tobacco), often homeless, more often than not facing violence during their pregnancies, frequently dealing with long-term ill health and often mental illness as well—became a symbol of everything that was wrong with the country. For all these reasons, it often seemed plausible that the children of "crack mothers" weren't doing well. Of course these infants were not doing well, but crack was a marker of their mother's distress, not the cause of the children's. As a public policy response to these mothers' pain, the punishment and opprobrium that rained down on their heads was disastrous. As Mindy Fullilove documents, women doing crack during their pregnancies in these years were almost uniformly trauma survivors, often of childhood sexual violence. In the public imagination and for the mothers themselves, crack use during pregnancy was a symbol of wretchedness and degradation. Regardless of whether it actually was the worst thing one could do during pregnancy, the widespread belief that it was shaped the contours of which women did it. According to the press, even some crack-using pregnant women were persuaded that jail was the best place for them.[38] The people Fullilove interviewed reported that their crack use waned and then waxed again with life disasters: a violent and abusive lover, the end of a relationship, the death of a loved one, losing a job, losing housing were all events that regularly triggered crack use, as the drug was not only cheap but comforting. Although many sought treatment during their pregnancy, relapse or even the suspicion that they were using or might use crack at some point in the future meant they could lose their children at birth—a loss that almost inevitably triggered them to use again,[39] no doubt confirming doctors' or social workers' decision to take their child and, presumably, the child of the next similarly situated woman that they encountered.

The entire edifice of the moral panic about crack babies rested on two statistics, both of which ultimately proved to be wrong. The evidence for a growing "epidemic" of cocaine use, rooted in the newly available, cheap form of the drug, crack, was a slight increase in a daily and weekly usage statistic provided by the General Accounting Office. These statistics were notoriously unreliable because they relied on very small samples. Even the slight increase reported proved wrong: the percentage of the U.S. population using crack remained absolutely stable between 1988 and 1994.[40] A second statistic showed a sharp rise in the mortality rate of African American infants in Washington, D.C., in the first half of 1989; officials later realized that a large number of these deaths had really occurred in 1988, and infant mortality rates had, in fact, stayed stable.[41] While the knowledge that the case for the crack "epidemic" wreaking havoc in inner cities and blighting a generation of babies was extraordinarily shaky was available for those who cared to find it even in the late 1980s, few did.

At the precise moment when the Reagan and (first) Bush administrations had all but succeeded in disallowing race as a legitimate term of political grievance through their attacks on supports such as affirmative action and AFDC, as the gutting of the public health system gave way to an AIDS epidemic disproportionately affecting communities of color and gay men—an epidemic that might, perhaps, have been quickly contained by the stronger public health systems of the 1970s[42]—and following decades of deindustrialization and the flight of jobs from cities that disproportionately affected communities of color, race emerged sharply in the Reagan era as a term by which to characterize pathology, indeed, a specifically biologized pathology. The terms of this discourse explained away a multitude of things caused by Reagan-era economic policies, such as homelessness and high infant mortality rates, especially among African Americans. The crack baby crisis invited people not to think about the economic causes that led working-class people to be involved in the drug trade or the ways that deindustrialization and cuts to social services and government transfer payments left working-class families scrambling. It also discounted another story one could have told about impoverished children in this era: the effects on youth of declines in real wages, and the steadily expanding work days that working-class parents had to put in to make ends meet. In its place, the crack baby epidemic offered bad parenting, moral failure, and a criminal recklessness about fetuses.

At the same time, while the crack baby crisis enabled conservatives to clearly identify scapegoats—black women with bad morals making outrageous claims on the public purse, demanding funds from the state for their irresponsible pregnancies, partially but never quite conflated with women receiving AFDC as a whole—the issue also revealed the dissonances between neoconservative and neoliberal agendas. Crack babies were poster children for the War on Drugs and an allegory for debates about abortion —Exhibit A for the conservative policymakers and prosecutors who wanted to show why small-time drug users were a danger to society as a whole and deserving of jail time (since what were being called "boarder babies" were putting an incredible strain on hospital finances in a time of shrinking allocations from the federal government in constant dollars, and once out the children were entitled to expensive special education classes at public expense)—and why fetuses needed to be protected from dangerous mothers who would kill them if they were lucky, to paraphrase the columnist Charles Krauthammer.[43] If single mothers were the epitome of moral danger to children in the 1950s and 1960s, the focus of concern shifted from children to fetuses in the 1980s and 1990s (when the exemplary U.S. citizens became fetuses and corporations, Lauren Berlant suggests with tongue only partly in cheek),[44] Federal and state governments were simultaneously building a massive prison system, in no small measure for these same children's parents—people using drugs, often people of color—and "crack babies," those littlest victims were part of the argument that drug use was a crime, not an illness or a personal choice.[45] This antifeminist and race-baiting agenda may have played well as a statement of a certain kind of conservative values, providing a productive cover story for why there was no meaningful social contract between the federal government and impoverished single mothers, why the state owed no debt of responsibility to *these* citizens. (Or only a negative, security-state one—William Bennett proposed boot camps and orphanages for youth born exposed to crack.)[46] Privatization in this instance meant giving up on commitments to racial egalitarianism in education and employment, attributing worsening racial differences in income and well-being, instead, to biology. It also provided the context in which, five years later, Newt Gingrich could urge that the state should take the children of welfare mothers and put them in orphanages, completing the cycle of the attack on wages for motherhood: not only was no one entitled to state support for raising their children, if they asked, they deserved to lose their children. But as an agenda for shrinking government, it was a disaster, promoting ever-more federal and state spending on jail and foster care.

At the same time, a parallel crisis was brewing with respect to alcohol and pregnancy, focused significantly but not exclusively on Native Americans. Since alcohol is a legal drug (one that, in fact, is used more frequently by white people with college degrees than those who are not white or less educated),[47] this moral panic ultimately took in middle-class white women as well, which, as we will see, made it more productive for neoliberal agendas. In 1989 the Native American scholar Michael Dorris published *The Broken Cord*, an influential account of FAS. Although FAS had been identified in the research literature as early as 1973, and had received passing mention in the media and in court cases, it was Dorris's book that put it on the map as a public health emergency. *Broken Cord* could actually be described as two entirely different books within the same covers. The first half is a tremendously compelling, novelistic account of the adoption of his son, a toddler with developmental delays, and the crashing to earth of Dorris's hopes that environment was everything, as his son, called "Adam" in the book, continued to exhibit growing health problems and learning disabilities. As Adam grows, the story shifts from the agonies of trying to appear the put-together parent for social workers and the pleasures of reconnecting Adam with his tribe of origin to Dorris's research on FAS.

The book reads as a parable of the inadequacies of the antihereditarian, racial justice politics of the 1960s and 1970s, a rethinking of the politics in which Martin Luther King Jr. could assert that the "sons of former slaves and the sons of former slaveowners" were created equal. Dorris, whose own beliefs were, at the outset, a product of the moment and milieu in which King expressed such dreams, charts in *Broken Cord* how he abandons that hope. In the beginning Dorris attacked the IQ tests Adam took as racially biased; he challenged the school as racist for labeling his son's behavior as disruptive and out-of-control; he argued that colonialism and deprivation on the reservation had caused any transitory troubles Adam might be experiencing. Eventually, however, Dorris concludes, sadly, that teachers and school officials were right, that Adam was doomed from before birth (although the cause was alcohol, not racial inferiority). Dorris becomes increasingly angry with Adam's birth mother in the course of the narrative, imagines her turning to alcohol again and again during her pregnancy, and wondered if she should have been incarcerated. He writes: "If she had come after him with a baseball bat after he was born, if she had smashed his skull and caused brain damage, wouldn't she have been constrained from doing it again and again? Was it her prerogative, moral or legal, to deprive him of the means to live a full life?" The book's emotional ending combines hyperbolic medical claims with tragedy. Dorris insists that as many as one in three American Indian children may have been irredeemably harmed by maternal drinking during pregnancy (while even the highest public health estimates put it between fifty and one hundred times lower),[48] and then he describes twenty-three-year-old Adam's death in a hit-and-run accident, caused he thinks by Adam's inability to remember to look both ways before crossing the street.

Dorris is an affecting writer, and the book was a bestseller. It received unprecedented media attention, won a National Book Critics Circle Award, and became an ABC-TV movie. *Broken Cord* initiated a wide public conversation in the United States about fetal alcohol syndrome, culminating in Congress requiring alcohol manufacturers to put labels on bottles warning pregnant women against drinking. A surprising number even of physicians reported that Dorris's book, not the medical literature, framed their understanding of FAS; one told sociologist Elizabeth Armstrong that "All I know [about FAS] is what I read in that book."[49] (Dorris also published an editorial in which he called crack-exposed children "remorseless" and "without a conscience.")[50] The debate over FAS had divergent effects, producing in essence two racialized classes of mothers and children. One set of effects were very much like those produced by the crack baby crisis, a racialized underclass that was understood to be stunted from birth; television and print media produced features that decried the child abuse and even "genocide" perpetrated by Native women, including a weeklong segment on NBC in 1989 entitled *Incident at Pine Ridge* (referring to maternal drinking—even though this is the same phrase used to refer to the month-long FBI siege and brief shoot-out with American Indian Movement activists in 1975). Pregnant alcoholic women, mostly Native American, went to jail to "protect" their fetuses, notwithstanding physician objections about the absolutely appalling fetal outcomes for women in prison. Mothers lost their children at birth to the foster care system. American Indian children with developmental problems were over-diagnosed with FAS; a genetic study on reservations in Arizona in 1994 found that between half and two-thirds of the children diagnosed with FAS had Down's syndrome or some other genetic developmental issue that would be entirely sufficient to account for the children's developmental delays; instead of looking to obvious answers like Down's syndrome, physicians turned to FAS as a catch-all diagnosis for children with developmental issues on reservations.[51]

The other set of effects, however, was that the debate terrified (mostly white) middle-class women who didn't drink very much. Historian of medicine Janet Golden has traced how FAS devolved from a problem diagnosed in the children of alcoholic women who drank an average of ten drinks a day to a warning to all pregnant women not to drink at all. Knowledge that alcohol caused disabilities, combined with medical uncertainty about how *much* alcohol caused fetal defects, Golden argues, emboldened some researchers, public health officials, and the media to claim that any alcohol use at all during pregnancy constituted fetal child abuse.[52] Dorris's partner, Louise Erdrich, embodied this strain of the debate when she said in an interview that the "one-glass-of-wine-a-day permissiveness of first-time yuppie mothers is still sufficient to cause brain damage in the fetus."[53] Nobody knows if that is true or not. But there is, perhaps, good reason to be suspicious, whether or not moderate drinking can cause negative fetal outcomes, that the entire discussion was overblown from a public health perspective. FAS is difficult to diagnose, making all claims about prevalence soft, but it is almost certainly quite rare. Among alcoholic women who drink continuously and excessively through their pregnancies, the likelihood of an infant being born with FAS is estimated at just 5 percent. Addressing poverty, inequality, and violence might be more effective in preventing FAS than blaming women who binge drink: more recent studies have suggested that alcohol is only damaging to the fetus when the mother is malnourished, stressed, exposed to environmental toxins, smoking, or any combination of these. If one were to pick the best way to improve fetal outcomes from a public health perspective, it certainly would not be addressing maternal drinking (or crack use); it would involve remedies for poverty, inequality, and violence against women and girl children. Yet as the two political scientists Jean Reith Schroedel and Paul Peretz point out, "Between 1989 and 1991 . . . the *New York Times* devoted a total of 853.5 column inches to fetal abuse . . . by pregnant women's use of illegal drugs and/or drinking. During the same period there was not a single column inch dealing with adverse birth outcomes as a result of the physical abuse of women."[54] Further, as with crack, women who engage in extreme binge drinking during pregnancy are already in terrible pain and trouble in their lives, unlikely to be able to respond to a little reminder note on alcohol packaging—FAS is so often an issue related to adoption because, according to some studies, *most* of the mothers that gave birth to infants affected by FAS were dead within a few years as a result of violence or alcoholism.[55]

The Expansion of Middle-Class Domestic Space

Yuppie mothers in the 1980s were never demonized in the way black or indigenous mothers were. Still, for them, the 1980s was a period of intensifying anxiety about their vulnerable children. In contrast to the 1950s, 1960s, and 1970s, child advice books aimed at middle-class mothers turned mean. Instead of the reassuring Dr. Spock, who told mothers that if they listened to their children and their own commonsense, all would be fine, mothers in the 1980s got Richard Ferber and T. Berry Brazelton. The new advice books warned of multiple dangers of bad parenting; urged disciplined approaches to making your child sleep alone and to potty train early; the need to educate oneself about developmental guideposts and how to tell if your child is late; how to set boundaries; establish discipline and consistency; the need for enrichment, piano lessons, and soccer, as well as careful monitoring of school work; all this, however, without over-doing it and stressing out your fragile child, which carried its own dangers. One title that perfectly captured this anxious vigilance with all of its double binds was *How to Get Your Child to Eat But Not Too Much*. This decade's emphasis on parenting as something learned, something easy to get wrong, and something that took tremendous amounts of time, thought, and work, was not a product of an expansion of leisure time that allowed parents to spend more time and be more attentive to their children. On the contrary, because of declines in real wages, even middle-class mothers were increas-ingly in the workforce, relying on daycare at younger ages and on children's good sense to care for themselves after school. As Susan Cheever writes in a *New Yorker* article about nannies and the changes in childrearing that made them seem necessary, "Our generation has made a religion of parenting. Our mothers had Dr. Spock; we have books to fill a ten-foot shelf. They had a family doctor; we have pediatric endocrinologists who specialize in glandular disorders. We love our children passionately, and for me, at least, leaving them—for a week, or even for a day—is the hardest thing I've ever had to do."[56] At precisely the moment when middle-class U.S. American mothers most needed them, sturdy, self-reliant children disappeared.[57]

The 1980s also marked the emergence of a host of new anxieties about child death and disability. Prenatal screening became widespread in the late 1980s, making many parents believe that disability was an avoidable problem—that with sufficient *prenatal* vigilance, medical care, and abor-tion in the event of bad genetic news, all children could be healthy, strong, and above average.[58] In continuity with the eugenics years, the problem most screened for was cognitive impairment, specifically Down's syn-drome. Sudden infant death syndrome (SIDS) began to attract great media attention in the 1970s, a symptom of rising middle-class parental anxiety even earlier, but it took a characteristic turn in the 1980s: it became associ-ated with congenital abnormalities and became, at least in public, a tragedy that was increasingly associated with working-class, poor, nonwhite infants and families, with smoking often identified as the culprit.[59] In 1984 uncor-roborated (and probably mythical) reports of poisoned Halloween candy, or candy with razor blades in it, inaugurated an era in which parents were to go out trick-or-treating with their children, and some communities cancelled Halloween altogether. Stranger kidnapping and sexual abuse generated countless news stories (although the far more common intra-familial sexual abuse never got much play). Mothers Against Drunk Driv-

ing identified alcohol-impaired driving as a threat specifically to children—
implicitly, in their photo campaigns at least, white and middle class—and
with growing success waged a campaign to change state laws and lower the
legal standard for inebriated driving. In 1986 medical journals began to
warn of the dangers of bicycle-mounted seats for toddlers, and in 1987
California became the first in a series of states requiring bicycle helmets for
children.[60] Public safety campaigns brought new laws in the late 1980s
requiring children to wear seat belts while riding in cars. Laws mandating
that very young children must ride in expensive child safety seats were
passed in all fifty states between 1978 and 1985, despite what some have
argued is little evidence that they are better than lap belts at reducing
fatalities in toddlers in car crashes.[61]

These were not friendly campaigns aimed at parents who might under-
standably be concerned about preventing accidents to their children.
Rather, they aimed to stir up public anger—and state intervention—on
behalf of children who were endangered by irresponsible parenting. A survey of eight hundred adult drivers conducted by the Air Bag and Seat Belt
Safety Campaign in November 1999 measured their effect, finding that 70
percent of adults felt *angry* when they saw unbuckled children in a car; 78
percent agreed with the statement that "people who fail to buckle up their
child passengers should be considered guilty of child endangerment."[62] Like
campaigns for eugenic marriage laws in the early twentieth century that
blamed men for visiting venereal disease on women and children and instituted blood tests for syphilis as a prerequisite for marriage licenses, an
anxious middle class simultaneously identified threats from without and
within. Mothers in particular, but fathers as well, were under increasing
pressure to produce healthy children and blamed for inadequate vigilance in
the event of disabling or fatal accidents, or even *congenital* disability. Tragedy as a category for understanding bad things that happened to children
disappeared, replaced with blame. White middle-class children in the
United States, free as never before in history from widespread killer diseases
or accidents, became the focus of obsessive concern.

These changes in the way U.S. Americans saw middle-class childhood
corresponded with what Barbara Ehreinreich termed "fear of falling" in her
book of the same name in 1989, the increasing tilt of the economic playing
field that was, for the first time in decades, expanding the ranks of the poor
and working class at the same time that a handful of people were becoming
very wealthy. Middle-class families were working more hours to achieve the
same standard of living. In this meaner economic landscape, middle-class

parents looked down the road at what the prospects were for their children and saw great payoffs for a few successful ones and failure for many. Narratives that rooted success or failure in the body—in the difference between the "bio-underclass" and the carefully protected and cultivated middle class —naturalized these futures, made them seem fair or at least inevitable, differences one could often see written on the surface of the body. However, it was not fully natural, something inevitable at birth, but something produced also by a certain kind of protective, intentional parenting.

The other thing that narratives about protecting vulnerable children did was to vastly expand the private sphere at a time when the number of middle-class mothers in the workforce was rapidly expanding—and new welfare rules were requiring poor mothers to be in the workforce for more hours per week. Maternal legitimacy was being defined very specifically in terms of time and class. Rather than taking children's increasing time unsupervised to be normative, these narratives invoked guilt and fear. They insisted that it actually required more work than previously to raise children, more time, thought, and concern. While feminist scholars have often commented on the ideological production of the difference between public and private in the nineteenth century, we have less reliably noticed that this line between public and private is a battlefield, that its location has moved and changed. The expansion of *the private* in the 1980s was at once an attack on feminism and impoverished mothers and the incursion of neoliberalism, replacing belief in public services with private, familial labor. At precisely the moment when there might have been a widespread demand for publicly funded daycare, for example, daycare became seen as a dangerous place where children were routinely sexually abused.[63]

What I am calling the expansion of the space of the private also had the contradictory effect of increasing the pressure on infertile couples to adopt or turn to reproductive technology (or adopt after trying reproductive technologies as its success rates are low). This ennoblement of the desire for a baby was generally directed at white families, however, and certainly those who were middle class; it was coupled with antiwelfare rhetoric that viciously degraded poor women and their families. This class and race pronatalism project put more pressure on some of those who were infertile, structurally or medically, to believe that their condition was untenable. In September 1984 *Time* ran a cover story titled "Making Babies: The New Science of Conception," which carried the inside title of "The Saddest Epidemic," claiming that "the incidence of barrenness has nearly tripled" in the last twenty years, rising to affect one in six couples, and blaming feminism and birth control as the cause.[64] As Susan Faludi pointed out in her book *Backlash*, the factual basis of the claim was nonexistent; infertility rates were actually decreasing. Faludi argued rather that it was a "political program" championed by the Republican Party.[65] And, precisely as a political project, it gained steam.[66] As the media declared from every street corner that (white) infertility left one "desperate," birth rates, rates of using infertility treatment, and pressure on adoption rose (and, as an unsought side note, many began to notice a "gayby" boom).[67]

Adopting Parents as a Market Segment

Following the reprotech model, adoption in the 1970s and 1980s became increasingly like a consumer market for parents and less like a solution for children in need. It was less likely to be arranged by an agency and social workers that "matched" a child to parents and more likely to be arranged by an independent agent, sometimes an adoption "facilitator," a lawyer, or a religious figure, without much screening of parents or children. Since the 1920s there has been a fight between agencies and social workers on the one hand and "independent" or "private" adoption facilitators on the other.[68] In "public," regulated adoption, agencies and social workers, working closely with the state, produce bureaucratic mechanisms to match the infants and children in their care with would-be adoptive parents, who are carefully screened. State-organized adoption is usually free or nearly so, but it tends to be slow and intrusive to adoption applicants; since the 1920s parents have been complaining about the shortage of adoptable children in this system.[69] On the other side a free-wheeling, market-driven private system run by a heterogeneous group of actors—lawyers, religious leaders, those who informally foster children, people trying to make money—has made many more children available, although it has always been expensive and subject to charges of baby selling.[70]

Just as neoliberalism was working to make "private" the name of a good and virtuous economic entity, and "public" was portrayed as wasteful, for the first time in the twentieth century "private" adoption was not being called "baby farming" or "black market adoption." Rather, it was a more efficient route to a healthy white baby, while "public"—as in public benefits—marked children who were not white, not babies, not healthy. Furthermore, public agencies were portrayed as part of the problem. "Publicly assisted child-care agencies get payments while a child is in foster care or

temporary placement, but those payments end with adoption," wrote the
New York Times in 1984. "This leads the system, [critics] say, to encourage
publicly supported foster care and to discourage adoption. 'Agencies don't
really want to place children,' said Irwin Wein, president of the New York
State Adoptive Parents Committee."

In 1955–56 the Kefauver hearings on interstate adoption had outlined a
series of unethical practices—birth mothers being coerced, birth certificates
being made that showed the adoptive couple as the birth parents, intermediaries being paid excessive high fees, medical problems in infants being
concealed—but any effort to regulate adoption by the federal government
was defeated; adoption remained (and remains) in the hands of states.
While private or independent adoption did not go away, the Kefauver
hearings and a series of scandals involving unethical placement and involuntary relinquishment (including individuals like Georgia Tann who personally earned over $1 million between 1930 and 1950, placing more than one
thousand children), and the rise of the authority of the technocratic expert
(in this case, social workers), made private adoption seem unsavory, the
conversion of what should be a philanthropic exercise into a for-profit
business, with all the incentives running in the wrong direction: with a
placement, agencies get a big payoff; no placement, financial loss.[71]

Even as late as 1980 private adoption was still illegal in twenty-five states,
a situation that underwent rapid change in the subsequent two decades.[72]
Would-be adoptive parents tend to like private adoption—they become
more like consumers, seeking a child and then paying a fee, and less like
petitioners, with every corner of their lives scrutinized, and even then
sometimes waiting long periods to adopt. In the decade between 1973 and
1983 independent adoption went from representing about 50 percent of all
adoptions to about 70 percent (and the norm in international adoption to
the United States).[73]

Not everyone thought independent adoption a good idea, however. It
increased the cost of adoption, making adoption increasingly the province
of the upper-middle class and wealthy, and all the financial incentives work
against protection of birth parents. Even well-meaning, ethical adoption
facilitators have to notice that a birth mother who decides to keep her child
means a financial loss for the facilitator or the agency; unscrupulous organizers of adoption have every reason to engage in exploitation, kidnapping,
and trafficking. Critics charged that the National Council for Adoption
(NCFA), the trade association for fee-charging agencies, has consistently
opposed federal regulation that would set reasonable limits on high fees

and abusive practices, pointing out that that the group even includes some of the same people and institutions targeted by the Kefauver hearings, like the Gladney home.[74] In 1998 Gladney was charging fees up to $30,000 to adopt, depending on family income; according to their marketing coordinator, their average fee in 1998 was $20,000. Gladney has built a massive campus for pregnant women, which included dormitories, an on-site health clinic, a chapel, swimming pool, greenhouse, banquet hall (which, ironically enough, they rent out for weddings and other functions),[75] and services that included high school and community college courses, vocational training, legal representation, and counseling.[76]

Advertising of the "couple seeks child to adopt" sort, as well as ads in the local yellow pages all over the country, brings women and girls to campuses like Gladney's, in Fort Worth, Texas, or Smithlawn Maternity Center in Lubbock, Texas. Most of these facilities are in Sunbelt states that tend to have looser regulation of adoption; many are run by evangelical Christian groups or have close ties to them and are part of their political commitment to providing an alternative to abortion. Critics, like the birthmother and writer Mirah Riben, charge that separating women from their families and housing them in fancy facilities where they are beholden to the agencies for their living costs is an implicitly coercive system and, sometimes, an explicitly coercive one. For example, Riben tells the story of a Tennessee couple, the Smoots, who were flown to Baton Rouge by Beacon House Adoption Services, where they were put up with their two children in a housing complex with other expectant, relinquishing pregnant women. On learning that she was carrying twins, Misty Smoot backed out of her contract with Beacon House for fear the agency would place the twins separately (doubling their fees), seeking an agency that would allow an open adoption instead. Beacon House sued the Smoots for breach of contract, seeking repayment for airline tickets, housing, and expenses.[77] Another woman, Christine Kilmer, responded to an ad for Adoption Insight in a free shopper's guide in Florida. She was relocated to an apartment in Sioux City, Iowa. When she decided to keep her baby, she was told to vacate her apartment, paid for by the prospective adoptive couple, and wound up in a homeless shelter. The lawyer and broker, Maxine Buckmeier, apparently notified the Iowa Department of Human Services (DHS) that Kilmer was homeless, and DHS stopped her from taking her newborn from the hospital. They then took the baby and Kilmer's four-year-old, who had been living with her in a homeless shelter.[78] In 1984 the Gladney Home went to court to get an eviction order for nineteen-year-old Barbara Landry, who refused to leave the facility without her newborn, saying she had signed relinquishment papers under pressure.[79] Some call adoption an "industry" with annual revenues in excess of $15 million dollars.[80] Although outright baby selling is illegal in all states, what constitutes reasonable expenses that agencies and would-be adoptive parents can pay vary widely from state to state, and adoption services and brokers tend to cluster—and relocate pregnant women—in states like Louisiana where there is essentially no upper limit to what can be charged. Fees of $100,000 are not unheard of.[81]

Agencies insist that such stories are the exception, that women back out all the time, that such expenses are just folded into the cost of doing business, and the fees charged for successful adoptions cover such things.[82] They also distinguish between licensed agencies and unlicensed brokers, who they say are less likely to be bound by the same ethical standards.

One thing that can certainly be said for the private system, though, is that it requires the birthmother's consent, at least at some point and under some set of conditions, however imperfect. Although adopting from the public system, from foster care, is often taken to be more virtuous—a self-sacrificial gesture involving adopting children who are older, poorer, sometimes sick, often with behavioral health issues—it is useful to remember that it almost always involves taking a child whose mother (and sometimes father) lost them involuntarily.

From Foster Care to Adoption: MEPA-IEP

In December of 1994 Speaker of the House Newt Gingrich threatened to take the children of welfare mothers and put them in orphanages as part of congressional welfare reform. The idea didn't sell well. For one thing, it evoked images of Oliver Twist—*Time* magazine's cover story the next week was "The Storm over Orphanages," as commentators and politicians rushed in to condemn Gingrich as heartless. Liberals were appalled; this seemed to symbolize exactly why they opposed his "Contract with America," of which the orphanage proposal was a part.[83] For another, it was expensive: analysis by the Child Welfare League of America suggested that while the average cost of keeping a child with her mother on AFDC in 1994 was $2,644 a year, with a foster family it would be $4,800, and in residential group care it would be $36,500.[84] No one on the Republican side of the aisle came to Gingrich's defense. Were Republicans serious about orphanages? "If they were, they have buttoned their lips. This thing has been mercilessly crucified. . . . I would not be surprised if they strike the provision from the bill, because it's given us so much grief," an unnamed House staffer told *Time*.[85]

Yet in 1996 a modified form of Gingrich's vision became law when two bills (originally one but subsequently split)[86] were enacted into law. One, the Personal Responsibility and Work Opportunity Act of 1996 eliminated AFDC, the program that since the New Deal had kept children out of orphanages by giving their mothers the support to raise them at home. The second was the IEP that amended the MEPA, hence it was known as MEPA-IEP. It was designed to make it easier to place foster children in adoptive homes. That act addressed what was widely regarded as an obstacle to moving children from foster care into adoptive homes—"race matching" policies that, many insisted, kept children of color from the most readily available adoptive homes: those with white parents. Another provision of the same bill included a tax credit of $5,000 to $6,000 for adopting families. These measures were followed in 1997 by the Adoption and Safe Families Act (ASFA) that, among other things, provided state child welfare systems with bonuses for placing children into adoptions and time limits to terminate parental rights.[87]

Taken together, these adoption reform measures set out to restructure foster care by providing an enhancement of one exit strategy for children in foster care: adoption, by undoing the work the NABSW had done the previous time the size of the foster care system had rapidly expanded and caseworkers began taking black children in considerable numbers. By eliminating AFDC as a benefit to children, these acts of Congress simultaneously made it more difficult for children to use the most common exit from foster care: family reunification. The adoption components were enacted with the full-throated support of liberals.

What happened? How did liberals go from attacking to supporting Gingrich's suggestion? The answer lies in the redefinition of the elimination of AFDC and the enactment of MEPA-IEP and ASFA from an assault on the preservation of families to a "racial equality" measure, and, arguably at least, the growing political clout of adoption's new class of adoption "consumers." In 1994 as Congress was debating MEPA, the earlier incarnation of the IEP, the influential child policy advocate Elizabeth Bartholet, in a letter to the *New York Times*, described the problem in this way: "this legislation . . . was originally developed in recognition of the fact that child welfare workers throughout the country are holding children of color in foster and institutional care for years at a time rather than placing them in permanent adoptive homes, solely because of their reluctance to place children trans-racially."[88] Well, no. Bartholet's argument seems to have lost track here of the fact that MEPA-IEP was originally part of the welfare reform bill. The goal of the legislation, as formulated in the Contract with America, ban-died about in the press, and discussed in conservative think tanks, was explicitly to take children away from single mothers.

Conservatives argued that only the muscular parenting of fathers could fit sons for the rough-and-tumble of life and employment in the formal sector, and single mothers, as we have heard since at least the 1930s, create weak-willed and pathological underclass children (able only to exist in the kinder, gentler world of gangs and guns).[89] There was a concerted effort to pin all social problems on single mothers. In an editorial in the *Washington Post* in 1993, Richard Cohen called crime "a clear consequence of illegiti-macy,"[90] while Charles Murray was railing against the "Coming White Underclass"—those trashy white women who were having out-of-wedlock births, children they would raise in poverty who would turn out badly.[91] The Contract with America promised to "discourage illegitimacy."[92]

Ironically, Bartholet *is* a single mother and a defender of the diversity of family structure in the face of conservative criticism.[93] Clearly, demonizing single mothers was not her goal, nor, for the most part, that of other liberal champions of MEPA-IEP. While conservatives fought a battle fraught with controversy to eliminate AFDC (albeit an ultimately successful one), MEPA-IEP enjoyed broad support, precisely because it changed the subject and nature of the debate, focusing not on the evils of welfare mothers or the need to take their children away but rather on children who discursively were always already in foster care and "languishing" or "waiting."[94] Al-though this was a bit of a rhetorical sleight of hand—children got into foster care *somehow*—it was extraordinarily useful to the conservative pol-icy agenda. It became such a commonplace that these children were just lingering about, seeking adoptive parents but prevented from doing so by wrong-headed policies, that Bartholet's influential book could carry the title *Nobody's Children*.[95]

Despite serious opposition from feminists, including both the National Organization for Women and the Feminist Majority Foundation, AFDC went down in flames without much acknowledgment that there even *was* a campaign to defend it, probably because the national Democratic Party refused to take a stand on it. Bill Clinton—who, as a former Arkansas governor, knew his Southern Democrats—had campaigned for the presi-dency in 1991 on the promise to "end welfare as we know it."[96] After the

midterm elections of 1994, Republicans and Democrats vied to outdo each
other in their opprobrium for "welfare mothers." In *The Politics of Disgust*,
the political scientist Ange-Marie Hancock analyzes the media coverage
and the floor debates of the welfare reform discussion and found that its
logic worked by stereotype—that recipients of AFDC were typically black,
unemployed, hyperfertile, and were or had been mothers in their teen
years. That none of these attributes were in fact typical of AFDC recipients,
Hancock notes, was simply irrefutable as the debate allowed little space for
dissent—only one article of the 149 she analyzed from major newspapers
across the political spectrum and around the country even noted that
anyone testified against the bill. The most revealing thing she found was
that no one in the congressional floor debate ever described AFDC as a
benefit for children.[97] Indeed, some states, in their enactment of the new
Temporary Aid to Needy Families (TANF) program included financial
incentives or explicitly encouraged caseworkers to pressure recipients of
TANF to relinquish their children for adoption.[98] Only by taking away their
financial support, medical coverage, and apparently their mothers as well
could these children be saved. Despite the fact that the actual prospects for
unmarried mothers had vastly improved since the 1950s and 1960s, the
discourse about it had not. If unmarried mothers were, perversely, going to
insist on raising their children rather than giving them up for adoption,
well, perhaps they could literally be forced to.

For the last half century, the idea of adoption across racial lines has
occupied a place in the U.S. national imaginary that has far outstripped its
significance as an actual practice. It seems to capture all of the things we
worry about—vulnerable children, drugs, questions of love and race, irresponsible parenting, the danger of losing one's children, law, and policy.
The legal scholar Twila Perry has made the insightful point that issues of
race and adoption pit two views of race against each other, both of which
have considerable purchase in the national public discourse—"race blind
individualism" versus "color and community consciousness."[99] So as we
tack into these hugely emotionally compelling waters, it is helpful to take
stock of what this debate is *not* about, despite the prevalence of claims to
the contrary.

It is not about whether white parents can adopt children of color in the
United States. Recent debates about so-called race matching policies, crys-
tallized in MEPA-IEP, addressed *public* adoption agencies, which is to say
adoption from foster care. This represents only 20 to 30 percent of children
adopted in the United States.[100] Only about three-quarters even of public

agencies ever had policies that preferred race matching, and such policies never had the force of law.[101] Private agencies, unless for some reason they receive public funds, are unaffected by MEPA-IEP and were always far less likely to have had race-matching policies.[102]

When we discuss children in foster care, we are not, in the majority of cases, talking about abused children; abuse is only alleged in a minority of cases (in 2003 it was 30.1 percent).[103] Most are removed for reasons of "neglect," which some argue includes simple poverty.[104] Neglect includes controversial categories like parental homelessness, domestic violence, or chronic illness.[105]

It is not about whether children of color should "languish" in foster care. The evidence that the demographics of foster care had much of anything to do with transracial adoption, basically, amounts to the following. A House report in 1990 found (as had earlier ones) that the length of time children spent in foster care varied by race, with black children spending a longer amount of time there. However, this primarily represents lower family reunification rates; black mothers, especially in the context of the crack babies hysteria, were far less likely to get their children back. At no time did all states have race-matching policies for children from foster care, and adoption only accounts for 10 percent of the *exits* from foster care.[106] Bartholet's article published in 1991, "Where Do Black Children Belong," cited personal interviews with adoption advocacy organizations and child welfare workers in a handful of states, predominantly in the Northeast, as well as California.[107] Whatever the significance of states like New York, Connecticut, Massachusetts, and California, however, it was misleading to make them stand for the nation as a whole. The question of the race of adoptive parents was essentially a red herring if the issue was getting children out of foster care—black children were spending a disproportionate amount of time in foster care because TANF and the moral panic around crack were separating them from their unmarried mothers as a matter of federal and state policy.

Two lines of argument diverted public attention from this fact and shaped the political case for MEPA-IEP—one, the arguments of Elizabeth Bartholet, Randall Kennedy, and others in law review articles that attacked state-level foster care systems (and to a lesser extent, private adoption agencies, by extension) for enacting what they said were non-explicit but pervasive race-matching policies, and, two, Rita Simon and Howard Altstein in their series of outcome studies of black children placed in white homes.[108] Both Altstein and Bartholet testified repeatedly in congressional hearings related to child welfare, and their respective positions became gospel as debating points in the media: that psychological outcome studies proved that black children did just as well in white homes as African American homes, and that black children languished in foster care because through a variety of measures, "most of them invisible to those who aren't intimately familiar with the workings of the child welfare system" (as Bartholet said she was), white parents who wanted them were being denied access to parenting black foster children. Specifically, their argument was historical: as a result of the NABSW statement, white parents were being prevented from parenting black children. Ironically, as we have seen in chapter 1, a close and historical reading of the NABSW position would have turned the question around in a way that would have been at least as productive in the 1990s as it had been in the 1970s: not who should adopt the black children in foster care, but how black mothers can keep their children.

But it was not read that way. As a result, the political question of the size of the foster care system was organized around a tremendously compelling but concretely not very significant question: should white families adopt black children? It was insignificant in the sense that compared to, say, examining the question of whether the child welfare system was removing children for poorly conceived reasons of "neglect" (which, critics charged, could be a synonym for poverty),[109] transracial adoption from foster care affected a small number of children. Evidence from the private adoption system indicates clearly enough that there is little white "demand" for black children.[110] But the "problem" in foster care was construed as black children, who represented about 45 percent of the children in foster care.[111] The argument became that black children "languish" in foster care because their route to "permanency" with white families was blocked by "racist" policies put in place after the NABSW statement about transracial adoption. But there is not much evidence that the size and racial demographics of the foster care population was greatly affected by race-matching policies in adoption. The most reliable predictor, of course, would be the numbers and demographics of children *entering* foster care. Second best would be the success rates of family reunification, since most children who leave the foster care system leave it when they reunite with their families.[112] Black children are far less likely than white children to be returned to their families.[113]

The reason there were so many black children in foster care, then, and the reason they stayed longer, had little to do with adoption. It had to do with how many black children *entered* the foster care system in the late 1980s and early 1990s and the fact that they were being returned to their mothers (and fathers, but usually mothers) at considerably lower rates. Did they need to be removed from their families? There is no baseline, logical number of children that *need* to be in foster care. Its considerable variation over the last half century suggests the extent to which it is a matter of policy. As I have suggested, there were almost no black children in foster care before 1961, but the authorization of unlimited federal funds for foster care sent 150,000 into care by 1962. Similarly, before the 1950s there were almost no Native children in foster care. Rules that scrutinized whether a mother kept a "suitable home" that sent so many black and Native children to foster and adoptive homes in the 1950s and 1960s were finally determined to be out of bounds,[114] but one wonders if a few decades from now we will find the current wave of concern over substance abuse just as suspect as "suitable home" rules. Perhaps we really are, again, just criminalizing the ways impoverished people get by. Alcohol use, for example, is far more common among white women than among black or Native women.[115] Perhaps that accounts for why mothers who drink don't elicit moral horror and the almost unchecked power of the state to take their children away.

ICWA

MEPA was written to exclude ICWA, but congressional Republicans made a major play to kill ICWA with the IEP. And while ICWA had barely dented the rate of out of home placement—the rate at which American Indian children were placed in non-Indian familial or institutional placement was higher in 1987 than it was in 1977, being more than a third of Native children[116]—ICWA had staunch defenders who believed that the situation might actually have gotten much worse over those two decades had ICWA not been in place. Because of the considerable controversy over amending and eviscerating ICWA, Republicans separated the two issues and went ahead and passed the IEP in 1996 with the hope of introducing new legislation in 1997 that would have made Indian families and children vulnerable to this new poverty policy of separating families in the same way it envisioned making black families vulnerable.

So in 1997 conservative think tanks, commentators, and representatives were making the case that ICWA hurt white adoptive families, even though tribal courts were regularly approving the placement of American Indian children with white adopters. The heart of it was, as with the IEP, to insist that ICWA's basis was racial—rather than about political status—and to invoke the question of strict scrutiny. The other strategy, invoked even by members of Congress, was to link it to the reviled NABSW statement.[117] The public campaign followed similar lines, arguing that ICWA was about race. For example, *The Encyclopedia of Adoption* describes Indian children as "the only group that continues to be deprived of the protections of MEPA-IEP."[118] In 1997 celebrity talk show host Laura Schlesinger (Dr. Laura) took a call from a white foster mother who was interested in adopting the Indian child she had been fostering but worried that ICWA would make that very difficult. Dr. Laura agreed that ICWA would make her adopting the child all but impossible, saying that it was a "stupid" and outdated law that had been passed in the 1800s.

Media coverage of a number of highly publicized cases in the 1990s suggested that ICWA was a barrier to specific adoptions because of race. In the Rost twins case a couple in Southern California adopted twin girls at birth. The birth father concealed that he was, and more importantly the twins were, eligible for enrollment in the Pomo tribe. Four months later, at the request of the girls' paternal grandmother, the tribe asked for the order of adoption to be vacated, saying it had not conformed with ICWA.[119] In another case two parents, both enrolled members of the Mississippi Band of Choctaw Indians, went off the reservation to have twins and, after their birth, signed a consent to adoption. Again the adoption was declared invalid because the case should have been heard in tribal court. These cases, which critics charged involved an abuse of racial classifications by parents and tribes to disrupt adoptions, motivated some to back amendments to ICWA. But as we saw in chapter 2, the appropriate analogy would not be to race or questions about the NABSW but to a birth parent who crossed state lines for an adoption. This was how the U.S. Supreme Court ruled in the *Holyfield* case (1989), again finding that it was a question of jurisdiction and sovereignty, not race.[120]

ICWA was built on a stronger foundation than the highly local policies that flowed from the NABSW statement; ICWA had lawyers, courts, and case law attached to it. Just as the racialization of Native peoples and African Americans has been different, the political and legal status of children—and child removal—was different. The legal scholar Randall Kennedy suggested that the disproportionate number of children removed from Native parents who wanted them might not be an injustice that the law should remedy but that one-third of Native mothers really were unfit (unwittingly echoing Dorris's unfounded claims about FAS) because of the "impact of disease, unemployment, violence and family dysfunction on Native Americans."[121] He could not, however, get the same political traction that he and others had gotten in asserting that a great many black families could not raise their children.

Conclusion

Considered together, the two halves of welfare reform, TANF and MEPA-IEP, went a long way toward enacting Gingrich's promise to take the children of welfare mothers and put them in orphanages but with a neoliberal twist that took seriously the emergence of the middle-class consumer market segment that fervently wished to adopt: it took the children of welfare mothers and gave middle-class people a massive tax break to adopt them. This chapter has been interested in how, and why, liberals and even feminists like Elizabeth Bartholet joined the campaign against "illegitimacy" waged by neoconservatives in the 1990s as part of the effort to get rid of federal entitlements that supported single mothers. As we have seen, the IEP was redefined to separate it from the previous controversy over Gingrich's remarks about orphanages and even, ultimately, from the measures to end AFDC. It was called, instead, as the legal scholar Joan Heifetz Hollinger defines it, a "law aimed at removing the barriers to permanency for the hundreds of thousands of children who are in the child protective system, and especially, for the African American and other minority children. . . . MEPA makes it clear that children in state custody are not exempt from the antidiscrimination principles embodied in . . . Title VI of the 1964 Civil Rights Act."[122] In the 1970s activists had worked to remind policymakers that those "barriers" were parental rights, deserving of protection from abuse by an overreaching state system. A great deal had changed in a handful of years.

Most disconcerting, though, was the way a liberal discourse of "color blindness" in adoption disabled what was, at least initially, sturdy opposition to policies designed to take children from their unworthy single mothers. To borrow from Twila Perry again, color blindness met community and color consciousness, and together they engaged in a lively and compelling debate that utterly obscured the larger issue: that black and Native mothers were losing their children in considerable numbers. In the meantime, as with the Flemming rule a generation ago, liberal concern about black and Native children met conservative willingness to provide significant funds to take them away—I am thinking here of the ways the Adoption Promotion and Stability Act of 1996, with its $5,000 tax break to families willing to adopt children of color or "special needs" children, was like ADC-Foster Care. As a result, we have created the conditions under which the foster care system could stabilize at its new, massive size (about five hundred thousand children), with a population much less white than a few decades earlier—a new generation's "browning of child welfare." As Dorothy Roberts writes: "Scholars who deal with Black children in the child welfare system tend to focus on social work practice—how children should be treated—rather than the politics of child protection—how political relationships affect which children become involved in the system. . . . Child protection authorities are taking custody of Black children at alarming rates, and in doing so, they are dismantling social networks that are critical to Black community welfare."[123] Making the NABSW the villain of the story, making that group responsible for why black children were disproportionately in the child welfare system, misses that the organization tried to call attention to the targeting of black single mothers by child protection systems and tried to defend those mothers.

Adoption was an ideal neoliberal solution to the problem of supporting impoverished children. Neoliberalism sought to privatize a variety of services, pushing them onto (sometimes already quite strapped) families. Medicaid and Medicare cuts limited services to people with disabilities and people who were ill, relying on families to pick up the slack. The failed effort to privatize Social Security pensions would have made wealthy people quite independent but left middle-class and working-class people who never made enough to save for years and years of retirement dependent on family care for their elder years.

A radical agenda of privatization was, of course, the heart of neoliberalism in two senses. First, there was the "privatizing" of resources for the benefit of business—such as the awarding of contracts to private companies for what have traditionally been government functions, such as a military activity. Second, privatization delegated to families and religious groups many of the post–New Deal functions of government, such as supporting single mothers with children. Together, these embody the domestic goals that Grover Norquist memorably phrased as making government small enough to drown in the bathtub. In order to accomplish these goals, however, neoliberal ideologues needed to build a broad consensus that middle-class domestic space was *not* going to shrink in the wake of women's move into the formal workforce, but on the contrary it was going to expand.

Adoption managed the contradictions of this position quite nicely, albeit more symbolically than actually (since adoption still represents quite a small fraction of familial reproduction). For middle-class families, it offers a way out of the conundrum of education, work, and the reduced success of late childbearing. For impoverished children and the child welfare system, it finds middle-class families to absorb the social cost of their care. Between 1986 and 1992 the size of the child welfare systems in the United States nearly doubled, from 276,000 in 1986 to 450,000 in 1992,[124] largely as a result of the "crack babies" scare. These kids were disproportionately children of color, and so the proportion of white children in the foster care system became progressively smaller.[125] The debate about MEPA-IEP was in significant part about how to stabilize this huge new burden on state budgets, especially since children were being taken at birth. If their mothers were being designated as singularly unfit, with little chance of getting their children back, adoption represented an important alternative to commitment by states to these children's support for as much as eighteen or even twenty-one years.

PART II

Transnational Adoption and Latin America

FOUR

From Refugees to Madonnas of the Cold War

In September 2009, Lisa Belkin posted a guest piece about infertility to her blog at the *New York Times* website. "Life After Infertility Treatments Fail" related Shelagh Little's struggles with grief after efforts at in vitro fertilization that did not enable her to get pregnant and the lack of support and space for childless women. The results were explosive: readers posted 369 responses. Few took Little up on her invitation to think about why U.S. culture in the first decade of the twenty-first century demands that all women be mothers and all families contain children or to consider the need for feminist spaces that celebrate childlessness. A surprising number of posts were not just unsympathetic but positively angry that Little had decided not to adopt. "CCC" was typical: "Your 'story' left me feeling like you need someone to shake the heck out of you because you can't get past the fact that you, like so many others, can't have your biological child, that no other child—adopted or surrogate—will do. People, including children, are dying from hunger, disease, war. Children are out there longing for a loving, protective home instead of the limbo of foster home after foster home and the abuses heaped upon them. You clearly have not experienced enough real tragedy in your life. Consider yourself lucky and me unsympathetic."[1] This visceral anger at those who "should" adopt (particularly from overseas, where children are "dying from hunger, disease, war") but do not has a history. It is the sedimented effect of nearly a century of stories of children who will die without "us"—middle-class folk in the United

States—who need the home and emotional investment that only "we" can provide. The second part of this book explores that history, beginning in this chapter with the 1930s, the decade that produced that passionate investment in adopting children from outside the United States.

This chapter argues that the interventionist history of overseas adoption to the United States was born during the Cold War, and it tries to illuminate some of the parameters of what that adoption meant—why it relied on separating children from their birth families permanently and irrevocably —by exploring its roots in evangelical Christian anti-Communism, and showing the defeated model on the left that preceded it, largely involving supporting refugee children until parents or other relatives could reclaim them. It begins by exploring how U.S. Americans learned to feel a sense of obligation for and longing to help children overseas. It follows the photographic traces of how those in the United States initially understood children in need, arguing that it began with Popular Front art that demanded reform in immigration and U.S. foreign policy, followed two decades later by an evangelical Christian Cold War impulse that demanded intervention overseas and sharpened a U.S. desire to rescue children (understood to be) orphans. This chapter also explores the law and practice these photos gave rise to: how the diverse forms of caring for refugee children that existed from the 1930s to the 1960s hardened into the kind of exclusivity we call plenary adoption—where a new birth certificate is written for the child, creating the legal fiction that the birth parents never existed. The chapter will argue that this was not an inevitable development. On the contrary, it was one among many possibilities that those who wished to help children were experimenting with in the 1930s and 1940s.

I begin the narrative of how transnational adoption came into being a bit earlier than most scholarly accounts do, which typically start after 1945 in the midst of the rise of Cold War anti-Communism.[2] From the great crash of 1929 to the end of the Korean War in 1953, the United States experienced seismic shifts in its economy and politics, from Depression to prosperity, and from left to right. In the 1930s, there were the Depression-era radicalism of the Popular Front, the Communist Party, the Abraham Lincoln brigades fighting Fascism in Spain, strikes, May Day marches, the "bonus army" of the unemployed encamped across from the White House, and New Deal liberalism. On the right, there was a vigorous conservatism, sometimes expressly racist, whose legacies included the ongoing failure of a federal antilynching bill, the renewal of the Ku Klux Klan, the trials of the

Scottsboro boys and Sleepy Lagoon, Father Coughlin's Southern populist proto-Fascism, the widespread deportations of Mexican Americans from California and the Southwest, and the anti-immigrant isolationism of the American Legion and other "100% American" groups. The 1940s saw the mobilization for the war, the visible entry of (white, married) women and African Americans into the wartime labor force, the *braceros* (guest workers) program for Mexican wartime labor, and the rise of urban gay communities, and then the ashes of Hiroshima, the birth of Truman's Cold War anti-Communism, the ascendancy of Joseph McCarthy, and the execution of the Rosenbergs. It was a period of political and cultural battles over Fascism, Communism, labor, racism, feminism, and sexuality that would mark the rest of the twentieth century.

In the United States (as elsewhere), two views of the world dominated this period. One was a left anti-Fascist internationalist front arrayed against German Nazism, Franco's war against the Spanish Republic, Mussolini and the invasion of Ethiopia, and the Japanese invasion of China, and sympathetic to the Mexican and Russian revolutions. The second was an anti-Communist position that opposed these same revolutions, saw the rising fortunes of the Communist Party in Europe and the United States (and to some extent, New Deal liberalism) as spread by open immigration, and opposed Roosevelt leading the United States into war against fascism. This latter political formation was isolationist before the war, openly anti-Semitic, and associated with a hard-line anti-immigrant position. After the war, however, this political formation supported an anti-Communist internationalism abroad and prosecution of suspected communists, "fellow travelers," and homosexuals at home. It was this conservative ascendancy that stopped international adoption to the United States before 1948, and promoted it thereafter.

Genealogies

One continuity across this era of abrupt shifts was the importance of visual images and policy initiatives aimed at helping children in distress, or sometimes mothers and children, to the various political formations. In the United States during the Depression, photos of children were leftist images that demanded attention for working-class lives. The gritty photographic realism of the 1920s and 1930s in the United States was characterized by a politics that railed against "business as usual." U.S. Americans first learned how to feel about foreign children from photos of sad eyed, often hungry or homeless kids. Before there was transnational adoption, there were photographs of children in need. This tradition in visual culture has become deeply familiar, not just because we recognize *Migrant Mother*, the Depression-era photo of a tough but desperate and careworn mother with her two children curled tight against her, but because these kinds of images persist as an iconic representation of "poverty" or "need." Call to mind an image of "famine" and chances are, if you grew up in the United States, you will picture a child or a mother and child. A Mexican newspaper columnist trying to explain U.S. Americans' obsession with "saving" children (which in his view gets turned into the naked exercise of the power of the dollar to buy them) wrote, not entirely unsympathetically, of how U.S. citizens are reared with "heart-rending black-and-white photographs of tiny, barefoot Latin American children, with large, sad eyes," and invitations to send five dollars a day to rescue "little Lupita" from life without running water or electricity.[3] Popularized by evangelical Protestant and United Nations child-saving agencies during the 1950s, 1960s, and 1970s, they have become ubiquitous, an enduring image of "hunger" and "need."

These images were popularized during the Depression as art created to demand attention and empathy for working-class lives, not necessarily patronizing pity. Dorothea Lange's *Migrant Mother* is a moving photo that works as an icon of the era because it echoes the successful political struggle to see those in need of "relief" as hardworking but down on their luck (figure 1). It was taken in 1936 while Lange worked for the Farm Security Administration (FSA), released for public relations purposes, and featured in articles with titles like, "Ragged, Hungry, Broke, Harvest Workers Live in Squalor" and "What Does the 'New Deal' Mean to This Mother and Her Children?"[4] The photo made the case more or less explicitly for the moral and political necessity of relief, at a minimum, or, as the second caption suggests, fundamental economic change. Although *Migrant Mother* was by far the most famous such photograph, Lange and the other FSA photographers like Russell Lee, Ben Shahn, and Jack Delano often chose women, children, or Madonna and child figures for their subjects,[5] producing an empathetic archive of the poor, migrants, and working people for a broad audience. Lewis Hine took pictures of children as part of the Child Labor Bureau's campaign to halt child labor practices, and his Ellis Island photos were designed to combat anti-immigrant sentiment. He used the Madonna and child and child alone (what we might call the "waif") figures prominently; the Ellis Island collection is full of Madonna images, while the child-

FIGURE 1.
Migrant Mother by Dorothea Lange.
Farm Security Administration Series, 1936.

labor photos feature images of tough, prematurely adult boys and girls dwarfed by the machines on which they worked (figure 2).[6]

Similar visual images had fought earlier foreign policy battles in Europe. In the immediate aftermath of the First World War, Allied powers continued to blockade Austria and Germany in order to force them to accept the terms of the Treaty of Versailles. A group in England founded the Fight the Famine Council—the organization that would become Save the Children—in response to news reports of hungry children in Germany and Austria subsisting on cabbage and of six-year-olds the size of two-year-olds. One of its founding members, Eglantyne Jebb, was arrested for handing out a leaflet showing a starving Austrian baby with the heading "Our Blockade Has Caused This." The organization that subsequently emerged sent relief funds from England to a host of unpopular places and peoples in the interwar years: Germany and Austria (as well as France and Belgium), refugees from the Armenian genocide, and the Soviet Union. Save the Children's public relations material agues that the group's singular success

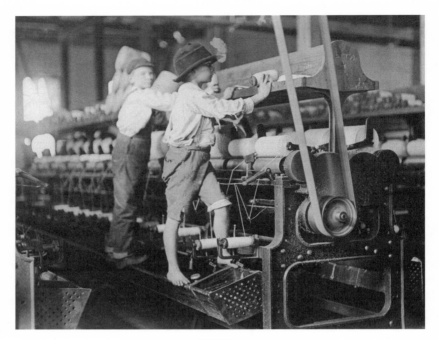

FIGURE 2.
Mill children in Macon, Georgia.
Photo by Lewis Hine.

—then as now—in fundraising for national "enemies," or at least those ill-liked, rested in part on its deployment of photography, its ability to send photographers to capture "hunger" on film.[7]

In the 1930s photojournalists in the United States and elsewhere used images of children to dramatize the effects of rising Fascism in Europe and Asia. The Associated Press photo archive records some of these haunting images: a bloodied, wailing infant in a railroad station in China destroyed by Japanese bombing in 1937 (figure 3); Jewish refugee children fleeing German-controlled areas in the *Kindertransport* (figure 4); Basque children fleeing the Fascist bombing in Spain (figure 5). Collectively and individually, these kinds of images built support for popular organizations and socialist movements. Like Pablo Picasso's agonized painting *Guernica*, they sought to be a call to conscience, raising the alarm over the rising Fascist persecution of popular movements, political tendencies toward socialism, and ethnic minorities like Basques and Jews. A few years later, British children targeted by German bombing of civilian populations would also

FIGURE 3.
A bloodied child cries in the ruins of Shanghai's South Railway Station
in China after a Japanese bombing on August 28, 1937,
during the Sino-Japanese War.
AP Photo/H.S. Wong.

feature prominently in U.S. newspapers and magazine. As discussed below, in a victory for race-based immigration restriction, Jewish, Chinese, and Basque refugee children were officially denied entry to the United States, while displaced British children were allowed visas.

Madonnas of the Cold War

The aftermath of the Second World War is often described as a retreat from the reformist or even radical period that preceded it into a cocoon of the Cold War, McCarthyism, suburbs, and nuclear families, and the fate of the Madonna and waif pictures was no different. They, too, made a turn from their reformist career to a defense of U.S. power. They became part of the architecture of Cold War liberalism, which constructed an overseas role for the United States that was at once compassionate and interventionist. If

FIGURE 4.
Three young refugees at a London terminus on May 14, 1940,
with their few belongings escape the Nazis in Holland.
AP Photo.

the United Nations was founded on principles that included noninterven-
tion in the affairs of sovereign states, the waif and Madonna photos con-
ceptualized the families within those sovereign states as in urgent need of
intervention, of rescue.

After the Second World War, the Madonna and child and waif images,
already common, became ubiquitous—tropes not only of journalism but
also of other kinds of visual culture. In 1947, shortly after the end of the
war, Truman sent telegrams to army commanders in Germany and Japan
asking them to take photographs "showing famine conditions, particularly
emphasizing children, women and aged, bread lines, emaciated conditions,
etc."[8] Meaning to answer critics who complained about providing food aid
to former enemies at a time when the United States was still experiencing
shortages (and congressional representatives who were insisting that there
were no starving people in Europe), the federal government sought a
simple, already popularized way of representing "hunger." Although sending members of the army out to take sentimentalized photos to document

FIGURE 5.
Some of the four thousand Basque refugee children from Bilbao, Spain,
who arrived at Southampton, England, on the *Habana* on May 23, 1937,
waving on arrival. They were sent to Britain to escape the Spanish Civil War.
AP Photo.

the devastation to women and children that they themselves had caused sounds almost like satire, it was a taste of things to come. In the years that followed, Americans became ever more schooled in how to believe that only U.S. intervention could solve the problems that U.S. intervention had wrought.

For example, the *Saturday Review,* a bastion of American middlebrow liberalism, published an article by Norman Cousins in 1949 on the atomic devastation of Hiroshima, the still-mounting casualties, and questions of American moral responsibility for orphans four years after the dropping of the atomic bomb. While not exactly an anti-bombing piece, it did suggest that something terrible had happened there for which Americans were, sadly, responsible. While Cousins took pains to say that the Japanese residents of Hiroshima endorsed the American view of the bombing—that it was necessary to prevent further casualties in the war in the Pacific and to bring down Hirohito's military government—he also reported the high end of the (very contested) figure for the number killed by the bomb, fixing it at as high as 250,000, and noted that none of millions of dollars in the Atomic Bomb Casualty Commission's budget was being spent on treating the people still dying from the effects of radiation, but rather on observing them. A similar gentle dissent infused his account of what he termed "moral adoption" of Hiroshima's children. He mentions that before he went to Japan,

> several people had told me they would like to adopt Japanese children orphaned by bombing. Under the Oriental Exclusion Act, however, these adoptions are not possible. I should like to suggest the next best thing—moral adoptions. By moral adoption I am thinking of Hiroshima children who would be adopted by American families and who would carry the names of the people adopting them. The children would continue to live in Japan—perhaps in some place like Mrs. Yamashita's [orphanage]—but the American families would be responsible for their care and upbringing. Then, later, if Congress passes a law permitting Japanese children to come to America, these morally adopted children could become legally adopted as well.

He said that the cost of taking care of a child at Mrs. Yamashita's orphanage was $2.32 a month and offered the *Saturday Review* to serve as facilitator to transfer donations to Hiroshima.[9] While Cousins clearly found the Asian Exclusion Act unjust and inhumane, he also powerfully believed in the fundamental decency of Americans, their capacity to resist the official xenophobia, and their ability to do right with respect to the victimized Japanese.

The response to Cousins's modest proposal was overwhelming and represented the full range of the sharply conflicted U.S. responses to the Hiroshima bombing and previous firebombing of Japanese civilians (that U.S. Defense Secretary Robert McNamara much later called a war crime).[10] Some denounced it. One woman enclosed a check as "a tragically small tax payment for my own share in the guilt of belonging to a race which dropped the first atom bomb."[11] A former pilot, Lawrence Malis wrote, "Having flown twenty-six B-29 missions over Japan, I have carried a guilty conscience for several years. First, because of the indiscriminate fashion with which we used to burn out slum areas with fire bombs; second, because of the atom bomb itself, and what I feel was its unwarranted and needless use. Your article . . . was interesting enough as far as it went, but it also presented an easy way to soothe an elusive feeling of collective guilt. I know I can't buy back my teen-age ideals for a small sum . . . [but] I am enclosing my check."[12] For some, "moral adoption" embodied a contradiction: the sense of collective guilt being too easily assuaged, yet at the same time, the necessity of doing *something*, and the difficulty of articulating what that might be.

At the same time, others described their participation in terms of U.S. (nationalist) domesticity, as part of the citizen-family with a husband, wife, dog, cat, and children. This Cold War ideal of the nuclear family is what the historian Elaine Tyler May calls "domestic containment," in which the ideals of national security and family security are conflated. The psychologist Joseph Adelson powerfully characterized the domesticity of the 1950s as both zeitgeist and a willed denial of some of the forces that shaped it. He wrote: "We had as a nation emerged from a great war, itself following upon a long and protracted Depression. We thought, all of us, men and women alike, to replenish ourselves in goods in spirit, to undo, by exercise of the collective will, the psychic disruptions of the immediate past. We would achieve the serenity that had eluded the lives of our parents, the men would be secure in stable careers, the women in comfortable homes, and together they would raise perfect children."[13] The contradictions in this account—as in the structure of feeling to which it refers—are interesting; willed serenity and psychic disruptions that lead to stability, comfort, and perfection. While "lying" might not be a fair or just description of a "willed serenity" that came out of such collective upheaval and pain, Adelson's description does reveal something of why the youth of the 1960s—their "perfect children"—attached the moniker of "hypocrisy" to so many of the beliefs and political policies endorsed by their parents of the 1950s.

Having a job, marriage, children, house, and a dog constituted the reassuringly normal, painfully conformist, consumer-oriented way of life that defined the "man in the gray flannel suit" and his stay-at-home, suburban wife who attached themselves to these clearly defined roles and expectations, proving that they were, if not happy, then American. (As William J. Levitt, developer of Levittown wrote, "No man who owns his own house and lot can be a Communist. He has too much to do.")[14] One respondent to Cousins's proposal of "moral adoption" took up precisely these kinds of terms, insisting:

> It seems like a wonderful plan to us . . . Any American family of the most moderate means could manage to squeeze out that small sum each month. We pledge ourselves to be financially responsible for some small orphan . . . I can think of no better way to teach our own

four-year old daughter a sense of responsibility for others in the world. . . . My husband is a ceramic engineer. He has been employed for ten years, with four years out for Army service. We own our home and are not in debt. We support our daughter, one dog, and two cats, so feel quite sure we can undertake another child."[15]

Thrift, good childrearing, engineering, home ownership, volunteerism (though not dissent), the letter writer, who signs herself as Mrs. John Snoddy (read, "wife"), produced a catalog of the earnest values of U.S. Cold War domesticity, emphasizing their difference from a "small orphan" for whom she hoped her daughter would feel a sense of (pity and) "responsibility," and conflated it with a foreign policy. Or, with a different emphasis but contending with much the same ideology, two "spinsters" (who may or may not have been partners), Etta Gibson and Myrtle Moore, wrote of their desire to support a child, and their concern that this would not be acceptable, saying "since we are spinsters I don't suppose we would be allowed to have a child over here, but if we could have him, or her, we would accept the responsibility and do our best to rear him happily."[16] Two other, more famous "spinsters," Helen Keller and Polly Thompson, also sponsored a child, "preferably a girl [because] women are the precious fruit trees of the future Japanese civilization [who need a] fair chance of healthy growth."[17] Presaging virtually every theme in contemporary debates in adoption and fostering, from political conformity to protest to feminism and questions about the shape and components of "legitimate" families, the response to the *Saturday Review* piece also rehearsed Cold War questions about "our" responsibility for "them."

The *Saturday Review* Hiroshima orphans were ultimately also incorporated into the regimes of visual culture. One of the principle distinctions between "them"—foreign, impoverished, war refugees, orphans, migrant laborers—and "us"—white Americans—is made visually with reference to the home. Where the letter writer cited above mentioned a dog, a cat, homeownership, and engineering as a series of equivalences, each reinforcing a claim to non-Communist, U.S. American normality, photographs treated the interior of the home as a synecdoche for the whole. Displaced and "foreign" children were outdoors; American families and children were represented inside homelike spaces.[18] Nine months after the original Cousins article, *Saturday Review* told a story about the resolution of the problem it had presented readers: all the orphans in Yamashita's institution had been "adopted" by American families, as had eighty others from orphanages

FIGURE 6.
Children sleep on Hong Kong's streets, May 8, 1958.
AP Photo.

elsewhere in Hiroshima. An accompanying photo-essay demonstrated the resolution of this narrative problem in a different way—pictures of the orphans outside, near buildings or flowering bushes, were presented alongside photographs of their American "families," parents and children or children alone inside houses. Japanese children had been moved, symbolically, into or at least almost into American homes.

Other Cold War uses of women and children were frankly ideological. Two Associated Press photos published on sequential days, May 8 and 9, 1958, point to how the discursive distance between "the free world" and "Communism" could be figured visually. The first (figure 6) showed almost-naked children sleeping on a piece of cardboard in the streets of Hong Kong, refugees from "Communism" in China. Communism caused this—nakedness, homelessness, children alone—the picture and caption declare (never mind that it could equally function as a placard for "capitalist" hard-heartedness, where children are not guaranteed a place to live, even years after they arrived in Hong Kong as refugees). The second photograph (figure 7) is a

FIGURE 7.
U.S. Vice President Richard M. Nixon is greeted by school children waving flags of
Ecuador and America at the airport in Quito, Ecuador, May 9, 1958.
AP Photo/Henry Griffin.

study in contrast—neatly dressed, well-scrubbed Ecuadorian children wave
American flags at Vice President Nixon, with the name of their school on a
banner and a new building rising in the background. Latin America and
development thrive because of "capitalism" and alliance with the United
States.

An even more dramatic shift came in the work of the Christian Children's Fund. It was founded in 1938 by J. Calvitt Clarke as the China
Children's Fund to assist the victims of the Japanese bombing. Clarke, a
Presbyterian minister, was at least nominally concerned with labor and
other leftist issues in the 1930s; one of his novels, written in 1935 about a
young girl preacher, revolves in part around how she is to respond to a mill
owner who cruelly exploited his employees.[19] Twenty years later, Clarke
recalled that the origins of his project lay in very Popular Front concerns:
"at that particular time," he wrote, "the Japanese occupied China, and there
were literally thousand of children starving to death." He remembered

himself saying to another minister, a Methodist, that "it's a shame America isn't doing more," and that the Methodist minister turned around and urged Clarke to do it himself. He did. As other U.S. Americans were driving ambulances and running orphanages in Spain, Clarke began raising money for orphans in China, and by 1950, he supported forty-two of them. The Christian, or China, Children's Fund was one of the first groups in the United States to use the "sponsor an orphan" appeal, and were quite successful at it: by the time the Mao Tse Tung government forced the organization out in 1950, they owned a million dollars in orphanage property in China.[20] Whatever his sympathies for leftist causes in the 1930s, however, he was an avowed anti-Communist by the 1950s. The Christian Children's Fund began to advertise the idea of sponsoring a child as itself a way to defeat Communism, because "the hungry children of the world are more dangerous to us than the atomic bomb," as a 1952, first-person narrative, signed by Clarke and featuring a photo of "hunger limp" infant argued. "I have returned from overseas with the realization that the Communists care enough to make very successful capital of democracy's failures and with the strong conviction that we Americans can not close our eyes or stop our ears to the cry of a hungry child anywhere in the world—black, brown, yellow, or white."[21] Another featured a photo of a painfully thin South Korean child, with the caption, "This picture is as dangerous as it is pitiful," arguing that the orphans of wartorn South Korea were vulnerable to Communist influence and ideas if "democratic" countries failed to alleviate their misery.

One of the greatest purveyors of Cold War images of waifs and Madonnas was UNICEF, which used them to raise money and build support for their mother-and-child health and child-feeding programs. Organized in 1946 to provide blankets and milk to child war refugees in Europe, the Middle East, and China, UNICEF quickly became, at the urging of representatives from the Third World, a permanent organization dedicated to combating disease and malnutrition. UNICEF had a tremendously high profile in U.S. magazines, newspapers, towns, and cities, in part because of its startling early success in combating yaws, tuberculosis, and leprosy with new wonders—vaccines and penicillin—but more broadly because it embodied the postwar dreams of eradicating poverty through technological, scientific means.[22] UNICEF worked hard at maintaining its high profile in the United States, raising money in visible, public places, urging volunteers to sell its Christmas cards, and soliciting children's donations at Halloween.

The story of the organization of the "trick-or-treat for UNICEF" campaign suggests how omnipresent UNICEF was as an organization in suburban life in the 1950s. According to UNICEF-USA's account:

> the idea that Halloween could be turned into "something good" first occurred to the Reverend Clyde and Mary Emma Allison in 1950 in a Philadelphia suburb. Clyde Allison was then a young editor looking for ideas for a national Presbyterian publication aimed at junior high school groups. One day, Mrs. Allison happened to be downtown when Elsie, the Borden Company cow, was parading along the main street. Mrs. Allison followed the cow to Wanamaker's department store, where a booth was set up to collect money for UNICEF's milk-feeding programs. Why not, she thought, have children collect money for hungry children through UNICEF?[23]

The alarming image of a cow in Wanamaker's notwithstanding, the indication that one could follow Elsie down Main Street in suburban Philadelphia and find UNICEF suggests how ubiquitous the organization was, and not only because it so perfectly embodied the ideals of postwar liberalism. The organization also put massive energies into public relations campaigns in the United States—appointing celebrities like Dannie Kaye, Audrey Hepburn, and Harry Belafonte as its "goodwill ambassadors," for example.[24] The United States was its principal funder and, after enabling legislation was passed by Congress in 1954, the source of great quantities of free milk from agricultural surplus. The popular press, like *Parents* magazine, marked and extended UNICEF's popular appeal through puff pieces about "Trick-or-Treating for UNICEF" that noted perkily: "This Halloween perhaps your youngster will join millions of boys and girls who will ring doorbells to collect pennies and dimes for the United Nations Children's Fund. This new style Halloween gives our own children an opportunity to aid sick and starving children in other lands." *Parents* magazine recommended hosting an internationally themed party afterward, complete with a discussion of games from many lands, borrowed, apparently, from UNICEF's "Youth Recreation Kit."[25] UNICEF's publicity machine was massively successful in insinuating the organization into everyday, domestic life.

UNICEF's most prominent public relations campaigns in the United States, however, were not Christmas cards or trick-or-treating but its extensive use of photographic images to demonstrate and generate support for its work. Perhaps more than any other single thing, the massive, repetitive use of Madonna and waif images by UNICEF in the 1950s accounts for the normalization of these images as the grammar of "hunger" or "need" in contemporary U.S. culture. UNICEF hired commercial photographers and sent them around the world to capture on film the things not there—the *absence* of yaws, the *absence* of tuberculosis, or hunger, or widespread infant mortality. Compounding the difficulty of this task was the work of capturing "strange lands" in ways that marked them as different but not other, to tell the story of foreign places in ways that did not reinforce the United States' historic tendency toward isolationism but rather excited pity toward and interest in these children. UNICEF photographers accomplished these tasks in part by repetition of the two images—the Madonna with child and the waif. They essentially reproduced the same photograph over and over in different places. The things that changed—complexion and clothing of the subjects—was rendered picturesque, while the essential interchangeability of children and mothers was stressed. These photos stand as testament to themes of liberal universalism and the family of man: we are all the same, with a few minor changes. Of course, they are *not* us; the lack that must be remedied through our intervention could be figured as a few facial lesions, in the case of yaws, or painfully thin infants. As often, though, the children, infants, and mothers appear curiously plump and healthy, if we consider that the point of these photographs is in part to talk about malnutrition and unmet health needs. Their lack, though, is still there— figured by the absence of interior spaces—they are not "at home," they are (always) outdoors or at the clinic. Where magazines like *Ladies' Home Journal*, *Parents*, or *Good Housekeeping* consistently pictured U.S. children inside home spaces, UNICEF's children are never indoors. The other striking contrast between "our" and "their" children can be seen with reference to activity and autonomy—in women's magazines even the youngest U.S. infants are sitting, sleeping, or playing at some distance from adults, if there are any adults in the picture at all—while UNICEF's infants are in the arms of, connected to, or at least within touching distance of a mother figure.

Other United Nations agencies, even those that did not run mother and child programs, also came to rely on Madonna and child images. After 1953, for example, the United Nations Korea Reconstruction Agency worked on typical development projects: vaccinating cattle, importing fertilizer, planting seedlings, supplying bicycles for forest guards, providing textbooks and supplies for universities and books for a literacy campaign, supplying spindles for the rehabilitation of the textile industry, building houses, providing laboratory facilities for mining, making nets available to fisherfolk, dredging a harbor, and providing flood control for farm land.[26] When the agency hired photographer Josef Breitenbach from New York and sent him to Korea for two years to take pictures and develop a photo lab that would send home pictures for publicity purposes, these were the projects they told him about. The agency's public relations arm described the problem that his photographs were meant to solve: "Since 1953 coverage of Korea is essentially restricted to short political new[s] items. There must, however, be a number of people who want to hear what happened to the Reconstruction projects of which so much was spoken during the war and on which close to 100 million dollars [of] American money and about 50 million from other U.N. countries was spent."[27] Like so many others, Breitenbach sent photographs back to New York that were dominated by Madonnas and children and kids in the street. So much so, in fact, that when he published under his own name a book of the photographs he took in Korea and elsewhere he called it *Women of Asia*.[28] The visual idiom of "development" was women and children, even if the actual site of it was flood control engineering.

Refugees and Law

What happened with visas when we were learning to feel—fear, pity, sympathy, identification—with the children and mothers of these photos? Much the same kind of transition occurred in child refugee and immigration law and policy as in the cultural significance of photographic images of children in the same period—a transformation in policy, hopes, and dreams for children from solidarity to rescue. The efforts to secure visas for refugee children spanned the period from the Kindertransport to Operation Pedro Pan, from fostering to adoption, from anti-Fascist activity to anti-Communist activity. These two kinds of programs and projects, I argue, produced the dimensions of possibility of meaning and practice for adoption to the United States.

Let us turn first to U.S. efforts to help Jewish children under the Nazis. In 1939 Congress debated the Wagner-Rogers Bill, which would have allowed twenty thousand German children, particularly Jewish and other "non-Aryan" children, to immigrate to the United States outside of the narrow quotas imposed by the Immigration Act of 1924 (and still more narrowly interpreted, during the Depression) and hence without jeopardizing the ability of adult refugees to migrate. Even sweetening the pot by insuring fully half of the proposed twenty thousand unaccompanied minor visas would go to Catholic and Protestant children was not enough to calm fears about admitting children of an "alien" race, and the measure failed.[29]

Anti-Communist, racist, and anti-immigrant forces—white-fear populism—had broad support in the United States in the 1930s, and these sentiments played a significant role in policy, from defeating the antilynching bill to delaying the U.S. entry into the war in Europe. Father Charles Coughlin's weekly radio address, claiming an audience of 3.5 million regular and 15 million occasional listeners, rallied anti-Semitism as an explanation for the Depression, claiming that Jewish financiers were responsible and that Jewish refugees were taking American jobs. Those selling his newspaper, *Social Justice*, provoked street attacks on Jews. The American Bund, composed largely of lower-middle-class German-Americans formed the American Nazi movement, complete with swastikas, goose-stepping marches, and storm troopers. The spiritualist William Dudley Pelley rallied old-stock American Protestants and former KKK members around protest of the "Kosher New Deal," the "communistic Jewish Reds," and "Yiddisher refugees" who were responsible for everything from unemployment to air crashes.[30] Seward Collins, a leading conservative intellectual, wrote in 1933 about the anti-Communist benefits of the rise of Hitler and Nazis in Germany:

> One would gather from the fantastic lack of proportion of our press— not to say its gullibility and sensationalism—that the most important aspect of the German revolution was the hardships suffered by Jews under the new regime. Even if the absurd atrocity stories were all true, the fact would be almost negligible beside an event that shouts aloud in spite of the journalistic silence: the victory of Hitler signifies the end of the Communist threat, *forever*. Wherever Communism grows strong enough to make a Communist revolution a danger, it will be crushed by a Fascist revolution.[31]

The combination of anti-Semitism, anti-Communism, and anti-immigration fervor (especially against what one group called the "refu-Jews") had a disastrous effect on efforts to get Jewish and other "non-Aryan" refugees out of the Third Reich, and in this period of widespread unemployment consular officials were instructed that anyone who was not wealthy or did not have wealthy relatives was "likely to become a public charge" (LPC) and hence should be excluded from immigration. Even the restrictive quotas instituted in 1924 were not fulfilled, and immigration ground virtually to a halt. Even when consular officials were finally instructed to interpret the

LPC exclusion more generously, just before the Nazis shut the door to emigration altogether, lack of personnel meant that applications went unprocessed.[32]

In the waning months of 1938, after the anti-Jewish pogrom known as *Kristallnacht* (the night of the broken glass) left no more room to equivocate about the murderous direction of Nazi policy toward the Jews, Britain promised a delegation of Jewish leaders that it would take in unaccompanied minors up to the age of seventeen in Reich-controlled areas. The program, run by the Movement for the Care of German Children, set up networks first in Germany and Austria, then Poland, Czechoslovakia, and the Netherlands. Organizations sought children in orphanages, teenagers, those with a parent in a concentration camp, and those whose parents had become too impoverished to care for them. In England, the BBC broadcast a call for foster homes for refugee children and more than five hundred households responded. Although some undoubtedly sought a maid or other household help, and no one seemed to think it mattered whether the children's religious or national heritage was respected and preserved, many of the homes were warm and supportive places. In all, nearly ten thousand children were rescued by the program. It was not an overwhelmingly generous project. Britain reassured its citizens' anti-Semitism with the proviso that the child's sponsor had to agree to send the child out of England after the war, and all financial responsibility for transportation, care, education, and board of the children was assumed by private Jewish groups. Still, the Kindertransport, as it was called, stands out as one of the few successful humanitarian efforts of significant scale in the days leading up to the Holocaust.[33]

In the United States, however, a similar measure was defeated without even being reported out of congressional committee. A volatile mix of anti-Communism, anti-Semitism, and anti-immigrant fervor defeated the bill, despite the backing of a wide and deep coalition of intellectuals, people of faith, and labor, women's, and child welfare groups. The Daughters of the American Revolution, the American Legion, and numerous ad hoc groups claiming to represent veterans and widows opposed the bill on shifting and various grounds that all ultimately claimed to be "Americanism." The *Nation* wrote that "a subtle and effective argument [against the bill] is the *sotto voce* contention that all the children are Jewish." Indeed, although anti-Semitism could be quite effective in polite company when it was not spoken, it wasn't altogether hidden, either. For example, John B. Trevor of the American Coalition of Patriotic Societies testified at the joint hearings on the bill that "the American-born child in many places must yield to the foreign-born refugee because of race affinity," referring to the allegation that Jewish businessmen and financiers were hiring their own, contributing to (white) unemployment.[34] Anti-Communism, too, played a role. The long list of supporters, while it included some prominent Republicans like former president Herbert Hoover, Grace (Mrs. Calvin) Coolidge, and former presidential candidate Al Landon, was mostly a profile of the American Old Left: Popular Front intellectuals like John Steinbeck and actors like Henry Fonda and Helen Hayes, John L. Lewis and the Congress of Industrial Organizations, the executive council of the American Federation of Labor, Dorothy Day's Catholic Worker, prominent women activists like Labor Secretary Frances Perkins, the Children's Bureau's Katherine Lenroot, and others from the YWCA and the National Child Labor Committee, newspaper editors, college presidents, Quakers, Unitarians, and religious leaders of all denominations.[35] And they were, inevitably, called Communists; Mrs. Agnes Waters of Washington, testifying on behalf of the widows of soldiers from the First World War, said that many of the people offering to foster or adopt German refugee children were "communists in this country. We have seven million persons here now who are boring from within," referring to the idea that immigrants were Communists and undermining the American way of life and government. "Of course the communist house would welcome a child."[36] The third form of "Americanism," and some have argued the most effective in defeating the bill, was the suggestion that if all these people wanted to provide foster homes for someone, they should be offering them to the children of sharecroppers and migrant laborers in the United States (regardless, apparently, of whether their parents wanted to give them up).[37] The Roosevelt administration was mostly silent, although the State Department opposed the Wagner-Rogers Bill, citing its administrative challenges.

The consequences of the failure of the bill were deadly, of course. By the end of the war, the United States had taken in only 240 child refugees from German-controlled areas (although 830 British children were admitted to protect them from the Blitz, clarifying, had there been any doubt, the central role of anti-Semitism and suspicion of "alien" socialist ideologies from Eastern Europe).[38] Although many countries did better than the United States in making visas available for Jewish children, none provided a degree of safe haven that made more than a token difference. In all, about 1.5 million of the roughly 6 million Jews who died in the Holocaust were children. Jews in particular but also Rom (Gypsys), homosexuals, Communists, trade unionists, sex workers, and people with disabilities perished in horrifying numbers. Other child refugees from Fascism—in Franco's war to win control of Spain and in Japanese-occupied China—did not even make it onto the radar screen of U.S. refugee groups, despite reports that Franco's forces specifically targeted the children of Republicans, kidnapping them to "save" them from the Communism of their parents, while Basque parents evacuated 20,000 children to Mexico, Europe, and the Soviet Union—the "Guernica generation" after the town destroyed by bombing and the Picasso painting.[39] Opponents of immigration were well aware of the unfolding refugee crises caused by the rise of Fascism, as those who testified against the Wagner-Rogers Bill suggested that one reason not to admit German refugees was the specter of being forced to admit Spanish or Chinese children. In the receding tide of Fascism after the war, there were calls of "never again"—not, sadly for the last time in the twentieth century—and more generous immigration policies for refugees.

However, if the racism associated with anti-immigrant policies receded somewhat, allowing the entrance of Jews, for example, the anti-Communism did not. Indeed, the period saw a replacement of anti-Semitic anti-Communism with a broader worry about Communists everywhere. Not that the anti-Semitism retreated entirely; it was not an accident that the most visible prosecution and execution of accused Communists and spies were of Jews, Ethel and Julius Rosenberg. Clearly the Cold War marked a new centrality to the politics of anti-Communism. But it is important to register that this was not a new note in U.S. American politics but the renewal of anti-Communism, the expansion of the role of the House Un-American Activities Committee, and a reversal of the largely sympathetic trend of U.S. liberalism toward socialism. In the aftermath of the war liberals joined with conservatives in condemning socialism and Communism.

Joining the refugee question to anti-Communism was what finally made transnational adoption possible. If it proved impossible to bring the refugees from Fascism to the United States, the refugees from Communism were more than welcome. First a trickle, then a flood of refugee children were welcomed into U.S. American hearts and homes, particularly as it became clear that "children fleeing from Communism" was a potent image for U.S. foreign policy. At the same time, the efforts to save children from difficult situations made a fateful turn: from fostering to adoption, from supporting children's return to their communities and parents when possible, to adoption, conversion, and finding them new identities as young Christian Americans.

In the immediate aftermath of the Second World War, the State Department began to issue refugee visas piecemeal, slowly breaking the solidity of the anti-immigrant position. What made the visas possible was mostly a growing anti-Communism. On December 22, 1945, President Harry Truman issued a directive to ease the processing of would-be immigrants who were refugees from the war, adding, "Of the displaced persons and refugees whose entrance into the United States we will permit under this plan, it is hoped that the majority will be orphaned children."[40] Although technically designed to help all displaced persons and refugees in Europe equally, the overwhelming majority of the roughly 1,300 children admitted to the United States under the program were those displaced from areas controlled by the Soviet Union's Army: Poland, Czechoslovakia, Hungary, and Germany.[41] In 1947 with the support of the Truman administration, Congress authorized another displaced persons program to ease migration in spite of quotas and proposed allowing countries to mortgage future quota numbers in order to admit refugees immediately. Restrictionist members of Congress, alarmed by what they (rightly) perceived as a slippery slope toward weakening and ending the quota system, demanded a focus on (what were perceived to be racially similar) ethnic Germans, including 3,037 nonquota orphans.[42] Nearly 1,400 Hungarian children were admitted in 1956, following the Soviet repression there.[43]

In addition to child-saving programs organized and supported by the U.S. State Department, liberal groups, similar in ideology to the supporters of UNICEF, and evangelical churches emerged as crucial, privatized middlemen in organizing adoptions. However privatized the *funding* had once been, those who dreamed of a Kindertransport to the United States had centrally involved the federal Children's Bureau, and the huge foster program for Hungarian children was coordinated in significant part through federal agencies. These new projects treated the federal government as simply a visa provider. Although no program could function without the involvement of the Immigration and Naturalization Service, they carved out a far more central role for private organizations than these earlier projects had. They, too, were trying to rescue children from Communism, particularly Amerasian children left behind by U.S. troops.

One of the most important midcentury liberal adoption efforts was Pearl S. Buck's Welcome House. Pearl S. Buck—well-known author of *The Good Earth* and outspoken advocate of a midcentury liberalism that combined concern for women's rights and improving race relations with a fierce anti-Communism—started Welcome House, a program that placed Chinese American children in U.S. families. Within a few years, with the U.S. war in Korea and U.S. troops still stationed in Japan, she and Welcome House were locating and placing Amerasian children from these nations; ultimately, Vietnam, Taiwan, and the Philippines would be added to the list as well. She also started the Pearl S. Buck Foundation, which supported Asian American children in their country of birth, their mothers' nations. Buck herself adopted several Asian American children.[44] Buck drew simultaneously on themes of rescue, anti-Communism, and American paternalist responsibility to overcome Asian "barbarism" to argue for increasing U.S. involvement in the lives of Asian American children.[45] "These children are isolated and alone, stateless and lost," wrote Buck. "I cannot see them grow up lost and angry without trying to do something about it. I know from history and experience that lost and angry children, especially if they have brains and beauty, grow up into dangerous people. Moreover . . . I cannot bear to see Americans, or even half-Americans, growing up ignorant and at the lowest level of Asian society, which is very low indeed. . . . Do we, their fathers' people, not owe them something?"[46] Buck argued not just for care for families or individual children but also argued for an anti-Communism located in caring families that can assimilate these children as Americans, not "low" Asians.

In addition to liberal internationalist organizations like CARE, UNICEF, and Welcome House, the other major transnational organization in the postwar period was the evangelical Protestant church. Evangelical Protestantism was undergoing a revival of sorts, growing as a key ally of political anti-Communism. A young minister named Billy Graham, one of a network of evangelical leaders and ministers in Youth for Christ, drew large crowds with a simple message: the Bible is the literal word of God, and it demands that we act in the world to stop godless Communism. It was a message and a mission that would inspire U.S. conservatives, including presidents from Nixon to Reagan to George W. Bush, all of whom were personally advised by Billy Graham. According to the journalist and media critic Ben Badikian, it was William Randolph Hearst and Henry Luce who "made" Billy Graham, plunging him into the limelight through their news empires because they liked his anti-Communism; Luce put him on the cover of *Time* in 1954.[47] Whether or not it was Hearst and Luce who were the kingmakers, Graham's message fit the tenor of the times, and evangelical anti-Communism became powerfully wed to conservative international politics.

Another minister in Youth for Christ, Rev. Bob Pierce, founded World

Vision in 1950, an evangelical development organization that focused on organizing U.S. Americans to send $5 a month to sponsor a child, beginning in China, then expanding into Korea. After the end of the Korean War, Pierce and World Vision sponsored the filming of "Lost Sheep," a documentary full of sad-eyed children in South Korean orphanages that was shown in evangelical churches around the United States. According to their own narrative, an Oregon couple, Bertha and Henry Holt, went to see that film one night in Eugene, and it changed their lives and, ultimately, the face of Christian transnational adoption. Through World Vision, the Holts first sent money to sponsor orphans, then began the arduous mission of legally adopting eight Korean orphans, ending, ultimately, in a special act of Congress to allow them to take in so many. The children, including one destined for another couple, arrived in Oregon to considerable fanfare. World Vision employed a publicist on their behalf, and photographers and journalists made their arrival a circus that spread the word far and wide. The work received considerable support in and beyond evangelical circles, spawning a number of books and ongoing media attention, and the Holts expanded their sphere of church-based child-rescue activism to include orphanage building in South Korea and running an adoption service, including placing a Korean child in the home of the actor Roy Rogers. After Henry's death the adoption service became what is still, half a century later, one of the largest international adoption agencies, Holt International.[48]

Operation Pedro Pan

One of the more startling episodes in the development of intercountry adoption was a Cuban American program dubbed by the press in Miami as Operation Pedro Pan—or Peter Pan by its opponents in Havana. Like virtually everything divided between the Cubans of Miami and Havana, the meaning of this one is ferociously contentious. The basic outline of the story, however, is not in dispute. Between 1960 and 1962 more than fourteen thousand Cuban children were sent alone, without their parents, to the United States under a unique visa program. After several false starts, the "visa" program ultimately consisted of a mere photocopied letter from Father Bryan Walsh of Catholic Social Services in Miami. Although virtually everything about Cuban visa programs in the United States in this period was unusual—from blanket amnesty in 1966 for Cubans in the United States without papers to the massive government subsidies supporting Cuban migrants (Florida in the 1960s went from having one of the worst-funded public welfare systems in the country to one of the best)— even by those standards, the child visa program was extraordinary. The writer Joan Didion caught the full flavor of this program by noting its temporal proximity to the CIA-supported invasion of Cuba: "at a time when . . . the 2506 Brigade was training in Guatemala for the April [Bay of Pigs] invasion, the United States Department of State granted to a Miami priest, Monsignor Bryan O. Walsh, the authority to grant a visa waiver to any Cuban child between the ages of six and sixteen who wished to enter the United States under the guardianship of the Catholic Dioceses of Miami."[49] Radio Swan, a CIA-run radio broadcast out of Honduras,[50] and members of the anti-Castro underground promoted rumors in Cuba that Fidel Castro was going to take children away from their families, either sending them to Russian camps or to government hostels far from their parents. "¡Madre cubana!" began a broadcast on October 26, 1960, "Listen to this. The next law from the government will be to take your children from the age of 5 to the age of 18. . . . Cuban Mother, don't let them take your child! . . . When they return them to you they will be masterialist monsters. Fidel will be converted into the Supreme Mother of Cuba."[51] The following day, Radio Swan's *Noticero para el Caribe* broadcast got even more melodramatic: "Cuban mother, they can take your clothes, your food, or even kill you, but the right to raise your children nobody can take away from you. Remember that there is no beast more ferocious than a mother defending her cub. Offer your life in a just cause like ours before you surrender your child to the beasts."[52] Members of the anti-Castro underground printed copies of a circular purporting to be the Castro government's new law "nationalizing" children. Rumors flew, abetted by the CIA. A group of fifty mothers in Bayamón were said to have signed a pact vowing to kill their children rather than let them fall into Communist hands. The rumors were reported in *Time* magazine and even scholarly journals as evidence of the Cuban people's fear of Castro. One woman remembered a day at the beach, when the story flew from one mother to the next that there was a van in the neighborhood picking up children to take them to a Russian boat sitting in Havana harbor, and they would not return to Cuba except as tinned meat. Within weeks, she said, all the mothers in her neighborhood had sent their children to the United States.

It was the era of "brainwashing," of psychological warfare, of CIA experiments with hypnosis and LSD, sensory deprivation and induced psychosis. The notion of "mind control" colored both what people feared and what it was acceptable to do. As the scholar María de los Angeles Torres, herself a grown Pedro Pan child, points out, one of the minor yet decisive skirmishes of the Cold War was the fate of the Hungarian Cardinal Mindszenty of Budapest in 1945. He denounced the elimination of Catholic schools and the state's requirement that all children attend schools that officially denied the existence of God, comparing it to Hitler's Germany, which "educated its youth as little pagans. They came home from their youth camps to laugh cynically at their parents when they knelt in prayer." After weeks in the custody of Hungary's secret police, Mindszenty signed his own confession, denouncing himself on charges of corruption. If this could happen to someone as outspoken as Mindszenty, asked members of the nascent intelligence community that would form the CIA, what could happen to their own agents—or, what could they make others do?

De los Angeles Torres has herself played a decisive role in our historical understanding of Pedro Pan. Following years of denials by the CIA of any official U.S. role in promoting the exodus of children from Cuba, historians in the United States and the Pedro Pan children have understood the flight from Cuba as simple fear of Communist brainwashing of vulnerable children, heroic efforts by the Catholic Church and various individuals in Cuba and Miami, and a generous visa program by the U.S. State Department. Two books by grown Pedro Pans, *Fleeing Castro* by Victor Triay and *Operation Pedro Pan* by Yvonne Conde, remember the effort in this way. De los Angeles Torres, however, filed a successful Freedom of Information Act suit against the CIA demanding documents relating to Pedro Pan. Because of the agency's commitment to secrecy and to classifying everything, it didn't yield much, but it yielded enough. The CIA was deeply involved with the anti-Castro underground on the island that promoted the rumors, the agency did so itself through Radio Swan in Honduras, and it was kept apprised of the success of the effort to bring thousands upon thousands of unaccompanied children to the United States.[53]

The State Department's decision in 1962 to halt flights from Cuba stranded about half of the children in the United States without their parents or other relatives, and what many had imagined as a short separation of a few months became permanent. And while many of the youngsters grew up in kind and caring foster homes, others were raised in orphanages, in refugee camps, in homes for troubled children, in Catholic monasteries. A scandal in Helena, Montana, involving a priest who sexually abused a number of children was quickly hushed up.[54]

Opinions differ as to the goals of the program. Wayne Smith, who worked in the U.S. embassy in Cuba in this period, told de los Angeles Torres that he believed that the goal of the visa waver program, and the rumors that Castro was going to take children away, was propaganda: "The idea was to frighten families and . . . strengthen anti-government actions and attitudes. And also it was good propaganda, all these children coming out, fleeing godless communism because the Cuban government might take them away from their parents."[55] Torres herself believes that the program had military origins, enabling members of the anti-Castro underground on the island, and those training in Guatemala for the Bay of Pigs invasion, to act without fear of what would happen to their children. Because issuing such visas telegraphed to the Castro government who was in the underground, however, it had to expand to encompass ever-larger groups of children to cover their tracks.

Vietnam: Operation Babylift

In significant measure as a result of the Holts' campaign to publicize the plight of Korean children, the Refugee Relief Act of 1953 and another law in 1957 allowed up to four thousand special visas for children to enter the United States.[56] In subsequent years immigration restriction eased for those entering the United States from Asia—symbolically in 1954, when the McCarren-Walter Act offered ridiculously tiny quotas, and actually in 1965. During these years smaller but significant numbers of Korean children also began to be adopted in Sweden, Norway, and the UK.[57] When the war in Viet Nam ended in 1975 more than two thousand children were picked up in Saigon and flown to adoptive families throughout the United States, Canada, and Europe. Many of them were of mixed ancestry, literally embodying the U.S. (and French) war there. Organized by Holt International and a host of other organizations, Operation Babylift (with a name that sounds like a military campaign) was warmly embraced by liberals and conservatives alike as an opportunity to salvage something from the horror of the war. Some witnesses expressed uneasiness, suggesting that children were hurriedly being picked up off the streets of Saigon and packed onto airplanes, without any effort to find their parents, as the city fell to advancing North Vietnamese troops.[58]

A decade later there was also considerable effort to bring the Amerasian children of U.S. servicemen "home" to the United States. In the early 1980s journalists returned to Viet Nam to do retrospective pieces on the effects of the war and were haunted by the Amerasian children they found in urban streets. "Who can forget," wrote the *Christian Science Monitor*, "the pitiful sight of those manifestly half-American children standing in the monsoon rain of Ho Chi Minh City and begging American TV crews to save them from a land where they are not wanted?"[59] An Amerasian amendment in Congress in 1982 won bipartisan support to provide visas to these children, with the support of groups like the Pearl S. Buck Foundation, Save the Children, and Holt International Children's Services. Although some hoped that the children's fathers would "take responsibility" for them, even at the outset this was understood as an effort mostly to promote stranger adoption. Congressman Romano Mazzoli described the purpose of the bill this way: "Many of them [Amerasians] will be reunited with fathers they have not seen in many years. Others will be adopted or sponsored by generous Americans who want to help these young people live happy lives."[60]

As Jana Lipman argues, although the Amerasian Immigration Act of 1982 passed, it ran into two problems immediately. One was that the Reagan administration and the Immigration and Naturalization Service hated the program, as it seemed to implicate them in normalizing political relations with a Communist Viet Nam, and so these agencies put their offices in Bangkok, which made processing visas almost impossible. The second reason, though, was that Amerasian children were imagined as orphans: there were no provisions in the law for them to migrate with their mothers or other family members. The congressional debate bypassed mothers altogether, emphasizing that these were American children with American fathers who were coming "home," erasing their Vietnamese ancestry and their Vietnamese families—mothers, siblings, stepfathers, spouses. As Kerry, an Amerasian who attempted to migrate under the program said, "I went with my wife and my mother, and we applied for the Orderly Departure Program. . . . I was accepted to go, but only me, not my mother or my wife. I would not leave them, I refused to go alone."[61] As Lipman writes, "The U.S. media and political establishment embraced Amerasians as innately American, shuffling their Vietnamese heritage to the side. The law made clear that American men mattered and Vietnamese women did not."

Yet if the war in Korea and its aftermath could be defined by an anti-Communist consensus, the U.S. war in Indochina mobilized the New Left, and Amerasian children and Vietnamese war orphans were an issue that concerned the Left as well as the Christian and anti-Communist Right. The left-of-center comic strip *Doonesbury* featured a Vietnamese war or-

phan, Kim, starting in 1975, who was adopted by the Rosenthals of Santa
Monica. Vietnam Veterans Against the War backed measures to offer visas
to Amerasian children. Criticism of the Amerasian Act resurrected the Old
Left legacy of seeing war refugees not as isolated children in need of rescue
and focused on the fact that the act broke up families. Five years later the
Amerasian Homecoming Act of 1987 was passed, securing an overdue recognition that Amerasian children had Vietnamese families and allowing
them to migrate with their relatives.

By the 1980s, though, the U.S. Left was largely focused on new wars:
those in Central America. As we will see in the next chapters, those wars gave
rise to new solidarity efforts and new child refugees adopted to the United
States and Europe. The right-wing governments of Central America and the
Southern Cone also disappeared children. Some of them found their way to
the United States and Europe, inaugurating an era in which the adoption of
Latin American children would briefly eclipse adoption from Asia.

Conclusion

From the 1930s through the 1970s, U.S. Americans learned a way to feel
about foreign children. Photographs and news about war zones in this era
taught U.S. Americans a certain powerful affective investment in children
in situations of "disease, poverty, war," to recall the phrase of the anonymous blog commentator who criticized Shelagh Little for failing to adopt
after in vitro fertilization treatments failed for her in 2008. The Korean War
marked the transformation in the nature of efforts on behalf of children in
war zones. In contrast to the committees that placed children in foster
homes during the Second World War, Holt and similar agencies understood the goal as adoption, the permanent removal of children from their
family, community, and country. Evangelical Protestants were committed
to religious conversion; the children would be raised Christian, whatever
the faith of their birth parents. While secular agencies provided no explicit
direction about the religious faith in which adopted children would be
raised, leaving it up to the adoptive parents represented a real decision to
promote or at least allow conversion.

International adoption entered U.S. consciousness forcefully between
the 1930s and the 1970s, far outstripping its significance as a practice
affecting actual children and families. Sad-eyed children and desperate
mothers became potent symbols of the tragedies of the era, from the

Depression to its wars, concentration camps, and refugee crises. These iconic images worked best, however, when they could serve anti-Communist ends. The failure to enact a Kindertransport to the United States and the CIA's engineering of Operation Pedro Pan provided the two political and ethical poles for child-saving operations to the United States.

FIVE

Uncivil Wars

International adoption from Latin America to the United States became more than an occasional practice beginning in the 1980s, at the same moment that the Reagan administration made Latin America a proving ground that Cold War anti-Communist military interventionism was not over. In response to what its conservative critics called the "Vietnam syndrome"—the foreign policy paralysis they felt followed on the left and the liberal call for the United States to abandon its imperial military role overseas—the Reagan administration instead pursued an aggressive policy of intervention in Nicaragua, El Salvador, Guatemala, and elsewhere in Latin America, even illegally continuing support for the Contras' war against the elected government of Nicaragua in the face of an outright ban on such activities by Congress.[1] After the collapse of the Soviet Union, U.S. military and political interventionism continued in Latin America and Asia, promoting U.S. strategic and economic interests in the name of antiterrorism, a War on Drugs, and free trade agreements. By the 1990s state policies related to free trade turned U.S. citizen-consumers into participants in this kind of globalization, which in turn shored up consent for interventionism abroad. International adoption was a good fit with the broad thrust of these policies, producing and relying on a renewed sense of American responsibility for those outside its borders and an easing of the movement of money and (some) people.

The children lost, kidnapped, and displaced by these wars and upheavals came, with increasing ease, to the United States (as well as Western Europe and other countries in Latin America, but we will focus here on the United States). From the 1930s through the 1960s one thing that made transnational adoption to the United States so intensely politicized was that unaccompanied children were admitted under refugee visas, which are intrinsically political. Missionary groups, the U.S. Children's Bureau, or churches would lobby the State Department or Congress on behalf of visas in response to humanitarian concerns related to a specific group of children. However, beginning in the 1950s, but emphatically in the 1960s and 1970s, the character of war, adoption, and visas all changed in similar directions: they became more privatized. The CIA and the U.S. military became increasingly involved in proxy wars, especially in Latin America, in which they fomented, funded, and acted as advisors to (and tried to maintain deniability about) civil wars, assassinations, and coups. At the same time the State Department increasingly made visas available to "orphans"— defined as children whose parents had died, abandoned, or relinquished them—from countries it negotiated arrangements with, specifically those that had, or agreed to develop, legal mechanisms to sever a child's relationship to birth families. By removing the question of whether they were "refugees"—a question deeply imbricated in the politics of their home countries—and instead producing a rather technical definition of "orphan" (in common speech we don't speak of relinquishment, much less "abandonment," in the context of fleeing the military, which might simply mean becoming separated in the confusion and the terror, as producing orphans), the State Department emptied the question of visas for adoptees of most of its political content.

Between 1973 and 1983 the number of intercountry adoptions to the United States doubled.[2] The largest number was still from South Korea, but Latin American countries were growing as a source and accounted for most of the increase. The most significant Latin American sending countries were Colombia, Peru, Guatemala, Chile, and Paraguay.[3] This is a striking list. In the 1980s each was run by a right-wing government with close ties to the United States; each was engaged in a civil war against leftist insurgents that included massive human rights violations against civilian populations and used "disappearances"—clandestine arrests, kidnapping, and murder—as a tactic of terror.[4]

As brutal wars pitted Latin American militaries (and semiofficial paramilitaries) against their own people, many of the children of those identified as "subversives" and "terrorists" washed up on foreign shores, adoptees who were sometimes kidnapped from their (at least supposedly) leftist parents to prevent the rearing of another generation of "reds." What was being struggled over was profoundly ideological and hence heritable: a notion of a redistributive state on the one hand and a nascent neoliberalism on the other. Anti-neoliberalism and neoliberalism, globalization and antiglobalization, grew up together in the clashes of Left and Right in Latin America. From Pinochet's Chile—where Milton Friedman and his "Chicago Boys," Latin Americans and U.S. citizens educated at the University of Chicago, first built a regime that tried an extreme free market ideology and divested itself vigorously of public services—to the birth of the "global assembly line" in the development policies of Puerto Rico, an ideological battle over economic policy was being fought up and down the Americas. While the socialisms that opposed it were heterogeneous movements, their basic building blocks included unions, neighborhood and community organizations, agrarian cooperatives, women's collectives, Christian base communities, Freirean educational initiatives, and, as the historian Greg Grandin writes, the dream of "democracy" that was "not a procedural constitutionalism but a felt experience of individual sovereignty and social solidarity."[5]

Emergent neoliberalism shaped the form of transnational adoption as well; between the United States and Latin America, it was privatized. In the absence of agencies with international reach, it was "private" or "independent" adoption that became the norm between the United States and Latin America. Most of those engaged in the efforts to negotiate international human rights frameworks for transnational adoption initially opposed allowing private adoption, arguing that it opened the door to all kinds of profit making and improper pressure on mothers; however, as the framework for the Hague Convention on Intercountry Adoption was elaborated in the early 1990s, U.S. negotiators prevailed, arguing that the convention could not exclude the most common route for U.S. adopters, and since the United States was the largest single receiving country for intercountry adoption in the world, the treaty would be effectively meaningless without U.S. participation.

Human Rights and Adoption

There were reasons, though, why an international human rights community was uneasy. For Latin American activists, adoption in the region in the

1970s, 1980s, and early 1990s has a very different meaning than it generally does in the United States. Networks of organizations of mothers of disappeared children and those disappeared span Latin America and Europe— the Asociación Madres de Plaza de Mayo (Mothers of the Plaza de Mayo), the Asociación Civil Abuelas de Plaza de Mayo (Grandmothers of the Plaza de Mayo), and Hijos e Hijas por la Identidad y la Justicia contra el Olvido y el Silencio (HIJOS; Sons and Daughters for Identity and Justice Against Oblivion and Silence) in Argentina; Comité de Madres Monsignor Romero (Comadres; Committee of Mothers), Comité de Familiares de Víctimas de Violaciones a los Derechos Humanos "Marianella Garcia Villas" (CODEFAM; Committee of Family Members of the Victims of Human Rights Violations), and Comité de Madres y Familiares Cristianos de Presos, Desaparecidos y Asesinados "Padre Octavio Ortiz—Hermana Silvia" (COMFAC; Committee of Mothers and Family Members of Prisoners, the Disappeared, and the Assassinated) in El Salvador;[6] Coordinadora Nacional de Viudas de Guatemala (CONAVIGUA; National Coordinating Committee of Widows) and Grupo de Apoyo Mutuo (GAM; the Group for Mutual Support) in Guatemala;[7] and, spanning the region, Federación Latinoamerican de Asociaciones de Familiares de Detenidos-Desaparecidos (FEDEFAM; Latin American Federation of Associations of Family Members of those Detained-Disappeared).[8] Since the war, court cases from Argentina to El Salvador have used the disappearance and adoption of children as the major—sometimes the only—civil war or Dirty War crime that can be prosecuted. Where amnesty laws and regimes of impunity have foreclosed many possibilities of legal action against war criminals, kidnapping followed by adoption are *ongoing* crimes—they continue, past the cutoff dates for crimes forgiven by retrospective amnesties, which has been a major tactic for "forgiving" and forgetting torture, disappearances, rape, and murder by militaries and officials.[9]

Organizations of family members of disappeared children and the grown children themselves have emerged as some of the most important groups in Latin America's movements demanding legal accountability for war crimes. In Guatemala, the truth commission report after the forty-year armed internal conflict marked the disappearance of children as a tactic of war, though others did not.[10] In El Salvador, La Asociación Pro-Busquéda de Niños y Niñas Desaparecidos won damages and a judgment from the Inter-American Court of Human Rights in 2005 that the Salvadoran military had indeed disappeared children, and the organization has been active in arranging meetings between children disappeared into transnational adoptions and their birth families.[11] In Argentina the Asociación Madres de Plaza de Mayo and then the Asociación Civil Abuelas de Plaza de Mayo and HIJOS mounted a fifteen-year campaign to establish the relationship of the adopted children of prominent families to disappeared leftists through DNA testing,[12] and in June 1998 former president Jorge Rafael Videla was arrested and convicted for running a government-sponsored illegal adoption operation during the Dirty War.[13] A ruling in 2006 that his pardon on war crimes was invalid has opened the way for a trial on wider charges.[14] In Mexico a slightly different kind of campaign for children—parents of teens and young adults who were disappeared, or who were shot in the massacre of students at Tlatelolco in 1968—resulted in July 2006 in the arrest of former president Luis Echevarría and the apparent collapse of the legal basis for the ex post facto amnesty.[15]

Consider the story of Jacinto Guzmán Santiago in Guatemala. In 2005 Guzmán, renamed Oscar Jacinto Rojas by his Ladino (nonindigenous) adoptive family, told the following story for a publication by Todos por el Reencuentro (known as just Todos; All for Reunion/Restitution), an NGO that was attempting to reunite children disappeared during the civil war by the military and paramilitaries and then adopted:

> In 1983, because of the armed conflict and the scorched earth policy that General Efraín Ríos Montt directed against the population of Nebaj, soldiers captured me at the Sumal Grande mountain. At that time I was nine years old. . . . During the years I was separated from my family I suffered a lot because the person who adopted me treated me very badly. I wasn't given food, I was beaten for every little thing, I was discriminated against because I didn't understand or speak Spanish . . . it was a lot of suffering that I lived through. I couldn't stand all that mistreatment, and for this reason I left the house. I was living for a few months with different people, but thank God, one day I met the family of doña Chona, Miguelito, her grandson, and Rosalaba, her daughter, and they had compassion for me and took me to their house. There, they treated me well, like a son, like a brother. I told them my story and they always encouraged me, they told me that one day maybe I would find my family.[16]

His mother, Petrona Santiago, told the story of what happened this way:

> Before the war we lived in the village of Vijolom. There we had a little ranch, our cornfield and some animals. In 1982 the soldiers came

among us and began to kill the people, burned the house, destroyed the crops with a machete, killed and stole the animals. We were terrified and for that reason we fled to the mountain, we hid ourselves, but the soldiers stayed a long time in that place. Afterward we went further, into the mountain of Sumal Grande, but our tortillas ran out, we had no food, we had no salt, now all we ate was grass with the children. For this reason one day in the morning, my late husband told me that he was going to go look for potatoes to eat, because if he did not go the children were going to die of hunger. I remember that that day Jacinto left with his father to help him, but, according to my late husband, there was a lot of fog and he didn't see that the soldiers were hidden in the mountains. They came out and grabbed him and Jacinto, who was nine, and then they didn't come back. From that moment on, I cried constantly. Suddenly, after four days, my late husband came back alone and I asked him where Jacinto was, and he said that he had stayed with the soldiers, that they didn't want to release him. I only remember that I became very sad and began to cry for my son. There were times when I thought maybe they were going to let him go and I was going to wait for him; but my Jacinto never came back. Thus they took my Jacinto.[17]

The renamed Rojas looked for his family repeatedly in the years after the signing of the Peace Accords in 1996, but he failed. The group that finally was able to help Rojas find his family in 2002, Todos, was a project of the Liga Guatemalteca de Higiéne Mental (Guatemalan League for Mental Health).

It was a particular history of Guatemalan governmental neglect and refusal to deal with the issue of children disappeared and then adopted during the war that required Rojas to turn to an NGO for help. The Guatemalan truth commission (called the Comisión para el Esclarecimiento Histórico [CEH], for its initials in Castilian;[18] the Committee on Historical Clarification), in its report of 1998–99, had called for a governmental agency to look for lost and disappeared children "with the function of searching for children disappeared, adopted illegally, or illegally separated from their family and to document their disappearance."[19] The Guatemalan government never formed one, despite the fact that the CEH had documented 183 children being kidnapped during the war—some of them "disappeared" into adoptions overseas, to the United States and Europe. It also quoted one army officer who stopped just short of admitting that the army had disappeared children and adopted them, saying, "The families of many army officers have grown with the adoption of victims of the violence since, at certain times, it was popular among army soldiers to take responsibility for little three or four year olds found wandering in the mountains."[20] An earlier report, *Recuperación de la Memoría Historica* (REMHI; Recovery of Historical Memory) that was commissioned by Oficina de Derechos Humanos de Arzobispado de Guatemala (ODHAG; the Archbishop's Commission on Human Rights), documented 216 children disappeared.[21] (The bishop who commissioned the report, Monsignor Juan Gerardi, was killed two days after its release, a crime for which members of the military were convicted.)[22] In 1999 a number of private groups came together to found what ultimately became Todos. Drastically underfunded, without access to the military, adoption, and other governmental records that would have made it imaginable to succeed in such an endeavor, Todos nevertheless set out to do what many thought was impossible: to find the children who had disappeared, alive.

The following year, Todos got a considerable boost from ODHAG, which published another report, *Hasta Encontrarte* (Until you are found). *Hasta Encontrarte* documented the disappearance of 444 children during the war, and suggested the possibility that there were many more cases. But most importantly, *Hasta Encontrarte* insisted that many of the children were alive. By 2008 Todos had certainly confirmed that belief, documenting more than 650 cases of children disappeared and locating more than 200 of them.[23] Its director, Marco Garvito, believes that with more funding they could find many, many more cases—that the group has not even begun working in vast areas of el Quiche, Alta Verpaz, Baja Verapaz, and the Mam communities around Huehuetenango—all areas where the war was very intense.[24] Human rights activists in Guatemala faced truly daunting challenges though: a very multilingual society, low rates of literacy, cultures of terror and impunity, all of which make the basic strategies used by groups in countries like Argentina or El Salvador impossible. Todos could not and cannot simply spread the word about their existence through official or civil society channels and expect people to respond. Ironically, Guatemala may be the Latin American country with the largest number of disappeared children who can be found alive, but the obstacles to even learning who was lost are daunting.

Not all of the disappeared children were still in Guatemala, however. The same year that ODHAG published its report, a representative from Amnesty International presented the UN Committee Against Torture with the testimony of Denese Becker, born Dominga Sic, who had survived a massacre in Guatemala in the early 1980s and been adopted in the United States. Becker was adopted at the age of eleven from an orphanage in Guatemala City by a Midwestern Baptist preacher and his wife and raised in Thompson, Iowa (population 670). When Becker tried to tell the story of fleeing a massacre in 1982 in her Maya-Achí community in the Baja Verapaz department (state), near Rabinal, the adults she knew in Iowa told her she was making it up. She tried to forget it, to become a "normal teenager" in Iowa; she married, had two children, and got jobs as a manicurist and waitress. Troubled by nightmares and memories, Becker finally got help from a cousin, Mary Purvis, who had grown up as a missionary kid and spoke fluent Spanish after a childhood in an indigenous community in Mexico and who had herself given up a child for adoption. According to interviews in a film made about her story, *Discovering Dominga*, her adoptive parents and husband, although initially stunned by what Mary Purvis and Denese were making them understand about Guatemala's past, were supportive of her search for information and surviving relatives.[25]

Purvis read extensively on massacres near Rabinal, the only place-name Becker remembered, and finally pieced together her community of origin —Río Negro—from her memories and published testimony. Fortunately for Purvis and Becker, the story of Río Negro was unusual among massacres in the highlands in that it had received widespread international attention because of the role of international agencies in making that massacre more likely. The community of Río Negro had been slated for destruction as a result of a hydroelectric project sponsored by the World Bank and the Inter-American Development Bank, the Chixoy Dam, but residents had refused to simply leave and demanded adequate resettlement plans and reparations. Because of this resistance the community was accused of being part of a guerilla organization and became the target of three separate massacres by the military; the first was aimed at murdering political organizers; the second, all the able-bodied men, including Sic's father, who were lured to a nearby market town and killed; and the third, the women and children, where a nine-year-old Dominga fled with her newborn sister on her back as her mother and other residents were killed by the civil patrols, paramilitary groups of local people organized in highland communities by the military. Sic hid in the mountains for weeks, alone, eating berries, trying and failing to keep her baby sister alive. Eventually she came upon other refugees from Río Negro in hiding, including an aunt. After months on the run, community members hid Dominga in a convent, and the nuns eventually sent her to an orphanage four hours away in Guatemala City, from which she was adopted to Iowa. Her family never knew what had happened to her. In 2000 another Río Negro survivor, Carlos Chen, was doing a U.S. speaking tour with Rights Action, and Sic contacted him. "We wondered and worried about what happened to you!" he told Sic. She began making plans for a trip to Guatemala, one that ultimately resulted in her becoming a human rights activist.[26]

When Sic found the survivors of her community, they had been relocated and were living under the shadow of a military garrison. The whole community turned out to meet her, and people began weeping when she arrived. She had forgotten her mother tongue, Achí, but with Purvis as translator she was able to use Spanish to reconnect with many of her relatives (although most did not know Spanish, some did, and could translate from Spanish to Achí). The next year and subsequently, she made many more trips to Guatemala and testified as a survivor that it was the military and civil patrols that murdered her mother and others in the community—not, as the military claimed, the "terrorists," the guerillas.[27]

Searching for Lost Children

Ironically, what most people in the international community know about the disappearance of children during the civil wars in Latin America is inversely related to the extent of what human rights activists believe happened in those countries. Where the problem was worst, we know the least. The kidnapping and subsequent adoption of children by the military in Argentina is well known through the activism of the Asociación Madres de Plaza de Mayo and the Asociación Civil Abuelas de Plaza de Mayo. The distribution in 1985 of the independent Argentine film *La Historia Oficial* (The official story) and numerous books and articles meant that people learned of it. Indeed, the Library of Congress classification system has awarded the Madres de Plaza de Mayo their own call number for the many books by and about the group.[28] The contrast with Guatemala is extreme, even though many more children were disappeared and subsequently adopted there: fewer than a dozen libraries in the United States hold any of the three books written by Todos through its parent organization, the Liga Guatemalteca de Higiene Mental.[29] The story of El Salvador's lost and kidnapped children has been discussed intermittently in the U.S. press beginning in about 1996 and received notice again in 2006 when the

University of California, Berkeley, sent out a press release about the work of Eric Stover, who, in the context of Physicians for Human Rights and then the Berkeley Human Rights Center, worked with Pro-Búsqueda as he had with Abuelas de Plaza de Mayo, developing a DNA database of the families of disappeared children.[30]

The work of bringing the knowledge of disappearances of children into the official historical record, at least in a way that enabled people to begin to look for them not just write their epitaphs, was to a significant extent pioneered by groups in Argentina and El Salvador. In Argentina the Madres de Plaza de Mayo provided what was for a long time essentially the only public protest against the military junta and the Dirty War, a clandestine counterinsurgency campaign by the military from 1976 to 1983 that relied on kidnapping, detention, torture, and murder. Driving Ford Falcons and dressed in plainclothes, representatives of the military and security forces would grab people off the street and from their homes. Judges refused to grant or enforce writs of habeas corpus, literally the demand to "produce the body" in court, an old innovation of English common law designed to prevent precisely these kinds of abuses by public officials. Lawyers who requested such writs in Argentina during the Dirty War disappeared themselves. Borrowing a term from even earlier in Guatemala, Argentines began in 1976 to speak of *los desaparecidos*, the disappeared. Disappearances served two kinds of functions simultaneously. On the one hand, the practice insulated those involved from defending themselves against charges of extrajudicial kidnapping and murder; if there was no body, how could there have been a crime? On the other, it served to increase the fear and horror that echoed through communities: accused of no crime, able to offer no defense, those who may or may not have been "communists" simply vanished. Family and friends could neither grieve their death nor hope for their return; they were forever caught in a tortured, unresolvable state of uncertainty.

In this climate, the protests of the Madres in the main plaza in Buenos Aires beginning in 1977 was an act of tremendous courage—women would dart out of the crowd, march with others for a short time, then try to vanish back into the crowds in central Buenos Aires—and many of the Madres were disappeared themselves. But the Madres were able to protest at all because they were afforded a measure of deference simply because they were (or acted as) older women, mothers, wearing white headscarves whipped out of pocketbooks with the names of their disappeared children embroidered on them. Although they were denounced in the press as crazy old women and bad mothers who had raised subversives, the military to some extent tolerated their protests because it simply could not figure out how to strike out at apparently defenseless old ladies. Analysts have alternately praised the tactical brilliance of the Madres as a feminism that "revolutionized motherhood" and exploited a weakness caused by sexism in an otherwise unopposable totalitarian regime, on the one hand, and argued that the mothers were "caught in bad scripts," on the other, limited in what they could accomplish precisely because they were constructed as *not* political actors by virtue of being women and mothers. It is telling that the Nobel committee, on receiving a nomination for the Madres, awarded the peace prize in 1981 instead to Adolfo Pérez Esquivel, a human rights lawyer from whom the Madres had sought counsel and legal advice. It was both their strength and weakness that they were seen as "just" women and mothers.[31]

Early on it was apparent that not all of the women prisoners who were pregnant when they were disappeared, or who became pregnant as a result of rape by their captors, had been killed right away. In a relatively small, generally monolingual country, much that went on in the "secret" detention camps was known, at least to human rights advocates; not all who were tortured were killed, and released prisoners provided those who cared to hear with reliable information about what was happening. What family members learned was both reassuring and horrifying: the military was running an adoption program, awarding the infants born to *las desaparecidas* to childless members of the junta and their associates or even sending them to orphanages, falsifying the children's identities in the name of the "best interest of the child."[32] Members of the military described the goals of the program in two ways, either as a desire to prevent the children from learning to be "subversives" from their parents or to forestall the growth of a generation of orphans that hated the military for killing their parents.[33] A small group that by 1980 was calling themselves the Abuelas de la Plaza de Mayo, the grandmothers, began demanding their grandchildren back. A number of them also sought children who had been disappeared together with their mothers who were also sent into adoptions. Much of the disappearance of children was done quite legally through the juvenile courts; one judge explained that since the parents of the children were "terrorists," and hence murderers, neither the parents nor the grandmothers had any rights to them.[34]

The incident that really galvanized those Abuelas that knew or suspected that they had missing grandchildren was the case of Anatole Julien Grisonas and his sister, Victoria, who had been disappeared with their mother at the ages of three and one, respectively, in 1976. They were found three years later with an adoptive family in Chile—with the help of the Committee for Human Rights of the Archbishop of São Paolo, Brazil (CLAMOR, for its initials in Portuguese)—and the adoptive family had no idea about the children's origins. The children, in fact, had been found wandering, abandoned, in a park in Valparaiso, Chile, before they were adopted. While the children stayed with their adoptive family, they also began to have extensive contact with the living relatives of their birth mother. It was, first, confirmation that the security forces in Argentina and Chile (and Paraguay, later, when children from that nation turned up in Argentina) were working together, but also that they were keeping children alive. In 1980 the Abuelas found two more children, Tatiana Ruarte Britos and her sister Laura Malena Jotar Britos, this time in Argentina, as a result of passing around pictures and their own detective work. Again the adoptive family had no knowledge of their background, and again the children stayed with the adoptive family but maintained contact with the birth family. In the process of making their claim to have the children's original names and identities legally restored, however, a sympathetic but cautious judge asked a critical question: how could the Abuelas prove that the children were who they said they were?[35]

This question set in motion a multinational search for scientists and methods to establish a relationship between a child and a possible grandmother. In 1980 DNA paternity testing was still in its infancy, although one of the Abuelas stumbled upon a mention of it in a newspaper in La Plata. Over the next several years, the group contacted a number of scientists, particularly in the United States, including Eric Stover of the American Academy for the Advancement of Science (AAAS), who had himself been briefly detained in Argentina in 1976, and Mary-Claire King at Berkeley. They believed that a "grandparentage" test, akin to a paternity test, could be developed.[36]

The following year, in 1983, the Dirty War ended with the election of Raúl Alfonsín as president, forensic anthropologists began to unearth mass graves, and the Comisión Nacional sobre la Desaparición de Personas (CONADEP; National Commission on the Disappearance of Persons) began its investigations for the report that would be called *Nunca Más* (Never again), ironically as it seems now, as the twentieth century echoed with its acknowledgments of murderous human rights abuses followed by vows, never kept, that it wouldn't happen again. The Abuelas got an invitation to King from CONADEP, and based on DNA and her mathematical formula the group was able to identify Paula Logares, adopted by a policeman, as the granddaughter of one of the Abuelas, and she was returned to live with her grandmother.[37]

The Abuelas have generally left the children with their adoptive parents if they adopted out of ignorance of the children's origins but demanded them back if the adopters were the torturers, collaborators, or responsible in some way for the disappearances. They have been remarkably successful at finding stolen babies, although some adoptive parents resisted DNA testing and tried to hold onto the children.[38] By 1987 the group had gotten a law through Congress approving a DNA databank to establish relationships for any type of dispute over parentage that enabled them that to identify many more cases. By 1990 they had located forty-eight children.[39] In the 1990s increasing numbers of adolescent children came forward because they remembered or suspected their origins. The group HIJOS, composed of the disappeared children themselves, became active on the left, engaged in *escraches* or "outings" of former officials of the Dirty Wars by surrounding their homes, drawing them out in public places, and denouncing them.[40] The adoptees struggle, on both sides, with an ideological division; their biological parents are construed as "subversives," their adoptive parents, torturers.

El Salvador

When the Madres and Abuelas approached the Argentine Catholic Church, individually or collectively, they were rebuffed and received no help in finding their children.[41] This was not true in El Salvador. The Catholic Church in El Salvador had been much influenced by the Second Vatican Council, which from 1962 to 1965 initiated a fundamental reform of the Catholic Church, most memorably transforming the Mass from Latin into the vernacular. But the change in language was emblematic of a larger shift most profoundly recorded in one of the last documents it produced, *Gaudium et Spes* or the Church in the Modern World, which said that not the clergy nor doctrine but the people—"especially those who are poor or in any way afflicted"—were the center of the Catholic Church.[42] The job of the church, then, was to act and speak on behalf of people, especially the poor. This had profound repercussions in the thinking of many theologians and clergy, particularly in Latin America where dependency theory was gaining power: the economic view promulgated by scholars like André Gunder

Frank, Raúl Prebisch, and Immanuel Wallerstein that economic under-development in the periphery was produced in relationship to the fantastic wealth of the metropole through processes that included colonialism, poli-tics, and economics; terms of trade and credit; the location of manufactur-ing; and the ways raw materials were obtained. The idea began to gain force: if the job of the church was to listen *especially* to the pain of those who were poor, and capitalist inequalities were making their countries systematically poor, perhaps the role of the church was to speak against that. While the Latin American Catholic bishops and clergy were traditionally representa-tives and spokesmen of the wealthy and those who governed, and in many ways still were, a series of documents produced by meetings of the Latin American bishops suggested the momentum of this idea: at a meeting in Medellín, Colombia, in 1968, the bishops wrote that the role of the church was "listening to the cry of the poor and becoming the interpreter of their anguish," and in Puebla, Mexico, in 1979, they wrote of a "preferential option for the poor"—a central concept of what was coming to be known as liberation theology.[43]

In El Salvador and in Guatemala the growing sense among many clergy that their first alliance ought to be with the poor rather than the wealthy got them branded as Marxists and targeted by the military as giving aid and comfort to the guerillas—when they did not suspect them of being gueril-las themselves. In 1980 El Salvador's Archbishop Oscar Arnulfo Romero was murdered as he celebrated Mass by a right-wing paramilitary with close ties to the government. In 1989 six Jesuit professors at the University of Central America, together with their housekeeper and her daughter, were killed in the middle of the night by the military. One professor, Father Jon Cortina, was away on a pastoral visit to a community and survived. He went on, five years later, to found La Asociación Pro-Búsqueda de Niñas y Niños Desaparecidos, a search group for the children disappeared by the military during the war.[44]

So mothers whose young children had been disappeared got a hearing from the church in El Salvador, and this affected the character of the activism to locate them. Where the Madres organized autonomous women's groups in some measure baldly because no one else would help them (they went to the Vatican, but Pope John Paul II literally refused to acknowledge them, greeting the groups on either side of them but ignoring the delegation from the Madres),[45] in El Salvador efforts to find lost children were part of a broad human rights movement with roots in the church. This is not to suggest that there was not an organized, and feminist (or at least female),

response to disappearances; Comadres, the Salvadoran Mother's Committee, was part of an international alliance of Mothers of the Disappeared that
spanned Latin America. Its full name tells the story of its origins, however:
El Comite de Madres y Familiares de Presos, Desaparecidos, y Asesinados
Politicos de el Salvador "Monseñor Oscar Arnulfo Romero" (the Committee of Mothers and Family Members of Prisoners, the Disappeared, the Politically Assassinated of El Salvador—Monsignor Oscar Arnulfo Romero),
being born of a conversation with Archbishop Romero, who urged them to
organize with other families; when he was murdered, they added his name
to their group's. They and the Madres de Plaza de Mayo were part of an
international network of family members of the disappeared, FEDEFAM.
Member organizations spanned Bolivia, Colombia, Guatemala, Honduras,
Mexico, Paraguay, Uruguay, Costa Rica, and Venezuela.[46]

Initially, Jon Cortina urged and facilitated the testimony of five mothers
who had lost children during the war before the truth commission when it
took testimony in Garjila, a resettlement community of displaced people in
the department (state) of Chalatenango. When it assembled the testimony
and published its report in 1993, however, the truth commission did not
repeat the stories of mothers who had seen their children carried off by the
military; on the contrary, it merely listed their children among the names
of the dead. In the aftermath of that disappointment, families who had seen
their children disappear continued to organize, with the assistance of the
Commission on Human Rights of Chalatenango, of which Cortina was a
member. Continuing to believe that their children might still be living,
even though most were younger than seven when they were taken, with the
commission's help they pressed demands on the state, even holding a press
conference and circulating flyers to orphanages. As a result, perhaps, of this
publicity—and a certain amount of simple luck—a young man named
Santos Mejía, originally from Chalatenango, working as a gardener at an
orphanage, recognized five of the children there as survivors of a military
attack on their community. While they were supposedly orphans, Mejía
believed that their parents were living. He was right. With help from the
orphanage director, the human rights commission, and members of the
Catholic Church, parents and children—mostly grown, in their final years
of high school—met again after eleven and a half years. One of the children,
Andrea, described that meeting for a publication of Pro-Búsqueda:

> [When the children arrived in a microbus at the plaza in Guarjila]
> there was a big group of people waiting for us. We got out and, in that

moment, the shouting and the hugging began. A tall man hugged [two of the orphanage children] Marta and Angelica so impetuously that his hat fell off. They started weeping too. [Another child] Juan Carlos disappeared into a group of women who all hugged him at the same time.

I didn't see anybody I knew, and nobody came over to me. Maybe my family had not come after all. I started to feel worried when someone told me that my family had come in [to the plaza] from the street. I don't remember if it was Father Jon [Cortina], the priest of Guarjila, who told me: "Those are your parents." I walked toward them. My parents came into the middle [of the plaza] and around them were walking so many children, big and small, who had to be my brothers and sisters. When I saw how much one of my little brothers looked like me, I could not contain my tears. We met at the edge of the little plaza and started to hug.[47]

News of the meeting—and that disappeared children had been found alive —spread like wildfire through rural communities. A few months later, in August 1994, families and their advocates founded Pro-Búsqueda. Within a few years, with the help of DNA testing through groups like Physicians for Human Rights and the hard, slow sifting and matching of newspaper stories and the archival records of orphanages, Pro-Búsqueda began finding these lost children—in adoptive families in France, in Spain, in the United States.[48]

For the "found" children, as well as their families, integrating their experiences and renewing their relationships was frustratingly difficult. After more than a decade of waiting, worrying, and wondering, it was hard to learn that relationships did not just start over where they had left off; often there was unresolvable pain about how the disappearances themselves had taken place. El Salvador and Guatemala were different from Argentina, in that in contrast to the fast, targeted, and orderly—albeit clandestine and violent—kidnapping of parents and children, in Central America militaries and paramilitaries targeted entire communities, resulting in scenes of murder, mayhem, and anguished flight. Andrea's story, which she wrote as part of a Pro-Búsqueda program to try to heal young people and their families after they had been found, is worth quoting at length. After months of gently pressing her parents, who were reluctant to share the story, and consulting with community members about the event know as the Guinda de Mayo (the flight in May [1982]), this is what she wrote:

[When the people got to a place called] Los Alvarenga, they couldn't get out. There were a ton of people, maybe a thousand, hidden in the vegetation of a tiny hill. It was only a question of time before the soldiers found us. Thus, they said that they were going to try to break through the wall [of the military]. The guerillas [who were trying to escort the people past the military] started to shoot and the people to run. In order to organize its ambushes, the army had hidden in a place where they believed the people would pass. My father had to pass through the middle of the shooting, running with me against his chest and [her sister] Carmen in his arms. My mother ran with [another child] Argelia in her arms and Arturo [the oldest son, ran] with my brother Luis, but with all the people they could not follow my father. The people ran, terrified. The dead fell before them and behind them. The wounded on the ground shouted, "Kill me, please!" because they did not want to continue suffering. In the road, you could see only the dead and wounded and the uproar of the people who fled, while the soldiers shot at them. Following an avalanche, my father came to a huge cliff. But the helicopters had arrived. Now they were shooting from the hills and from the air. The people were throwing themselves off the cliff, a fall of many meters. They were falling on top of each other, hitting each other, shouting in pain. At the edge of cliff, around my father, the dead and the wounded were piled up. Others threw themselves without even looking, as if they didn't realize there was a cliff in front of them. My father thought that if he threw himself holding both girls, we would surely all three die. In this moment, he decided to leave me. He lay me down under a tree [she had been seriously wounded days before by a rocket attack on their community, and couldn't stand] at the edge of the bank, gave me a final kiss, and jumped with my sister in his arms. . . . My father was the one who suffered the most from my loss. He spent months crying and lamenting for having left me. He felt very guilty. Personally, I think he made the correct decision. Nevertheless, it is a decision that no one, no human being, ever should be forced to make, a decision of life or death, save one or the other.[49]

Andrea ultimately found herself in an orphanage, where she lived throughout her childhood. Because of her injuries, she lost her arm.

On a practical level, reunion did not resolve the loss or grief. Parents' and children's lives had developed trajectories that were not overlapping.

Andrea, for example, intended to go to college with help from the orphanage. Although she and her parents and siblings took great pleasure from their meetings, and their subsequent connections, none of the children in that early group went to live with their parents again. Seeing each other continued to be important, but finding each other did not heal all the wounds; their lives had taken separate paths for more than a decade. In birth families new children had been born, sometimes a mother or father had died and the surviving partner had remarried. As Pro-Búsqueda grew there was mutual support but also friction and resentment when some families found their children and others did not. All—children, parents of found children, parents of lost children—had been through tremendous upheaval, loss, and trauma. Some had lost children as a result of guerilla forces, while the majority had lost their children to the army. The strength of Pro-Búsqueda, though, was that it simultaneously emphasized political and mental health approaches and, in fact, did not see the two as that different from each other. In support groups, participants would try to sort out the political context that gave rise to their own, and others,' actions and feelings. Responding to critics who wanted to know why Pro-Búsqueda couldn't just leave the question of lost children alone so many years after the kidnapping, Jon Cortina always spoke in terms of wounds that parents, children, and the society as a whole carried that could not heal until people knew the truth and justice was done.[50]

On March 1, 2005, Pro-Búsqueda won a significant battle in seeing the military held responsible for the kidnapping of children. The military had long insisted that it had only acted in humanitarian ways, picking up lost children and taking them to the Red Cross; under unusual circumstances, raising war orphans in military barracks and teaching them skills.[51] In 2005, though, the Inter-American Court of Human Rights issued a decision condemning the Salvadoran government in the case of the Serrano Cruz sisters, Ernestina and Erlinda, who at the ages of two and seven were taken from their family at gunpoint during the military's Operación Limpieza (Operation Clean-Up) in 1982. As they watched, family members said, soldiers took the little girls into a military helicopter, which flew away and disappeared. The girls have never been found nor have the individuals responsible been identified. Their mother initiated the case but did not live to see its fruition, but their sister, Suyapa, was able to testify in her stead. The Salvadoran government, for its defense, suggested that the girls never existed—the logical culmination of the process of "disappearance." The court ordered the Salvadoran government to apologize to the family, to make monetary restitution, to open the military archives to searchers, and to develop a state-level organization to find El Salvador's lost children.[52]

Guatemala

Guatemala ultimately had both the longest-enduring and largest Latin American transnational adoption program. It also had the worst anti-Communist civil war in terms of the number of people killed, despite the fact that it was a small country with a relatively tiny guerilla force (perhaps as small as two thousand people).[53] As some have said, it was as if they used napalm to destroy an anthill. According to the report of the Commission on Historical Clarification, two hundred thousand people were killed in Guatemala during the armed internal conflict in "acts of genocide," and 93 percent of the dead were killed by the military or others working for the state—more dead than El Salvador, Nicaragua, Chile, and Argentina combined.[54] Yet the tag line on the bottom of the military's emails reads: "There was no genocide in Guatemala." And no newspaper in Guatemala recorded the massacres in the 1980s. Guatemala was not only an epicenter of transnational adoption but of political repression, silence, and lies.

Through most of the period of the civil war, it was a broadly ideological struggle, with the chief targets being students, trade union leaders, leaders of agrarian organizations, and political activists, mostly urban, some Mayan, some Ladino, that were "disappeared," detained, tortured, and killed. By the mid-1970s the war was also targeting rural people in the highlands, and in the early 1980s entire indigenous communities were massacred under the "scorched earth" policy first of Romeo Lucas García then, after the coup that removed him, of Efraín Ríos Montt. Ríos Montt, a friend of U.S. Christian Right leaders Jerry Falwell and Pat Robertson, was an evangelical preacher associated with the California-based Church of the Word—Iglesia Christiana Verbo, in Guatemala—an avowed anti-Communist Christian Right organization. He was also a graduate of the U.S. military's School of the Americas, as well as the head of the Guatemalan Army and the leader of a military junta that ran the country. Perhaps most horrific of all, the military organized paramilitary civil patrols (PACs) in indigenous communities throughout the highlands. Many of the massacres in the highlands—more than ten thousand people dead and one hundred thousand forced to flee in the first six months of 1982 alone, according to Amnesty International— were carried out by neighbors, men under arms in PACs in nearby communities, or individuals who were targeted because of their betrayal by *orejas* (ears, military spies) in their own communities. Ríos Montt and the war offered a bitter pedagogy of survival to indigenous communities: join the evangelical church (Catholic clergy and lay leaders—catechists—were killed in such numbers that in 1982 Bishop Juan Gerardi shut down the entire diocese of the state of el Quiché, saying its leaders were sitting ducks), practice a visible political apathy, and denounce anything out of the ordinary lest you be identified as a Communist yourself.[55]

In his aptly titled *Silencing the Past*, the Haitian philosopher of history Michel Rolph Trouillot asks how silences are produced, the ways sources, narrators, archives, and historians omit things, through accident or judgment that they lack significance. More insidiously, ideas or events are silenced precisely because they *are* significant, that certain kinds of knowledge would have consequences in the present. Trouillot's insight is important because it brings to our attention the processes of producing silences, making us pay attention to the things that are unintelligible, not quite knowable. Throughout the period of attempted genocide in Guatemala's highlands, conspicuously 1980–1982, the government denied, the newspapers silenced, and the international community largely did not know that entire communities—men, women, and children—were being systematically killed by the military and state-sponsored paramilitaries.[56] Guatemala's history is structured by its silences, the things suppressed and obscured; this is the insight of the report produced by the truth commission —*Guatemala: Memoría del silencio* (Memory of the silence). The truth commission itself was given the name, revealingly, of the Commission on Historical Clarification.

The work of producing testimony about what happened in the 1980s has been—and remains—tremendously contested, and adoption was no different. Thus, this part of the chapter has to be written backward, beginning with testimony produced after 2000 then turning to the harder to read evidence from the 1990s. The effort is to try to produce an account of the 1980s, when hundreds, probably thousands of children were kidnapped and adopted in Guatemala and adopted to Europe and the United States. In the 1990s, through extraordinarily contested efforts, people began the dangerous work of bringing the story of the indigenous targets of genocide into history, of rendering these events representable as fact. Forensic anthropologists dug up mass graves. The United Nations Verification Mission in Guatemala (MINUGUA) and ODHAG collected oral testimony. Groups like Witness for Peace were finally able to get into the highlands. The accounts that foreign newspapers and human rights groups had produced during the war—always instantly contested—were largely verified.

But it is only barely an exaggeration to say that the 1980s has no history of indigenous people in the highlands, never mind a history of the kidnapping and adoption of children—not in the sense of authorized speech, an official history—only an ugly, brutal period of subalternization. Todos por el Reencuentro wrote in 2003 in the introduction to one of its collections of *testimonios* about lost children of the problems of writing a history of these events, one that my account has had to struggle with as well. "These testimonios locate us in [the speakers'] yesterday and today, as a demonstration of this history that is constructed and deconstructed in the present. A past/present that the official history minimizes or denies. Each testimony speaks of the past in relation to the present, and in this way the versions of the past are spoken, shared, debated, validated, and hence pass on to form part of the social imaginary that is expressed in the oral tradition of our communities."[57]

Further, there is the question of language: many who might have wished to speak of massacres and disappearances in the 1980s were essentially disallowed by definition because they did not speak Spanish, the "official" language of Guatemala, but one of more than a dozen indigenous Mayan languages that essentially had no written form except, now, in linguistic institutes. (It is not surprising that since the end of the war, compiling written grammars of Mayan languages has become a major movement; in the contest over truth in the 1970s, 1980s, and 1990s, one of the sites of that struggle was bringing Mayan speech into the official, written, historical account.) Among the Comunidades de Poblaciónes en Resistencia (CPR), a highland indigenous resistance group formed of refugees during the war, narratives of the 1980s that I heard in 2006 still had the quality of testimony —of articulating a story for me as a historian, sometimes in the present tense, often with startling immediacy—a story that could not pass into memory until it was heard, received, made real.

In the decade after 2000, Todos published three books of testimonios about disappeared, adopted, and (sometimes) reunited children.[58] For example, Tomás Choc, a father who lost his children in 1984, relates his story:

The army surprised us when we were in Guacamayas, Uspantán. It was a day in which the army surprised the [community's] lookouts, and when we knew what was happening, there were soldiers throughout the camp. Bullets flew everywhere. The only thing we could do was to go out running. When we succeeded in liberating ourselves from the danger of the soldiers, we started to look for our children. After a few hours I ran into the terrible surprise that the children were not with my wife. She didn't have more than one of our four children. We looked for them all night and all the next day, but nothing. . . . We spent several weeks looking for them but failed. Sometimes it was me who gave up hope and cried, and when she saw me, my wife also collapsed. Other times it was her, she would cry and her sorrow was contagious to me.[59]

Years later, he would find one daughter, Ana, married to a soldier; the children had been adopted by families in other indigenous highlands communities. But it was not until 2001, and with the help of Todos, that he would learn the fates of all of them. The youngest, he learned from the adoptive family, had sickened and died. The two other daughters, they found.

Choc's story points out one of the features that made the Guatemalan experience of losing children so painful and complicated: even if they could be found, not only were they grown strangers, but they almost always had lost their mother tongue. "The experience of being reunited with my daughter made me realize the harm the war did to the whole family. In addition to the death of my wife, [my children] Magdalena and Jose, this violence changed us, made us different from each other. Today my children have other identities: Ana is Ladina, Julia is Q'eqchi, Catarina is Kiché," said Choc, who is Ixil.[60] His children, like many found by Todos, had been kidnapped by members of the PACs. Indeed, at one point after their kidnapping, Choc learned where his children were but was afraid to even contact them. He was a member of the CPR, hiding from the army in the mountains, and the community where they had been taken was "pure patrollers [PACs]. . . . The bad thing was that they saw us in the CPR as guerillas in that community, they hated us . . . it was very dangerous to enter that community."[61] In an atmosphere of excruciating paranoia—in which, according to the CEH, entire indigenous groups, like Maya-Ixiles, were targeted as belonging to guerilla groups—many describe members of the PACs as essentially conscripted, that refusing instructions to form or participate in these paramilitaries would be a virtual death sentence, for themselves and their communities. At the height of the military's "counterterrorism" effort in the *altiplano*, it is estimated that as many as half of the able-bodied men in the

highlands were under arms in the PACs.[62] Many analysts, including Rigoberta Menchú, have suggested that the goal of the counterinsurgency program was the destruction of Mayan culture and their communities, pointing to the military's own admission that 440 indigenous communities were
destroyed.[63] Certainly, turning neighbor against neighbor and kidnapping
children would be a way to ensure the disruption of the intergenerational
transmission of a way of life while destroying communal networks and
organization.

Yet Pedro Santiago, another Maya-Ixil man, tells a moving story about
trying to reconstruct such relationships even in the aftermath of a child's
forced disappearance. In 1984 he and his three-year-old daughter Rosa
were wounded by the same bullet as he carried her on his back and they
were caught in a shower of bullets shot by soldiers. Both were taken to the
hospital but separated. Rosa was picked up by the military and left in
another hospital, while her father searched for her in the first, and she was
subsequently adopted by a family from Aguacatán, Huehuetenango. It was
twenty-one years before Pedro Santiago saw her again, and she arrived for
the reunion with her parents wearing the traditional clothing of another
place and people.

One of the ways race or ethnicity is measured in a Guatemalan context
is by clothing. In the context of the encounter between Spanish and Maya
in the nineteenth century, according to historian Greg Grandin, the Ladino
version of "race" won out: the thing that makes someone Ladino rather
than indigenous is not something about body or ancestry (as Mayan
peoples might have it) but rather what they wear and what language they
speak.[64] As a result, among Mayan peoples, especially women, identity,
community, and place are sharply marked by adherence to tradition in
clothing and weaving, the colorful *traje* that tourists find so picturesque.
Men in most communities, though not all, are more likely to speak Spanish
and wear the clothing of their Ladino countrymen.[65] While some, generally
men, might change clothes on the bus ride from the highlands to the
Ladino areas and then back again, thus slipping from one "race" to another,
women are far more likely to guard the community's history and identity
by wearing traje, with its distinctive local patterns, in all contexts. The
Mayan genius for survival and resistance in the face of five hundred years of
often violent encounters with Europeans and their descendents is tied to
the cultivation of a fierce loyalty to traditional teachings, some of great
antiquity, and this becomes visible through traje; many women still make
their own *huipiles*, or blouses.

In this context, for Santiago, seeing his daughter in the "wrong" traje was an event invested with significance. He narrates the story of meeting her again, in its full context of community celebration, this way:

The day that they were coming, early in the morning some of our brothers from the evangelical church came, and all morning we had a musical group and a religious service to give thanks to God for the life of our daughter. My wife and other women from the community started making little tamales really early. I think that they had made a thousand tamales, maybe more. They killed a chicken and made a stew. At about noon three cars arrived. Then we lit fireworks and went to meet Rosa. She arrived wearing traje from Aguacatán and her three daughters with traje from Cobán. When I saw her . . . my eyes filled with water and she hugged me. After that my wife received her and her husband. It was a really happy thing and it brought tears from us. Then we began the activities . . . [they prayed, told stories about their lives]. Afterward, my wife took Rosa inside the house and together with other women they dressed her as an Ixil. For us it is very important that one day little Rosa returns to her traje from Nebaj and I hope that she can learn to speak our language, because now she can't.[66]

When Rosa narrates the story, she too tells a moving narrative of community that dwells on the traje:

When we got there, there were like two hundred people in my parents' house, they had arranged everything for me. Later I understood that many were my family members. My family sure is big! Many people spoke; my father spoke to everybody in Ixil and Don Pedro [from Todos] was translating for us so I could understand; my father told how they shot at us both, but the best was to realize that my family had always loved me and that they too had suffered because of the war. They dressed me in Ixil traje; I was nervous but I liked it . . . in front of everyone they put a wide ribbon through my hair. After that, many of the people who were there came by and greeted me and gave me money, gifts, food. I was very emotional.[67]

Traje was one marker of Ixil identity and community that both father and daughter held up; it was a concrete symbol of the greater violation, the way the social relations of family and land that marked who they were had been disrupted. The shame and the grief of losing a child or a family was intensified in that it was woven through the fabric of what it meant to Mayan.[68] Although distance, poverty, and differences of language prevented them from growing close, both tell a story in which finding each other was meaningful and an act of resistance against silence and disappearance.

The question of why child disappearance followed by adoption happened across so many different countries is troubling to contemplate. Perhaps it was simply direct communication among these states during their reigns of terror. Maybe it was rooted in these governments' ties to Fascist Spain; Franco, too, targeted the children of Republicans to rid the country of a future generation of "reds";[69] and Hitler's swastikas were on the walls of Argentina's secret detention centers. Perhaps it was a common debt to U.S. counterinsurgency tactics and training at the School of the Americas.[70] There is indirect evidence that child disappearance was part of the lexicon of U.S. counterinsurgency tactics: according to two of the low-level military police accused of abusing prisoners at Abu Ghraib prison in Iraq and interviewed in Errol Morris's *Standard Operating Procedure*, children of purported terrorists in Iraq in 2006 were being kidnapped—disappeared—by the U.S. military and held at Abu Ghraib.[71]

Monster Stories

Guatemala returned to civilian rule in 1986, and both allegations of the commodification of children and human rights-based efforts at adoption reform were not far behind. Especially in Guatemala, there was not always a bright line separating the war from the postwar period. Is it a meaningful difference if it is criminal organizations rather than the military that are being accused of kidnapping children and "selling" them into adoptions? What if, as Deborah Levenson-Estrada argues, much of the extraordinary rise in criminality in Guatemala can be attributed, directly or indirectly, to a demobilized military?[72] As a Spanish journalist explained it, "The traffic in children in Guatemala began to consolidate itself—according to the investigations by lawyers, journalists, and human rights organizations—in 1982, with the coup d'etat of General Ríos Montt and was supplied by so-called orphans from the highlands, a great quantity of children that were left without parents as a consequence of the killings by the army, which was eliminating peasants accused of collaborating with the guerillas. These orphans were sold into false adoptions. Later, the mafia was better organized and—in addition to buying and stealing children—came to include pregnancy for hire."[73] Already in 1989, for example, Congressman Mario Tarcena, president of the legislative commission for the Protection of Minors, was insisting that the primary threat to children and the integrity of the adoption process was not the military but what the newspaper *Prensa Libre* characterized as the need "to eliminate, or at least reduce, the profit made on children and to strengthen the controls to get rid of the problem that children available for adoption are stolen from their mothers, attacking it together with a growing traffic in children."[74] He dated the presence of significant "traffic in children" from about 1986, with the easing of the genocidal violence in the highlands ("the massive repression has given way to carefully selective repression," as a critic put it) and the coming of economic crisis in the aftermath of the elimination of price controls as a result of IMF-mandated restructuring. Year after year the efforts at legal reform of adoption, to institute a central authority and stricter scrutiny, failed, because, said Tarcena, there were deputies in the legislature with ties to the adoption business.[75]

Adoption was quite easy, written into the legal code in 1977 to require only the presence of a notary, not a judge, to record the transfer of a child from one family to another. One could perhaps make an argument for why it should be simple, given the imperfect (at best) penetration of state bureaucratic access in Guatemala, the linguistic isolation of the indigenous peoples who make up a majority of the population (when all official business is done in Spanish), and the absence of courthouses or ways of getting birth certificates within even a day's travel of most people in the highlands (one estimate had it that about 18 percent of children born did not even have their births registered).[76] But if easy legal standards for adoption might have been an accommodation to the weakness of the civilian state in relationship to impoverished or indigenous peoples, it also undoubtedly eased the way for the military and "mafias" who engaged in transnational adoption.

Beginning in the 1980s newspaper articles regularly referred to the large quantities of money being paid by adoptive parents from the United States in particular—high even by international adoption standards but astronomical compared to most Guatemalans' income—and, by the late 1990s, to the fact that children's pictures could be found on the Internet. There was also a good deal of debate about whether family courts were moving too quickly in finding that children were neglected; what, exactly, does neglect mean in a context where impoverished families for generations have had to leave children in the care of older children in order to work, either in the fields or in urban commerce or manufacturing? What does it mean when more than half of all children are malnourished?

The first real evidence that made it into the international press that something was terribly awry about transnational adoption from Guatemala was much less clear than the testimonies about lost children adopted else- where. In March of 1994, six years before Denese Becker (Dominga Sic) was able to tell her story and two years before the peace accords, a human rights activist from Alaska, June Weinstock, was beaten and nearly killed in a mob attack in a small indigenous community in highland Guatemala as a result of allegations that she was stealing children and taking their organs. Weinstock, an environmental and indigenous solidarity activist, had gone to the region to support the Zapatista uprising and had probably gone to Guatemala to attend a language school to help her in that endeavor; that at least was her intention, as she described it to a Salvadoran solidarity activist, José Gutier- rez, in an email the month before.[77]

The whole thing was horrific; while Weinstock survived the attack, she lived with a brain injury and other permanent disabilities as a result of the attack. Weinstock's lynching (*linchamiento*) was televised; a cable station ran live videotape while a mob chased Weinstock into a bathroom at a courthouse. As U.S. Embassy personnel apparently watched on television, unable to figure out how to get a helicopter from Guatemala City out to the rain-locked highlands, Weinstock spent six hours hiding until the mob broke down the door, dragged her out, beat her, raped her with a stick, and left her for dead while they burned the courthouse. In response, the U.S. State Department issued a statement urging tourists to stay away from Guate- mala, denouncing the "urban legends" about organ theft that poor, rural people in Guatemala believed. The attack on Weinstock received wide- spread attention in the international press, and in subsequent years this story has continued to provide one of the grids of intelligibility through which questions about the legitimacy of adoption or the trafficking of children from Guatemala are understood: poor, illiterate people believe irrational things; organ transplants take place in hospitals, there are trans- plant registries, organs cannot be stored out of the body for very long, it is all a very rational and bureaucratic system, and so forth. One U.S. journalist described rumors of children being kidnapped as "magic realism on acid."[78]

Yet with the benefit of hindsight, it seems more likely that the attack on Weinstock was part of the effort to halt the work of human rights activists, that the whole thing may have been orchestrated by the Guatemalan mili- tary. By my count, Weinstock was the ninth person attacked by a mob that month because of allegations that she was stealing children. The attacks were widely dispersed geographically, and while Guatemala is not a large country, poor or nonexistent roads make communities relatively isolated from each other. Newspapers and government officials spoke of a "psychosis" gripping the country, but collective insanity seems like a weak explanation for a series of events that give every appearance of being coordinated. Furthermore, as the anthropologist Abigail Adams points out (as did some journalists), "the rumor cycle was largely perpetrated by Guatemala's most literate; [it was] the authorities who filled Guatemala's columns and airwaves and newspaper with the organ-harvesting stories."[79] Lynching in the U.S. context implies violence that is at once extralegal and officially sanctioned, which may be correct here. *Prensa Libre*, the nation's largest circulation daily, ran a particularly ghoulish version on March 13, two weeks before the attack on Weinstock, complete with an organ price chart.[80] In fact, the press accounts in Guatemala throughout March seem distinctly schizophrenic, alternately stoking the rumors and mocking the people who believed them.

Three weeks earlier, the tiny town of Santa Lucia Cotzumalguapa in the southern sugar region had also been rocked by a mob attack on a U.S. tourist, this one named Melissa Carol Larson, accused—according to the mocking press accounts in Guatemala—of being an ogre and a child trafficker. In fact, it was the police who had accused her of kidnapping children to traffic their organs and subsequently released her to the mob; the mob also burned the police station to the ground. This attack, too, incredibly, was videotaped (this is not Los Angeles, most rural people do not own video cameras). The army arrived to restore order, and in the very early morning the following day soldiers apparently dragged sixty people from their homes, beat them, robbed them, and jailed them, claiming that they had been seen on the news video the night before, according to the Unidad de Acción Sindical y Popular.[81] In the days that followed, government officials[82] and the Policía Nacional warned people about the danger of child kidnapping, saying that there were networks of people stealing children for their organs and that they were organized by U.S. women. The Policía Nacional told people not to let strangers into their homes, to watch for cars with polarized windows cruising in residential areas or near schools, and particularly warned about people alleging that they were photographers. The police also said that they had found bodies of newborns and were investigating dozens of possible infant kidnappings.[83] Graffiti appeared in Guatemala City, on the road from the airport charging that "gringos roba chicos"—

gringos steal children.[84] The police arrested three men in Santa Catarina Pinula for attempting to steal children from a public school, suggesting that they were in the company of a U.S. woman who was never found, and a mob gathered and threatened to kill the men—until the disturbance was put down by a large group of policemen.[85] In one neighborhood in Guatemala City, reports began cropping up of unknown cars following children; parents who went to the police station to ask for increased vigilance in their neighborhood were turned away.[86] The Ministerio Público announced that it had received sixty-six allegations of children kidnapped in 1994 and that its investigations had brought seven child kidnapping rings to justice.[87] Four more foreigners, engineers and scientists studying Guatemala's chain of volcanoes, were attacked as possible members of a child trafficking network.[88] The Policía Nacional announced its concern about the safety of tourists during Semana Santa (Holy Week, culminating in Easter) and its intentions to protect them.[89] When, the following day, a mob attacked June Weinstock in San Cristobal Verapaz, the police withdrew, and several hours later the army came and put down the disturbance after Weinstock had already been nearly killed.[90] The military put nearly sixty people in jail by nightfall. The next day the government was proposing the imposition of a state of emergency or, in its memorable phrasing, a "state of exception,"[91] threatening to reimpose military rule in defense of women (tourists) and (Guatemalan) children.

It was peculiar but convenient for the military that the two mob attacks on Americans were videotaped, that the military, whose power was in danger of being curtailed by the anticipated arrival of MINUGUA and the demilitarization demanded by the peace process, was suddenly crawling all over small towns again, arresting large groups of people. The Policía Nacional and the Ministerio Público seemed to have done everything imaginable to make these events more likely, from arresting people for child and organ trafficking to telling people to watch out for U.S. women to announcing the expectation that another attack would occur during Semana Santa.

It was a volatile and complicated time in Guatemala. There was a new ambassador in the U.S. embassy, Marilyn McAfee, the first since Clinton's election, and growing pressure from the United States that the government of Guatemala clip the military's wings, curb the death squads, and sign a peace agreement with the Unidad Revolucionaria Nacional Guatemalteca (URNG; Guatemalan National Revolutionary Unity), the united front organization of the guerilla groups. Neoliberal business leaders sought to be included under a Central American version of the newly enacted NAFTA agreement between the United States, Canada, and Mexico and feared expensive sanctions if the war were not ended. The military, which had controlled the presidency, the courts, and the terms of civic discourse more often than not over the course of the previous thirty years, to say nothing of having an extensive network of informers and henchmen up and down Guatemala, was not pleased with this state of affairs.

International human rights activists were all over the country, banking on the belief that it would be too costly for Guatemala if foreigners were killed, challenging the authority of the military and charging it with crimes. A few months before, for example, Witness for Peace had sent a group into the rainforests of the department of Quiché to certify that the refugees that had come together to form the CPR were civilians—not guerillas, as the military charged—and demand that the military stop shelling and starving them and allow them to return to their homes. Days before the attack on Weinstock a major newspaper in Guatemala repeated the charges against Larson—that she had kidnapped children to murder them for their organs —under the headline (in English), "Yankee Hippees [Hippies], Go Home!" The same day Weinstock was attacked, the Tuesday before Easter, an agreement was signed between the government and the URNG that would allow a human rights verification mission by the United Nations. On Good Friday, Judge Epaminondas González Dubón, president of the Constitutional Court, was gunned down at point blank range in front of his home. It was a murder that many attributed to death squads, as González had played a key role the year before in returning the country to civilian rule after former president Serrano's coup. Serrano had shut down the press, the Congress, and the courts and sent the military into the streets; González had declared Serrano's "self-coup" illegal. (When the new Serrano government collapsed, a few days later, the military took power; it in turn was replaced by the solicitor general of human rights and the Constitutional Court under González.) Now, nearly a year after the coup and the emergence from hiding of the CPR— many of the same Maya-Ixiles whose testimonios about their kidnapped children would emerge years later, as we have seen—pressure from international forces was again threatening to put the power to curb the military into the hands of "Yankee Hippees" through a truth commission and human rights verification process.[92]

Analysts argued that the military was the only organization with sufficient networks throughout the country to orchestrate attacks like those on Carol Larson and June Weinstock.[93] Allegations that there were members of the Guatemalan military intelligence (M-2) in the crowd at San Cristobal

Verapaz and Santa Lucia Cotzumalguapa were reported in the *New York Times*, *Miami Herald*, and the activist news service *NicaNews*. "The army wants to appear as the savior for the people, but they are chief accomplices," Rosalina Tuyuc, director of CONAVIGUA, told the press.[94] Fernando Lopez of ODHAG told the *Miami Herald* that child stealing was common enough, "but it is not foreigners who are involved. It is Guatemalans, mostly lawyers and military officers."[95] José Gutierrez, the Frente Farabundo Martí para la Liberación Nacional (FMLN; Farabundo Martí National Liberation Front) activist who corresponded with Weinstock, believed that given the intensive international surveillance of FMLN solidarity groups, Weinstock may have been targeted in Guatemala because of her association with him.[96] One indigenous community started to escort Peace Corps and solidarity workers to protect them.[97] According to the journalist and human rights activist Daniel Wilkinson, conventional wisdom in U.S. circles in Guatemala at the time had it that the baby-stealing rumors were deployed to imperil the work of the human rights workers who were unearthing mass graves in the highlands or collecting testimony of army atrocities; this might account for rumors that targeted photographers. Wilkinson himself, researching a history of the origins of the civil war, was briefly detained as a *robachicos* (child stealer) and reported that throughout that year the organ-stealing story made his work more difficult.[98] The anthropologist Diane Nelson writes that it was for her a startling and abrupt reversal of the expectation of the magical immunity of gringas to the violence all around.[99] Perhaps it was supposed to be.

This is speculation, of course. A lot of people were blamed in Guatemala in the days following the attack on Weinstock. The Catholic Church blamed government officials. Government officials blamed Communist agitators and also unions—specifically road crew workers in Santa Cruz Verapaz, which, they said, urged on the mob that lynched Weinstock. The U.S. State Department blamed the Guatemalan press, superstitious folk beliefs, and—this is my personal favorite—the Soviet Union, which no longer existed.[100] Because stories of organ theft are horrifying, they command attention and demand an interpretation: are they true or not? The anthropologist Nancy Scheper-Hughes, studying the circulation of these stories among poor people in Brazil, or myself, in the context of Mexico, have said: well, it is not impossible.[101] In Guatemala, though, these stories took such a definable route through official sources (police, newspapers, and radio) that it seems more important to ask: what work did they do and for whom? My suspicion about the circulation of these ghoulish stories in Guatemala is that their explosion in 1994 served the goals of the military—remilitarization, the threat in fact of military rule, and contributed to the climate of fear of speaking to foreigners in the context of the truth commission process.

Yet I also suspect they resonated for another reason: children really had disappeared, and torture and murder had occurred with impunity. If, as I suspect, the rumors were circulated by the military or other authorities, perhaps the goal was to provide an alternative account about who was stealing children to the one many believed: that it was the military, government officials, and other illegal networks connected to them. As allegations circulated in the national and international press that mafias associated with government officials were kidnapping children and engaging in a highly lucrative business of sending them into international adoptions, rumors accusing gringos of the same thing were circulating in isolated communities.

Efforts at Legal Reform

If the rumors that gave rise to the attacks on Weinstock and others were an effort at misdirection, a prose of counterinsurgency designed to distract attention from the involvement of the military and civilian authorities in illegal adoptions, they were not entirely successful. There were numerous efforts to prosecute "illegal" adoption cases through the courts and legislative measures to limit it. By 1994, numerous efforts, large and small, to reform adoption had failed.[102] Allegations about child trafficking in Guatemala were nearly continuous by the mid-1980s, once civilian rule was reestablished and the worst of the repression in the highlands was ended.

The Guatemalan press ran dozens of stories in the first months of 1994 about children being kidnapped, about illegal adoptions and illicit nurseries that "fattened" children for international adoption, and about mothers losing their children to the state for abuse and neglect that seemed dubious. At the time the attorney general, Telesforo Guerra Cahn, was arguing that children were being sent into international adoptions through a network of baby traffickers that included many of the wealthiest and most powerful people in Guatemala, including the president of the Supreme Court, Juan José Rodil Peralta. "We've tried to prosecute him, but it's hopeless because he controls the court system and the judges," *Time* magazine quoted Cahn as saying. "He's also protected under parliamentary immunity."[103] Peralta's successor in the Supreme Court in 1994, Ricardo

Umaña, was also alleged to be deeply involved in a network of child traffickers; his then-spouse, Susana Luarca de Umaña, was a successful adoption attorney who became prominent in the international politics of promoting adoption from Guatemala.

Most of the legal cases designed to halt adoptions went nowhere. For example, in 1995 the adoption attorney Rubén Darío Ventura Arellano was arrested for "trafficking" and stealing children. Neighbors reported that children were frequently seen arriving and leaving an address in Guatemala City, and when investigators interviewed domestic workers there, they found they were caring for two newborns. The workers reported that they frequently cared for young children, usually newborns, at this location and another, and said they had no knowledge about where the children came from or where they went. The police were able to locate the parents of one child but not the other.[104] This case was typical of many cases in the 1990s; the police responded to neighbors' alarm at what appeared to them to be a child trafficking depot with an arrest, but the police, confronted with children whose parentage was unnamed and perhaps unnameable, declined to investigate the matter further.

Since foster homes required neither licenses nor paperwork showing where their charges came from nor where they went, the matter was simply dropped. With legal requirements so slight, Darío Ventura Arellano could say, in all truth, that there was nothing illegal about what was happening in the foster homes. Still, they disturbed the conscience of the neighbors and the press, who understood as well as anyone how unlikely it would be for someone impoverished—particularly if she or he were from a rural community, spoke an indigenous language, or was in a combat zone—to be able to successfully press a missing person claim. So, as happened so often, the neighbors and press complained, the police made arrests, and then courts quietly dropped the charges.[105]

The most serious debates related to adoption began nominally in 1990, but really in 1995, and were over international human rights treaties. By the 1990s Guatemala was striving for international legitimacy on human rights questions. Civilian rule was at least nominally the order of the day, although the military continued to play an oversized role in governance. Business interests feared that the emergence of George H. W. Bush and Bill Clinton's New World Order would leave them out if the country did not make at least a marginal effort to acknowledge international human rights norms. So in 1990 Guatemala signed the Convention on the Rights of the Child. The following year the attorney general for human rights created a commission to enact the convention, although nothing happened for another five years. Early in 1995, though, the commission wrote enabling legislation, the bill for the Rights of the Child, which was approved by the congressional Commission on Women, Children, and the Family. That was the beginning of the end, however. As we will see in chapter 6, by 1996 the evangelical church had declared war on the convention, and, as one newspaper put it, the bill to enact it was "stillborn."[106]

The United States: The Stories We Tell

How did the U.S. families who adopted from Latin America during the height of these disappearances understand their relationship to these events? Not always well. As we saw in the introduction, Elizabeth Bartholet's account of adopting her two boys from Peru relies on a combination of anti-Communist fear of Sendero Luminoso and an erasure of the birth parents. Similarly, when I went to the offices of Pro-Búsqueda in San Salvador, a young man there, himself a "found" child, told me that when they trace a child or young person to adoption by a U.S. family, less than one-third of the adoptive parents will let the child have any contact with their Salvadoran family.[107]

Some U.S. citizens, however, went to Latin America because they were leftists and wanted to raise the children, especially from Central America, that the war had left parentless. It is painfully clear how little control those on the left had over the circumstances of these adoptions, the context in which children in El Salvador or Guatemala were adjudicated "orphans."[108]

Much like those in the 1930s, strategies for narrating intercountry adoption from Central America in the 1980s by those on the U.S. left located it within a crucible of solidarity. In contrast to the earlier decade, what had changed—both in the war and in the meaning of adoption—is the context of complicity with right-wing forces. Where in the 1930s it was possible to hope that the United States could take up a defense of, say, the Spanish Republicans and admit refugee Basque children, in the 1980s it was painfully clear that the United States was backing the right-wing governments and death squads that were devastating civilian populations and that the context of adoption was at the mercy of these state actors. Within these constraints, however, people on the left related what I would call a narrative of witness, which occupied a space of dissent by naming the massacres of civilians by militaries and paramilitaries, the involvement of the United

States, and upholding the legitimacy of kinds of peasant and labor organizing that was being brutally suppressed.

Under the pseudonym of Lea Marenn, Helen Fehervary—herself hidden from the Nazis in Germany as a child—wrote such a narrative of
witness in her book *Salvador's Children*. It begins by noticing that the
orphanage where she found her daughter in El Salvador was next to the
women's prison, which housed political prisoners. "On dark Ilopango
nights, I thought to myself, the women must whisper secrets and crawl over
the prison wall to visit with their children," she wrote, aware from the
outset of the uneasy complicity of the prison and the orphanage.[109] She
goes to the orphanage to pick up the eight-year-old girl who will be her
adoptive daughter, whom she calls María de Jesús, together with a couple
who will adopt María's younger brothers, Ramón and Aurelio. Ramón is in
the care of María, and the adults and these two children go to the older
boys' barracks. But when they find Aurelio, all is not well; Aurelio will not
join them. She narrates an incident that frames the moral and narrative
problem of the book: "It was clear that there was a special reason for
Aurelio's suffering. He appeared to be waiting for somebody, something.
The tears had begun to trickle down his cheeks. . . . We could have forced
Aurelio down the stairs and dragged him into the car . . . but it would have
remained imprinted on his mind forever. Or he could have stayed at the
orphanage, [but] the next station for the older boys in the orphanage was
inevitably the army. . . . Suddenly, I had an idea. It would implicate me
forever in this colonial history of North-South rationalizations and exchanges." With that, Marenn sends María and Ramón, hand in hand, to
bring the following message to Aurelio, with instructions to take his hand
and lead him to the car: "Tell him they are going to the United States to live
with new parents who will care for them and love them. They will have
clothes, a nice house, and food . . . he will be living together with Ramón
and she will be close by." The plan succeeds, and Aurelio goes quietly to the
car with his brother and sister, but the incident haunts Marenn. "For a
moment, I stood alone at the bottom of the steps and turned to look up at
the adolescent boys who still watched the scene, leaning awkwardly, tentatively, against the orphanage wall. Now we were the ones who would never
forget."[110] Clothes, a nice house, and food in exchange for losing people
and places one loves; this is the bargain they have to offer, and the naked
materialism of that offer shames Marenn, implicating her in the "colonial
history of North-South rationalizations and exchanges."

The book proceeds in three parts. The first, including this scene and a memorable one where the embassy people who process the visa for María's adoption are compared to the soldiers and members of the paramilitary Guardia, is called "Yankee Itineraries"; the second, where a traumatized María narrates her life in El Salvador in bits and pieces, including descriptions of massacres and being caught in the fighting, is called "Homage to Cándida," María's mother; Marenn agonizes over whether to counsel forgetting or to just be present to María's pain. In the final section, "Underground Railroad, Southward," Marenn actively begins to look for the lost members of María's family, to conceptualize her relationship to this eight-year-old girl in terms simply of solidarity with her family's and community's struggle, and to insist—against the dominate terms of political debate in the early 1980s—that María's stories of the rape and murder of women, children, and the elderly by the military were true. It is in this last section that we understand the full meaning of that scene at the orphanage, as she unfolds the suspicion that one of the older boys hanging back against the wall was the children's brother. This is not a narrative of regret for her specific actions but of the unbearable, impossible complicity, of the lack of options for Americans on the left in this situation, except to bear witness by telling the stories of violation and loss.

The anthropologist Emily Noonan offers a different reading of the narratives of U.S. adopters in Guatemala, looking at postings on adoption listservs. These listservs offer a political counterpoint to Marenn's. Following the literary critic Mary Louise Pratt, Noonan is interested in what she terms "anti-Conquest" narratives, stories that simultaneously reject explicit statements of superiority while conveying the writers' wealth and power in relationship to the people and places they describe. Characterizing one such story, Noonan says of the author, "she simultaneously constructs the country as unimportant and inferior, a place one 'could hardly locate on a map,' and as the valuable and benevolent home to 'gracious people' who gave a 'lifelong gift.' Through this type of narrative, parents set themselves up as appreciative of Guatemala, but convey their belief that they will be able to provide better for the child than anyone in the birth country."[111] This is the tradition of the Holts and anti-Communism, the Right's vocabulary of adoption that introduces difference and superiority. Where Marenn sees offering a child material inducements to cooperate with adoption as part of a shameful and deceitful history of colonialism, this narrator and others Noonan cites construct a story of their innocence and superiority.

Whether from left or right, though, the "class" of adopters that had emerged in the United States late in the twentieth century did not con-

struct the terms on which adoption from Latin America took place (or, for
that matter, the economic conditions under which they found themselves
completing their families through adoption). Or rather, to reiterate the
insight of the Madres, some adopters more than others were in a position
with the power, or the ability to negotiate with those with the power, to set
the terms of these extensively privatized (and even militarized) adoptions.
Neoliberalism was hardly an inevitable outcome of the ideological struggles in the Americas (as elsewhere), any more than plenary, private adoption was the only possibility for forms of transnational family making or
solidarity politics. But for most adopters, those decisions happened at
considerable remove from them.

SIX

Latin American Family Values

On July 24, 2008, the Associated Press (AP) in the United States reported on the case of Ana Escobar, whose daughter, Esther Sulamita, was reportedly kidnapped by Guatemalan "traffickers" and then nearly adopted by a couple from the United States. After searching orphanages and hospitals for her for six months, Escobar found a girl she said was her daughter: Esther was about to be taken out of the country by her would-be adoptive parents. DNA tests subsequently established that Escobar was right, that the girl was her daughter. The AP paraphrased a Guatemalan official, Jaime Tecu, as indicating that "the test results represented the first time officials had directly linked a baby reported stolen from its mother to the country's fraud-plagued adoption system."[1]

This is an odd sentence by the AP writer. Was Guatemala's adoption system known to be "fraud-plagued" even before officials linked a child about to be adopted to a birth parent whose child had been kidnapped? There were many in the United States and Guatemala who took the position that there was no fraud in Guatemalan adoptions, especially before the Ana Escobar case, and some who continued to insist on it even afterward. The story goes on to clarify that (unnamed) "authorities have long said that children were stolen or bought before thousands of pending adoptions were frozen in May." Authorities, then, are proven right; a logical and (now) largely transparent system is in place, in which authoritative knowledge could be relied upon first to close down adoptions and then, given the proper opportunity to halt the whole system and conduct careful, unhurried investigations, to find evidence for what they had suspected. The next sentence takes us once again into the world of unproven claims: "The child's mother, Ana Escobar, said armed men locked her in a closet in March 2007 at the family's shoe store north of Guatemala City and took the 6-month-old." Mothers *say*, they make claims that cannot be verified; officials produce *test results* that *directly link*.

Reading this story across multiple national presses is revealing. The BBC, for example, repeated the claim that it was "the first time" such a story had been confirmed but filled in additional details: Ana Escobar had gained access to international media as an activist, demonstrating with other mothers in front of the new Consejo Nacional de Adopciones (CNA; National Adoption Council) building (the CNA being the central authority authorizing adoptions brought into existence by Guatemala's efforts to accede to the Hague Convention on Protection of Children and Co-operation in Respect of Intercountry Adoption [or the Hague Convention on Intercountry Adoption]). Escobar had first spoken to the BBC in November 2007, when she and other mothers of kidnapped children, members of Fundación Sobrevivientes (Survivors Foundation), had demonstrated with their empty baby strollers in a conscious echo of the *Madres de Plaza de Mayo*, saying that their children had been stolen and sold into adoptions. Further, when the adoption of Esther Sulamita was "reviewed" by the new system, it had already been approved, including through the use of two (apparently) falsified DNA tests. Finally, the BBC tells us in "Adopted Guatemalan Baby 'Stolen'" that it was not the review process—not officials at all—but the child's mother, Escobar herself, who uncovered the kidnapping and fraud. She saw her daughter with a U.S. couple and went to authorities and demanded a new DNA test, which found that the girl was, indeed, her daughter.

While the story of Ana Escobar marked considerable but not surprising differences between the U.S. and British press (by 2004, after the widespread ratification of the Hague Convention on Intercountry Adoption by most European Union countries, few adoptions took place between Guatemala and the EU),[2] the difference between this story and the one the Guatemalan press was telling is still more remarkable. As we have seen, the Guatemalan press had been telling the story of disappeared children since 1994 and before (and, as we have seen, the Comisión para el Esclarecimiento Histórico [CEH] and Oficina de Derechos Humanos de Arzobispado de Guatemala [ODHAG] had likewise written human rights reports about extensive kidnapping by the military during the armed internal conflict). So it is not surprising that the

Guatemalan press had sympathetically and extensively told the story of Fundación Sobrevivientes. According to *Prensa Libre*, Fundación Sobreviventes was born out of opposition to *machista* violence against women and children and understood itself as a feminist group. Its founder, Norma Cruz, came out of Coordinadora Nacional de Viudas de Guatemala (CONAVIGUA, the political organization of the widows of those disappeared during the war) and, through CONAVIGUA, was part of the history since even before the Madres in Latin America of the assertion of the moral authority of women whose family members had been disappeared. Cruz told *Prensa Libre* that she founded Sobrevivientes when her daughter was sexually abused by her then husband, a leftist, because, she said, women needed to speak up about violence in the family, akin to but broader than disappearances by the military and paramilitaries. The group also took up the issue of femicide, the chilling and growing number of murders and disappearances of women in Guatemala, building on the Mexican feminist movement's denunciation of femicide (particularly but not exclusively in Ciudad Juarez). Finally, it began demonstrations against the kidnapping and disappearance of women and children, which it said the police were failing to prosecute. Further, the group argued, the massive numbers of children being adopted transnationally could only be accounted for if some of those kidnapped children were being adopted (and others compelled to do sex work).[3]

There was also yet another, and perhaps most curious, response to the Ana Escobar case. The website of the Asociación Defensores de Adopción (ADA), the network of Guatemalan lawyers, maintained—in English—significantly for a U.S. audience and extensively cross-referenced with the adoptive parents' listserv at guatadopt.com, simply called the whole story a lie. At this website, the attorney Susana Luarca de Umaña reported approvingly of a legal motion filed to demand that the child be returned to those organizing adoption proceedings, saying that Escobar "claimed that the child looked like the one she lost, even though she could not tell the same story twice and could not remember the date when she lost her child." Nearly a year after the international press carried the story of how Ana Escobar's daughter's DNA test had proven her relationship to Escobar, the ADA's website still called for the child to be returned to the would-be adoptive parents, characterizing Escobar and her claim to the child in the following way: Escobar was "a woman sponsored by a group called Sobrevientes (Survivors) whose battle cry is the killing of women, but lately switched to attack adoptions with empty cribs and women lamenting the loss of their children for illegal adoptions."[4] In this account, those who claimed that there was fraud or kidnapping in adoption were liars and opportunists out to harass well-meaning people who had children's best interests at heart and sought to facilitate adoptions.

This is a fascinating set of narratives, which represent the range of strategies for making sense of transnational adoption that were in play in the decade after 2000. There is the United States, the neoliberal security state, in which officials know best and ultimately root out danger and stop bad things from happening to people. In this account adoption is a contract that has to be freely entered into from both sides, and it is the job of the state to enforce contracts and ensure their legitimacy—in this instance by preventing kidnapping and fraud on the Guatemalan side. There is the European human rights regime, in which individuals protest injustice and thus force the state—understood to be transparent, benevolent, and an honest broker between competing interests—to do the right thing. From the Guatemalan and feminist side, though, there is a belief that there are no real guarantors of safety for women and children—not the Guatemalan state, certainly, not the family, not fathers, and not the law. There is, however, collective action and the formation of groups, especially of women, who will fight for each other. Finally, there is the well-practiced tactic of the powerful in Guatemala: silencing, the simple and categorical denial that anything bad has happened.

This chapter is interested in how adoption, gender, and social movements were negotiated at the end of the Cold War and the dawning of the era of neoliberalism between the United States and Latin America (and to a lesser extent Europe), looking particularly at Guatemala. First, I explore the history of debates over adoption reform legislation in Guatemala, beginning in 1996, and trace three moves. One move was a conservative, evangelical Christian, "Guatemalan family values" position that tried to facilitate transnational adoption. A second insisted that there were tremendous communal resources in indigenous communities to adopt and raise children and opposed international adoption as contrary to Mayan interests and values. Finally, as the above stories intimate, there was a transnational discourse (U.S. and Guatemalan, mostly) that focused on silencing the allegations of kidnapping, abuse, and criminality. This chapter develops a genealogy of how it became possible, in the face of a vigorous counterdiscourse, to imagine that the Ana Escobar case was the first such case in Guatemala—or even that it was a lie. This chapter also explores the other post–Cold War alternative, enacted in virtually every country in Latin America except Guatemala, which included the production of a new way of understanding children and international adoption through human rights treaties. Starting with the presumptions like those of the BBC—that where there are illegalities or trafficking, the state and the rule of law will eventually prevail over them—this chapter considers the "victories" against exploitation elsewhere in Latin America and asks whether things really were better for impoverished mothers in, say, Brazil or whether these states substituted a national transfer of children—and reform of impoverished families—for a transnational one. Finally, this chapter turns to the United States and explores the stories we tell—how we narrativize knowledge about the pain and sometimes the violence of transnational adoption.

My intention here is not so much to write an Amnesty International–style exposé of "where babies (really) come from"—although there is certainly an important role for such things. But this chapter explores the longings and anger that question generates. I am interested in the anxieties, frustrations, violences, and political struggles over the production of adoptable babies in Latin America in the context of transnational adoption, alongside the "closing" of nations to intercountry adoption. Adoption is about the fate of impoverished children and what happens to the mothers who gave them birth; as such it carries tremendous symbolic significance, including, in the post–Cold War moment, questions of how we should understand the closing of the socialist and welfare-state dream that states would care for impoverished women and children, how the economic transformations of structural adjustment and neoliberalism heightened inequality, leaving some, particularly women and children, without economic resources or even a fig leaf of support from the state. For liberals in the United States (and, increasingly, the EU), the ethical dilemma of this state of affairs, together with an ideological cynicism about the value of state support for communities and families, leads to NGOs and adoptions, privatized solutions to what used to be collective problems that needed solutions at the level of the community or the nation. This chapter is about how the violence of the Cold War moment, running as much through paramilitaries, churches, and the politics of family as through the state and the autonomous individual, gave rise to the violence of post–Cold War neoliberal regimes.

Guatemalan Family Values:
Losing Children, Parental Rights, and Human Rights

While Latin America's civil wars may have launched transnational adoption, in terms of sheer quantity the really significant number of adoptions from Latin America occurred after the wars, as "markets" were "opened." Guatemala accounted for most of it. After staying relatively constant at around 400 adoptions to the United States per year for most of the decade, in 1997 there were 788 Guatemalan adoptions to the United States; in 1998 there were 911, and rates quickly shot up after that, with 3,783 Guatemalan adoptions to the United States in 2005.[5] From 2004 to 2007 tiny Guatemala led the world in adoptions to the United States, and in 2007 one out of every hundred Guatemalan babies born was being raised as an adopted child in the United States, a rate of foreign adoption utterly unrivalled in the history of any nation.[6] In 1996 the signing of the peace accords marked the consolidation of a new era in economic policy. The historian J. T. Way has argued that Guatemala is the state in which neoliberalism advanced the furthest, with its hallmarks—the shrinking of the state, privatizing health and welfare functions, economic disparities, a growing prison-security apparatus, and what is often called a "favorable" business climate (the absence of unions, taxation, and worker or environmental protections)—well developed in the aftermath of the war.[7] By 1996 NGOs born from within as well as outside Guatemala had begun, piece by piece, to replace any social welfare programs that the social movements in the forty years from the 1950s to the 1990s had sought to make the responsibility of the state (from health care to clean, running water), and the number of adoptions to the United States really took off. Adoption to the United States became the alternative to a civilian child welfare system, which seems bitterly fitting given the role of U.S. military aid in helping to destroy those with an alternative vision of the Guatemalan state.

As we have seen, beginning in the mid-1990s, the Guatemalan press had run stories, sometimes many times a week, of children disappeared, kidnapped, and often adopted. My file of clippings from the Guatemalan press of children allegedly kidnapped who sometimes found their way into international adoptions is an inch and a half thick—more than three hundred articles. And that is only the decade from 1993 to 2003. After that the press is digitized—any number of searches on, say, the *Prensa Libre* website (www.prensalibre.com) with words like "robo y adopciones" (theft and adoptions) turn up hundreds more articles—a far cry from the claim by the AP or the BBC that Ana Escobar in 2008 was the "first."

To dip into this archive is to get a sense of it: In 2001, according to the press, three-year-old Kimberly Xiomara Pineda was kidnapped from her home and offered in adoption to a Spanish couple, Rodrigo Espósito and Luz Maria Rodríguez. Kimberly was reported missing to a number of agencies, but it was only when her mother, Rebeca Arbizurez, persuaded her employer (she worked at the Colegio Julio Verne) to call the head of the General Office of Migration, Luis Mendizábal, who confirmed that the child had been issued a passport and was due to leave the country any day; the tickets had already been purchased. In fact, incredibly enough, a family court judge had approved the adoption six weeks before the child had been kidnapped, when she was still living with her family; an employee at her daycare center had taken the child to all the necessary appointments. Kimberly's mother, Rebeca, was both persistent and lucky; while she, a person of humble means, was not the sort of person who could get Luis Mendizábal to take her calls, she won the sympathetic ear of someone at the Colegio Julio Verne who could—not identified in the press—and because of that bit of good fortune, she got her daughter back (Mendizábal was identified some years later in *La Prensa Gráfica* in San Salvador as a liaison between those linked to death squads in El Salvador and those similarly situated in Guatemala; yet other reports had him smuggling guns to the FMLN. He has also been reported to be simply an *oreja*, a spy, someone who knew everyone and everything that happened in Guatemala).[8] Even afterward, though, the family was terrified—they moved houses in hopes of escaping their daughter's kidnappers. A few days after Kimberly was recovered, the woman who had posed as her mother to the court disappeared; she had been detained but then was released from jail by the police. The family received death threats and entered the witness protection program of the Public Ministry. While this may have made the parents and their four children safer, it did not protect the whole family. Seven months later Kimberly's two uncles were shot and killed by strangers who found them at a local community fiesta. The killers ran off into the woods and hid. The neighbors gave chase, but they were never found.[9]

This case elucidates a number of things that many Guatemalans, and certainly the press, believed about adoption. First, that it can involve kidnapping. Second, that if you report the abduction of a child, the criminal group that sponsored it may retaliate. Third, that the police and judges are involved, so there is impunity for those caught engaging in such crimes. This helps explain something that is often hard for those from outside Guatemala to understand: the mob violence against those accused of child stealing (and any number of other crimes, but it is the mob attacks on the midwives and *jaladoras*—arrangers—that made the international press, including but not limited to the June Weinstock incident). Communities believed that they could not rely on the police for justice or for protection against criminal violence, and so they take matters into their own hands. Finally, the other thing that is interesting here is the more or less complete impotence of the press: nobody thought that shining the bright light of public scrutiny on this incident was going to result in prosecutions of those who were, after all, named in court papers—hardly anonymous or hidden perpetrators—or result in safety for the family.

Legal Reform Efforts

By 1994, fifteen adoption reform bills had already failed in the Guatemalan legislature.[10] Beginning in 1996, the position exemplified by the press—that adoption proceeded through violence and degradation—had new champions in the legislative arena in the form of leaders of the groups of family members of the disappeared. But it also had renewed opposition: the conservative, Christian Right formation that had been a significant part of the anti-Communist ruling junta during the armed internal conflict. The elections in 1996 brought the historical adversaries of the civil war into the legislature together, and adoption reform was an arena in which they squared off. One of the chief proponents of transnational adoption was Efraín Ríos Montt. One of the major figures proposing adoption reform was Nineth Montenegro, a human rights activist and one of the founders of the Grupo de Apoyo Mutuo (GAM; Group for Mutual Support), which provided solidarity and support for family members of those disappeared ("modeled somewhat after the Mothers of the Plaza de Mayo," as writer Francisco Goldman puts it). Montenegro had become an activist after the disappearance of her husband, the student and labor activist Edgar Montenegro García, and she began sitting in at government buildings and demanded accountability from the police and the military for disappearances, somehow surviving even as other members of GAM were being targeted as subversives and murdered themselves.[11] One of the first issues this newly elected Congress struggled over was the enactment of the Convention on the Rights of the Child.

Evangelical Christian groups proceeded to articulate what I want to call a "Guatemalan family values" position that was much like the Christian Right position in the United States in the 1980s. The family was the foundation of church and society, and women and children needed to be protected from the corrupting influence of the state and other secular influences. Although the U.S. Christian Right has focused obsessively on legal abortion—which was not an issue in Guatemala, where abortion was illegal except to save the life of the mother—it also elaborated positions on adoption in the 1980s and 1990s that were concerned about making it easy, secret, and free from state influence (in opposition to Bastard Nation— styled after Queer Nation in both name and ability to drive the Christian Right to distraction—which urged open records and other restrictions on "secret" adoptions).[12] As the journalist Michelle Goldberg has argued, the early 1990s were a period of intense transnationalization of U.S.-style "culture wars," as Christian Right groups pushed to take issues like abortion, birth control, and homosexuality to ever more countries. Goldberg cites particularly the example of El Salvador's extreme antiabortion law that makes abortion illegal even to save the life of the mother, which forces emergency rooms to withhold life-saving treatment for women who spontaneously miscarry until the fetus no longer has signs of life.[13] We could equally say that the fight over *adoption* in Guatemala maps the new transnational activism by the Christian Right over proper family forms, in which single mothers should give up their children and relinquishing a child for adoption is the ultimate expression of parental authority. Human rights treaties—especially those governing adoption—were regarded as international meddling in the authority of the family.

Beginning in 1996 a number of evangelical churches and the two conservative parties—the Partido de Avanza Nacional (PAN; Party for National Advancement) and the Frente Republicano Guatemalteco (FRG; Guatemalan Republican Front, Ríos Montt's party)—had declared the Convention on the Rights of the Child an agent of the destruction of the authority of the family.[14] In 1998, after the signing of the peace accords and with the election of a still-larger reform-oriented legislative delegation drawn from the Left, there was a serious effort to reform adoption and document abuse. That year, when enabling legislation for the Convention on the Rights of the Child was slated to go into effect, a number of opposition groups sprang up, including the Associación Pro-Patria (Association for the Homeland), the Asociación por el Poder Local (Association for Local Power), and the Madres Angustiadas (Anxious Mothers), a group of well-to-do conservative women who argued that the convention would make it impossible for them to control their children, since it would give children freedom of religion, travel, expression, and a right to privacy over their space. "It would destroy the family," insisted the Madres Angustiadas spokesperson José Luis González.[15] The Alianza Evangélica de Guatemala (Evangelical Alliance of Guatemala), a coalition of evangelical Protestant churches, also opposed the legislation. "It is the responsibility of all Guatemalans to struggle against a law that undermines the family as the foundation of society and the church," the group said in a statement.[16]

Fernando Linares Beltranena, a conservative lawyer and columnist for *Prensa Libre*, expanded on this position: "The most surprising thing about the [children's] code is that it pretends to help children . . . but the majority of it, with euphemisms and ambiguous terminology, with pretensions of legislating altruistically, and with foreign values, disintegrates family values, handing family authority over to the state, to a great bureaucratic network." He went on to insist that it prevented parents from taking any action if their children swore, wore miniskirts, got tattoos, or cross-dressed. Only with an order from a judge, he insisted, could parents go into their child's room to look for drugs, guns, pornography, or sex toys. Linares also worked to construct a pan-Guatemalan account of these "family values," arguing the not so obvious position that this autonomous nuclear family that just wanted to be free from outside influence was as Mayan as it was Ladino, "Indigenous families, who are trying to preserve their values and customs, also will be especially affected [by the code] in the loss of their authority to halt this exercise of freedom [i.e., to wear miniskirts and use drugs] by their children."[17]

Proponents of the convention took a different view, arguing that the family argument was a red herring and the real issue was the abuse of power that resulted in fantastic money-making opportunities in adoptions, not parental authority. In Congress, Nineth Montenegro argued that her commission on Women, Minors, and the Family could document irregularities in 440 adoptions, and that lawyers were making a fortune: US$30,000 per adoption. "Groups with economic power are involved [in adoption], and when their interests are threatened, each time there is an effort to legislate in relation to that institution [of adoption], the proposals get bogged down and don't do well," said Débora Cóbar de Alvarado, the state's attorney for children and youth. "The process, as it is, is very simple. Any notary can do it, and in this way it is made into a simple matter of paperwork, in which the child is converted into a good [in the sense of something that can be sold] rather than treated as a human being."[18] Montenegro and others associated with families of the disappeared, working with UNICEF and child advocacy groups, held press conferences, reached out to international human rights activists and demanded reform, linking adoption to organ theft and the murder of street children by the police and military.[19] In a press conference in 1997 the human rights activist Bruce Harris of the Catholic children's home, Casa Alianza, Attorney General Acisclo Valladares, and Carmela

Curup, the attorney for minors, denounced the attorneys involved in trans-national adoption, with reference to a series of specific cases. In one a lawyer had submitted the same birth certificate for multiple babies. In another five babies being sent into adoptions in Canada by a single lawyer were revealed, through DNA testing, to be unrelated to the "mothers" who were supposedly relinquishing them. The third lawyer singled out in the press conference was Susana Luarca de Umaña, wife of the president of the Supreme Court, who was accused of using her influence to affect relinquishment proceedings. Harris noted the sheer volume of her work: she was sending about ten babies a month into adoptions, and Harris calculated that she was receiving US$10,000 to $15,000 for each adoption.

The BBC broadcast a Canadian report, "The Body Parts Business," that followed disappeared street children and argued that there was a consider-able traffic in children—in adoptions and possibly also in the theft of body parts—through organized criminal networks and with the collaboration of the police.[20] A Spanish journalist likewise denounced a Guatemalan traffic in children for organs, compiling his articles in a book he titled *Niños de Repuesto*—Children for Spare Parts.[21] The evidence was sufficiently robust that children really were being kidnapped and carried into the United States as adopted children that the U.S. State Department began to require a DNA test establishing that the woman relinquishing the child truly was its mother before issuing a visa for an adopted child (establishing, ironically, a requirement that U.S. officials certify maternity before declaring a child an orphan, suggesting some of the basic strangeness of the "orphan" visa).[22]

The Mexican journalist Karen Avilés wrote in *La Jornada* that women, notably sex workers, were being paid to get pregnant, "renting out their wombs," in her memorable phrase.[23] She also suggested that Mexican children were getting swept into Guatemalan adoptions, writing about the transport of Mexican children across the border to "orphanages" in Guate-mala, with no record of how the children were obtained. She wrote a series of articles detailing the traffic in children in Guatemala, describing an extensive network of eighty Guatemalan professionals and government officials—lawyers, social workers, judges—who benefited from these opera-tions. She also told stories of those who kidnapped children, the birth mothers who sold children for as little as US$250, homes where birth-mothers stayed through their pregnancies with the understanding that their newborns would be adopted out. She quoted Carmela Curup of the federal Attorney General's Office of Guatemala describing the difficulty of proving the existence of an international traffic in children but admitting the shady nature of much of what goes on: "everything [about adoption procedures] is legal, all, in inverted commas, is 'legal.' " She added, "We see with concern the number of people who get here, into Guatemala who, for a few *quetzales*, manage to procure a child." Avilés also wrote of the other side of the equation, hotels filled with foreign guests, each one of whom carried an about to be adopted, brown-skinned infant, an image worthy of Borges repeated daily in Guatemala.[24]

Within Guatemala, others, like Carmen Rosa de Leon, the director of the government agency to support refugees, offered a less sensational account, but one that ultimately was rooted in an explanation that was just as much about violence—but structural violence rather than kidnapping. She stressed the ways transnational adoption emerged from the desperation of the very impoverished. "Why is there a traffic in children?" she asked. The answer, she thought, was because there are so many families who have more children than they can feed. She told the story of a couple with ten children, in which the oldest left to do sex work at the age of eighteen. Another young woman married an older man at the age of fourteen to ensure that she would continue to eat regularly. Most of the other children worked after a couple of years of schooling to contribute to the family income. De Leon argued that in families like these, adoption could be a gift, both to a family that could not have children and to the family that had too many. She urged reform of adoption, though, to remove the financial gain from it and to make it possible for Guatemalan families to adopt.[25]

The basic structure through which children came into transnational adoption made it difficult to distinguish between legitimate adoptions—or at least those where the parents had fully and willingly consented, however much that consent may have been conditioned by war's aftermath, community dissolution, refugee status, poverty, violence, or other kinds of desperation—and those that happened as a result of kidnapping, threats, or bribes. The adoption process was fiercely neoliberal, resting on a notion of contracts in which consent could be freely given—but in this instance, consent to something that particularly indigenous people did not and had not reliably or freely controlled, especially where the war was intense: their children. Typically, a midwife or jaladora (facilitator) learned about newborns or young children that might be adopted and arranged for them to be sent to a foster mother employed by a lawyer who worked with adoption agencies, usually from outside Guatemala. The head of the section on minors and disappeared persons of the Policía Nacional complained to the press that the law barely distinguished between legitimate and illegitimate adoptions—there was simply no way to bring charges against those involved in adoptions, even if the children had been kidnapped. Any lawyer, he said, can obtain a signature of a woman who says she is relinquishing a child for adoption. The only thing that can be prosecuted, he said, is if a lawyer rents out a house and hires people to care for children without obtaining a license to make it a nursery. The police also tried arresting jaladoras who were recruiting pregnant women to relinquish their babies (at times having them give birth at a private clinic set up for the purpose). Guatemala's orphanages were not a usual source of children for adoption; children were usually too old by the time they might enter an orphanage. Indeed, Mother Inés Ayau, a nun who ran an orphanage, complained fiercely about the unregulated character of the private adoption arrangements that took newborns from their mothers, finding children for childless Americans rather than finding homes for homeless children, saying that one should not "play with the future of any child."[26]

Mayan Family Values

Indigenous groups offered a different analysis, one that imagined neither transnational adoption nor a state-based social welfare or human rights system. A Pan-Mayanist movement had arisen during the era of the peace negotiations (1987–96) that rejected the guerilla movement's principally class-based analysis in favor of one that focused on indigeneity and colonialism, calling attention to the systematic disenfranchisement of the Mayan majority—linguistically, religiously, socially, and politically. Much of their political force derived from the demand to take Mayan lifeways seriously.[27] This demand extended to adoption. In 1998, as part of legislative debate about displaced children, the Maya-Kaqchikel human rights activist Rosalina Tuyuc—formerly the outspoken head of CONAVIGUA and by 1998 also a member of the legislative assembly—said that Mayan communities could and would care for children displaced and abandoned as a consequence of the war: "Within the social system of each of the communities, and as a tradition within indigenous law, the Maya do not have the problem of children without protection or support for their development. In Mayan tradition, [if a child is orphaned or abandoned] one resorts to the *compadres* or godparents of the children, or the closest family members, but the reality is that indigenous societies have always shared responsibility for vulnerable community members, giving support to their families."[28] Or, similarly, another Mayan deputy in the assembly, Ricardo Choy Ajquehay (also president of the Commission of Indigenous Communities) made the same argument: "In indigenous communities . . . it is understood that adoption is practiced voluntarily/informally, and when a child becomes an orphan in the social group, a close family member of the abandoned or orphaned child is spoken to, and the adoption is made official with a ceremony."[29] Since informal adoption was the norm in indigenous Guatemala, they argued, legal and transnational adoption did not solve a problem for children, it only introduced a new kind of exploitation of children and their parents.

The documentation of more than two hundred "found" children by Todos por el Reencuentro is certainly an endorsement of Tuyuc and Choy's argument that indigenous communities informally adopt children at the same time that it rather thoroughly disrupts any romanticism one might entertain about their position. Over and over again, we find in the work of Todos, particularly in indigenous communities but also among Ladinos, the paramilitary groups (PACs) and the military actually ran a highly effective adoption bureaucracy, if we want to call it that. Every one of the hundreds of children they disappeared was "placed" in a family, with only occasional recourse to ancillary institutions—orphanages or, for older boys, military barracks. Hundreds, perhaps thousands of Guatemalan families, particularly but not exclusively Mayan, adopted children in the 1980s and 1990s and raised them as their own. For better and for worse, they taught them a new language, fed them, clothed them, educated them, and dressed the girls in the *traje* (or Ladino dress) appropriate to their communities.

Indeed, the stories from the civil war simultaneously suggest that there is something implausible about the arguments frequently mounted by the ADA and other proadoption groups: that Guatemala has no "culture of adoption" and lacks the capacity to build a bureaucratic state apparatus to place children within the country. The disappearance and placement of children by the military and PACs reveal the extent to which it was certainly a highly functioning bureaucracy, well funded, multilingual, and with national reach—one that ironically puts the state's civilian child welfare system to shame. Children the military disappeared to terrorize their families and communities did not get dumped on the streets of Guatemala City. Guatemala has a culture, and a history, of state-sponsored adoption. It just does not have a history of *civilian* state-sponsored adoption. Or rather, the state has relied on churches, NGOs, and the massive private, for-profit network of notaries and facilitators that offer their services when U.S.

adoption agencies come calling. It is not the case that Guatemalans won't adopt. It's that the military stopped running its program, the civilian government has resisted creating anything resembling a welfare-state style system of child placement, and private adoption entities found during and after the war that it was not nearly as profitable to arrange adoptions within Guatemala as outside of it.

The Post-Postwar Period, 2000–2008

At the end of 1999, the FRG swept into legislative and presidential power, marking an important transition for human rights groups and those on the Left. While human rights groups were not entirely defeated by the election of the FRG, it was a clear statement that they were on the defensive again. The condition of adoption reform reflected this state of things. By 2002–2003, as we will see, every other Latin American nation had bowed to the necessity of instituting international human rights norms in adoption—however disingenuously or with whatever negative consequences for impoverished people—but Guatemala still had not.

In 2000 Efraín Rios Montt, as president of the Congress, held a press conference to announce an agreement with the Supreme Judicial Court that the enabling legislation for the Convention on the Rights of the Child, the Code for Children and Youth, would not go into effect. He cited the cost, claiming that it would require seven hundred new courts to enact. The general and pastor declared a comprehensive program for youth, but one centered in churches, not the state: "The idea is that the state will give housing and food, and the churches will be in charge of recovering, educating, and preparing youth, widows, orphans, and street children." The Evangelical Alliance and the Patriotic League cheered; the Catholic Church's conference of bishops, Nineth Montenegro, and human rights advocates criticized the position, saying the supposed cost of putting the code in force were ridiculously inflated. "*Es mentira*," said Marvin Rabanales of Coordinadora Institucional de Promoción por los Derechos de la Niñez (CIPRODENI; Institutional Coordinator for the Promotion of Children's Rights), the group coordinating children's rights activities. "It's a lie."[30]

Defeated in the legislature and in the courts in Guatemala, the locus for activism for adoption reform in Guatemala shifted further into the international arena. In 2000 Guatemala was repeatedly criticized in international forums for its record on human rights and adoptions, and, judging from the angry responses in the Guatemalan press, the denunciations stung. First, the Special Rapporteur on child pornography, prostitution, and adoptions of the United Nations, Ofelia Calcetos-Santos, issued a report presented to the UN Human Rights Commission in April 2000. The UN was hardly universally popular in Guatemala; the United Nations Verification Mission in Guatemala's (MINUGUA) human rights monitors were loathed by the military (as we saw in chapter 5, some of the suspected targets of the mob violence that victimized June Weinstock were MINUGUA representatives). Calcetos-Santos reported that, initially, members of the Guatemalan Bar Association refused to even meet with her. The report found that the buying and even stealing of babies for international adoption was widespread. For example, it reported: "In Escuintla, the Special Rapporteur was told of the case of a prostitute who was pregnant and was threatened with death by the owner of the bar where she worked if she did not give up her baby for adoption. The bar owner worked in cooperation with a midwife, and the pregnant woman was taken to the house of the midwife and kept there under lock and key with other pregnant prostitutes until she gave birth. She did not see her baby again."[31] The Latin American Institute for Education and Communication (ILPEC), together with UNICEF also issued a report some months later, commissioned by the Special Rapporteur. The international bodies stressed the legally defective nature of a procedure in which the same lawyer could be responsible for procuring the child, making arrangements for it to be fostered by someone he or she paid, then represent the birth mother and adoptive parents, and notarize the entire proceeding. The ILPEC report also cited improper pressure on birth mothers, sale of babies, and hasty abandonment or neglect proceedings, such as this one in which the report accused Susana Luarca de Umaña:

> In October of 1997, Mrs. Iris Xiomara Borrayo was taken to the hospital and she left her baby under the care of neighbors. During her stay in the hospital, the neighbors delivered her 8-month-old child to the Minor's Court Judge. The judge declared the child, Marlen Sofía Díaz Borrayo, in the "state of abandonment" on February 13, 1998. The baby was delivered to the orphanage Los Niños de Guatemala and they immediately sought to place her in adoption to a family in the United States. Desperate to recover her baby, the mother stated her opposition on May 19, 1998 and requested revocation of the abandonment sentence through the Second Court of Minors. In the ruling pronounced a day later, the court accepted the request for revocation of the abandonment sentence and ordered the president of the Los

Niños de Guatemala Home to consider the previous ruling invalid. The court also ordered the attorney involved with the adoption process to suspend activities. In an attempt to recover the baby's eligibility for adoption, the Los Niños de Guatemala Home pursued [two more motions, until the court] on December 1, 1998 ruled that the "motion for protection should not proceed." The judge of the Minors Court of Chimaltenango ordered the Los Niños de Guatemala Home to deliver the child to her mother on February 17, 1999 [seven months after the mother first sought the return of her child].[32]

The report also cited the dramatically low rates of adoption from orphanages and within the country, which it suggested pointed to a private network soliciting children, some of them before birth—their mothers then living in homes and clinics until their birth—and then spiriting them out of the country: "Institutions are saturated with children who are not being adopted. It would be worthwhile to further investigate this circumstance since those actually being adopted are, to a large extent, being 'produced' for this end, while those who are truly in need of a family are being condemned to institutionalization until they reach the age of adulthood. It is also necessary to consider that the majority of institutionalized children are awaiting a formal abandonment ruling which can take up to seven years. This fact dramatically reduces their possibilities of being integrated into a family, particularly since most prospective adopters tend to seek children less than one year of age."[33] These reports were reviewed by the Hague Special Commission monitoring compliance with international treaties. The report by that body condemned the process of adoption in Guatemala, saying Guatemala was out of compliance with both the Convention on the Rights of the Child and the Hague Convention on Adoption.[34] In the wake of all these reports, European nations began to systematically shut down avenues for legal adoption from Guatemala.[35] The coordinator of the Catholic Church's social ministry, Guillermo Monroy, together with Elizabeth Gibbons, the coordinator of UNICEF in Guatemala, the Anglican Church, and the attorney general for human rights, among others, held a joint press conference calling for the legislature to shut down adoptions from Guatemala until such time as it could accede to the Hague convention by requiring that adoptions be reviewed by judges, not just notaries. Nineth Montenegro again introduced legislation, and again it failed.[36]

This scenario was repeated, with slight variations, twice more in the next eight years. In 2003 the signatory states to the Hague Convention on

Intercountry Adoption met in Holland and sharply condemned Guatemala's lack of compliance with the convention, although it was nominally a
signatory. In response the Guatemalan legislature passed the Protección
Integral de Niños y Adolescentes (PINA) law, the law for the holistic
protection of children and adolescents, which abolished the notarial system of adoptions, and approved the Hague convention. The Procuraduría
General de la Nación (PGN; the Attorney General's Office) halted adoptions for six months but, as a result of political pressure inside Guatemala,
resumed adoptions without the promised overhaul of the system. The
Constitutional Court, never independent of politics, declared that acces-
sion to the Hague convention violated Guatemala's constitution. This left
Guatemala in the peculiar position of having a state divided over whether
the PINA was in force. Notaries continued to authorize international adoptions, and the U.S. Embassy in Guatemala continued to issue those children IR-3 visas, visas for children with complete adoptions. The solicitor
general for human rights, however, held that the PINA was in force, and so
all notarial adoptions from that point forward were illegal. In 2005 the
Hague Special Commission again met and again considered Guatemala's
relationship to the treaty that it had signed but not enacted. This time
(because history does not repeat itself, except as farce) Guatemala actually
sent a delegation to the meeting, which was, by some reports, embarrassing
for all concerned. In 2006 Holt International—institutionally more closely
aligned with those in Guatemala who had promoted adoption reform than
those who had resisted it—nevertheless issued a report describing a need
to develop alternatives to "child abandonment" and the need to accede to
the Hague Convention on Intercountry Adoption. That same year legislation finally made it illegal to participate in irregular adoptions, criminalizing the selling and buying of children.[37]

Beyond Courts, Legal Reform, or International Human Rights Treaties:
Adoption and Highland Communities

There was also, in a sense, a long-running guerilla war over the adoption and
procuring of children; the lynchings of supposed adopters or jaladoras in
rural communities that had made international headlines in 1994 never
stopped. For example, in the summer of 2007 a string of mob attacks on
Guatemalans and detentions of foreigners suspected of being involved in
kidnapping children for adoptions and organ stealing told a similar story. In
the middle of June, to pick only one of six or seven stories we could tell from

that two-week period, residents of Camotán, Chiquimula, found the muti-
lated body of a nine-year-old girl along the side of the road. The girl, Mishell
España, had been missing since the previous day, when she disappeared
between her family's house and a nearby store. The residents of Camotán
knew her well and had been searching for her, together with residents of
nearby Jocotán, which had also recently lost a child under similar circumstances. When the body was found, residents accused three of their neighbors of the crime, saying that these women were known to be involved in
trafficking children into international adoptions, and the mutilation made it
clear that the purpose was to steal their organs. A mob burned one of the
women to death, a second was disappeared and presumed dead, and a third
was rescued from a beating by the police. Residents then burned a police car
and the police station, saying that the authorities were complicit and that
numerous similar incidents in the past had been ignored. The Policía Nacional denied any knowledge of previous incidents, but the national commission on human rights admitted they had six reports from past years in
Camotán, including the quite specific information that go-betweens were
being paid Q$2,000 for girls and Q$3,000 for boys.

One would like to know a great deal more about what happened to
Mishell. She seems old to be adopted to the United States, as U.S. adopters
mostly came to Guatemala with the hope of adopting infants or younger
children. However, she seems young to be running away or to be spirited
away for prostitution, although none of these scenarios seem impossible.
Above all what is striking about the story is how little anyone beyond
Camotán and Jocatán cared about finding the answers to these questions,
when you compare it to, say, President George W. Bush making phone calls
to the family of the disappeared Elizabeth Smart in Salt Lake City. One
national newspaper in Guatemala ran a couple of articles but lost their
enthusiasm for the subject when one of their reporters was detained by the
mob. Other incidents—in Sayaxche, Petén, and Chicaman, Quiché, a couple of weeks later and Jocotán earlier—received almost no mention at all.
The U.S. Embassy sent out a note to American citizens in Guatemala telling them not to talk to children, spinning the events largely as a potential
threat to U.S. Americans.[38]

Halting Transnational Adoption (Again)

Later that year, a powerful coalition of human rights groups finally brought
the issue of adoption to a head. As we have seen, Fundación Sobreviventes

began their demonstrations with empty baby strollers outside the CNA that riveted the attention of the British (if not the U.S.) press. The Fundación Myrna Mack (Myrna Mack Foundation) joined Sobreviventes in 2007 in producing a report on adoption and the disappearance of children entitled *Adoptions in Guatemala: Protection or Business?* Even if the press could be routinely discredited by adoption's advocates, Helen Mack and her colleagues at the Fundación Myrna Mack have a great deal of credibility in Guatemala and beyond it as serious researchers; Helen Mack's determination that the military would be prosecuted for the murder of her sister, the Guatemalan anthropologist Myrna Mack, resulted not only in the first conviction for all those hundreds of disappearances during the war but also in forcing the military and the state to reveal a great deal about how and why they did what they did. In this effort, Fundación Sobreviventes and Fundación Myrna Mack were joined also by a group with arguably still more gravitas, ODHAG (the Archbishop's Office of Human Rights), author of the REMHI report and among those who prosecuted high-ranking military officers for the murder of Bishop Juan Gerardi. The report was also the work of Casa Alianza, the Social Movement for Children and Adolescents, and the Social Welfare Secretariat.

In it, investigators report on two different kinds of child disappearances —adoption cases and young people who wound up in sex work and pornography—and the 230 cases of kidnapped children reported to the solicitor general of human rights in the first six months of 2007. Carefully footnoted, with detailed case studies, the report offered the imprimatur of social science on silenced or discredited accounts. Here we find stories of a child trafficking ring and jaladoras in Camotán, accounts of women approached when pregnant and vulnerable, in line to visit husbands and boyfriends in prison, or tricked out of their babies in line at the Roosevelt, the public hospital. Here are the women drugged, raped, kidnapped. From Sobreviventes we learn of husbands, boyfriends, and rapists who convince, coerce, or trick a woman into giving up her child. It notes numbers that don't match: the PGN issued more visas for children to leave the country and go to the United States than the United States admitted. The report examined diverse kinds of material—adoption files at the PGN, the case files of these diverse organizations, international press accounts, and its authors conducted interviews with those who alleged nonconsensual adoptions, exploitation, coercion, or kidnapping who could be located and had not been interviewed previously by these groups—the classic methodology of human rights groups in Guatemala during the war. Then it aggregated the cases to produce a *social*, rather than an individualized, account of how child trafficking was occurring: the kinds of isolation (geographical, linguistic, and familial) that make women vulnerable to losing their children and children vulnerable to being lost. Like the UN report in 2000 and the press accounts, it is an effort to make fact out of subalternized narratives, to bring the disenfranchised onto a world stage.[39] In 2007 another UN report, the *Report of a Fact-Finding Mission to Guatemala in Relation to Intercountry Adoption*, began by noting that most of what could be said about adoption in Guatemala in 2007 had been said in the ILPEC report in 2000.[40] In 2007–8, again with great fanfare, Guatemala promised to halt all adoptions (as of December 31, 2008) and come into compliance with the Hague Convention on Intercountry Adoption.

History of a Silence

In 2007 guatadopt.com, one of the primary U.S. discussion boards for those adopting from Guatemala, commented on the Fundación Myrna Mack report in the following way:

> A new report has been released by a group consisting of Casa Alianza, Bienestar, the Myrna Mack Foundation, and the Human Rights Office of the Archdiocese. I've been unable to find a copy of the actual report anywhere. Based on media reports, it basically states that adoptions are a huge organized crime syndicate. Media sensationalizes things, so I don't want to attack the report without reading, though there are obviously some of the usual suspects involved. Nonetheless, Myrna Mack and the Archdiocese are not commonly involved in the adoption debate. The newspaper *La Hora* seems to be on an anti-adoption rampage. They have run a number of stories, some of which cover truly atrocious things done to mothers and children. However, I don't see any of these showing that these children were to be adopted. It would make sense, but when a child is stolen and no DNA is ever taken, it seems tough to say the kids were joining families in the US, where almost all children go. So, these cases could be old and before the 2nd DNA [mandated by the U.S. embassy in August 2007]. If so, I am at a loss for what to do other than be thankful for that second test and to reiterate—what took so long in instituting one? Or these children could go through abandonment proceedings. If that's the case, then the children are in the courts and someone in law enforcement—find

them and throw the perpetrators behind bars! ADA has issued a new statement on their website about all of this, primarily the report mentioned above. It is very strongly worded and full of the passion we know and love of Susana [Luarca de Umaña]. So while I personally have a hard time with some of it, the ADA's voice is one always worth having.

This post is among the more moderate and concerned of the discussions by adoptive parents from Guatemala. Yet for all its gestures at evenhandedness, there is a verbal shrug over the extensive and detailed reports of kidnappings of children and murders of their mothers in the Fundación Myrna Mack report, the belief that Guatemalan adoption attorney Susana Luarca de Umaña is a better source than either local newspapers or international human rights groups, the belief that DNA tests are not falsified. The wholesale denial of what "the usual suspects" are saying echoes unnervingly close to what the U.S. State Department and the Reagan administration said about human rights reporters' insistence that two hundred thousand indigenous people were massacred in the highlands in the early 1980s: Reagan's assertion that Ríos Montt was getting a "bum rap."[41]

This post followed a well-worn groove among U.S.-based online discussion groups for parents of children adopted from Guatemala. For a decade, they had suggested that the critics of adoption were lying and that groups like Casa Alianza and UNICEF were just NGOs trying to justify their salaries and raise money for their organizations, with the press and international UN-affiliated groups their willing dupes. For example, a posting to the guatadopt.com website in October 17, 2004, argued: "As seems to be a near annual event, UNICEF has once again called for the government of Guatemala to place a moratorium on adoptions. Last year this was via the Procurador de Derechos Humanos [Attorney General of Human Rights] when he falsely claimed that PGN had approved 1,500 adoptions in 10 days. . . . For the most part, the content seemed to be more of the sensationalized claims that have become commonplace for UNICEF. [Critiques of] these claims are all well documented and quite frankly not worth repeating."[42] Since the source is UNICEF, the criticisms of adoption being raised by human rights activists in Guatemala are "not worth repeating." Possibly the only context in the United States where UNICEF—bringer of Christmas cards and images of adorable children—could be controversial was at a conference in 2007 on Ethics and Adoption in the United States, where an organizer admitted that bringing someone from UNICEF in Guatemala was potentially quite explosive.[43] Guatadopt.com offered members a flyer to distribute for UNICEF's annual Halloween collection, trick-or-treat for UNICEF, complete with jack-o-lantern and black cat graphics. It reads: "UNICEF is known to be the world's most respected child aid organization. In reality, this is not so. As you read this, UNICEF is actively working to end international adoptions from Guatemala, leaving thousands of innocent children a year with no chance for a decent life. UNICEF endorses legislation that severely restricts a woman's right to choose an adoption plan for her child as well as her right to privacy. Unfortunately, UNICEF offers little advice on how countries like Guatemala should care for the children who would otherwise live secure lives with a loving family."[44] They argue that the truth is closer to the following, posted to Guatemala.adop tionblogs.com in response to critical news coverage in 2007: "Adoptions from Guatemala have been going on for over twenty-five years, coming into existence during the brutal Civil War (1960–1996) when so many children were orphaned. There was little hope for these destitute children and adoption was a viable option in a country that had nothing in place to accommodate these homeless children."[45] The children were orphans, in this view, and there is no adoption system in Guatemala, which requires that they be sent to the United States.

The truth commission report about the armed internal conflict in Guatemala was titled *Memoría del silencio* (Memory of the silence). How was the silence around allegations of children being illegitimately whisked into adoptions produced? The audience that had to be persuaded that adoptions were legitimate and free of coercion was not just Guatemalan but transnational. As we have seen, this silencing on the whole failed in Europe, which largely shut down transnational adoption from Guatemala as corrupt and exploitative. However, it mostly succeeded in the United States, where until 2007 accounts of illegitimate adoptions were answered by organized parents' groups (these sites also organized opposition to what they considered erroneous or uninformed press accounts). The Guatemalan ADA and Susana Luarca de Umaña in particular were vigorous in informing and organizing this opposition, but these seeds fell on fertile ground. I am curious about the suppression of narratives of what opponents called child trafficking, and how this was produced.

Francisco Goldman writes of the "suffocating atmosphere of paranoia" in wartime Guatemala[46] (incidently, he documented the disappearance and subsequent adoption of children, albeit novelistically, in his *Long Night of the White Chickens*). Paranoia made every claim to truth instantly subject to hypervigilant scrutiny. A symptom of this, albeit one with a particularly U.S. twist, was the David Stoll and Rigoberta Menchú controversy. In 1992 Rigoberta Menchú, a Maya-K'ichee' woman, won the Nobel Peace Prize for her account of the civil war in *Me llama Rigoberta Menchú y así me nació la consciencia* (*I, Rigoberta Menchú* in its English version). Without going into a controversy that has been discussed at great length elsewhere, suffice it to say that claims about violence and exploitation in wartime Guatemala were subject to formidable critique in the United States. The urge to discredit claims against the military or the government spilled out of Guatemala as claims about individuals, their character, and their personal stories, and into the international context—even after the publication of the REMHI and CEH reports underscored the incredible scale of murder by military and paramilitary forces.

Noting the barrage of accusations that were launched against Menchú is relevant to trying to understand adoption from Guatemala. Two of the leading critics of the adoption system in Guatemala that have gotten some notice on a world stage—UNICEF in general and Bruce Harris of Casa Alianza in particular—have also been the object of vigorous campaigns to discredit them, both in Guatemala and internationally. Just as with Menchú, the context has been attacks on the messengers rather than engagement in a substantive refutation of their arguments.

Although the only charges that have been arrayed against UNICEF—that their information is inaccurate and that as an NGO their staff is receiving salaries, which means they "profit" individually from the controversy—are vague and nonspecific, the charges against Bruce Harris were very specific and effective. In 1997, as we have seen, Harris denounced Susana Luarca de Umaña by name in a press conference for being part of a network of lawyers and judges who were hastening children into adoptions illegitimately. This was a fateful decision. De Umaña answered him in the press: "This is a desperate way to get into the limelight, but adoption processes have been transparent. The only thing the Association [for Children, her adoption group] has done is to ensure the well-being of children. If there are more adoptions overseas, it is because there are not people in [Guatemala] that want to adopt them." Then she filed a legal complaint against him for libel.[47] Although she lost the case, it was an enmity that would have ongoing, serious consequences.

In 2008, his biographical entry in Wikipedia began, "Bruce Harris is the disgraced former executive director of Casa Alianza . . ." Harris ran shelters for street children in Central America for fifteen years and was vocal and vigorous in his denunciation of their abuse by police and what he believed was the disappearance of children into adoptions. That is, until 2004, when he was accused of attempting to buy sex from a young man—either eighteen years old or twenty-one, the reports varied—in a park one night in Honduras. The imputation that Harris was homosexual, and hence presumptively a child abuser, got him dismissed from his post as executive director of Casa Alianza and widely excoriated by the Christian Right in the United States and Guatemala.[48] It didn't help Harris that the man in question had, as a child, spent time in a Casa Alianza shelter in Honduras. In the United States the pro-Guatemalan adoption community posted things like, "You would think that since Bruce Harris has been exposed for the lech [sic] he is, and that since much of UNICEF's 'information' seems to come through him, they might question his motives and this 'truth.'" In Guatemala the ADA and others involved in adoptions have added their voices to his denunciation. Still, those concerned about intercountry adoption note that during and even after the war, military intelligence had a unit devoted to discrediting people by generating allegations of sexual impropriety. For example, when Bishop Juan Gerardi was murdered in 1998, he too was accused of being homosexual, and there was an effort to pin his murder on a lover rather than the military.[49]

Others point to previous efforts in Guatemala to silence critics of adoption. For example, according to human rights groups and even the U.S. State Department, a Universidad de San Carlos professor and the founder of gender studies there, Mayra Gutierrez, disappeared in April 2000, and her family believed it was because she had met with Ofelia Calcetas-Santos as part of the preparation of the report published in 2000.[50] In 1989 the offices of Casa Alianza were sprayed with machine gun fire after Harris brought charges against the police for the murder of a thirteen-year-old street child; in 1997 there were the libel charges against him by de Umaña, of which he was exonerated in 2004, and the offices of Casa Alianza in Guatemala were repeatedly broken into; Harris received death threats, forcing him to live outside of Guatemala.[51] There is no doubt that Susana Luarca de Umaña considered Harris a serious enemy; in addition to her pursuit of him in court, she—and through her U.S. adoptive parents, as represented on their websites—considered him the source of all the negative international reports, a one-man disinformation campaign who had somehow persuaded the rest of the world, unfairly, that there were irregularities in transnational adoption. When I was in Guatemala in 2005 I attempted to interview de Umaña and had an odd conversation with her, veering toward paranoia. When I introduced myself as a scholar doing research on Guatemala, her first question, reasonably enough, was how I had gotten her number. I said I had gotten it from Hector Dionisio, the attorney at Casa Alianza. I admitted that I had spoken with him but said I wanted to understand "both sides" of the debate over adoption. "If you think there are two sides to adoption then you are against it." I assured her that this wasn't true and added that I didn't see how one could read the newspapers in Guatemala and not get the idea that there were those who supported and those who opposed international adoption. "You are a lying journalist, and you are trying to trick me, but I won't let you!" she said, and hung up the phone. (At the time of this writing, in 2010, de Umaña is under house arrest in Guatemala for her role in adoption fraud.)[52]

Post–Cold War Alternatives: Adoption Reform

Guatemala was anomalous in Latin America in its postwar treatment of adoption. While many Latin American nations had significant adoption programs during the Cold War, the post–Cold War years saw political organizing to curb or even end transnational adoptions in most of the region. These were couched as human rights discourses (most significantly in the Convention on the Rights of the Child and then the Hague Convention on Intercountry Adoption) or efforts to address criminality or trafficking or both. In 2002, for example, Juan Díaz González, a commissioner of the Mexico City legislative assembly, had proposed a reform of police procedures to address child disappearances, saying "This is a very serious problem because beyond the [child] theft, we are also dealing with issues related to the child pornography network, the trafficking of organs and the sale of children into illegal adoptions."[53] He warned readers and officials that twenty thousand children disappear each year from Mexico City. Although his numbers may be hard to verify, Díaz González's statements were part of an extensive public discourse throughout Latin America about child kidnapping, illegal adoption, sexual exploitation, and traffic in children's organs.

Through the 1980s, as we have seen, Latin America was the major region (aside from Korea) sending children into international adoptions. By the 1990s it was eclipsed by China, Romania, and the nations of the former Soviet Union. Of the ten leading nations sending children overseas into adoptions between 1980 and 1989, six (Colombia, Brazil, Chile, Guatemala,

Peru, and El Salvador) were in Latin America. By 2004 only Guatemala and Colombia were part of the ten leading nations.[54] What happened in Latin America in the 1990s that transformed it from a leading region in transnational adoption to a small player? In nation after nation there were scandals about selling babies into international adoption, involving allegations about the exchange of considerable amounts of money and weak or nonexistent consent by the birth parents.

Brazil

In the 1980s Brazil was the fourth-largest supplier of children for international adoption, offering approximately two thousand children in 1989. Nancy Scheper-Hughes documented illegal adoption practices there. "In the shantytowns of Brazil I encountered several cases of coerced adoption and (in 1990 alone) two cases of child stealing by wealthy 'patrons,'" she writes, one of whom was a boss who requested the presence of a worker's child overnight "for [her] amusement." When the child failed to return, the *patrón* told the parents that the child had been adopted by an American couple and told them that they were being "selfish" and denying the child an opportunity for a better life in the United States. In the context of this kind of pressure, threats, and the omnipresent reality of paramilitary murder of shantytown residents who cause too much trouble, the parents let the matter drop, although years later, Scheper-Hughes noted, they still grieved. At the other end of the adoption business, in 1989 Scheper-Hughes spoke to staff at an "orphanage" run by American missionaries. She writes: "When I asked, directly, about the Brazilian 'traffic in babies,' the director admitted that aspects of the adoption process were murky. Sometimes, she had to fight with mothers to release their children. Some birth mothers resisted signing the adoption papers even when they know it would be best for their child."[55] Why, exactly, adoption was "best" for their child is left unstated, as if it were simply a given that any working-class, shantytown resident parents in Brazil were intrinsically worse than middle-class or wealthy parents in the United States, Europe, Israel, or Australia.

In 2000, however, the number of infants and children leaving Brazil for international adoption had been reduced to a trickle. As the anthropologist Claudia Fonseca has pointed out, with only four hundred children adopted transnationally a year by 2003, Brazil was no longer even among the top twenty sending countries.[56] In 1988 the Brazilian Congress had commissioned a parliamentary inquest into allegations of trafficking in children. In

1990 Brazil adopted a new children's code that ratified and enabled the
International Convention on the Rights of the Child, expressly preferring
intracountry adoption to transnational adoption. Another significant event
was the emergence of a new activism by mothers of children lost into
adoptions. In 1998 low-income mothers from the city of Jundiaí, in the state
of São Paulo—compared in the press to the Madres de Plaza de Mayo—
began regular vigils outside the courthouse, protesting the loss of their
children to international adoptions. Investigation found that in the previous six years, one judge, working with an Italian agency, had sent more
than two hundred children into intercountry adoptions, usually after a
summary judgment that declared the child abandoned. Journalists reported on the conditions that, in the judge's mind, had justified finding the
child an Italian home; one had a mother who worked as a stripper; another
lived in a home "with broken windows and roaming dogs."[57] Impoverished
single mothers, this movement charged, were losing their children in ways
that amounted to little more than judicial or extrajudicial kidnapping.

If the hallmark of Brazil under the military dictatorship was creating
order among the poor—to the extent that, as Nancy Scheper-Hughes argues, the military would roam the *favelas* and murder those believed to be
juvenile delinquents—democratic Brazil understood itself as more sympathetic to impoverished women and children. The scandal of the mothers of
Jundiaí whose children had been "abducted" by an unjust state, expressly
compared to the disappeared of Argentina during the Dirty War, put an
end to adoption in the last state in Brazil that was still doing them in any
significant numbers. While organ theft rumors may have prompted a reex-
amination of international adoption practices (particularly in 1987–88 and
1993–94, when these rumors seemed to emerge with particular vehemence
up and down Latin America), there were also much more quotidian questions of whether it was the exploitation of impoverished mothers that
provoked real struggles.[58]

Mexico

In the Mexican state of Jalisco a similar scandal unfolded in 2000. The
Consejo Estatal de la Familia, a state agency, was found to be transferring
children very quickly to waiting adoptive parents in Spain in what their
mothers thought amounted to legal kidnapping. Children were being taken
from their families without a hearing and transferred to orphanages far
away; there, officials were obtaining new birth certificates for these chil-

dren without their family names and placing them through an Andalusian adoption agency. When officials were caught, they defended themselves on moral grounds, arguing that these were street children left unsupervised all day by impoverished and lax single mothers. Europeans would take these older, difficult children, officials argued, and they would never have a decent life in Mexico. Yet some of these children's mothers were very involved in their lives and tried to stop the process, but apparently they remained invisible to social workers and officials *as* mothers.[59]

Not all children whose adoptions raised eyebrows were sent across borders legally, of course. Throughout this period, northern Mexico and the Southwestern United States continued one of their centuries-long relationships: using the differences that borders produce in value and jurisdiction to create smuggling opportunities. In October 1998, Mexican newspapers began to report on an illegal adoption network operating along the Mexican-U.S. border, for the most part through the contiguous cities of Agua Prieta, Sonora, and Douglas, Arizona.[60] The U.S. Immigration and Naturalization Service (INS) investigated the allegations, and in March 1999 a woman named Margarita Soto was arrested crossing the border into Douglas, transporting an unrelated child whom she claimed was hers. Soto worked for a lawyer named Mario Reyes, who practiced on the Agua Prieta side of the border but lived in Douglas. He was arrested shortly thereafter. He was probably lucky to be arrested and tried by U.S. authorities rather than Mexican ones, who accused him of smuggling five hundred unlawfully obtained children and angrily demanded his extradition.[61] Two Long Island women, Arlene Lieberman and Arlene Reingold, were held on similar charges for their roles in acting as go-betweens with New York families and Reyes.[62] The INS assured the Long Island families from the very beginning of the investigation that they would be able to keep "their" children,[63] and they seemingly made no effort to locate the birth parents of illegally adopted children, even refusing to allow a group in Mexico dedicated to finding kidnapped children to obtain photos of the Long Island adoptees.[64]

The INS charged Reyes with mail and wire fraud and illegally transporting seventeen children and placing them with U.S. adoptive families. Reyes had apparently sought out desperate mothers in the burgeoning *colonias* around Agua Prieta, people who had come looking for work in the *maquiladoras* but found only a poverty grown more painful because they had moved far from friends and family. He had persuaded a few to relinquish their children for a few hundred pesos for food for their other children and grandiose promises, never kept, of building them decent homes.[65]

In thirteen other high-profile legal cases between 1979 and 2000 people were prosecuted for unlawfully bringing a child from Mexico to the United States, all apparently into adoptions.[66] But the best description of the scope of child smuggling from Mexico to the United States, at least as those of us who have lived near that border understand it, is a comment from a U.S. customs official describing what his staff noticed in the one hundred thousand cars a day that pass through his port of entry, only a small number of which are detained. "We've been encountering two or three minors a day," said Roger Morin, the port director in Eagle Pass, Arizona. "We're talking about situations where maybe the husband is already in the United States illegally and maybe the wife and children are trying to reunite with him, and of course they don't want to cross the river [with the child] because it is dangerous," he said.[67] Those of us who have walked the migrant trails in Arizona know that among the piles of trash left by people making the perilous journey across the desert, there are always baby strollers. Most of these children are crossing into the United States with the goal of being reunited with parents or other relatives. But the extensive, daily movement of children from Mexico to the United States makes it very easy to engage in less innocent, more commercialized traffic in children, and it shows how fundamentally absurd it is to imagine that there is no clandestine traffic in children for illegal adoption.

Compared to places like Guatemala, El Salvador, or even Brazil, Mexico was clearly less affected by the Cold War, and the struggle for a democratic opening was likewise less dramatic. But the Mexican state, which had struggled for legitimacy continuously after the shooting by the army of hundreds of protesting students at Tlatelolco in 1968 and the disappearance of many, many others in its "dirty war,"[68] faced sharp crises of legitimacy in the 1980s and 1990s. The government's slow response to the earthquake in Mexico City in 1985, particularly in impoverished neighborhoods, renewed calls for political reform and accountability. In 1988 activists and the press charged that Carlos Salinas of the ruling Partido Revolucionario Institucional (PRI; Institutional Revolutionary Party) had stolen the election from Cuahtémoc Cardenas of the leftist party, who had been the projected winner until the computer counting the ballots crashed. A symptom of the burgeoning popular resistance to the status quo of the *priístas* was the translation on the street: *se cayó el sistema* (the system crashed) became a synonym for political fraud. In 1994 the southern state of Chiapas saw the Zapatista uprising, begun to correspond with the effective date of NAFTA and opening both a military and a political battle against neoliberalism.

The years 1994 and 1995 also marked a kind of scuffle in the streets in urban areas like Mexico City over wealth and poverty issues. The collapse of the peso and an abrupt recession (the sort that are the hallmark of neoliberalism, according to economists like Joseph Stiglitz[69]) resulted in a sharp rise in crime and an effort to "crack down" on the poor.

At the same time the Salinas government that had negotiated NAFTA was also linked to a number of high-level political murders, including, some said, Salinas's own heir apparent, Luis Donaldo Coloso, the PRI's candidate for president in 1994—perhaps because he was behind in the polls, perhaps because Coloso was too much the populist and an advocate of democratic renewal at a time when Salinas's legacy was threatened by the ways the Zapatista uprising had caught the imagination and hopes of the Mexican people. A few months later Salinas's brother was arrested for the murder of José Francisco Ruiz, the secretary general of the PRI (it helps to remember that from 1929 to 2004 the PRI was the sole ruling party in Mexico, so there was at least as much political intrigue and bad blood within the party as there was between it and any others). Whatever the truth of the matter, the allegations against the Salinas brothers represented—and further stirred— a substantial political shift away from the presumption of impunity for PRI leaders. According to *Newsweek*, Ernesto Zedilla, the man who succeeded Coloso as the PRI candidate and Salinas as president, told Carlos Salinas, "From now on, neither you nor I nor anyone else in this country will be above the law again."[70] While that may have been altogether too optimistic, it nevertheless signaled the sense at that moment that something powerful had shifted.

Transnational adoption rates declined alongside the palatability of political impunity, in the moment of Mexico's version of the post–Cold War democratic opening. In the 1980s Mexico was eleventh in the world in sending children to other countries for adoption, with about 1,500 over the course of the decade.[71] In the 1990s there was tremendous alarm in the press about the possibility that children were being kidnapped and sold for their organs; activists charged that there were private clinics in Ciudad Juarez providing organ transplants for wealthy clients from all over the Americas from the bodies of missing and murdered street children. At the same time, there were also calls to require children adopted transnationally to be presented at the Mexican Embassy each year so they could be monitored.[72] Perhaps in part as a result of this suspicion of the grisly exploitation of children, Mexico quickly adopted international treaties that regulated private adoption and enacted a preference for in-country over international adoption. By 2002 Mexico had all but halted intercountry adoption: according to Sistema Nacional para el Desarollo Integral de la Familia (DIF; National System for Integral Family Development, the state agency regulating child welfare matters) there were fifty-five international adoptions from Mexico that year.[73]

Peru

In the 1980s Peru ranked ninth in the world in the number of intercountry adoptions, with about 2,200.[74] By 2003 the flow of children from Peru had been reduced to a trickle.[75] The number of children adopted in the United States from Peru continued to climb from 1990 to 1991, began to drop in 1992 and 1993, and finally plummeted in 1994 and 1995, dropping off the top-twenty list.[76] Until 2000 the numbers of children being sent to Spain and Italy continued to grow slightly, although the total number of children being adopted from Peru by all countries never matched the high of 1991.[77]

In the early 1990s, in Peru as elsewhere, there was a significant public outcry against the trafficking of children and the suspicion of the involvement of government officials, particularly judges and lawyers. Like the rest of Latin America (and some of Europe), the outcry in Peru was fueled by fears of organ theft, rendered in the Andean idiom of *pishtacos* (fat stealers) and *sacaojos* (eye stealers), mixed with concerns, perhaps well-founded, of child theft and kidnapping.[78] In 1991 the Peruvian legislature conducted an investigation into illegal adoptions and found considerable irregularities. In the eighteen months from January 1990 to July 1991, there were 126 adoptions in the central region of Junin. Of this number, 117 were adopted by people from outside the country in a process that took an average of a month; nine were adopted by Peruvians in a process that took an average of a year. Of the adoptions by foreigners, the legislators found that 57 of the adoptions were not valid for various reasons; either the adults relinquishing the children were not their parents or the biological parents were not notified of the hearing. A judge, Adelaida Bolivar, in a separate report, found 310 irregular adoptions in 1991 in the town of Huaral alone, out of a population of only 50,000.[79] The arrest of a U.S. lawyer—James Gagel (who was later acquitted)—in 1992 intensified the pressure by the Peruvian population for the government to do something about what was perceived as the "sale" of their children.[80]

In contrast to Mexico and Brazil, Peru at the end of the twentieth century was still very much governed by the Right. Sendero Luminoso, a small but profoundly violent Maoist guerilla group that probably never enjoyed much popular support, continued its campaign of random bomb-ings throughout the 1990s, perversely ratcheting up support for an anti-Communist Right, which stayed in power until the turn of the millennium. On April 5, 1992, with the help of the military, Alberto Fujimori engineered what was called an *autogolpe* (self-coup) or even the *fujigolpe*, keeping himself in power but suspending civilian rule. At first adoptions were slowed as a side-effect of the autogolpe: when Fujimori removed judges who did not belong to his party, it snarled the courts. Later, though, reforming adoption became an explicit goal. It is a measure of how impor-tant human rights discourses about children had become, even in Peru. While by all accounts Fujimori continued to use the Cold War tactics of the Latin American Right—disappearances, death squads, and paramilitaries— his administration cracked down on international adoption. Enabling legislation was quickly passed in response to the Hague Convention on Intercountry Adoption of 1993, and Peru enacted a legal preference for in-country adoption over the next decade.[81]

In each of these nations, then, cries were raised about organ theft and selling the nation's future, and international adoption was recast from humanitarian child saving to a national embarrassment. In broad strokes, the story was the same in most Latin American nations, with individual variations, nation after nation in Central and South America that had developed a large international adoption program in the 1980s saw it shrink in the 1990s—with the exception of Guatemala. In a handful of years following the elaboration of the Convention on the Rights of the Child in 1989 and the Hague Convention on Adoption in 1993, Paraguay, Colombia, Peru, Brazil, Mexico, Costa Rica, and El Salvador made "private" adoption illegal, meaning that would-be adopters had to work with a state agency within the country, rather than merely arrange an informal agreement between parties, and had to appear before a judge. What had long been a small matter of family law, requiring little attention from judges or the state, had become a question of significant international commerce, popu-lar nationalism, fear, and exploitation. The Hague Convention on Inter-country Adoption provided a renewed international legal framework that established a preference for in-country adoption. It required that the birth family be shown to be unable to care for the child, not just impoverished relative to potential adoptive parents; that consent for relinquishment be freely and irrevocably given; that the relationship of those claiming to be the relinquishing parents to the child be clearly demonstrated, preferably through DNA testing; and that both sending and receiving countries have a central authority that regulates international adoption. Human rights activists also tried to put some brakes on unregulated adoption intermediaries, although U.S. negotiators in the Hague process ensured that some "private" adoption would be allowed to continue.[82] For most Latin American countries in the late 1980s and early 1990s, transnational adoption came to stand for all the ills of neoliberal globalization and the ugly civil wars that preceded it.

Of States and Markets: The Post-Reform Era

The kinds of exploitation of mothers and children that seemed to be taking place in Guatemala and elsewhere in Latin America certainly suggested to many people that some kind of legal and human rights protections might be desirable. They demanded the intervention of states, international human rights treaties, improved policing, and careful consumerism by would-be adopters. One of the hallmarks of these reforms was a preference for strong state bureaucracies dealing with child welfare, vigorous judicial processes, and a preference for in-country rather than transnational adoption.

Yet it is not altogether clear that strong state involvement in adoption necessarily produces different or better outcomes for impoverished mothers. After all, the analysis of the mothers of Jundiaí insisted that the state is *not* an impartial guarantor of fairness and an end to exploitation but rather, in this context, is implicated in what they called "legal child trafficking."[83] From this perspective the fight over adoption in Latin America inaugurated by human rights discourses could be said to be about whether children should be adopted within the country or outside of it, whether they were a national treasure or in need of international aid—but not whether impoverished mothers (or fathers) ought to be able to raise them. The anthropologist Barbara Yngvesson takes up this question in relationship to Sweden and argues that human rights treaties themselves contribute to the commodification of children. One of the things that makes children adoptable, she suggests, or free to be trafficked, is that the treaties themselves require states to create mechanisms through which children can be legally estranged from their birth parents through the judicial system, so new birth certificates can be issued and new parents assigned, whether this is accomplished internationally or within a nation.[84]

One of the significant ramifications for the reproductive rights of impoverished women, their ability to raise (or not raise) their children as they saw fit, of the shift from a less to a more formalized adoption bureaucracy run through the states and the courts, was to disrupt the ordinary, informal circulation of children as an economic survival strategy. (Gay families, too, often organized just outside legal forms—not married, often with only one or neither member of the conjugal couple the legal parent of children they raise—find themselves vulnerable in these regimes, as will be discussed further in chapter 7.) As Claudia Fonseca has argued for Brazil, and Jessaca Leinaweaver has pointed out for Peru, in most times and places the usual practice of adoption was and is to leave a child with another adult, perhaps temporarily, perhaps more permanently, without involving the courts.[85] The increasing bureaucratization of adoption, they suggest, is resulting in hardships for families raising unrelated children, even within Latin America, that sometimes actually criminalize informal adoption practices. (In Guatemala, in 2000, the military threatened that those who do not carry their children's birth certificates could be arrested as child traffickers—even though estimates are that as many as 18 percent of children don't even have them.[86]) People trying to cross international borders with an informally adopted child can also be arrested for trafficking.

For example, in the early 1990s, a woman named María de la Luz Guerrero Gómez was living in Mexico City and working as a street vendor; she had eight children. She sold various things on the street and came to know another woman in the neighborhood, Paula Cruz Santiago, who said she was desperate because her husband often did not have work. Paula had a newborn baby. Although working as a street vendor with eight children must have kept them on the bare edge of survival, María de la Luz tried to help out; sometimes she gave Cruz things to sell. They got to know each other fairly well, and one day six months later Cruz brought the baby, named Marcos, to de la Luz, frightened, saying that the baby was sick, had a high fever, and there was no money for a doctor or medicines. De la Luz took Marcos to the clinic, got his medicines, and waited for Cruz to reappear. She ran into her almost by accident three days later, and Cruz asked de la Luz to keep the baby, which she did, eventually moving to Tijuana with him. One day several years later, for reasons we do not know, the police in Tijuana knocked on her door and accused her of stealing the child. When she could produce no birth certificate or any legal guardianship agreement, the police put her in jail, tortured her, and took all nine of her children.[87]

This sort of routine policing and harassment of working-class people, while in many ways nothing new, is also a face of the heightened role of policing in the post–Cold War neoliberal state, particularly in Mexico where in the aftermath of the economic crisis of 1994–95 a crime wave swept Mexico City. As NAFTA went into effect, jobs disappeared overnight, the mortality rate of children under five doubled,[88] some Mexican businessmen like Carlos Slim became billionaires, and crime became a way that poor people slowed the abrupt upward redistribution of wealth. In 2003 Mexico City hired Rudolph Giuliani, former mayor of New York City, to help design more effective policing. While his consultancy arguably did little to halt crime in Mexico City, it did very effectively criminalize the work and maternity of street vendors like Maria de la Luz.[89]

At the same time that there is more policing *of* impoverished families, there is less policing *for* the poor, of the sort that might protect families from losing their children to kidnapping or disappearances. Officials suggest that the popular classes are excitable and ignorant, that children don't just disappear. The Fundación Internacional de Niños Robados y Desaparecidos of Mexico City, which has grown into a very successful search group, was founded by two mothers who were both told by the police that they were crazy and hysterical, that their daughters could not possibly have been kidnapped because that sort of thing does not happen.[90] Working-class women in Latin America offer different stories. Children do just disappear. If a mother leaves small children alone all day in order to put food on the table, she hopes that they are all still there when she returns. Children die of malnutrition and treatable illness or run away to the streets and are never heard from again. The state takes them away for no reason at all.[91] But from the dirty wars to the commercialized movement of children into adoptions, there is the production of a silence about the reality of these disappearances.

The United States: The Stories We Tell

How do people in the United States manage the contradictions of the prominence of child trafficking stories in the international press when the dominant narrative within the United States is that children are being rescued from the Third World? An article in *Newsweek* from July 2002 suggests a complicated story. It begins with Kathleen and Richard Borz, who adopted a child, Fabiola—whom they renamed Holly—from Guatemala, even after her birth mother told U.S. Embassy officials that she had been paid to relinquish her child and had understood that she could expect to see Fabiola monthly. The *Newsweek* article charged that Susana Luarca de Umaña paid working-class families to relinquish and that both embassy officials and the Borzs understood that fact. Not only did they keep Fabiola, but the Borzs mounted a campaign with their congressman to adopt her brother as well. After two years, they did succeed in adopting "Holly's" brother, as well as seven-year-old "Rico," when a Guatemalan judge found that his mother neglected and abused Rico, charges she disputed. The judge found the maternal grandmother an unsuitable parent because she is a lesbian, and a maternal aunt was rejected because, it was said, her husband had hit the child. Apparently no one inquired after the biological father. When he resurfaced, Bruce Harris and Casa Alianza charged that the child's "abandonment" order was improper, but no judge would agree to rehear the case. Furthermore, the birth father told *Newsweek* that he was attacked on a bus by two machete-wielding men who told him to stop trying to reclaim his child.[92]

While the *Newsweek* article casts the adoptive parents as beleaguered innocents, duped consumers in a globalized marketplace, it also raises sharp questions about transnational adoption.

> With dad proudly watching and the coach shouting his name, "Rico! Rico!" a scrawny 12-year-old crouches into position at second base. . . . With his team up 8–0, Rico glances over to the first-base line. Dad smiles. What could be more perfect than a father and son at a Little League game in the Pittsburgh suburbs? Every few months, however, the bliss is shattered when yet another reporter calls wanting to know if it is true: was Rico stolen? Kathleen and Richard Borz, Rico's parents, almost always refuse to comment and hang up the phone. Like the growing number of Americans who go overseas to fulfill their dreams of parenthood, they believe that adoption—especially from an impoverished country—is inherently a good thing for the child.

The article tells the story of the couple's loss of a child to a neurological illness, Rico's good grades, and some difficult behavior problems like hoarding food. It quotes Henry Hyde, the very conservative representative from North Carolina, well known for his opposition to abortion and one of the people, many suggested, most responsible for U.S. military support for right-wing governments in Central America,[93] as saying, "there is nothing to be gained by forcing innocent babies to spend the rest of their childhood in orphanages instead of with loving parents in the United States." Yet the article suggests something rather different, telling the story of his father's effort to get him back, and suggesting that his single, impoverished mother, Flor, might be as much a victim of tough economic circumstances as a bad mother. It relates how she "earned less than $50 a month handing out food samples in grocery stores. Home was a one-room cardboard-and-corrugated-tin shack. Rico attended school sporadically. Flor had little choice but to leave him in charge of his baby half brother, Jeffrey." While less than a confident account that he should have stayed with her, the *Newsweek* article refuses any simple stories about Latin American orphans and their North American rescuers.

A second, even more interesting account emerges from another adoption narrative, from one of the U.S. families in the Mario Reyes and Long Island cases. David Kruchkow tells part of this story in his *When You Wish Upon a Star*, which he published on the Internet as a resource to other families. Kruchkow emerges with a sharp critique of international adoption, charging that international adoption agencies are profiteers and that the U.S. State Department is not particularly interested in investigating potential illegalities. His narrative is ultimately both compassionate about the hard choices made by birth parents and angry that his adoptive child will not have any future opportunity to have contact with hers.

He began, as many U.S. adopters do, with a desire to do good and a much more acute sense of the domestic politics of race than of the controversies over U.S. adoption of Third World children. He wrote: "Neither of us wanted to deal with the social issues of being white parents of an adopted black child, so we looked in the direction of Eastern Europe and Latin America. . . . Sara felt she would be comfortable parenting a Latin American child as she has a dark enough complexion to pass as Hispanic. My degree in Anthropology focused on the peoples, cultures, and prehistory of the Western Hemisphere, so I had no objections and felt that I could help our child stay connected with its culture and heritage."[94] It didn't turn out to be that easy. After a referral from a local adoption facilitator, he and Sara poured tens of thousands of dollars into an attempt to adopt and ultimately went to Mexico where they took custody of an undocumented child. They essentially smuggled her across the border and wandered unwittingly into an international controversy. The Kruchkows subsequently became quite intimately acquainted with the politics of international adoption, when they, along with sixteen other Long Island families, became the focus of an INS investigation of an illegal adoption operation between Mexico and the

United States—and Kruchkow suggests, though the allegations were not investigated, several other Latin American countries as well.[95]

What happens to people's sense of family when there is a compound story about the child's origins—that she or he might be authentically Mexican as well as American or even instead of American? In the Long Island cases there were at least two responses: those that insisted ever more strongly that the children were "really" American and theirs, and those, like Kruchkow, that negotiated more interesting and hybrid answers. As mentioned above, the INS was not interested in returning children to their birth families, making it clear that the Long Island families could keep "their" children.[96] On the other hand, one Long Island family, the Libertos, returned their adoptive child, nine-year-old Flor Azucena, to the birth mother the child missed fiercely even before the illegalities of the adoption ring were revealed. The Libertos told the *New York Times* that they decided to return their child to her family because Mrs. Liberto understood, firsthand, how painful it could be to be "rescued" from one's working-class family: "Mrs. Liberto cried when she was asked why she agreed to let Flor Azucena go. The decision, she said, arose from memories of growing up poor and being sent every year to a summer camp in Pennsylvania. It was the most beautiful place she had ever seen, Mrs. Liberto said. But after a few days, she recalled, she was crying and pleading to go home. 'A family bond is something you cannot break,' she said." For her, it was not self-evident that poverty was a reason to separate children from their birth families, nor that the child was "really" hers or "really" American. At the same time, the Libertos' response was not about a kind of racial purity that rendered Mexican children inalterably different from their American family; they got drawn into the INS case because they subsequently adopted Flor Azucena's little sister.[97]

Yet most of the press coverage of these cases refused this kind of complexity, relying instead on ideological moves that rendered the birth parents unfit and discountable, inscribing the adoptive parents as heroic rescuers in a sentimental mode. An article in the *Arizona Republic*—with similar intent but more flourishes than a great many similar news articles about the Reyes case—uses the Kruchkows to suggest the logic of keeping the children in the United States and implicitly points to the kind of nationalist rhetoric that can govern transnational adoption:

> Sara and David Kruchkow of Flushing, N.Y. . . . fear the child they adopted from Mexico more than a year ago may be taken from them.

... The couple already has been through an emotional wringer. ...
Twice, the adoption group told the couple there was a child available,
only to dash their hopes a few months later. [Sara is] happy to tell
how delighted the Kruchkows were a year and a half ago, when they
met a bright 20-month-old girl with a sense of humor. They named
her Shelly, and "she took to us immediately," Kruchkow said. A few
things about her new life in New York startled the little girl at first.
"When she saw running water, she started screaming and jumping up
and down and saying, 'Agua, agua,' so evidently where she was there
wasn't running water," Kruchkow said. ... Now, she said, "My biggest
fear is I'm not going to be able to keep the child I was meant to have."

The article goes on to explain that the couple spent $30,000 on the adop-
tion, and that Reyes operated from a desire to help children and an opposition to abortion.[98] The *Arizona Republic* writer tells us in multiple ways
that Shelly (originally named Maria Soledad) "really" belongs with the
Kruchkows and not her birth parents, stressing her birth parents' poverty
and the Kruchkows' economic stability. The article says nothing about the
birth parents who lost this child; the only relevant emotional investment is
the Kruchkows', who have "been through an emotional wringer."

David Kruchkow, though, did not write this kind of narrative. On the
contrary, he railed against the corruption of the transnational adoption
industry, raised questions about coercion and illegitimate pressure on birth
parents in places like Guatemala and Mexico to relinquish their children,
and mourned the loss of the possibility of contact with his daughter's birth
parents due to the shady dealings of Mario Reyes and his associates. He
wrote about the local politics in Agua Prieta that had first allowed Mexican
officials to ignore Reyes's illegal adoption operation and then to demand
his prosecution. He had, in a few years, been transformed into a close
analyst of the political and affective economies of intercountry adoption.[99]

Kruchkow is not alone among U.S. adoptive parents in calling for reform
or in becoming steadily more critical with respect to the politics of the
practice—these kinds of sentiments are regularly raised in the context of
adoption groups like Ethica, Parents of Children from China, or Connections, articles like those by David Smolin as well as on adoptive parents'
listservs and in their books and stories.[100] Raising an adoptive child born
outside the United States sometimes seems to bring U.S. parents into a
complex, critical relationship with conditions in those home countries and
U.S. foreign policy. For all their power in mobilizing potential parents to

consider "saving" a child, or to account for why and how they ought to adopt from overseas, sentimental narratives seem to do a surprisingly poor job of providing a satisfying narrative of how to raise them. And this unexpected outcome, of the very heterogeneous politics of *raising* adopted children, opens doors for more critical accounts of how the process of getting them could be different.

PART III

Emerging Fights over the Politics of Adoption

SEVEN

Gay and Lesbian Adoption in the United States

In the 2008 presidential election campaign, when Republican candidate John McCain was asked about his views on gay adoption, he told the *New York Times*, "I think that we've proven that both parents are important in the success of a family so, no I don't believe in gay adoption,"[1] reminding us that the way gay couples are different from straight couples is that gay couples are composed of only one person. But aside from the essential strangeness of McCain's response, inadvertently but revealingly conflating gay parents with single parents (mothers), it reminds us that gay adoption has been a persistent campaign issue in presidential elections, with, until 2008, both parties being varying degrees of opposed. Interestingly, in 2008 Democratic candidates Barack Obama and Hillary Clinton both indicated their support for gay adoption, the first time any major contender for the U.S. presidency has. For both queer folk and their right-wing opponents, children have been a persistent issue; perhaps if it hadn't been for HIV/ AIDS, it would have been the defining issue for a lesbian and gay freedom movement. And, in some ways, it has become that—to a significant extent, the question of gay marriage is centrally about the raising of children, for its supporters among LGBT folk, for its Christian Right opponents, and even for the judges writing decisions about it.

In the 1990s, some of the people who were disproportionately likely to be adopting the babies of indigenous or impoverished mothers in Guatemala were gay and lesbian. The wide-open, neoliberal markets of Guatemala were one of the few places that did not have bars to gay and lesbian adoptive parents. Ironically, as the outgrowth of a fierce fight to keep their own children in the seventies and eighties, LGBT people began articulating a "right" to parent that began to extend to fostering and adoption—which seemingly implied a "right" to take other people's children. The irony was not entirely lost on queer folk, whose parenting continued to be denigrated (they were everybody's first choice for "hard to place" children) and vulnerable, without legal recognition (as "second parent" adoptions were, in 2010, still allowed in only eighteen states). LGBT people did manage to have one of the most robust spaces of debate, at least, about the sources of these children. Furthermore, although this chapter will focus on the United States, it bears noticing that the fight for gay and lesbian adoption has been a transnational one, centered at least as much outside the United States as inside it. In South Africa, Canada, and in about one-third of the European Union countries, there are no legal barriers to gay and lesbian adoption. In Mexico and Brazil, as in the United States, whether gay and lesbian people are able to adopt depends on the state and the judge.[2] In short, this chapter tracks the trajectory of the status of gay and lesbian parents in the United States over the forty years beginning in 1970, from being a group that often lost their children to one that could often adopt and be foster parents, despite the furious objection to it by the Christian Right (which continues to assert and imply that gay people are child molesters or at least bad for children's mental health). This chapter explores the very neoliberal terms of that inclusion—in which gay people with sufficient financial wherewithal are seen as a resource for the state to avoid supporting children, a consideration that has in part driven the gay marriage decisions in various states. In what ways, it asks, have LGBT families (imagined to be white, whether or not they actually are) become the ultimate safety valve for a neoliberal U.S. state that has for decades been quite harsh toward communities of color, taking away the children of poor families, and now delivering them as "hard to place" children that lesbian and gay families will be desperate enough to take off the hands of states that do not want to pay for them? Or, how are LGBT families seen as the alternative to a civilian welfare state that nations like Guatemala refused to build, first taking the children of the "communists" who dreamed more collectivist dreams, then of those too impoverished to raise their own children or mount an effective defense against those who kidnapped children?

Divorce Cases, Lesbian Moms, Gay Dads: The First Fight

Although parents who came out or were caught with a homosexual lover had lost children for decades, in the 1970s the nature of the question of gay parenting changed, as queer folk for the first time in real numbers began insisting that they could live openly as gay or lesbian and keep their children, too. In 1974 the first issue of the newsletter *Lesbian Connection*—hand-typed then photocopied onto colored paper and stapled—announced the formation of a group called the Lesbian Mothers' Defense Fund (LMDF). It was a network of lesbians who were sharing information about custody battles with their children's biological fathers. It promised to "Give help with court costs, child care costs, food, clothing, attorney's fees. Insure lesbian mothers from all parts of the country fair representation in court. In cases pending in extremely hostile territory, allow a competent and sympathetic attorney transportation from one state to another state."[3]

The LMDF was contesting the ways courts were using a mother's admission that she was a lesbian as a reason in itself to deny custody, often imposing onerous restrictions even on visitation whenever a presumptively heterosexual spouse contested custody in divorce cases. Homosexuality was per se said to be damaging to children. Women who came out in the context of marriage in the 1970s faced stiff penalties. Before the era of no-fault divorce, a woman's lesbianism itself was grounds for a divorce. Fathers, and even grandparents or other relatives, who asked for child custody almost always got it. Some lesbian mothers fled illegally with their children, disappearing into new cities and new lives. Others stood and fought.[4]

The LMDF—soon the Lesbian Mothers' National Defense Fund (LMNDF)—was part of an emergent movement by lesbians in particular (but also gay men) to defend what they insisted was their right to parent. While the visible spokespeople, organizers, and public test cases in this movement were usually white, many of the people who sought their help were not.[5] In the 1970s, the flowering of a feminist movement offered some women the courage and context to come out and leave marriages; it also provided a community from which women gathered the resources to try to keep custody of the children from those marriages. The LMNDF helped more than two hundred lesbian mothers try to keep their children in their first two years alone. The organizers, like many of the women they defended, were strikingly young—one of their first fundraisers was a celebration of the twenty-first birthday of one of the founders, Geraldine Cole.[6] Like many women of their generation, the organizers not only married young but also emerged from divorce without simple practical skills like setting up a bank account.[7] But they learned and taught others, even developing a handbook for those who wanted to support lesbian mothers around the country. They also started a newsletter, *Mom's Apple Pie,* that shared strategies for winning custody or visitation, raising children in lesbian families, or, more painfully, surviving life without one's children.

While the LMNDF was holding fundraisers in Seattle and sending information and lawyers from one state to another, other groups were springing up around the country. One couple made a film, *Sandy and Madeleine's Family* (1973), which was distributed as an educational piece to use in courts. By showing judges how normal a lesbian family could be, the reasoning went, they could persuade them to grant custody. Sandy and Madeleine themselves had a tough fight. Both fundamentalist Christians who met in the context of the children's Sunday School classes, they fell in love, divorced their husbands, and sought to make a family together with their children. In 1971 their ex-husbands went back to court to try to obtain custody of the children, beginning a running battle that had them living with various kinds of restrictions (being forbidden to live together, for example), but the couple ultimately prevailed. The film, with its pretty blonde children, wholesome religious education, and vigorous outdoor activities, became a staple of courtroom battles and showings in lesbian communities around the country.[8] In San Francisco a law firm called Equal Rights Advocates formed a Lesbian Rights Project in 1977 that focused on custody issues. Lambda Legal Defense in New York advised people on the East Coast—and nationally—in custody disputes. Smaller groups, like Custody Action for Lesbian Mothers (CALM) in Pennsylvania, formed, often in response to high-profile custody fights in their communities.[9]

Many gay parents lost children over these decades; some cases were well known, most were deeply personal, invisible outside an immediate circle of family and friends. In 1974 Bruce Voeller, executive director of the newly formed National Gay Task Force (subsequently NGLTF), had severe restrictions imposed on his visitation with his children—they could not go to his home, his lover could never see them, and they could not go to any location where there were other gay men. In 1975 Mary Jo Risher lost custody of her nine-year-old son in Texas that resulted in a made-for-TV movie, *A Question of Love*, which aired in 1978 and, perhaps surprisingly, portrayed Risher as a loving, hurting mother who had lost her child.[10]

Legally, one of the crucial issues in gay and lesbian parenting and custody issues was sodomy or, rather, laws criminalizing sodomy. If gay sex was against the law, then lesbian and gay people with partners were presumptively criminals. Courts in states like Pennsylvania, Missouri, and Virginia were consistently awarding child custody in contested divorces to a heterosexual parent over a lesbian or gay one.[11] Even in the 1980s and 1990s many gay parents were still giving up their children to a heterosexual and even an abusive ex rather than face a bruising, humiliating, and public divorce.

In 1987 the U.S. Supreme Court shocked gay activists and legal groups by upholding the constitutionality of sodomy laws in *Bowers v. Hardwick*. The majority opinion argued in the most dismissive way imaginable that to say that homosexuals had a privacy right to engage in consensual sex in their bedrooms and "to claim that a right to engage in such conduct is 'deeply rooted in this Nation's history and tradition' or 'implicit in the concept of ordered liberty' is, at best, facetious."[12] Sodomy was not a crime much prosecuted in the 1980s and 1990s—aside from anomalous cases like that involving Michael Bowers, which seemed to involve a police officer with a personal homophobic vendetta repeatedly coming to Bowers's house to serve an invalid warrant for throwing out a beer bottle in a public trash can outside the gay bar where he worked and finally one time "catching him" having oral sex with another man. The most significant effect of the *Bowers* case, though, was that it resulted in the continued destruction of lesbian and gay families. For example, sodomy laws were important to the Sharon Bottoms case, which was vigorously publicized and contested by gay rights groups. Bottoms lost her two-year-old son to her estranged mother—the child's grandmother—when a Virginia court found Bottoms to be an unfit parent on the grounds that she was a lesbian. The juvenile court ruling was appealed to the circuit court. That judge, citing sodomy law and *Bowers* said in 1993, "The mother's conduct is illegal and immoral and renders her an unfit parent." The court-appointed guardian for the boy also called her "immature" and impoverished, "an irregular job holder." Bottoms's mother also objected because the boy, Tyler, called Bottoms's lesbian partner "Dada."[13]

Gay Parents as Morally Dangerous

Throughout this period there were public and political campaigns to define gay people as dangerous to all children, not just their own—indeed, as pedophiles. The first and most explicit was in 1977 when Anita Bryant organized in opposition to a gay and lesbian antidiscrimination ordinance in Dade County, Florida, with a campaign called Save Our Children. She argued that "the recruitment of our children is absolutely necessary for the survival and growth of the homosexual movement." On June 7, 1977, the ordinance (which had only tried to prevent housing and employment discrimination, having nothing to do with parenting or children) was repealed on a popular ballot. The next day the state's governor signed a ban on gay adoption that still stands in 2011. Subsequently, Oklahoma banned gay men and lesbians from teaching in the public schools. The Arkansas legislature even debated a bill that would not only have fired all gay teachers but also stripped gay pediatricians, youth psychologists, and psychiatrists of their licenses.[14] Further, in Margaret Thatcher's Britain as much as Ronald Reagan's America, the combination of gay people and children made the perfect emblem of moral danger, and in 1988 Britain passed Section 28, which caused waves on both sides of the pond. It made it a crime for local officials—including, perhaps especially school officials—to promote homosexuality as "pretend family relationships."

While the New Right made political hay out of finding gay child abuse lurking in employment nondiscrimination laws, Democrats were no strangers to making an issue of gay people raising children. In Boston, a Democratic governor, social service bureaucracy, and legislature mobilized in the mid-1980s to take away a gay couple's foster children and try to prevent all future gay fostering or adoption. At the height of the hysteria about Satanic ritual abuse of children at day care centers, with its secret tunnels and adults who could fly,[15] the U.S. obsession with blaming any but the most likely perpetrators of child sexual abuse—parents and other relatives—turned on gay folks with vengeance. Not only Bryant and Southern conservative Christians, apparently, but also liberal Democrats in Massachusetts could generate a sexualized moral panic about gay folk and children. Where the Save Our Children campaign resulted in the first law banning gay people as adoptive parents, the Massachusetts policy was the first to prevent lesbian and gay people from being foster parents.[16]

In May 1985 Governor Dukakis removed two little boys from the home of David Jean and Donald Babets following a front-page *Boston Globe* story critical of the decision to place the boys with gay foster fathers, even though the boys' birth mother had approved the placement. The Department of Social Services (DSS) sent social workers to pick the children up the next day while news cameras rolled.[17] The *Globe* reporter, Kenneth Cooper, was responding to a tip from Ben Haith, a neighborhood activist who was reportedly trying to drum up publicity for an intended second city council campaign.[18] Haith reportedly objected that the neighbors weren't consulted about this controversial move, and he felt that the residents of the predominantly black Roxbury neighborhood where Babets and Jean lived were being treated as "guinea pigs" in a sociological experiment.[19] Babets and Jean (and the boys) were white and lived in the traditionally white and gay corner of Roxbury known as Fort Hill.

Although the boys were never returned to the men's home, the incident galvanized lesbian and gay activists in a broadly progressive effort that mobilized networks of gay and black activists that had been allies as part of the first rainbow coalition only two years earlier—the progressive black activist Mel King's mayoral bid in 1983. The Rev. Grayland Ellis-Hagler, a black minister, called a press conference where black city councilman Bruce Bolling also spoke up for them. City Councilor David Scondras, the only openly gay politician at the city or state level in 1985, also spoke out.[20] Seven of the nine members of the Roxbury Highland Neighborhood Association, Haith's group, wrote the *Boston Globe* in support of the couple.

The *Globe* followed up their revelation with an editorial calling for a policy that preferred a "normal" home, insisting that "the most normal home setting—even if it is no longer statistically the most prevalent—is clearly that of a married man and woman with two or three children of their own. If the foster children are below school age, the setting will be most normal if the woman stays home as a full-time caretaker." If it is hard to tell whether the defining characteristics of "normal" here is gender or sexuality (as it clearly does not have its plain meaning, defined, as it is, *against* the statistical norm), the editorial tries to clarify: "Social Services' consideration of a lesbian household as a foster-care placement could rightly ignore the sexual preferences of the two women and grant approval if one of the women performs the role of full-time caretaker of the child, thus making the household close to 'normal.' . . . Applying that test to the case that has brought this matter to the public's attention, the two homosexual men would have been rejected as foster parents not because of their sexual preference, but because of the deviation of their household—consisting of two working men."[21] Gay people who make a "normal" nuclear family could be approved, perhaps, if one of them can be construed as a stay-at-home "wife." The supposedly progressive *Boston Globe* reiterated all the tropes that had animated antifeminist and anti–civil rights efforts to take people's children away—gay folk, single mothers, and women who worked were all likewise bad parents.

The gay community in Boston mobilized, forming the Gay and Lesbian

Defense Committee (GLDC), which launched a Foster Equality campaign. The group organized street demonstrations, a petition drive, held a picket outside Dukakis's home on Father's Day, and organized people to write letters to the newspapers and ask questions about the issue at events where Dukakis spoke. They sought, and won, a meeting with the Health Department Secretary Philip Johnson, who explained the policy to them by way of a story about a heterosexual mother who passed HIV to her child during pregnancy. Although this would seem to be an argument against heterosexual reproduction, Johnson's point was less rational than that—queer folk, tainted with AIDS, would undoubtedly communicate it to foster children in their care.[22] In January 1986 members of the GLDC were denied a meeting with Governor Dukakis, and, after a full-day sit-in in his office, thirteen were arrested by capitol police. In 1987 after Michael Dukakis sought and won the Democratic Party nomination for president, he received more or less constant heckling on the campaign trail by the GLDC, who followed him across the country in a quixotic effort to force a change in Massachusetts policy.[23]

The entire debate was, of course, organized around assuming lesbians and gay men were all or mostly pedophiles. Two weeks after the boys were removed the Massachusetts state House passed an amendment that would have banned lesbian or gay foster parents because "a homosexual preference shall be considered a threat to the psychological and physical well-being of a child." Said Scondras, "In effect it's saying that gay people are legally defined as child molesters. It's the most bigoted thing I've seen in my life."[24] Although the measure failed in the state Senate, at the governor's direction DSS created a policy that instituted a hierarchy of child placement. For the first time a state policy used sexuality as a defining characteristic for placement. Until then no state had explicitly inquired after the sexual identity of foster parents.[25] Following a Dukakis order to come up with a policy that emphasized what he called a "traditional family" setting,[26] the DSS foster-care placement policy did essentially what the *Globe* and the state House had called for. It made a heterosexual couple with parenting experience, and a stay-at-home female caretaker the first choice for placement, followed in descending order by two working heterosexual parents, followed by a single heterosexual woman with parenting experience, all the way down to gay and lesbian couples, who, the DSS secretary told gay activists frankly, would be "extremely unlikely" to ever have a child placed with them.[27] Nearby New Hampshire followed suit, with an executive ban on gay foster parents in 1986 and a legislative one in 1987. In the context of that debate one New Hampshire state legislator claimed that gay and lesbian people sought to foster or adopt children so they could "raise their own meat" to sexually molest.[28]

Tragically, the Babets and Jean case also demonstrated the real costs to foster care systems of antigay policies. The two boys, whom Babets and Jean had been willing to foster as long as there was need, were moved five more times in the eighteen months they were in care. Their mother was still very much in the picture, but the boys were ultimately moved across the state where she could no longer visit them. In their last stop in more "traditional" families, they were allegedly sexually abused; indeed, according to some sources, they were abused by more than three people in their travels through the foster care system.[29] From consistency to visitation to safety, a system that relied on "normal" families failed the boys and their mother at every turn.

How the Christian Right Learned to Hate Gays

While Anita Bryant's campaign in Dade County in 1977 used the language of fundamentalist Christianity, her group was pioneering a movement on the Christian Right, not emerging out of any existing religious tradition. As the analyst Didi Herman has rightly pointed out, the leading evangelical magazine, Billy Graham's *Christianity Today*, was as likely to decry "homophobia"—a word it used—as to endorse it before 1990. Although as early as the 1950s and 1960s one could find denunciations of homosexuality as unbiblical, and find individuals arguing that homosexuals were recruiting children in the schools (especially after 1963, with the Supreme Court's decision banning organized Christian prayer in the schools), there were also in the 1960s and 1970s articles by those involved in "ex-gay" ministries that called for laws outlawing employment and housing discrimination against gay and lesbian people.[30]

But one important pastor was drawn to the Save Our Children campaign, the televangelist Jerry Falwell. Falwell got his start as a public presence in radio and then a television show, *The Old Time Gospel Hour*, in the 1950s in which he denounced the civil rights movement and Martin Luther King Jr. After 1977 gay rights became his new issue, together with opposition to abortion and support for Israel. He had found a national platform in 1971, when his television show went national, and he transformed national politics when he founded the Moral Majority in 1979.[31] Although a later generation of evangelicals would consider Falwell a sometimes embarrassing figure who never really understood how to talk to a national audience—his attacks on the children's show *Teletubbies* character, Tinky Winky, as gay because he was purple and carried a purse, for example, did not play well in non-evangelical circles, and he was forced to apologize for attributing the 9/11 terrorist attacks to the influence of gays, feminists, and abortion in American life—the Moral Majority's campaigning for Ronald Reagan brought the Christian Right a seat at the Republican table.[32]

The Moral Majority, together with groups like Concerned Women for America and Phyllis Schlafly's Eagle Forum (with the crucial assistance of the Mormons—the Church of Jesus Christ of Latter-day Saints, or the LDS church, as they prefer to be known—which halted the momentum of the Equal Rights Amendment by defeating it in Utah in the late 1970s), forged a Christian Right out of disparate anti-Communist, anti-Catholic, anti-Semitic, and anti–civil rights forces united around opposition to feminism, abortion, and gays. Their agenda, in positive terms, was to insist on what they called traditional family values, the nuclear family, which they argued was not just *a* way of organizing social life but the natural way, ordained by biology and God. (Oddly, they also claimed a biblical basis for this way of organizing the family, a bold argument in the context of the normative polygamy of the Hebrew Bible.) A family consisted of a submissive woman and a dominant man plus children. U.S. culture was trying to pervert the way of God and of nature—through feminism and women working outside the home, through abortion, and through homosexuality. God's chosen warriors had to fight to bring this state of affairs to an end. It was a winning combination, politically; they brought evangelicals into the public sphere and out of their political quietism and forged a coalition that could fight a "culture war."

Another veteran of the Save Our Children campaign was Tim LaHaye, also a key figure in the founding of the Moral Majority, on whose board he served. In 1978 LaHaye, inspired by the Save Our Children campaign, wrote *Unhappy Gays* (later reissued as *What Everyone Should Know about Homosexuals*). In it LaHaye argued that queer folk are both deeply miserable and dangerously deviant. In addition to being selfish, lonely, and depressed, LaHaye warns that homosexuals prey on boys, as scout masters and as teachers (all homosexuals are men in his account).[33] LaHaye also founded, in the early 1980s, the Council for National Policy, a sort of right-wing steering committee that had a huge influence on national politics, which "brought together cold warriors, moral majoritarians, John Birchers, dispensationalists, anti-government libertarians, free-enterprise zealots, and national-security hawks under one roof, [and became] the incubator for the conservative movement's political strategy, and an essential stop for Republican presidential aspirants."[34] LaHaye is now one of the best selling novelists in the United States with his *Left Behind* series (a series of twelve adult and numerous juvenile novels; seven of the adult books have reached number one on the *New York Times* bestseller list), and the Council for National Policy is a critical component of the Republican Party's policy wing.

Following LaHaye's early entry into the field, by the late 1980s the fundamentalist Right began to branch out from televangelism to other mass media forms, what Herman called "the emergence of a new [Christian Right] cultural genre, consisting of books, videos, and special reports, specifically dedicated to identifying the gay threat, and calling Christian believers to arms."[35] One piece that was endlessly circulated in this genre was so perfectly suited to their child and family agenda that it's hard to believe that the Christian Right didn't write it. But they didn't. In 1987 Michael Swift wrote a piece in *Gay Community News* called "Gay Revolutionary" that promised to demonstrate "how the oppressed desperately dream of being the oppressor" and contained the immortal lines:

> We shall sodomize your sons, emblems of your feeble masculinity, of your shallow dreams and vulgar lies. We shall seduce them in your schools, in your dormitories, in your gymnasiums, in your locker rooms, in your sports arenas, in your seminaries, in your youth groups, in your movie theater bathrooms, in your army bunkhouses, in your truck stops, in your all male clubs, in your houses of Congress, wherever men are with men together. Your sons shall become our minions and do our bidding. They will be recast in our image. They will come to crave and adore us.

Most of this piece was subsequently read into the *Congressional Record* as evidence of the "homosexual agenda," was circulated endlessly in fundraising letters, and was read aloud in an important video, *The Gay Agenda*, produced by a group called the Report, complete with ominous music and pictures of blonde children. All of these, of course, omitted the crucial first line that described the piece as "madness, a tragic, cruel fantasy, an eruption of inner rage."[36] Irony has never been the strong suit of the religious Right, even if children were.

By the 1990s "fundamentalist" had become a pejorative term, with evangelical preferred even by Falwell, who had made it a household word. The

Moral Majority had ceased to exist. But the Christian Right's antigay agenda was more solidly entrenched than ever. The mainstream of evangelical Christianity, as represented in *Christianity Today*, had stopped loving the sinner very much at all and had become vigorously antigay, focusing on the Clinton administration's "don't ask, don't tell" policy in the military, and, as ever, gay and lesbian recruitment of children: "The National Education Association is training teachers how to offer 'equal opportunities' to gay and lesbian students. Lesbian couples are reading politically charged children's books to San Francisco kindergartners during story time. In fact, around the United States, homosexual activists—seasoned by their political successes over AIDS, abetted by the educational and social-work establishments, and strengthened by the support of the Clinton administration—are pushing harder than ever for schools to promote their sexual orientation as being on the same moral plane with heterosexuality."[37] The epicenter of Christian Right organizing in the 1990s was Colorado, which put an antigay rights initiative on the ballot for 1992. A number of important and emergent antigay organizations were in Colorado Springs in the 1990s. James Dobson's Focus on the Family radio empire (with a subsidiary in Guatemala) moved there in 1991. In 1995 so too did the Family Research Institute, directed by Paul Cameron, the controversial source of many of the "facts and figures" the Christian Right uses to talk about homosexuality and its effects on children. Largely debunked in academe—Cameron was thrown out of the American Psychological Association for violating their ethical guidelines and censured by the American Sociological Association for posing as a sociologist—he remains an influential if controversial figure for the Christian Right.[38] Another was Gary Bauer's Family Research Council, which began its life as a subsidiary of Focus on the Family but had become independent by the mid-1990s. Their first act in 1991 was to ensure that the organizing for the ballot initiative was shifted away from the "less effective" organizers in Denver and centered in Colorado Springs. Other groups that were represented in the Colorado Family Values Coalition were headquartered elsewhere but sent representatives to Colorado Springs, including Lou Sheldon's Traditional Values Coalition and Schlafly's Eagle Forum.

   The ballot measure, Amendment 2, passed by a narrow margin in 1992 with Colorado voters, but it was then caught up in a protracted legal fight, which the prominent Christian Right activist Jim Woodhall called "the *Roe v. Wade* of the homosexual issue."[39] In 1996 the amendment was struck down by the Supreme Court in *Romer v. Evans*.[40] Amendment 2 was designed to prohibit any jurisdiction in Colorado from creating any kind of antidiscrimination protection for gay and lesbian people. It read, in the relevant part: "Neither the state of Colorado, through any of its branches or departments, nor any of its agencies, political subdivisions, municipalities or school districts, shall enact, adopt or enforce any statute, regulation, ordinance or policy whereby homosexual, lesbian or bisexual orientation, conduct, practices or relationships shall constitute or otherwise be the basis of, or entitle any person or class of persons to have or claim any minority status, quota preferences, protected status or claim of discrimination." The Colorado Supreme Court stopped it from being enacted on the argument that it failed to meet a "strict scrutiny" standard. The Supreme Court decision went much further, saying it didn't need to evaluate it based on a "strict scrutiny" test; it failed even the more minimal "rational basis" test. Justice Kennedy, writing for the majority in a 6–3 decision, said, "Its sheer breadth is so discontinuous with the reasons offered for it that the amendment seems inexplicable by anything but animus toward the class that it affects; it lacks a rational relationship to legitimate state interests."[41] For the antigay Christian Right, *Romer* was a disaster; it effectively closed off future efforts in this direction to stave off lesbian and gay antidiscrimination ordinances through statewide legislation.

It is worth noting, again, how central children were to the case the Christian Right tried to make for Amendment 2, however. In court briefs the Christian Right made essentially three arguments. First, that Amendment 2 was necessary to protect freedom of religion, since their religion apparently required them to discriminate against gay and lesbian people. Second, it was necessary to protect familial privacy, which they argued meant not only preserving the right of parents to teach their children that homosexuality was reprehensible but also to prevent them from being exposed to any contradictory values. Finally, they argued, Amendment 2 protected heterosexual marriage by sending the signal that no competing norms—like queer relationships—would be tolerated by society. It was still all about protecting the children. Although the courts rejected all these arguments, they formed the basis of the next major offensive by the Christian Right—one that would prove much more successful.

In 1996 Charles Colson (founder of Prison Ministry Fellowship) made a crucial argument in *Christianity Today*: that the next major initiative by the Christian Right should focus not on gay rights but on gay marriage. As an initiative to recognize gay marriage in Hawaii—based on an argument that it was acknowledged within Native Hawaiian customary law—wound its way through the political process and the courts there, many in the mainland United States began to expect that legalized gay marriage there would bring massive numbers of gay and lesbian people to the islands to wed and then demand recognition for their marriages under the Constitution's full faith and credit clause. Reiterating an argument that David Coolidge had made in the Christian Right's *Crisis* magazine, Colson laid it out for the broader readership of *Christianity Today*: "If same-sex marriage wins the day legally, it will exert enormous pressure throughout society to move from the *Complementarity* to the *Choice* model. The message will be built into the law itself that there is no objective moral order, that marriage is a human invention. And if people believe marriage is just an invention, then they will feel free to change it, redefine it, or even discard it. The *Choice* model would inevitably weaken men and women's commitment to the institution of marriage."[42] Whether or not Colson was right about marriage, he was right about politics. The Christian Right began a full-court press on gay marriage, and it proved their most successful issue ever. Later that year the Defense of Marriage Act sailed through the Republican Congress, and President Clinton signed it. It represented the kind of overkill that would become the hallmark of the Christian Right family initiatives: although gay marriage was not yet legal anywhere, it assured that full faith and credit would *not* be given should it ever become legal. As we will see, it became a defining issue during the second Bush administration. First, though, let us explore the story of gay organizing on family and children questions.

Pushing Back: Affirming Gay Adoption and DIY Reproductive Technology

The nationally publicized Anita Bryant campaign also did more than anything since the police at the Stonewall in 1969 to organize a gay liberation movement. The mainstream media started using the word "gay" and talking about gay issues as politics (rather than criminal deviance or mental illness); gay rights groups sprang up around the country. In 1978 gay activists mobilized to deal the Christian Right its first setback, defeating a ballot initiative in California—the Briggs initiative—which would have created a law that would make a positive or neutral remark about homosexuality by a public school teacher cause for dismissal—essentially, an attempt to fire all gay teachers and their supporters. With a rallying cry of "come out, come out, wherever you are!" gay activists like Harvey Milk in San Francisco urged closeted lesbians and gay men to talk to their families, friends, and neighbors about who they were and why they opposed the initiative. Against all predictions, the measure failed, breaking the momentum of the New Right.[43]

Gay family law attorneys crafted legal strategies to win in divorce and custody cases with some successes—notably in California, Washington, Maine, Ohio, Oregon, and South Carolina. In 1976 the District of Columbia passed a statute that prohibited the use of sexual orientation as a basis to deny custody or visitation. Two things helped. First, in the context of changing sexual norms and the feminist movement, family law attorneys had begun arguing in heterosexual custody and divorce cases that lifestyle issues that didn't affect a parent's relationship with his or her child—that for example being an atheist or belonging to the Communist Party should not affect custody or visitation decisions.[44] Second, in 1973 the American Psychiatric Association, in a sharply contested decision at their annual meeting, declassified homosexuality as a mental illness. Lesbian and gay parents were no longer, by definition, mentally ill.[45]

In 1989 the lesbian poet Minnie Bruce Pratt published *Crime Against Nature*, which took its title from the statute against homosexual sex that was the basis for so many divorce decrees that removed children from their lesbian mothers and a small but significant group from gay fathers. Pratt gave up custody of her two boys voluntarily to the husband she was divorcing, rather than risk losing the ability even to visit them. "I paid for my freedom with my children," she wrote. The poems are wrenching, telling the story of her anger and shame in that loss, while simultaneously celebrating pleasure, sexuality, and life as a defense against pain. It was a measure of the growing legitimacy of queer folks' parenting that the book found an audience—it was the Lamont Poetry Selection that year.[46]

Throughout this period lesbians and gay men insisted on their fitness not only to raise the children they had conceived in marriages but also to adopt and foster children with lesbian and gay partners. Often, in the 1970s and 1980s, like-minded queer parents and would-be parents found each other through small-circulation magazines like *Mom's Apple Pie* and *Lesbian Mother* and compared notes and strategies for getting pregnant or adopting. By the 1980s it was planned queer families that were becoming the subject of debate, as gay men and lesbians increasingly formed families through adoption, fostering, surrogacy, and, for lesbians, donor insemination or in vitro. Information about alternative insemination for lesbians began circulating in the 1970s, with mimeographed pamphlets advising women about how to do it yourself by using a needleless syringe or a turkey baster to self-inseminate, getting semen from a friend or even an anonymous donor (with a mutual acquaintance acting as go-between).

While the brave new world of reproductive technology was almost entirely unregulated, in the 1970s and 1980s most reprotech clinics nevertheless chose to operate within the terms set by adoption agencies, which is to say, they refused to serve anyone they believed would be turned away as an adoptive parent. As a result most sperm banks refused to serve unmarried women, and even more turned away lesbians. There were, however, a handful of feminist health services that did provide help with donor insemination by the late 1970s—the Feminist Women's Health Center in Los Angeles, the Vermont Women's Health Center, and the Chelsea Health Center in New York. In 1979 *Lesbian Health Matters* devoted a chapter to alternative insemination. In 1982 Fenway Community Health Center, a gay and lesbian health center in Boston, started an alternative insemination (AI) clinic for lesbians. From time to time the issue irrupted into popular media as well: in 1979 a lesbian couple who had had a child by AI appeared on the *Donahue* show; in 1980 it was the subject of a *New York Times Magazine* article; by the late 1980s the media was pronouncing the existence of a "gay baby (or gayby) boom." Further, as HIV/AIDS entered the national consciousness in the late 1980s, many were celebrating the new chastity and suggesting that a politics of sexual liberation was giving way to a new emphasis on family and children. Richard Goldstein of the *Village Voice* (the voice of bohemia, apparently) was quoted in the *Washington Post* as saying that gay men would be taking up a "very traditional heterosexual model. The big issues [of the 1990s] will be the rights of couples, adoption, laws involving inheritance and real estate —the so-called 'gay family' issues."[47]

Although Goldstein missed the ways those were also the big issues of the 1970s and 1980s, he was right about the 1990s. In 1987 the Lesbian Rights Project won a major victory, persuading a California court to let two out lesbians adopt together.[48] By the early 1990s, such successes were becoming more common and not just in California. For better or worse, though, lesbian and gay parents were being steered toward hard-to-place children. "Typically, lesbians and gay men who are open about their orientation are steered very strongly toward 'special needs' children," wrote one observer in *Mom's Apple Pie*, "older, handicapped, emotionally disturbed. They may, in fact, be presented with a veiled ultimatum: the only child they can adopt is a 'crack baby' or a terminal AIDS baby or some other child which the agency feels isn't likely to be placed." Many of those were children of color. Those would-be gay adoptive parents who didn't want to deal with the potential problems of a "special needs" child in the 1980s turned to international adoption—usually from Latin America, where the restrictions on gay or single parents were looser than in places like Korea or China.

There was a surprisingly extensive debate in the pages of queer periodicals about the politics of transracial and transnational adoption—surprising in the sense that gay and lesbian folk who sought to be parents often had few choices, and the legal strength of their ties to their biological children or adopted children was often tested in court and found wanting. It is interesting to note, in contrast to the often robust refusal to consider the pain of birth mothers that we have seen in other political struggles over the legitimacy of contested adoptions, the care with which queers sometimes debated these politics. In the newsletter *Conceptions*, for example, in 1993 one writer noted:

> The incidence of lesbian/gay adoption. . . . has far out-paced the provision of community forums for reflection about the social and political issues involved in these family arrangements. . . . What is going on in the countries of origin that cause so many children to be available at certain specific times? And what are the relationships between these countries and the U.S. that perpetuate social and economic conditions in which it is so difficult for women to raise their own children? Is the availability of children due to policies that restrict women's control over their reproductive lives, e.g., lack of access to contraceptives and abortion? . . . How can one be sure that the birth mother gave her child up "freely"? And what is "freely?" . . . What does it mean to be a consumer in a free market economy where white babies "cost" more than babies of color? How does this supply-and-demand economy of adoption reinforce and perpetuate notions about who is valuable? In the past, many white adoptive parents did little or nothing to familiarize themselves or their adopted children with the child's culture of origin. This resulted in many children feeling disoriented and alienated from their cultures. Is this alienation different when parents involve themselves and their kids in their culture of origin? What are some of the ways that adoptive parents can bridge the cultural, linguistic, and religious gaps that might exist? Is it really possible to bridge these gaps? Does this really matter?

How do parents acknowledge racism with their kids and empower their kids to deal with it, when parents want to protect their children, particularly from the cruelties of racism? When children learn how skin color is ranked, how do they deal with the difference between themselves and their parents and feel like their parents can empathize, not just sympathize, or that they have to protect their parents from their experiences? The National Association of Black Social Workers and other groups in the black community have taken a position against the placement of black or bi-racial children with white families. What are the debates about this position? Adoption agencies report a 9–1 to 13–1 gender preference for girls over boys in international adoptions, which usually involve white parents adopting children of color. What are the explanations for this spontaneous preference? . . . Gender differences and white people's perceptions of people of color? . . . What is the challenge to the gay/lesbian community posed by the presence of multi-racial families among us?[49]

The reasons for these kinds of concerns lay in the kinds of politics out of which gay and lesbian adoption was being championed: it was born in sometimes fragile coalitions, and understood itself as broadly opposed to the New Right. "Homophobia is one aspect of socially conservative politics that is also racist and sexist," read the notes of one of the speakers at the GLDC forum on building coalitions from 1986, "and often works hand-in-hand with economically conservative politics."[50] In 1987 the demands of the March on Washington for Lesbian and Gay Rights included an end to funding for war and an end to Apartheid in South Africa.[51]

Throughout the 1980s and 1990s and into the decade after 2010, gay family law attorneys continued to win victories, expanding options for LGBT people to adopt or foster, first as veiled "single parents" who hid their lovers and later as gay couples. In an interesting epilogue to the events in Boston, the ensuing court case, *Babets v. Johnston*, rallied local gay community support for a fledgling group called Gay and Lesbian Advocates and Defenders (GLAD), a public interest law firm. In 1990 GLAD won the *Babets* case, and Massachusetts finally returned to a "best interests of the child" standard for placing foster children. Thirteen years later GLAD continued its work in queer family law, winning *Goodridge v. Massachusetts Department of Public Health*—the first gay marriage case. One could call it an outgrowth of Donald Babets and David Jean losing their foster kids.

A Defining Wedge Issue: The United States in the Aughts

Although gay marriage would become the paradigmatic gay issue of the decade after 2000, ironically some of the feminist family law attorneys who had crafted strategy in lesbian custody and adoption cases were not exactly thrilled by the turn to marriage.[52] The exact things that made marriage so appealing for the antifeminist Christian Right tempered its appeal among feminists in the LGBT movement. The long feminist critique of marriage— that it colonized questions of love, yoking them to a property-based contract with the state, instantiated relations of submission and dependency, including abuse and exploitation, and tied people to a "forever and ever" version of relationship that often does not predominate in matters of the heart, meaning essentially that people were agreeing to sustained periods of misery after the love part wore off—meant that some of the LGBT movement's best intellectuals and sustaining activists were uninterested at best.[53]

Gay folk having children was not universally embraced, either. In 1998 it was possible for gay activists to complain that all the press about a "gay baby boom" was part of the promotion of an assimilationist agenda that attempted to minimize the difference between gay folk and straight and marginalize the screaming queens and butch dykes who didn't look or act like straight people, didn't want marriage, didn't have children, and for whom gay and lesbian liberation meant sexual freedom, not family. When Elizabeth Birch of the Human Rights Campaign and Troy Perry of the Metropolitan Community Church proposed a Millennium March that would emphasize "faith and family" as LGBT values, some objected that the lesbian and gay movement was being sold out—after a march in 1979 calling for "Breaking the Chains" and a march in 1987 to "Come Out for Freedom," was it really a good idea to move to faith and family?[54]

By the middle of the 2000s, though, the political landscape had shifted so dramatically that such an argument seemed utopian—gay folk should be so lucky as to be able to push an assimilationist agenda that promoted faith and family. Anything that sounded like queer religiosity was furiously, almost hysterically, smacked down. That year New Hampshire's Episcopal Church (affectionately called "the Republican Party at prayer," and not without reason) elected a gay bishop, Gene Robinson—a move that proved so explosively controversial to evangelicals (and even a minority within the Episcopal Church) that he wore a bulletproof vest to his consecration, so pervasive and persuasive were the death threats.[55] In 2004 NBC and CBS refused to air a television advertisement by a mainline Protestant denomination, the United Church of Christ (UCC), because they deemed its message of inclusion of gay men and lesbians so offensive. CBS executives wrote to the UCC: "Because this commercial touches on the exclusion of gay couples and other minority groups by other individuals and organizations and the fact the Executive Branch has recently proposed a Constitutional Amendment to define marriage as a union between a man and a woman [though the ad said nothing about gay marriage], this spot is unacceptable for broadcast on the [CBS and UPN] networks."[56] A year later a lesbian conservative Jewish family lighting Sabbath candles on a children's television show, *Postcards from Buster*, was banned from the airwaves, because apparently religious observance by lesbian families had become too controversial even for PBS; the CEO of PBS was forced to step down and federal funding was imperiled when Secretary of Education Margaret Spellings criticized the episode.[57]

Also in 2003 gay marriage became a "wedge issue"—something deliberately manipulated by conservative strategists to divide people. On May 15, 2003, a Gallup poll found "the highest level of acceptance of the legality of homosexuality measured over the 26 years Gallup has been asking [whether] homosexual relations between consenting adults should be legal." Gallup said that 60 percent of Americans supported decriminalizing homosexual sex, and on civil unions, they were divided, 49 percent opposed and 49 percent favored giving same-sex couples "some of the legal rights of married couples." On June 7 Robinson was elected bishop. On June 26 the U.S. Supreme Court found in *Lawrence v. Texas* that there was no compelling state interest that permitted the criminalization of sodomy. On July 30 a CBS News poll reported that 40 percent of respondents favored same-sex marriage, while 55 percent opposed it. Sometime between May and July was the high point of support for gay unions in 2003 (CBS and Gallup asked slightly different questions, so it's hard to say). What happened after that is easier to read: support for gay marriage and civil unions fell precipitously. On August 14 a *Washington Post* poll said that "public acceptance of same-sex unions is falling," and only 37 percent of Americans supported civil unions. By January 2004 a Gallup poll found only 34 percent of Americans favored civil unions, with 41 percent opposed, and 25 percent expressing no opinion.[58] Opposition to gay marriage reached its high point in 2004 with 63 percent of Americans opposed in a February Pew poll, just after the Massachusetts Supreme Court ruling making gay marriage legal in that state.[59] CBS found even less support for gay marriage in November 2004 with only 21 percent supporting gay marriage.[60]

What happened from the summer of 2003 through the 2004 elections in

November? How did gay marriage, family, and faith issues go from being the assimilationist agenda that many gay activists didn't much like, and New Hampshire Episcopalians and a conservative Supreme Court could endorse in 1998, to something so horrifying that the day after the elections in November 2004 Democrats were blaming gay people and the gay marriage issue for their losses (even though Democrats had not been conspicuously supportive of either)? As we have seen, casting about for a new antigay strategy after their rout in *Romer*, the Christian Right was looking at gay marriage. On July 30, 2003, George Bush indicated his support for a constitutional amendment banning gay marriage in a press conference that day. Many believed it was the work of Karl Rove, the Bush administration strategist and master of the wedge issue. "The sacred institution of marriage should not be redefined by a few activist judges," Bush added, in a speech, as the Democratic primary season wound down, in May 2004. "The need for [a gay marriage] amendment is still urgent, and I repeat that call today."[61] Christian Right groups, like the Traditional Values Coalition and the Family Research Council, hammered away at the issue, saying that heterosexual marriages were shaky and endangered. In state after state, Christian Right activists won "mini-DOMAs"—state-level bans on recognition of gay and lesbian marriage—and even state constitutional amendments. While a federal constitutional amendment was an effort clearly doomed even in the antigay, high drama days of 2003–2004, the presidential endorsement was sufficient to mobilize the Christian Right to transform the focus of the election from a war in Iraq that was growing more unpopular by the day, from the questions of torture, the scandal of policies at Abu Ghraib prison, racism and Hurricane Katrina, to gays.

For the Children: Gay Marriage as
Privatizing Responsibility for Child Support

During the NBC coverage of the Summer Olympics in 2000, a major market for TV advertisers to tell sentimental stories of liberal internationalism, two separate corporate sponsors showed ads telling stories of Chinese children being adopted by U.S. families, suggesting some of the power of adoption to capture our imagination about what is good about neoliberal globalization. One of the ads, by the insurance company giant John Hancock, told a story of one these "new" American families by showing lesbian parents. It was first aired during the pre-Olympic gymnastic trials and then became the site of a struggle between the Christian Right and gay and gay friendly activists. While right-wing groups urged boycotts, the e-mail that circulated on leftist and liberal listservs urged recipients to contact Hancock over their "courageous" ad, and described the ad this way: it "shows two women at the airport where they are just bringing home their newly adopted Asian baby. They are so loving and it is so sweet you can't help but cry. They congratulate each other on what great moms they'll be, etc." Hancock compromised; they showed it once during the Olympics. This paradoxical conjuncture—of a lesbian, cross-racial baby story that the conservative Right hates, sponsored by a Fortune 500 global corporation—suggests something of the terms being realigned in the first decade after 2000: economic globalization, sex, queer folk, and virtue.

As we have seen, the 1990s and thereafter saw the decisive success of neoliberalism, with its preference for the dominance of markets and the shrinking of the state and of public spheres. The libertarianism in this ideological movement provided much of the force of the opposition— including among conservatives—to the antigay adoption and marriage forces in the Christian Right. Nikolas Rose, in his masterful close reading of the ideological architects of neoliberalism, Friedrich von Hayek and Alexander Rustow, among others, argues that the problem neoliberalism sought to solve was the excessive moralism and interventionism of the liberal welfare state. Under this logic, then, what we should expect to see under neoliberalism with respect to gay adoption is a backing away from the interventionist scrutiny into gay and lesbian families, allowing the market to neutrally regulate adoption without its haunting by the mythical gay pedophile—essentially making it possible for those who can afford it to adopt. At the same time the essentially moral claims about the human rights abuses of impoverished children and their families, represented in their most extreme form in the insistence that kidnapping is one of the things feeding the adoption market in Guatemala, we would anticipate to have less purchase in a neoliberal regime, where market logic saturates the public sphere. And, indeed, to some extent that is what happened.

However, anthropologists like Aihwa Ong have invited us to think about the unevenness of neoliberalism's advances.[62] Neoliberalism's dominance has been far less complete than it might appear from looking at the leadership and policies of major nation-states like the United States, Mexico, and Canada. Even in Central America, where neoliberal dominance seemed absolute, activists, as we have seen, have succeeded in using questions of adoption and the disappearance of children to press broad human rights claims. At the same time the libertarian aspects of neoliberalism, the effort to roll back the moralism of the welfare state, is also far less extensive than we would predict. For one thing, something peculiar happens when neoliberalism encounters the family. As Lisa Duggan and Richard Kim have argued, neoliberalism, in shrinking state entitlements for those who cannot work—children, the elderly, people with physical and emotional disabilities—relies on an expansion of the role of the family as the site of the privatization of dependency.[63] Children, then, need to be enclosed in a family that is sufficiently affluent to provide for their education, health care, nutrition, and so forth without relying on a (disappearing) welfare state. But obviously not all families equally, or we would not have such a large child welfare system. From "welfare mothers" with a "man in the house" in the 1960s to the crack hos and skeezers of the 1980s, deviant sexualities continued to be a cultural fault line in who would be allowed to raise children and who would be prevented by case workers and courts. And all of this of course begs the question of what happens to those families—the majority—who lack the resources to do so.

Here, then, we begin to see the paradoxical effects of neoliberalism, the precise opposite of what its original proponents imagined: as neoliberalism produces an ever greater polarization of wealth, it needs a massive security apparatus—private security forces guarding gated enclaves, immigration restriction, massive imprisonment of impoverished people, expanding militaries and paramilitaries.[64] The force of this policing is peculiarly moral as it plays out in the lives of impoverished families—and even not-so-poor families—as hyper-bureaucratization. Ordinary, informal circulation of children as an economic survival strategy is disrupted by human rights treaties, replaced with legal, bureaucratic adoption. Further, as market logic dominates adoption, there is even greater reason to be concerned about trafficking and exploitation—and the state, ever more reliant on the moral logic of the demonization of the poor, addresses these concerns by silencing them. Neoliberalism, in this account, does little to nothing about commercialization and exploitation of children and, oddly, subjects poor families to extensive moral regulation through the apparatus of security. Yet the terrain of this morality and policing have shifted—from what kind of sex one has to how much money. Middle-class LGBT people were no longer presumptively child molesters, and their growing moral and economic stature expanded the state's confidence in allowing them to adopt or become foster parents. Yet while many people from various points on the U.S. political spectrum came to accept as commonsense the immorality of the poor and the respectability of upstanding, coupled, well-educated, and middle-class gay folk, one powerful constituency at least continued to insist on sex as the grounding of morality: the Christian Right, which meant that the broad cultural question remained emphatically unsettled and subject to contestation.

By 2006 some evangelicals were predicting that gay adoption was going to be the wedge issue of the national elections of 2008, hoping for a reprise of the way gay marriage energized the homophobic Republican base in 2004 (not suspecting that the issue was going to be race and praying for Bristol Palin's unborn baby). It failed, though, even though in some ways gay marriage and gay adoption are not really separable issues, especially for courts and states, which have affirmed repeatedly that the gay marriage question turns on children. The fact that it didn't succeed as the same kind of Democrat-destroying issue was undoubtedly a result of the particular circumstances of the 2008 election rather than any new "softness" in support for the argument (the Christian Right won that year on a measure opposing gay adoption and fostering in Arkansas, and gay marriage bans passed on popular ballots in three states). However, the arguments that emerged in the context of the Arkansas campaign, alongside the gay marriage decisions, suggest that the counterposition, even among those defending LGBT people, is neoliberal. The state has an interest in ensuring that children are provided for, because the alternative is that they become the responsibility of the state. If gay people have children, then the state has an interest in safeguarding the legal status (and hence, presumptively, the stability) of the relationships in which they are raised, inheritance, and orderly divorce and custody arrangements. So, at least, has been the reasoning of some state Supreme Court justices who have written for gay marriage.

In some ways this logic was revealed most sharply earlier, in states' relationship to placing foster children, and organizing foster-adopt relationships, with gay parents. The long march away from the Babets and Jean–style antigay foster policies has been conspicuously about saving money for shrinking governments. In the 1990s the newly expanded number of children in the child welfare systems in the aftermath of the crack babies "crisis" had begun to take their toll on state budgets. White queers (or those rhetorically imagined as white in policy debate) disproportionately served as the safety valve in this system, unburdening child welfare agencies of their "hard-to-place" children, either as foster parents or as adoptive parents. There was substantial overlap between "hard to place" and "kids of color," as even federal law recognized; by the mid-1990s, as we have seen, the federal adoption tax credit allowed those who took in "special needs" children to deduct all the associated costs from their taxes —and children of color were all defined as special needs.

In debates over gay adoption there was an emphasis on the role of gay people in taking "hard-to-place" children who would otherwise "languish" in foster care, where they would be a burden on the public fisc. In Massachusetts in 2006, for example, Catholic Charities, which had actually been placing children for adoption with gay people for nearly two decades, announced its intention to seek an exemption from state antidiscrimination statute in order to begin banning gay people from adopting.[65] In the firestorm that ensued Catholic Charities ended its role as an adoption agency,[66] and proponents of gay adoption reminded everyone of the crucial role of gay people in taking "hard-to-place" children, telling stories like this one about a lesbian couple who took in "Jesse" at the age of ten: he had "been to six schools, could barely read and was in special education. He'd lived in a homeless shelter with his drug-addicted birth mother and in eight foster homes."[67] Even as impious and un-earnest a commentator as Dan Savage (author of the weekly syndicated column "Savage Love") wrote in the *New York Times* about a white gay plaintiff in a Florida case to legalize gay adoption in that state and his three African American kids, two of them HIV-positive. "Gay and lesbian couples in New York, New Jersey, Oregon, Illinois and other states that allow them to adopt are not snapping up all the available babies or even the 'best' babies. It is an open secret among social workers that gay and lesbian couples are often willing to adopt children whom most heterosexual couples won't touch: HIV-positive children, mixed-race children, disabled children and children who have been abused or neglected."[68] Although Savage has the good grace to put the cringe-worthy "best" babies in quotes, there is no escaping the social calculus to which he points us—second-class parents, second-class children, and an argument for gay adoption that relies on the ways that "good gays" will relieve the state of a burden.

The gay marriage cases, likewise, have been fairly explicit in making this argument, that the goal of gay marriage is to relieve states of a burden. For example, in the opening lines of *Goodridge*, the Massachusetts gay marriage ruling, the court began by affirming that the decision is as much about children as it is about couples: "For those who choose to marry, and for their children, marriage provides an abundance of legal, financial, and social benefits." A few pages later it affirms the interest that the state has in organizing people into married couples, arguing, "Civil marriage anchors an ordered society by encouraging stable relationships over transient ones. It is central to the way the Commonwealth identifies individuals, provides for the orderly distribution of property, ensures that children and adults are cared for and supported whenever possible from private rather than public funds."[69] Couldn't be clearer than that: from the point of view of the state, the function of the family is to privatize dependency.

The California Supreme Court case in 2008 that affirmed the legality of gay marriage (before the Proposition 8 ballot initiative reversed it), *In re Marriage Cases*, positioned gay marriage quite similarly (although less succinctly):

> Society is served by the institution of civil marriage in many ways. Society, of course, has an overriding interest in the welfare of children, and the role marriage plays in facilitating a stable family setting in which children may be raised by two loving parents unquestionably furthers the welfare of children and society. . . . Furthermore, the legal obligations of support that are an integral part of marital and family relationships relieve society of the obligation of caring for individuals who may become incapacitated or who are otherwise unable to support themselves.[70]

And in a footnote it makes the argument even more explicit: "Although the legal system has shifted its focus from families to individuals, society still relies on families to play a crucial role in caring for the young, the aged, the sick, the severely disabled, and the needy. Even in advanced welfare states, families at all levels are a major resource for government, sharing the burdens of dependency with public agencies in various ways and to greater and lesser degrees."[71] And this critique was the heart and soul of the "Beyond Same-Sex Marriage" statement of 2006, in which LGBT activists and intellectuals put forth a sustained argument for not making gay marriage the center and focus of queer activism. Marriage, they suggested, was a poor substitute for a social safety net.

Weirdly, even in cases where courts rejected gay marriage, the opinions were solicitous of the well-being of gay people's children and their relationship to the state and the role of the state in safeguarding the raising of children. New York's gay marriage ruling in 2006, for example, followed New York City in noting that gay people were particularly unlikely to be careless about procreation or the well-being of their children and hence did not need state support or intervention. Heterosexual relationships, the court lamented, were "all too often casual or temporary" and hence could not guarantee the well-being of children.[72] For this reason, the court said, heterosexual relationships needed a special status to protect the vulnerability of children in them—marriage. By extending marriage to gay people, apparently, the specialness of heterosexual marriage and its excellent protection of the innocent and helpless children of irresponsible heterosexuals would be weakened. The law professor Kenji Yoshino is unstinting in his condemnation of the intellectual poverty of this argument; at the time he wrote: "When an Indiana court introduced this seemingly heterophobic logic last year in upholding a state ban on same-sex marriage, I thought it was a cockeyed aberration. But after both New York City and New York State presented similar logic in oral arguments, and the court followed suit, I began to understand the argument's appeal: it sounds nicer to gays. It also sounds more desperate."[73] But, as Yoshino points out, this argument was widely used. Apparently, whether one agreed or disagreed with gay marriage, the key point about it was that it turned on questions about the fiscal responsibility for raising the children of gay couples.

And, indeed, there was further evidence that gay marriage was inseparable from gay adoption in 2008, when voters in California passed Proposition 8, backed by Dobson's Focus on the Family, the Family Research Council, and the usual panoply of right-wing groups, bolstered by $20 million in donations from the LDS church, and the proposition disallowed gay marriage in California. Their ads focused on those predictable fears—children and public schools—claiming, among other things, that children would be taught about same-sex marriage in the public schools. Before that ad ran, Proposition 8 faced double-digit opposition in polls; by election day, it narrowly passed.[74] And the same day Arkansas voters passed their ballot measure prohibiting all unmarried people—gay or straight—from adopting or fostering children.

It remains to be seen whether the success of Proposition 8 in California and the Arkansas gay adoption ban will be to the LGBT movement what the *Romer* decision was to right-wing forces: a call to renewed, more successful activism on a slightly different tack. Massive demonstrations, especially in the West, indicated a groundswell of support for LGBT activism around family and children issues. The "Beyond Same-Sex Marriage" statement in 2006 indicated powerful support among LGBT activists and intellectuals for recognition of the many forms of relationship in which queer folks and many non-LGBT folks form family and raise children (including single parenthood, partnership that does not resolve itself into marriage, extended families, and created families) that the statements' drafters and signers argued ought to form the nucleus of access to public benefits, like health insurance and social security, and in which the constitutional right to privacy—to be left alone—ought to inhere.[75]

Relative to 1980 there is little doubt that LGBT people were being allowed freer access to adoption in 2010. There has been a reduction in the equation of nonheteronormative sexualities with child abuse (shuffled off onto the creepy neighbor, apparently), although that shift is by no means stable. For example, the success of the Arkansas referendum (overturned by an Arkansas court in 2010) suggests that there is power in this position yet. But the interesting thing is that even the Arkansas opposition group, composed of queer folk and their allies, made the argument that LGBT people were a good resource for state government, pointing out that gay people provided homes for hard-to-place children.[76] In this vision queer folk are invited to provide a safety valve to states in their decades-long wars on impoverished people and communities of color and their ability to raise their own children. This seems a far cry from the long civil rights struggle of LGBT people in the 1970s, 1980s, and 1990s to be able to control what happened to their own children.

U.S. Immigrants

The Next Fight over Race,
Adoption, and Foster Care?

On August 19, 2009, a friend of mine, let's say her name is Mercedes, was pulled over in a routine traffic stop (brown people with older cars get stopped a lot in Arizona, to the point where many people refer to the crime of "driving while Mexican"). When they realized she did not speak English, the Tucson Police Department questioned her about her immigration status (which they were not supposed to do).[1] She showed them her border-crossing card; as a resident of the border state of Sonora, she had applied for and gotten permission to enter freely to visit family and friends. They asked to see the birth certificate of her two-year-old daughter, Stephanie, who was in the car seat in back. Because Mercedes understood the protocols of harassment and fear that characterize the potential consequences of putting a brown child in your car in a border city (as I had learned, too, years earlier), she did something few white suburban parents could do: reached into the glove compartment for the copy of Stephanie's birth certificate that she kept there. Stephanie, it showed, was born in Tucson, and Mercedes was indeed her mother. The police officers said the birth certificate indicated that Mercedes was really living in Tucson, which is not permitted under the terms of her visa. They turned her over to Immigration and Customs Enforcement (ICE).

ICE whisked Mercedes off to an immigrant detention center seventy-five miles away. They weren't gentle, and being manhandled was frightening enough. But most terrifyingly, they took Stephanie away. They told Mercedes she would not see Stephanie again unless she named names: Who was she working for? Where did she live? What relatives were living in the United States? Mercedes kept asking where her daughter was, who was with her, whether she was safe, but no one would tell her. Mercedes admitted to her own sins—yes, she had lived in Tucson since Stephanie's birth—but refused to implicate anyone else. She wasn't working, she had no relatives in the United States. They told her that since Stephanie was a U.S. citizen, they could take her and put her in foster care and deport Mercedes. A call from her immigration lawyer, who had been trying to help Mercedes get a student visa—she wanted to be an elementary school teacher—made no difference; friends and family could learn nothing about Stephanie's whereabouts, either. Finally, after four days of this, ICE officials gave up, returned the baby to Mercedes, and dropped them both in the streets of Nogales, Sonora, a sometimes-rough border town, at 3 a.m. They hadn't eaten and had nothing but the clothes they were wearing. Mercedes borrowed a cell phone from a stranger and called her family. Her mother drove the fifty miles from Tucson to Nogales that night and brought her clothes and cash and a blanket for Stephanie. A couple of days later Mercedes's husband got her other two children ready, packed hastily, and they moved back to a small town in Sonora, joining the estimated one hundred thousand parents of U.S. citizen children who have been deported in the last ten years.[2] Mercedes now ekes out a meager existence for herself and her family working as a street vendor. They have joined the ranks of the very poor again.

These events took place nearly a year before Arizona made headlines nationally for Senate Bill (SB) 1070, a law that attempted to authorize exactly what the Tucson Police Department (TPD) did to Mercedes. The passage of SB 1070 sparked a debate in which TPD promised to stop, suggesting that the effect of the controversy, ironically, was to halt the very practice it seemed to authorize. While opponents of SB 1070 argued that this kind of questioning of immigrants ought not be in the hands of local law enforcement, which certainly seems a point worth making, it bears noticing that the "proper" authorities at ICE, those whom SB 1070 opponents were arguing *should* be in charge of immigration enforcement, were the ones who held the baby hostage. Mercedes's treatment apparently represented the new, reformed kind of terror practiced against immigrants under the Obama administration in contrast to the Bush administration's harsh policies—this was two weeks after a press conference in which ICE and the Obama administration had promised reform. One of the proximate causes of this renewed commitment to humane treatment was that an Amnesty International report earlier that year had found child migrants spending years in detention without judicial review of their claims to stay in the United States, housed with juveniles convicted of crimes, reportedly beaten by guards, and subject to solitary confinement for infractions like poor sportsmanship, swearing, or even grammatical mistakes.[3] Children as young as seven were brought to immigration hearings in shackles, with belly chains and leg irons.[4] The administration promised to stop sending immigrant families to the inaptly named T. Don Hutto Residential Center, a detention center near Austin, Texas, that had become a symbol of the abusiveness of the system, the subject of a class action suit, and even two years after a consent decree demanding reform, a judge found that the facility was still not in compliance. At Hutto children of refugees awaiting hearings on asylum claims were denied schooling and held in cells with their parents with no recreation facilities. They weren't even allowed crayons or pajamas. The Obama administration, however, failed to answer the basic question of why children and refugee families were locked up at all, rather than released into the community pending hearings on whether their asylum claims would be honored. They also promised to send families instead to the Berks Family Shelter Care Facility—a former nursing home —where guards allegedly disciplined children by sending them across a parking lot to a criminal juvenile detention facility and held families for as long as two years. A year after Hutto stopped detaining families and be- came instead a female immigrant detention facility, a new investigation suggested widespread sexual assault by a guard. Finally, the administration promised to take steps toward removing immigrants accused of status offenses—those awaiting hearings only on claims that they may (or may not have) overstayed a visa or worked without papers—from the more than 350 jails and prisons where they are currently held, mixed in with those accused or convicted of crimes.[5]

This chapter explores how the U.S. citizen children of immigrants— especially Guatemalans, ironically—are starting to become very vulnerable to being sent into foster care and adoptions. By treating the status offence of overstaying a visa (or even not being able to present documents proving your citizenship or some other recognized status at the drop of a hat) like a crime, and making any effort to hide undocumented status a genuinely prosecutable crime, officials are pushing children into state protective ser- vices and foster care. In a way that would be familiar to Native peoples and particularly African Americans, immigrants, as the largest de-nationalized labor force since slavery, have been mobilized to provide labor in the context of neoliberal globalization, but visas, illegality, and now the danger of losing children have been deployed to ensure their continued vulnerability and low wages. Yet at the same time, this is still a fight, a question; immigrant children are not seen as a cute, innocent, victimized population that just by virtue of their circumstances are seen as adoptable, not in the way that, say, Haitians were after the earthquake of 2009 or reservation kids were in the 1970s. Like LGBT folks, immigrants also represent an as yet unsettled and uncertain question about who is vulnerable to losing their children and who can adopt.

Mercedes's story is not anomalous, and while she ultimately got Stephanie back, other immigrant mothers have not been so lucky. Encarnación Bail Romero, one of 136 immigrants detained in a workplace raid of a poultry processing plant in Missouri in April 2007, had parental rights to her six-month-old son terminated as a result. Hers was among the first raids the Department of Homeland Security pursued as part of a campaign they called Operation Return to Sender, which promised to aggressively prosecute "crimes" related to false identification, to sentence and hold people on those crimes, to conduct workplace raids, and to deport people whose status was suspect. So Bail was charged with possessing a fake ID and served a year and a half in jail for that crime, waiting to be deported after she had served her sentence.

At first, her baby, Carlos, stayed with two aunts. But they were sharing a tiny apartment with six of their own children and had very little money. When a teacher's aid at one of their children's schools offered to find someone else to care for Carlos, they agreed. Three months later the aid visited Encarnación in jail, saying a couple with land and a beautiful house wanted to adopt Carlos. She said no. A few weeks later an adoption petition arrived at the jail, in English. Encarnación was not literate in Spanish, never mind English. Still, with the help of a Mexican cellmate, a guard, and a bilingual Guatemalan visitor, she prepared a response to the court: "I do not want my son to be adopted by anyone," she wrote on a piece of notebook paper. "I would prefer that he be placed in foster care until I am not in jail any longer. I would like to have visitation with my son." Although she repeatedly asked judges and lawyers for help, it was a year before she found a lawyer who would take the case. By then, it was too late. The couple caring for Carlos complained that she had sent no money for his support and had not contacted him. A year and a half after she went to jail, a judge terminated her parental rights and permitted the other couple to adopt him. "Her lifestyle, that of smuggling herself into the country illegally and committing crimes in this country," Judge Dally wrote, referring to the false ID, "is not a lifestyle that can provide stability for a child. A child cannot be educated this way, always in hiding or on the run."[6]

Encarnación became a symbol of how immigrants lose their children to the child welfare system when she told her story to a House of Representatives briefing in November 2009, and the adoption was subsequently put on hold. But hers is hardly the only one; arrests and deportations have become more common since the Immigration and Naturalization Service was transformed into the Department of Homeland Security. Since 2003 hundreds of thousands of immigrants have been deported by ICE. As even seeking health care or social services for your child leads people to become ensnared in immigration enforcement—694 people in Arizona were reported to the Office of Special Investigations of the Department of Economic Security (which administers Temporary Aid to Needy Families, services for children with developmental disabilities, Medicaid, and so forth) in a single week in November 2009, to be investigated for suspected immigration violations[7]—these questions arise over and over. In another closely watched case, María Luis, a Guatemalan Maya-Kiché woman in Grand Isle, Nebraska (the site of another large workplace raid, although Luis had come to the attention of authorities earlier), had her parental rights terminated as well, following her arrest for lying to the police and subsequent deportation. María had taken her one-year-old daughter, Angelica, to the doctor for a respiratory infection. Although she was a Kiché-speaker, the doctors instructed her in Spanish about how to care for the child. When she failed to arrive for a follow-up appointment, social services went to her house with the police. When asked if she was her children's mother, María, frightened that she would be in trouble because of her immigration status, said she was the babysitter. The police arrested her on a criminal charge for falsely identifying herself, and she was deported. Angelica and Daniel, seven, went to foster care, and state social services began proceedings to terminate her parental rights. Federal immigration officials gave her no opportunity to participate in those proceedings, and she lost the children. In April 2009, four years after the children were originally sent to foster care, the Nebraska Supreme Court restored her parental rights, saying that federal immigration officials had denied her due process rights in interfering with her ability to participate in the state proceedings and that state officials had never provided her with an interpreter, never explained the process through which she could seek custody of the children, and never made any effort to reunify the family, largely because social service workers "thought the children would be better off staying in the United States."[8] In an echo of the fight over the Indian Child Welfare Act, people under federal jurisdiction—in this case, those suspected of immigration status violations—are losing children to the states and, precisely because of the jurisdiction problem, are powerless to defend their children.

Stories like these are unusual, in that the mothers finally were able to obtain effective counsel and were able to contest the state social services efforts. National organizations sent out press releases; the cases were publicized in national media and on the Internet. More commonly, no one hears about these cases except the people who know the family and the officials involved. The Urban Institute, in two recent reports, has suggested that there may be hundreds of thousands of children affected by federal immigrant deportations, an unknown number of whom may also be caught in state social welfare cases.[9] An estimated 4.5 million children in the United States in 2005 had at least one undocumented parent.[10]

George W. Bush, who had begun his presidency promising immigration reform, ended it as a global symbol of harsh tactics and even immigrant abuse, from "Black sites," where the CIA flew migrants who were suspected of being terrorists in order to turn them over to be tortured, to secret detention centers in the United States into which people disappeared, even those who had merely overstayed a visa, where family and friends and even members of Congress could not find them because ICE kept no centralized databases and the locations of the sites themselves were secret.[11]

Between 2004 and 2008, by some estimates five thousand U.S. citizens were deported as well for failing to produce the proper documents when they were questioned by ICE.[12] One day I had a glimpse of how easily that could happen when my daughter was briefly detained by ICE. It was 2004 and I was in Guatemala and had just that day been stopped at a military checkpoint, which prompted my traveling companion to tell me a story about how he had watched as the authorities detained and disappeared people off buses during the war. Troubled and wanting to hear that the people I loved were safe, I called and talked to my daughter, then sixteen, who was in school in Phoenix. She had been home in Tucson visiting earlier that day, and after her other mom bought her a ticket, watched her get on the Greyhound bus, and left, ICE held the bus and removed my daughter for questioning. She was (and is) constitutionally allergic to holding onto her birth certificate—something to do with her deeply conflicted feelings about who is supposed to be listed as her mother—and all she had was a school ID. She persuaded them that she was a U.S. citizen even without a birth certificate, and everything was fine, but I still have nightmares about her being deported to Mexico, where she has only been on day-trips to go shopping with me. She spoke no Spanish at the time.

The most visible symbol of the Bush administration's harshness toward immigrants were the massive roundups at workplaces that deported even people with credible claims to remain in the United States, who often chose to take "voluntary" departure because they felt that long confinement awaiting an immigration hearing would harm their family more than deportation. (Many Guatemalans who spoke only a Mayan language were quickly deported as well, never understanding the charges against them or having a translator.)[13] When George W. Bush went to Guatemala in March 2007 to promote free trade, he was confronted by angry crowds, press, and even politicians over a raid at a New Bedford, Massachusetts, plant that had resulted in the detention and deportation of many Guatemalans. Demonstrators dogged Bush wherever he went; the largest group, about five hundred people, burned the president in effigy. Some were angered by the deportations after that raid; others asked why the detainees were sent so far away from their families and communities—some in leg irons—to Texas.[14] Most, though, were mobilized by a photo that ran in *Prensa Libre* three days after the raid: a little girl, about two, clutching her mother tightly, waiting to hear what would happen to her father, who was picked up in the raid and accused of being in the United States without proper papers. She is adorable with her pig tails, clutching a green Dora the Explorer blanket, a well-loved and well-cared for child, but she looks straight into the camera, eyes full of tears and wide with fear. This picture of baby Tomasa, taken by Peter Pereira, a photographer for the *New Bedford Standard-Times*, became a symbol of ICE workplace raids for those inside and outside the United States.[15] Migrants under the age of eighteen who were working at the plant were taken into Massachusetts Department of Social Services custody. In Guatemala, Bush was grilled about the children of those migrants who had been left behind, which was reported in the Guatemalan press, some of whom were stranded at school, daycare, or even alone at home.[16] In response to a question from President Oscar Berger about children being separated from families in the context of the raid, Bush denied it. "*No es la verdad,*" he claimed. "That's not the way America operates. We're a decent, compassionate country. Those kinds of things we do not do. We believe in families, and we'll treat people with dignity."[17] The next day, Senator Edward

Kennedy, in Washington, demanded that Homeland Security release the single parents who had been flown to Texas, stranding their young children alone in Massachusetts. The Guatemalan press called Bush a liar.[18]

Workplace raids that target large employers are stressful for entire communities, citizens, and migrants alike. In the New Bedford and the Postville, Iowa, raids, schools, unable to get lists of who had been detained from ICE, tried frantically to arrange backup caregivers for children they guessed might be affected so no child went home to an empty house to await parents who were not coming back. In Los Angeles, U.S. citizens and legal residents complained that they were held against their will in another raid, and one U.S. citizen mother who had brought her young children with her to work, on her way to a parent-teacher conference, complained that her children were traumatized after being detained while ICE officials questioned employees and led some away in handcuffs.[19] The aftermath of a raid is a lot like a natural disaster. Social services, churches, and community-based organizations rally and try to get people information, income supports, and housing, especially at first. Families left behind report disruption, posttraumatic stress symptoms, loss of income, loss of homes, moving in with relatives, and even hunger.[20]

Some of the most shocking things that have happened to immigrant mothers and children have been done by local law enforcement agencies, conspicuously the Maricopa County Sherriff's Office (MCSO), under 287(g) arrangements, named for the section of the administrative code that permits them. These agreements involve deputizing local law enforcement to act as immigration agents. The other way that immigrants come under the purview of state and local police departments is in the context of detention. Federal immigration officials have begun to detain immigrants suspected of civil status offenses rather than releasing them on their own recognizance until their hearings, creating an unsustainable burden on federal detention facilities. An estimated four hundred thousand people a year were being held in 2009, only a fraction of them in federal, civil immigration facilities, the rest in a combination of private, for-profit lockups and local jails and prisons designed for those charged with or convicted of criminal offenses.[21]

In Maricopa County, local officials have required pregnant women accused of immigration offenses to labor and give birth in shackles. In 2008 Alma Chacón, picked up and accused of an immigration violation after a routine traffic stop, went into labor two days later. Transported to the hospital in shackles, she gave birth tied to her bed with a twelve-foot chain.

Her baby was removed as soon as she was born and placed in foster care for seventy-two days. Chacón had been in the United States for eighteen years. Although both the Arizona Department of Corrections and federal policy forbid restraining a laboring woman, the MCSO is a law unto itself. "Let's assume someone is faking labor—that's a hypothetical—and she then chose to escape and hit or assault the hospital staff," said Jack McIntyre, a deputy sheriff with the MCSO. "She could do that easily because it's an unsecured area."[22] A year later that policy was still in force. Miriam Mendiola-Martinez gave birth under the same conditions just before Christmas in 2009.[23] The previous August the Rapporteur on the Rights of Migrant Workers for the Inter-American Commission on Human Rights (IACHR) of the Organization of American States raised the question of whether the federal government actually had enforceable authority in Maricopa County. The IACHR delegation, conducting a fact-finding mission on immigrant detention, asked questions that many had about whether the MCSO was exceeding federal limits in its 287(g) immigrant sweeps: "The Rapporteurship is concerned that the federal government was unable to facilitate the Maricopa County visit, as it raises serious doubt about the control federal authorities have over how local law authorities enforce federal civil immigrations laws. The Rapporteurship is concerned that the federal government might be unable to hold local law enforcement properly accountable for enforcing immigration laws with respect for basic human rights."[24] Although the federal government modified its 287(g) agreement with Maricopa County a few months after this, it did not terminate it, leaving the IACHR's question hanging: to what extent are local police departments accountable to anyone for activities associated with immigration enforcement?

Finally, it is important to note how anomalous this kind of immigration policy is in the history of the United States. It is unlikely that Mercedes and Stephanie would have been deported at any time prior to 1996. Before 1920 there were no laws regulating the entry of residents of Mexico into the United States. Immigration enforcement, such as it was, was aimed at blocking entry of Chinese nationals and returning anarchists and Communists to Europe, so Mercedes could have come and gone as she pleased. In 1929 the U.S. Border Patrol began looking for migrants from or through Mexico who had failed to pay the head tax or evaded the hated baths, in which people were "inspected" while naked, their hair shorn, and they were subject to chemical regimens supposedly to detect lice—but probably having more to do with racial beliefs about "dirty" Mexicans, since they were not required by law and were not enacted at other ports of entry.[25] However, since the Immigration Restriction Act of 1924 did not set a quota restriction on Mexicans (as it did most non–Latin American nationalities), and considering that Mercedes had applied for and received a border crossing card, we could probably conclude that Mercedes would have been unaffected by these forms of immigrant restriction in the 1920s. In 1929 (as in 1986) those who had lived in the country for a long time were eligible for an adjustment of status, so had Mercedes been here at either of those times she would have been a U.S. citizen.

In the 1930s immigration officials began to adjust the status of immigrants whose deportation would cause a hardship to a U.S. citizen child, allowing parents who had lived in the United States for seven years or more to briefly leave and then reenter legally, but in 1938 that administrative provision was cancelled for Mexicans, and limited to Canadians and Europeans, when a U.S. consul in Juarez complained that many of the Mexicans were "of the laboring class." In the 1940s and 1950s, though, in exchange for an annual registration procedure, instituted as a wartime measure, migrants who registered were exempted from deportation.[26] Under such a practice Mercedes would have stayed, as she never hid her comings and goings (she and, even more so her children, had spent much of the summer before with their grandparents in Mexico).

The massive immigration reform of 1965 reversed the thrust of immigration reform since the 1920s and made immigration to the United States significantly easier. It also enshrined the principle of family unification as a centerpiece of U.S. immigration law, meaning that U.S. citizens could migrate their brothers and sisters, spouses, children, and parents. (In 1976, though, Congress amended the Immigration and Nationality Act to require that only those over twenty-one could petition for entry of their parents.)[27] Still, throughout the 1970s and 1980s immigration law for the most part got progressively more generous toward letting people stay. One key provision that remained from the 1930s was the principle of preventing deportations if they caused "extreme hardship"; in practice this meant that a parent with a U.S. citizen child would not be deported. This all came to a screeching halt in 1996 when the Illegal Immigration Reform and Immigrant Responsibility Act began sharply limiting any previous generosity extended to migrants. Specifically, it sought to limit parents' ability to stay in the United States with their minor children. As the conference committee wrote: "the alien must provide evidence of harm to his spouse, parent, or child substantially beyond that which ordinarily would be expected to result from the alien's deportation. . . . Similarly, showing that an alien's

United States citizen child would fare less well in the alien's country of nationality than in the United States does not establish 'exceptional' or 'extremely unusual' hardship and thus would not support a grant of relief under this provision."[28] Immigrants in mixed status families no longer had any presumed right to stay together. It was only really in the years since 1996, then, that Mercedes and her U.S. citizen daughter could be dropped in the streets of Nogales at 3 a.m.

In the Contract with America climate of hostility to welfare mothers, the press was also running significant numbers of stories about women coming across the border to have their babies, then using their U.S. citizen children as an excuse to stay. As Elena Gutiérrez argues, a discourse of immigrants "breeding like rabbits," mothers who are hyperfertile "breeding machines" emerged sharply the late 1990s, not for the first time but at an amplified volume.[29] It was a period of a recession in California. In an effort to criminalize migration offenses, voters passed Proposition 187, which sought to deny health care and education to migrants and their children, although it was rolled back by a judge as unconstitutional. Still more draconian legislation, never passed, sought to deny birthright citizenship to migrants' children who were born in the United States.[30]

As I write this in 2010 we do not yet have a discourse that would signal that the U.S. citizen children of immigrants are adoptable children, although some of the foster parents discussed above clearly do see these adorable Guatemalan and other immigrant babies as adoptable. Reflecting on why this is so tells us something about what the conditions of possibility are for the production of a population of babies and children that are severable from their parents and perhaps something of how close or how far the United States is from seeing immigrant children as adoptable.

I have been arguing that with black and Native children several things made them adoptable. One was the long durée of historical circumstances that made them not belong to their parents—beginning with slavery, for African Americans, and boarding schools, for Native communities. That is only sometimes the case for immigrants, either as an undifferentiated group or as Latin Americans in particular. In the 1930s and 1940s, for example, once they got to the United States, even if immigrant children were on the street or in the workplace, socialists and liberals mostly saw them as their parents,' in need of child labor law reform perhaps, or maybe as the tough but sturdy characters in Louis Hine's Popular Front photos of boys in the street. On the other hand, Orphan Trains that moved an estimated two hundred thousand children from East Coast cities to Western ranches, families, and farms did open up that possibility. The second thing that made black and Native children adoptable, I have suggested, was a discourse that scapegoated their parents as part of seismic shifts in the structure of the economy in the post–Second World War period and then again in the late 1980s, one that held up children as the little victims (of crack), downstream from the harm caused by government benefits—hence forming a rationale for downsizing the state. With immigrants we certainly see a racializing panic in the late 1990s that identified immigrants with high taxes and illegitimate use of resources, but migrants' children were as much the target of these attacks as the migrants themselves. They were not victims in need of rescue. The Proposition 187 campaign included bitter rhetoric about the cost of educating Latino children, seemingly extending even to U.S. citizen children. While even a few years earlier, the potential that deportation could harm a U.S. citizen child could serve as a justification for a whole immigrant family to stay, by the early 1990s there wasn't much support in the anti-immigrant camp for seeing the children of immigrants as victims. Indeed, there were discussions of how to evade the constitutional requirement of birthright citizenship for the children of immigrants born in the United States.

I have also been arguing that in the Latin American fight to instantiate a neoliberal rather than a socialist version of the state, indigenous Guatemalan people (and other supposedly left-leaning ethnicities and communities) lost their children to kidnapping and adoption, both as a tactic to frighten them into loyalty to the state and for the children's own good—so they would not become socialists, first, and be in need of the support of a welfare state, later. Here the discourse about immigrants seems quite confused. These children should be sent back to Guatemala, despite the fact that once they get there Americans regard them as potentially adoptable.

The other interesting thing that has apparently mitigated against the anti-immigrant efforts turning into rescue efforts for the children is that the anti-immigrant movement is overwhelmingly secular. Evangelicals for the most part have been building transnational denominations abroad and at least trying to build multiethnic churches and coalitions in the United States. The Catholic Church has long been one of the main groups providing support to immigrants, and in 2006 Cardinal Roger Mahoney of the archdiocese of Los Angeles was credited with providing some of the spark for that spring's mass marches for immigrant rights by pledging that his churches would defy a U.S. House bill making it a felony to aid immigrants, if it passed. It did not. As I have been suggesting, it is Christian church people and gay men and lesbians who do much of the adopting in the United States, and there is not much interest in either group, at least not in an organized way, in turning immigrant's children into adoptees.

It is probably also a factor that immigrants to the United States are still predominantly understood as men, as workers, rather than as single mothers. As we saw with African American children, from civil rights to the Moynihan Report to the welfare reform debate, the thing that made black children "need" to be adopted was the pathologization of their single mothers. Native children did not belong to proper nuclear families either, in the sense that they were being raised by tribal communities or extended families. In the times and places in Latin America where adoption has been prevalent, children are often construed as orphans by those from outside the country, but these "orphans" are often the children of single mothers.

It is of course not true that immigrants are all or even mostly men, and some of the same factors driving transnational adoption are bringing increasing numbers of immigrant mothers to the United States—changes in household labor and economies. As we have seen, there were significant shifts in economies of care work among (mostly but not exclusively white) middle-class women in the United States that created a "need" for domestic workers here. To offset declining real wages among men, increased numbers of heterosexual mothers entered the labor force, setting off what many saw as a gendered labor crisis at home.[31] Women were still doing most of domestic labor and, according to Arlie Hoschild in *The Second Shift*, fighting with their husbands about it. At the time many feminists thought that in order to resolve this crisis, men were going to have to do more childcare and housework—women's wages were becoming a non-negotiable part of domestic economies. It turned out, though, that there was actually another way of negotiating this problem for middle-class families: delaying childbearing until a time when a mother's wages would presumably be higher,[32] and then the family could hire a nanny from outside the United States, as her wages would be significantly lower from what a middle-class U.S. woman could earn.[33] As we have seen, this is a risky reproductive strategy, as both partners' fertility declines as they age, most conspicuously for women beyond the age of thirty, more or less exactly the moment when she might be getting established in a career, giving rise to a class of people who turned to reproductive technology and adoption to complete their families. This narrative is also relevant for lesbian and gay families, who, while they might not have a specifically gendered labor crisis at home, are nevertheless caught up in the same

problem of managing domestic and waged labor in the context of childrearing and a structural "infertility."

At the end of the twentieth century growing numbers of households in
the United States included domestic workers; these were increasingly likely
to be middle-class, rather than wealthy, households and the workers were
most likely to be of Latin American origin or ancestry.[34] This situation had
the effect of shifting the crisis of reproductive labor either economically
downward in the United States—to bring the "who's watching the kids"
question to a greater number of working-class and/or Latino households
in the United States, or to carry it across nation boundaries, as mothers
leave young children in their home countries to support them by doing
domestic work elsewhere. Those who bring their children, or who have
them once they reach the United States, do have an actual or potential
child-care crisis, depending on the extent to which they have friends or
family that are not in the labor force and can afford to watch the children.
To the extent that they cannot—as poor families in the United States so
often have not been able to—they are vulnerable to losing children to an
unforgiving social welfare system.

This book has been arguing that the production of adoptable children is
an index of vulnerability, particularly of single mothers. Studying how people lose their children suggests that gendered, racial, and political order is
revealed and in some ways enforced through the actual or potential taking of
children, whether it is sending Native children to boarding schools to "civilize" them and make them learn English or punishing black communities in
the civil rights era by taking the children of mothers who applied for welfare.
The "crack babies" hysteria and fetal alcohol syndrome crisis tell us a great
deal about how welfare reform was accomplished, how a controversial
argument ("Reaganomics") for massively shrinking government became
mainstream through a national pedagogy on how government benefits like
Aid to Families with Dependent Children create little victims, as crack use
was tied to black mothers and black mothers became the paradigmatic
welfare users. It also tells us how the War on Drugs became a massive
program to incarcerate poor people, and how even white and middle-class
mothers became persuaded that anything less than anxious, vigilant hyper-
parenting was tantamount to child neglect.

Adoption also helps us track the broad stories of fights over collectivist
notions of the state versus neoliberalism outside the United States as well
as inside it. It gives us a different way of narrating the real human cost of
the Cold War and its civil wars in Latin America, as well as the ways

neoliberalism's ascendancy made virtually everything available for commercialization, even children. It reminds us that there have been, since the 1930s, at least two traditions in the United States for understanding our responsibility for "their" children. One imagined rescue and conversion. Another reached for solidarity with refugees. If that latter tradition has never actually represented the way U.S. visa policies worked for refugee children, perhaps it should have. Finally, the contemporary controversies over adoption and fostering—whether gay and lesbian people can get children, whether immigrant (usually single) mothers should lose them or, on the contrary, whether their children should be denied citizenship and so create a permanent, multigenerational class of marginal people—reveal something of the current cultural fault lines in the United States. If adoption has often been a symbol of hopefulness and new beginnings, it is worth noticing that it is also an event in which long histories of inequality and social marginalization are sedimented, frozen in time and then made into family stories.

Notes

INTRODUCTION

1. Tauber and Wulff, "Angelina Adopts a Girl," 61.

2. Hall, "Zahara's Biological Mom."

3. Silverman, "Angelina Jolie."

4. Gibbs, "With Her Malawi Adoption."

5. Peretti, "Madonna, Mercy and Malawi."

6. Bainbridge, "U.S. Adoption Agent"; U.S. Department of State, Office of Children's Issues, "Intercountry Adoption: Cambodia."

7. Gibbs, "With Her Malawi Adoption."

8. Graff, "The Lie We Love."

9. Associated Press, "None of 33 Kids Taken by U.S. Baptists Is an Orphan."

10. See, e.g., Egan, "The Missionary Impulse."

11. Wander, "Love and Haiti."

12. Karen Dubinsky helped me understand how these narratives work. See Dubinsky, "Babies without Borders."

13. See Solinger, *Wake Up Little Susie*; Carp, *Adoption Politics*; Fessler, *Girls Who Went Away*.

14. John Triseliotis, "Intercountry Adoption: In Whose Best Interest?" in *Intercountry Adoption: Practical Experiences*, ed. Michael Humphrey and Heather Humphrey (London: Routledge, 1993), 129–37, cited in Solinger, *Beggars and Choosers*, 24.

15. Chandra et al., *Fertility, Family Planning, and Reproductive Health of U.S. Women*.

16. Berebitsky, *Like Our Very Own*, 132.

17. *New York Times*, "Hoover Backs Bill to Waive Quota Act for Reich Children."

18. U.S. Congress, *Hearing before the Subcommittee to Investigate Juvenile Delinquency, Interstate Adoption Practices*, 3.

19. See Solinger, *Wake Up Little Susie*; Bailey, *From Front Porch*; and Berebitsky, *Like Our Very Own*. Barbara Melosh stresses the extent to which the young women in the case records she reviewed were not forced, but rather felt happy and relieved to be relinquishing their babies. While she would disagree with this point, I would argue that her account and Solinger's story of young women compelled to relinquish by social conditions and experts actually don't contradict each other significantly; it is not surprising that pregnant girls were as persuaded as the rest of the society that it was shameful to be unwed and pregnant and impossible to raise a child as a young, single mother and that the desire to do so probably represented an abnormal psychological condition. Who wouldn't be relieved to be rid of that burden? The fact that the number of girls "choosing" to relinquish their babies declined sharply as soon as social conditions shifted slightly would seem to make that point rather indisputably. See Melosh, *Strangers and Kin*.

20. Stolley, "Statistics on Adoption in the United States."

21. For "moral panic," see Cohen, *Folk Devils*; for mugging, see Hall et al., *Policing the Crisis*.

22. See Gilmore, *Golden Gulag*; Davis, *Are Prisons Obsolete?*; and Sudbury, *Global Lockdown*.

23. See Kim, *Adopted Territory*; and Dorow, *Transnational Adoption*.

24. Selman, "The Movement of Children for International Adoption."

25. I am much indebted to John T. Way for this framework for thinking about Guatemala as a future, not a past, in the context of development policy and globalization; see Way, "The Mayan in the Mall."

26. Kane, "The Movement of Children for International Adoption."

27. Grandin, *Empire's Workshop*.

28. See Morgan and Roberts, "Rights and Reproduction in Latin America"; Goldberg, *The Means of Reproduction*; and Solinger, *Beggars and Choosers*. See also, *Juno*; thanks to Lisa Duggan for conversation about *Juno*.

29. Sevilla and Ingley, "Adoption Suspect Ordered to NY."

30. Goldman, *The Art of Political Murder*.

31. Selman, "The Movement of Children for International Adoption."

32. Graham and Domon, *I'm Pregnant*, 48.

33. See the conversation between Bartholet, "International Adoption," and Oreskovic and Maskew, "Red Thread or Slender Read," and between Ethica: An Independent Voice for Ethical Child Adoption, http://www.ethicanet.org/adoption/ethica-views/position-pape rs, and the Harvard Law School Child Advocacy Program (CAP), http://www.law.harvard .edu/programs/about/cap/law-reform/index.html, on legal reform, currently embodied as the "Families for Orphans" act that would reject the Hague Convention norms and allow the United States to set child welfare policy, globally and unilaterally, offering, for example, debt relief essentially in exchange for children.

34. Bartholet, *Family Bonds*, 40; 17–18.

35. The phrase is Signe Howell's; see Howell, *The Kinning of Foreigners*.

36. Bartholet, *Family Bonds*, 42–44.

37. Solinger, *Beggars and Choosers*, 28.

38. Bartholet, *Nobody's Children*, 15.

39. Ibid., 47.

40. Ibid., 90–94.

41. A note of clarification: subsidized adoption, which we had, does in principle maintain access to Medicaid programs. However, in our state Medicaid is subcontracted, and the shift from foster care to adoption changed our plan and provider. The effect was to get her many fewer services. Proposals to means tested adoption subsidy, if enacted, would only make that worse (some nontitle IV-E subsidy is already means tested).

1. AFRICAN AMERICAN CHILDREN AND ADOPTION

1. Kennedy, *Interracial Intimacies*, 396. For very similar arguments, in almost the same words, see Bartholet, *Family Bonds*, 94–95, 97; and Macaulay and Macaulay, "Adoption for Black Children." The contrast would actually be more significant than that; 3,310 represents 20 percent of adoptions from the public system, which Hansen and Pollack carefully analyzed to try to confirm the "whiteness" of the family (no mixed-race couples or individuals) and the "blackness" of the child (no mixed-race children); see Hansen and Pollack, "Transracial Adoption of Black Children." According to the Adoption and Foster Care Analysis and Reporting System (AFCARS) report, the number of black children adopted from the public system that year was 16,554; see U.S. Department of Health and Human Services, AFCARS *Report FY 2003*. But the numbers from the 1970s were not computed the same way, as many more children would have been counted as "black," so we could guess that by 1970s' standards quite a large number of "black" children were adopted by white families in 2003.

2. Hansen and Pollack, "Transracial Adoption of Black Children."

3. Howard, "Transracial Adoption," 515.

4. Neal, "The Case Against Transracial Adoption."

5. National Association of Black Social Workers, "Position on Interracial Adoptions," 9–10.

6. U.S. Department of Labor, *The Negro Family*.

7. With some notable exceptions. See especially Solinger, *Beggars and Choosers* and *Pregnancy and Power*.

8. See Gailey, "Ideologies of Motherhood and Kinship in the U.S."; Patton, *Birthmarks*; Day, *The Adoption of Black Children*; Shepherd, "Adopting Negro Children"; and *Newsweek*, "Adopting Black Babies."

9. Young, *Out of Wedlock*, 147.

10. Ibid., 16, 24.

11. Billingsley and Giovannoni, *Children of the Storm*, 141.

12. Ibid., 141–43.

13. Laurie Green, " 'Two Dimes a Day': Saving Babies and Mothers, from Guatemalan Villages to Memphis Neighborhoods," paper presented at "Making Health, Making Race: Historical Approaches to Race, Medicine and Public Health," University of Texas, Austin, November 13–15, 2008.

14. Billingsley and Giovannoni, *Children of the Storm*, 145–46.

15. Ibid., 147–53.

16. Ibid., 157–73.

17. Grow, *A New Look at Supply and Demand in Adoption*.

18. Billingsley and Giovannoni, *Children of the Storm*, 180.

19. Ibid., 180.

20. See Simon and Altstein, *Adoption, Race, and Identity: From Infancy through Adolescence* (1992), 5; and Herman, "The Adoption History Project."

21. Billingsley and Giovannoni, *Children of the Storm*, 198.

22. Grow and Shapiro, *Transracial Adoption Today*, iii.

23. Ibid., 20.

24. Grow and Shapiro, *Black Children, White Parents*, 29.

25. Ibid., 45.

26. Ibid., 73.

27. Ibid., 53, 102.

28. Ibid., 54, 112.

29. *Newsweek*, "Drip, Drip, Drip." The incident was made into a young adult novel and taught in high schools; see Neufeld, *Edgar Allen*.

30. Reliable numbers do not exist; these represent good guesses based on available data. Numbers for 1968–74 come from *Opportunity*, Division of the Boys and Girls Aid Society of Oregon, cited in Simon and Altstein, *Adoption, Race, and Identity: From Infancy to Young Adulthood* (2001). Numbers for 2006 are based on analysis of Cornell University data in Clemetson and Nixon, "Breaking through Adoption's Racial Barriers." The estimate of twelve thousand for all the years before 1975 comes from Herman, "The Adoption History Project."

31. Orleck, *Storming Caesar's Palace*, 33.

32. Mink and Solinger, *Welfare*, 146.

33. Lawrence-Webb, "African American Children in the Modern Child Welfare System."

34. Paul, "Return of Punitive Sterilization," 89.

35. Ibid.

36. Student Nonviolent Coordinating Committee, "Genocide in Mississippi" (Atlanta: Student Nonviolent Coordinating Committee, n.d., c. 1965), 4. Available through the University of Michigan's pamphlet collection and the archives of the King Center in Atlanta.

37. The birth control movement likewise opposed them. In the Student Nonviolent Coordinating Committee pamphlet members of Planned Parenthood and others are mentioned as constituting the opposition.

38. With notable exceptions. See, e.g., Robin D. G. Kelley, *Yo Mama's*; Solinger, *Pregnancy and Power* and *Wake Up*; and specific discussions of the Relf sisters in note 45 below and Fannie Lou Hamer, below.

39. Student Nonviolent Coordinating Committee, "Genocide in Mississippi."

40. Paul, "Punitive Sterilization," 92; Lee, *For Freedom's Sake*, 190; Roberts, *Killing the Black Body*, 90; and Mills, *This Little Light of Mine*, 76.

41. Lee, *For Freedom's Sake*, 90–91.

42. Samuel Yette, *The Choice: The Issue of Black Survival in America* (1971; reprint, Silver Spring, MD: Cottage Books, 1982), cited in Littlewood, *Politics of Population Control*, 80.

43. Gans, *The War against the Poor*.

44. Torpy, "Endangered Species," 20, citing Edward J. Spriggs, "Involuntary Sterilization: An Unconstitutional Menace to Minorities and the Poor," *Review of Law and Social Change* 4, no. 2 (1974): 127–51.

45. For excellent histories of the Relf sisters, see, e.g., Gutierrez, *Fertile Matters*, 38; Solinger, *Beggars and Choosers*, 227; Davis, *Women, Race, and Class*; Stern, *Eugenic Nation*, 202.

46. Trombley, *Right to Reproduce*, 176. A study published in 1974 by the ACLU found that few hospitals were following the informed consent guidelines; many did not even know about them. See Krauss and ACLU, *Hospital Survey on Sterilization*; and *Relf v. Weinberger*, U.S. Court of Appeals, District of Columbia Circuit, September 13, 1977.

47. U.S. Congress, *Green Book*.

48. Kelley, *Race Rebels*, 95.

49. Mink and Solinger, *Welfare*, 195–98.

50. Lawrence-Webb, "African American Children"; Babb, *Ethics in American Adoption*, 51–54; O'Neill Murray and Gesiriech, "Brief Legislative History." See also the footnotes to *King v. Smith*, 392 U.S. 309; thanks to Anna Marie Smith who flagged this for me.

51. From Bureau of Public Assistance, *Illegitimacy and Its Impact on the Aid to Dependent Children Program* (Washington, D.C.: U.S. Government Printing Office, 1960), in Mink and Solinger, *Welfare*, 188.

52. Altstein and McRoy, *Does Family Preservation Serve a Child's Best Interests?*, 6–7; Schene, "Past, Present, and Future Roles of Child Protective Services." This pattern was not limited to the South; in New York City, for example, the percentage of black and Puerto Rican children (versus white children) also soared after 1960. See Grant, *The Politicization of Foster Care in New York City*, 31.

53. Lawrence-Webb, "African American Children."

54. Boehm, "An Assessment of Family Advocacy in Protective Cases," 15.

55. Brissett-Chapman and Issacs-Shockley, *Children in Social Peril*, 49.

56. Nelson, *Making an Issue of Child Abuse*.

57. A fascinating glimpse of how this worked is in Michael Allen Rembis's research within the records of the Illinois State Training School for Girls at Geneva, which provided institutional care for "feebleminded" girls, some of whom, it was clear, social workers understood were being sexually abused by a family member. They sought custodial care of the girls as much to stop the abuse as to regulate the sexuality of the feebleminded. See Rembis, "I Ain't Been Reading While On Parole."

58. Kempe et al., "The Battered Child Syndrome."

59. And in 1974 Congress authorized massive funding to investigate and separate children in families where social workers believed there was abuse with the passage of the Child Abuse Prevention and Treatment Act; see Nelson, *Making an Issue of Child Abuse*; Gordon, *Heroes of Their Own Lives*; Sealander, *The Failed Century of the Child*; and Pleck, *Domestic Tyranny*.

60. See Cloward and Piven, "A Strategy to End Poverty."

61. U.S. Department of Labor, *The Negro Family*.

62. Muncy, *Creating a Female Dominion in American Reform*.

63. For a wholesale critique of this sociological tradition, see Ferguson, *Aberrations in Black*.

64. See Rainwater and Yancey, *The Moynihan Report*; Moody, *Coming of Age in Mississippi*; Jacobs, Child, and Yellin, *Incidents in the Life of a Slave Girl*; Yellin, *Women and Sisters*; Orleck, *Storming Caesar's Palace*; Dollard, *Caste and Class in a Southern Town*; and Frazier, *The Negro Family in the United States*.

65. *Chicago Defender*, "Black Renaissance."

66. Johnson, "Group to Battle 'Anti-Blackism.'"

67. Billingsley, "Elements of a Comprehensive Program for the Welfare of Black Children."

68. On King, see Rainwater and Yancey, *The Moynihan Report*; on Rustin and Farmer, see Scott, *Contempt and Pity*, 148–50.

69. Johnson, "Group to Battle 'Anti-Blackism.'"

70. Clines, "Group Will Seek Militants' Fund"; Fraser, "Black Social Workers."

71. Fraser, "Black Social Workers."

72. Ibid.

73. National Association of Black Social Workers, "Position on Interracial Adoptions."

74. Billingsley and Giovannoni, *Children of the Storm*, 76.

75. Du Bois, *The Negro American Family*, 21.

76. Quoted in ibid., 25.

77. Gilbert, *Narrative of Sojourner Truth*, 134.

78. Frederic Bancroft, *Slave-trading in the Old South* (Baltimore, MD: J. H. Furst Co., 1931), cited in Elkins, *Slavery*, 54n45.

79. Billingsley and Giovannoni, *Children of the Storm*, 29.

80. *New York Herald*, July 19, 1865, quoted in Schwalm, *A Hard Fight for We*, 249.

81. Ibid., 249–52.

82. Du Bois, *Some Efforts for Social Betterment among American Negroes*, 82.

83. Ibid., 82.

84. Gutman, *The Black Family in Slavery and Freedom*, 488, 500; Jones, *Labor of Love, Labor of Sorrow*, 126.

85. Circular posted on Maryland's eastern shore by a Union general, December 6, 1864; letter from Andrew Stafford, November 4, 1864, in Berlin and Rowland, *Families and Freedom*, 211–13, 220–21; Edwards, *Gendered Strife and Confusion*, 42–44, 47–54.

86. Schwalm, *A Hard Fight for We*, 250–51.

87. For stunning oral histories of this experience, see Orleck, *Storming Caesar's Palace*. One woman, asked why she left the South, replied, "Honey you don't want to hear that because, oh God, it'll make you cry" (7). See also Foley, *The White Scourge*; and Kelley, *Hammer and Hoe*.

88. Billingsley and Giovannoni, *Children of the Storm*, 75–76.

89. Quoted in Jones, *Labor of Love*, 80.

90. Gutman, *The Black Family*, 450, 502; Jones, *Labor of Love*, 88.

91. Kornbluh, *The Battle for Welfare Rights*; Orleck, *Storming Caesar's Palace*; Quadagno, *Color of Welfare*; Solinger, *Wake Up Little Susie*; Mink, *The Wages of Motherhood*; and Mink and Solinger, *Welfare*.

92. Schoen, *Choice and Coercion*.

93. Billingsley and Giovannoni, *Children of the Storm*, 75–76.

94. Ibid., 70.

95. Ibid., 94–96.

96. Ibid., 88.

97. Fraser, "Blacks Condemn Mixed Adoptions."

98. From Bureau of Public Assistance, *Illegitimacy and Its Impact on the Aid to Dependent Children Program* (Washington, D.C.: U.S. Government Printing Office, 1960), in Mink and Solinger, *Welfare*, 174–90.

99. Maas and Engler, *Children in Need of Parents*.

100. Leavy, "Should Whites Adopt Black Children."

101. Lawrence-Webb, "African American Children."

102. Simon and Altstein, *Adoption, Race, and Identity: From Infancy through Adolescence* (1992), 5–6; Grow and Shapiro, *Black Children, White Parents*, 5.

103. *Chicago Defender*, "Adoptive Parents."

104. Weaver, "From the Weaver" (1972); and Weaver, "From the Weaver" (1973).

105. *Ebony*, "The Fight for Black Babies."

106. Weaver, "From the Weaver" (1972).

107. Ibid.

2. INDIAN CHILD WELFARE ACT

1. Melosh, *Strangers and Kin*, 181–83. The most successful and political deployment of this historical genealogy was in the context of the public debate over the Multiethnic Placement Act of 1994 and the related Interethnic Provisions of 1996 (MEPA-IEP). There was one contemporaneous deployment of this historical argument (see Simon, "Assessment of Racial Awareness, Preference, and Self-Identity among White and Adopted Non-White Children"), which suggested that opposition to Native kids being placed with white families could be traced to "a group of American Indian leaders" and a meeting in Ann Arbor, Michigan, in July 1972.

2. Bartholet, "Where Do Black Children Belong?," 1181–82.

3. Bartholet, *Nobody's Children*, 124.

4. Simon, "Assessment of Racial Awareness," 45.

5. See, for example, Howard, "Transracial Adoption."

6. "Survivance" is Gerald Vizenor's term—a neologism that brings together "survival" and "resistance" because, he says, they have been inseparable in the continuance of tribal peoples. See, for example, Vizenor, *Survivance*.

7. See Jacobs, *Engendered Encounters*; Jacobs, "The Eastmans and the Luhans"; Philp, *John Collier's Crusade*; Kelly, *The Assault on Assimilation*; Collier, "Red Atlantis"; Collier, "The Pueblos Last Stand"; Sargeant, "Last First Americans"; Henderson, "Death of the Pueblos"; Fergusson, "Crusade from Santa Fe"; Lawrence, Letter; Collier, "Plundering the Pueblos"; Collier, "No Trespassing"; Collier, "Our Indian Policy"; Collier, "America's Treatment of Her Indians"; Collier, "American Congo"; Correy, "He Carries the White Man's Burden"; Collier, "The Pueblos' Land Problem"; Sargeant, "The Red Man's Burden"; Austin, "The Folly of the Officials"; Sergeant, "Big Powwow of Pueblos"; Duberman, "Documents in Hopi Indian Sexuality"; Jacobs, "Making Savages of Us All"; and Daily, *Battle for the BIA*.

8. Quiroz, *Adoption in a Color-Blind Society*; and Melosh, *Strangers and Kin*.

9. Goldberg, "Descent into Race."

10. *Morton v. Mancari*, 417 U.S. 535 (1974).

11. Ibid., 554.

12. *Washington v. Yakima Indian Nation*, 439 U.S. 463, 500–501 (1979), cited in Hawkins-Leon, "The Indian Child Welfare Act and the African American Tribe."

13. *Cherokee Nation v. Georgia*, 30 U.S. 1 (1831) at 15–16.

14. Cohen, *Handbook of Federal Indian Law*; emphasis in the original.

15. See Archival Sources: Associate Solicitor, "Memorandum to Justice Department."

16. As happened, for example, in the Jessica DeBoers case, in which a child was ordered

removed from the foster parents who wanted to adopt her in response to questions of jurisdiction. The mother had tried to evade the father's wishes, placed the child for adoption, then regretted the decision within weeks. See Wilkerson, "Michigan Couple Is Ordered to Return Girl."

17. See Johnson, "List of Federally Non-Recognized Tribes."

18. Barsh, "The Indian Child Welfare Act of 1978."

19. Hager and Law, *Handbook on the Indian Child Welfare Act*; Child Advocacy Clinic, *Child Advocacy Handbook*. Although this right of Anglo parents to the enhanced protections has not been uniformly upheld, it has been recognized fairly consistently. See, for example, *In re N.S.*, 474 N.W. 2d 96, 100 (S.D. 1991), where an Anglo woman who had admitted to her public psychiatric hospital counselor fears that her brother might sexually abuse her child was reported to the Department of Social Services, who removed her child, saying that she was an alcoholic, had borderline personality disorder, and the child was acting out and had developmental delays. The mother successfully argued that she was entitled to the enhanced protections of ICWA since the child was one-quarter Indian.

20. *Fisher v. District Court* 424 U.S. 382 (1976).

21. *In re Lelah-Puc-Ka-Chee*, 98 F. 429, 431 (N.D. Iowa 1899).

22. Deloria, *Custer Died for Your Sins*, 171–74.

23. Prucha, *Documents of United States Indian Policy*, 107.

24. For more on the railroads, see Matthiessen, *In the Spirit of Crazy Horse*.

25. Theodore Fischbacher, *A Study of the Role of the Federal Government in the Education of the American Indian* (San Francisco: R and E Research Associates, 1974), cited in Adams, "Fundamental Considerations," 3.

26. *Indian Family Defense*, "Historic School Victory."

27. Lomawaima, "Domesticity in the Federal Indian Schools," 229.

28. Archuleta et al., *Away from Home*.

29. Smith, *Conquest*.

30. Philp, *Collier's Crusade*, 81.

31. Brookings Institution, *The Problem of Indian Administration*. On allegedly rich Indians, see Bonnin, Fabens, and Sniffen, *Oklahoma's Poor Rich Indians*.

32. Brookings Institution, *The Problem of Indian Administration*, 15.

33. Canby, *American Indian Law*.

34. Philp, *Collier's Crusade*, 131; Lomawaima, *They Called It Prairie Light*, 7–8.

35. Wilson, *The Earth Shall Weep*, 330–58; Philp, *Collier's Crusade*, 135–60; Deloria, *Custer Died for Your Sins*, 54–77; and Daily, *Battle for the BIA*, 80–100.

36. Cohen, "Public Assistance Provisions for Navajo and Hopi Indians."

37. Harry W. Hill, commissioner of the Arizona State Department of Public Welfare, quoted in Lyter, "No Citizenship, No Welfare."

38. Berrick, *Faces of Poverty*, 169.

39. Cohen, "Public Assistance Provisions"; and Lyter, "No Citizenship, No Welfare."

40. Lyslo, "Background on Indian Adoption Project," 36–37.

41. *Indian Affairs*, "The Destruction of Indian Families."

42. On "liquidation," see Wunder, "Review: Kenneth R. Philip, *Termination Revisited*"; and Cowger, *The National Congress of American Indians*. Quote on equal rights is from the House Concurrent Resolution 108 (1953), cited in Officer, "Termination as Federal Policy," 114.

43. Officer, "Termination as Federal Policy."

44. Bertram Hirsch, "Keynote Address," paper presented at the Indian Child Welfare Act, the Next Ten Years: Indian Homes for Indian Children, UCLA, August 22–24, 1990, 25; Mankiller and Wallace, *Mankiller*.

45. Fanshel, *Far from the Reservation*.

46. Lyslo, "Background on Indian Adoption Project," 36–37.

47. *Indian Affairs*, "AAIA and Devils Lake Sioux Protest Child Welfare Abuses."

48. *In re* Whiteshead, 124 N.W. 2d 694 (N.D. 1963).

49. Fanshel, *Far from the Reservation*.

50. Strong, "What Is an Indian Family?"; Westermeyer, "The Ravage of Indian Families in Crisis"; Ira Berlin and Evelyn Blanchard, "Long-Term Effects of Out-of-Home Placement of Indian Children," paper presented at the Indian Child Welfare Act, the Next Ten Years: Indian Homes for Indian Children, UCLA, August 22–24, 1990; and Balcom, "Logic of Exchange."

51. Bensen, *Children of the Dragonfly*.

52. This problem has particularly plagued the legal and psychological scholarship on ICWA; some feminist scholarship on black and white women and girls has started with mothers, notably Solinger, *Wake Up*.

53. *In re* Whiteshead, 124 N.W. 2d 694 (N.D. 1963).

54. Hirsch, "Keynote Address," 23–24; and *Indian Affairs*, "AAIA and Devil's Lake."

55. *Indian Family Defense*, "Devil's Lake Sioux Resistance," 6.

56. Native American Training Institute, "30 Years of ICWA: How Are the Children?," conference poster, North Dakota, 2008; *Indian Affairs*, "AAIA and Devil's Lake"; and Byler, Deloria, and Gurwitt, "Another Chapter."

57. Bertram Hirsch, "Keynote Address," 25.

58. *Indian Affairs*, "HEW to Study Child Welfare Abuses"; *Indian Family Defense*, "Devil's Lake Sioux Resistance"; and Hirsch, "Keynote Address," note 55.

59. Byler, "Destruction of American Indian"; Hirsch, "Keynote Address," note 55; and Mannes, "Factors and Events."

60. Beiser, "Hazard to Mental Health"; *Indian Affairs*, "Indian Child Welfare"; and *Indian Affairs*, "Boarding Schools Assailed."

61. See Johnson, *Native Children and the Child Welfare System*.

62. Balcom, "Logic of Exchange."

63. See Archival Sources, United States: Association of American Indian Affairs, "Indian Child Welfare Act [1976]."

64. Deloria, *Custer Died for Your Sins*, 17.

65. *Akwesasne Notes* (multiple items): "The Latest in the 'Social Genocide' Field" [Late Autumn 1972]; "Comment on Indian Children"; " 'Far from the Reservation' "; "Saskatchewan Native People"; "Rift in N.W.T. Council"; "The Latest in the 'Social Genocide' Field" [May 1972]; "We Cannot Be Critical"; and "Michigan Indian Groups Searching."

66. *Indian Affairs*, "Destruction of Indian Families"; and *Indian Family Defense*, "Court Actions."

67. *Indian Family Defense*, "Court Actions."

68. U.S. Bureau of the Census, "Statistical Brief."

69. *Indian Affairs*, "AAIA Reunites Five Indian Families."

70. Richard Haney, personal communication with the author regarding Benita Rowland, March 17, 2005.

71. Frederick M. Van Hecke, interview with the author, March 16, 2005.

72. *Indian Affairs*, "Destruction of Indian Families."

73. *Indian Family Defense*, "Abduction of Benita Rowland."

74. Myers, *They Are Young Once but Indian Forever*, 92–93.

75. U.S. Congress, "Testimony of Harold Brown," 205.

76. Jones, " 'Redeeming' The Indian."

77. Fee patent land on the Navajo reservation is a remnant of land titled to non-Navajos between the recognition of the Navajo nation's boundaries under the Treaty of Guadalupe-Hidalgo in 1848 and the Indian Reorganization Act of 1934's extension of that land, creating islands of non-Navajo land in the middle of the reservation. See *Atkinson Trading Co. v. Shirley* 532 U.S. 645 (2001). See also Pavlik, "Of Saints and Lamanites"; and Navajo Tribal Council, "Tribal Policy on Adoption."

78. U.S. Department of Health, Education, and Welfare, *Indian Child Welfare*.

79. See Archival Sources: Association of American Indian Affairs (AAIA), "Testimony of Sister Mary Clare Ciulla."

80. See Archival Sources: Association of American Indian Affairs (AAIA), "Testimony of Faye La Pointe."

81. For the Leonard Peltier story, see Matthiessen, *Spirit of Crazy Horse*. See also *Incident at Oglala*.

82. U.S. Congress, *Revolutionary Activities with the United States*.

83. *Incident at Oglala*.

84. *Indian Family Defense*, "Book Review"; and Goldstein, Freud, and Solnit, *Beyond the Best Interests*, 108, 111.

85. Beiser, "Hazard to Mental Health."

86. *Akwesasne Notes* (multiple items): "Social Genocide, Challenge"; "Social Genocide, Someone"; "Good Intentions"; "Prairie Native Groups"; and "Potawatomis Assert Jurisdiction."

87. *Indian Family Defense*, "NACA Report."

88. Ira Berlin and Evelyn Blanchard, "Long-Term Effects of Out-of-Home Placement of Indian Children," paper presented at the Indian Child Welfare Act, the Next Ten Years: Indian Homes for Indian Children, UCLA, August 22–24, 1990; Unger, *Destruction of American Indian*; Strong, "What Is an Indian"; Blanchard, "Question of Best Interest"; and Myers, *They Are Young Once*, 90. Blanchard's article published in 1977 is lamenting that more was not done at the national level. However, this seems like a half full, half empty question; what she identifies as "not enough" seems a tremendous advancement over earlier years.

89. *Akwesasne Notes*, "Social Genocide, Someone."

90. *Indian Family Defense*, "Senate Probes Child Welfare."

91. Westermeyer, "Ravage of Indian Families."

92. Hager and Law, *Handbook on the Indian Child Welfare Act*.

93. See, for example, the much-cited first line of the decision in *Mississippi Choctaw Indian Band v. Holyfield*, 490 U.S. 30 (1989): "On the basis of extensive evidence indicating that large numbers of Indian children were being separated from their families and tribes and were being placed in non-Indian homes through state adoption, foster care, and parental rights termination proceedings, and that this practice caused serious problems for the children, their parents, and their tribes, Congress enacted the Indian Child Welfare Act of 1978 (ICWA)."

94. *Indian Family Defense*, "Senate Probes Child Welfare."

95. Ibid.; U.S. Congress, "Child Welfare Statistical Survey"; and U.S. Congress, *Indian Child Welfare Act*.

96. U.S. Congress, "Child Welfare Statistical Survey."

97. Ibid.

98. U.S. Congress, "Statement of Eric Eberhard"; and U.S. Congress, "Statement of Beatrice Gentry."

99. See Archival Sources: Association of American Indian Affairs, "Indian Child Welfare Act [1976]"; and Association of American Indian Affairs, "Indian Child Welfare Act [1977]."

100. See Archival Sources: Associate Solicitor, "Memorandum to Justice Department." See also U.S. Congress, "Statement of Raymond Butler."

101. Ibid.; see also Barsh, "Indian Child Welfare Act."

102. Plantz, *Indian Child Welfare*.

3. "CRACK BABIES," RACE, ADOPTION REFORM

1. For more on the emergence of the neoconservative movement, see Omi and Winant, *Racial Formation in the United States*.

2. For two different accounts of the emergence of the neoliberal movement into policy in the United States, see Duggan, *The Twilight of Equality?*; and Harvey, *A Brief History of Neoliberalism*.

3. This was a complicated proposal, which on the one hand seemed to offer support for welfare benefit but on the other was sold as an opportunity to get welfare into the hands of the "working poor"—which meant white men. New York's National Welfare Rights Organization opposed it in the form that it came before Congress, as it would have meant a significant cut to benefits in states like New York. For a smart analysis of it—including Nixon's ambivalence about it—see Kornbluh, *The Battle for Welfare Rights*.

4. Stolley, "Statistics on Adoption in the United States"; and Chandra et al., "Fertility, Family Planning."

5. Murray, "Coming White Underclass."

6. On Bastard Nation, see Carp, *Adoption Politics*; on birth mothers organizing to protest the loss of their children, see Solinger on Concerned United Birthmothers in *Wake Up* and *Beggars and Choosers*.

7. Not a constant decline—there were years with slight increases—but, overall, it was a steady decline. See Working Life, "Wages and Benefits: Real Wages (1964–2004)."

8. Hochschild, *The Second Shift*.

9. Women's age at first child has been climbing steadily since 1970, actually increasing almost every year, from 20.1 years of age in 1970 to more than 25 years of age in 2002. It has increased more and faster for white women than for black women, with women "of Hispanic origin" in the middle. This would be consistent with it being a strategy for maintaining middle-class status, as more white women than black or "Hispanic" women are middle class rather than working class. In 2002 the *average* age of first birth for all white women was almost 27—getting surprisingly close to ages at which fertility is difficult. See Centers for Disease Control and Prevention, National Vital Statistics System, "Birth Data," http://www.cdc.gov/nchs/births.htm.

10. See *Time*, "Saddest Epidemic"; Faludi, *Backlash*, 27–32; Chandra et al., "Fertility, Family Planning"; and Selman, "The Movement of Children for International Adoption."

11. Franklin, *Embodied Progress*.

12. McGirr, *Suburban Warriors*.

13. Duggan, *The Twilight of Equality?*

14. The argument is Robin D. G. Kelley's; see Kelley, *Yo' Mama's Disfunktional!*; "Chocolate City" is from the Motown song of that name by Parliament.

15. Moreton, *Between God and Wal-Mart*.

16. Harvey, *A Brief History of Neoliberalism*; Klein, *The Shock Doctrine*; and Equipo Maíz, *El Neoliberalismo*.

17. Kornbluh, *The Battle for Welfare Rights*.

18. Solinger, *Wake up Little Susie*; and Solinger, *Beggars and Choosers*.

19. *Time*, "Dan Quayle vs. Murphy Brown."

20. See, e.g., Duke, "Crack Abuser's Baby Is Born"; and Duke, "For Pregnant Addict, Crack Comes First."

21. For a detailed review of the news programming of 1989, see Humphries, *Crack Mothers*. Some characteristic newspaper articles include Long, "Bennett: Take Infant"; *Chicago Tribune*, "Pregnant Drug User"; Raspberry, "Addicts and Babies"; and Rosenthal, "How Much Is a Baby Worth?"

22. Humphries, *Crack Mothers*, 21, 42–47.

23. See, for example, Jackson, "America's Shameful Little Secret"; and Duke, "For Pregnant Addict."

24. Frank, Augustyn, and Knight, "Growth, Development and Behavior in Early Childhood Following Prenatal Cocaine Exposure," 613.

25. Chavkin, "Cocaine and Pregnancy."

26. Koren et al., "Estimation of Fetal Exposure to Drugs of Abuse, Environmental Tobacco Smoke, and Ethanol"; Accornero et al., "Behavioral Outcome of Preschoolers Exposed Prenatally to Cocaine"; Azuma and Chasnoff, "Outcome of Children Prenatally Exposed to Cocaine and Other Drugs"; Kaltenbach, "The Effects of Maternal Cocaine Abuse on Mothers and Newborns"; Askin and Diehl-Jones, "Cocaine: Effects"; Hutchings, "The Puzzle of Cocaine's Effects Following Maternal Use during Pregnancy"; Heffelfinger et al., "Visual Attention in Preschool Children Prenatally Exposed to Cocaine"; and Jacobson and Jacobson, "Prenatal Alcohol Exposure and Neurobehavioral Development." The one study to show negative effects was Singer, Arendt, and Minnes, "Cognitive and Motor Outcomes of Cocaine-Exposed Infants."

27. Chavkin, "Cocaine and Pregnancy." The conclusions of Frank and others have not gone entirely unchallenged; Singer, Arendt, and Minnes, "Cognitive and Motor Outcomes," offer contrary evidence, though an attendant commentary suggests that it might have something to do with the kind of drug that was available in Cleveland, in particular, where Singer and colleagues' study took place; see Zuckerman, Frank, and Mayes, "Cocaine-Exposed Infants and Developmental Outcomes."

28. Krauthammer, "Crack Babies Forming Biological Underclass."

29. Jackson, "America's Shameful Little Secret"; and Raspberry, "Addicts and Babies."

30. Koren et al., "Bias against the Null Hypotheses."

31. Humphries, *Crack Mothers*; Roberts, *Killing the Black Body*.

32. *Ferguson v. City of Charleston*, 532 U.S. 67 (2001).

33. Paltrow, Cohen, and Carey, *Year 2000 Overview*; Humphries, *Crack Mothers.*

34. Paltrow, Cohen, and Carey, *Year 2000 Overview*; Roberts, *Killing the Black Body.*

35. For the size of the child welfare system, see U.S. General Accounting Office, "Foster Care," 9; for the race of the child welfare system, see Roberts, *Shattered Bonds.*

36. *Boston Globe*, "More U.S. Children Using Foster Care."

37. See, for example, Shirk, "Foster Parents Struggle with Babies in Pain."

38. *Chicago Tribune*, "Pregnant Drug User Glad for Jail."

39. Fullilove, Lown, and Fullilove, "Crack 'Hos and Skeezers."

40. Humphries, *Crack Mothers*, 44–45.

41. Duke, "D.C. Revises Infant Death Figures."

42. Garrett, *Betrayal of Trust*, 268–377.

43. Krauthammer, "Crack Babies."

44. Berlant, *The Queen of America Goes to Washington City.*

45. There is a considerable and growing literature on the "prison-industrial complex." See, e.g., the brilliant and incisive Gilmore, *Golden Gulag.*

46. Krauthammer, "Put Cocaine Babies in Protective Custody."

47. Armstrong, *Conceiving Risk, Bearing Responsibility*, 173.

48. Ibid., 5; Golden, *Message in a Bottle*, 64; Dorris, *Broken Cord.*

49. Armstrong, *Conceiving Risk*, 111.

50. Michael Dorris, "A Desperate Crack Legacy," *Newsweek* (25 June 1990), 8, cited in Golden, *Message in a Bottle*, 106. This takes on particular poignancy in the context of Dorris's subsequent suicide, reportedly in the aftermath of the threat by a daughter, also diagnosed with FAS, to publicize allegations of sexual abuse by Dorris that many insisted were untrue.

51. Erikson, "Doctors Mislabel Defects"; and H. E. Hoyme, L. Hauck, and D. J. Meyer, "Accuracy of Diagnosis of Alcohol Related Birth Defects by Non-Medical Professionals in a Native American Population," paper presented at the David W. Smith Morphogenesis and Malformations Workshop, Mont-Tremblant, Québec, 1994, 29–33.

52. Golden, *Message in a Bottle.*

53. Trueheart, "Marriage for Better or Words: The Dorris-and-Erdrich Team, Creating Fiction Without Friction," *Washington Post* (October 19, 1988), cited in Golden, "An Argument That Goes Back to the Womb," 281.

54. Jean Reith Schroedel and Paul Peretz, "A Gender Analysis of Policy Formation: The Case of Fetal Abuse," *Journal of Health Politics, Policy, and Law* 19 (1994): 335–60, cited in Golden, *Message in a Bottle*, 114.

55. Armstrong, *Conceiving Risk*, 7, 82.

56. Cheever, "The Nanny Track."

57. Stearns, *Anxious Parents*; Starker, *Oracle at the Supermarket.*

58. Rothman, *Tentative Pregnancy.*

59. Stearns, *Anxious Parents.*

60. Sargent, Peck, and Weitzman, "Bicycle-Mounted Child Seats." See also U.S. Department of Transportation, National Highway Transportation and Safety Administration, "Bicycle Helmet Use Laws."

61. Leavitt and Dubner, *Freakonomics.*

62. *New York Times*, "Drive to Push Seat Belt Use by Children."

63. See Solinger on this point, *Pregnancy and Power*, 14–17.

64. *Time*, "The Saddest Epidemic."

65. Faludi, *Backlash*, 27–32; Chandra et al., "Fertility, Family Planning."

66. Elmer-DeWitt, "Scandals the Cruelest Kind of Fraud"; and Lemonick, "Trying to Fool the Infertile."

67. Salholz, "The Future of Gay America."

68. Herman, *Kinship by Design*, is brilliant on this point.

69. Most people assume that the "shortage" of adoptable infants, called the "white baby famine" by some, is of recent, post-1973 vintage. Hardly. It has been a persistent feature of the adoption landscape back to the 1920s and is better described as frustration by would-be adopters with the bureaucracy of adoption. For a 1920s example, see Berebitsky, *Like Our Very Own*.

70. Perhaps the best-known example in the U.S. context was Georgia Tann, who arranged adoptions from and ran the Tennessee Children's Home and who was subsequently found to have been brokering adoption for a fair bit of money, and without their parents' consent. See Raymond, *The Baby Thief*; Austin, *Babies for Sale*.

71. U.S. Congress, *Hearing Before the Subcommittee to Investigate Juvenile Delinquency*.

72. Fleming, "New Frontiers in Conception."

73. Rule, "Couples Taking Unusual Paths for Adoption."

74. See Maureen Flatley, "Why the Federal Government Must Regulate Adoption," Adoption.com, http://library.adoption.com/articles/why-the-federal-government-must-re gulate-adoption.html.

75. See Gladney Center for Adoption, http://www.gladneyfacilities.com.

76. Mansnerus, "Market Puts Price Tags on the Priceless."

77. Ibid.; Mirah Riben, *Stork Market*.

78. Gearino, "Hope and Risk: Money, Hope Lost in Failed Adoptions." See also Lee Rood, "Look Out for Scam, Couple Tells Would-be Adopters," *Des Moines Register* (July 15, 2006), cited in Riben, *The Stork Market*, 67–68.

79. *San Diego Union-Tribune*, "Unwed Mom Fighting to Keep Infant."

80. Freundlich, *The Market Forces in Adoption*; and Modell, *A Sealed and Secret Kinship*.

81. Mansnerus, "Market Puts Price Tags on the Priceless."

82. Spar, *The Baby Business*.

83. McGrory, "Orphanage Idea Has Many Parents."

84. Van Biema, "The Storm over Orphanages."

85. Ibid.

86. For the long version of the legislative history, see Patton, *Birthmarks*, 38.

87. Hollinger and National Resource Center, *A Guide to the Multiethnic Placement Act of 1994*; Patton, *Birthmarks*, 38; and Greene, "Move toward Adoptions."

88. Elizabeth Bartholet, "Letter," *New York Times* (December 8, 1993), cited in Patton, *Birthmarks*.

89. For more on the conservative argument in the 1990s, see McKenzie, "Revive the Orphanage"; McGrory, "Orphanage Idea Has Many Parents"; Zuckerman, "Effects on Parents, Children"; and Besharov, "The Worst Threat Is Mom Herself." For the highlights of the sociology of single mothers, see U.S. Department of Labor, *The Negro Family*; Frazier, *The Negro Family in the United States*; and Dollard, *Caste and Class in a Southern Town*.

90. Cohen, "Dealing with Illegitimacy."

91. Murray, "Coming White Underclass."

92. *New York Times*, "The 1994 Election."

93. Bartholet, *Family Bonds*.

94. This language is endemic to the conversation. Consider Kim Forde-Mazrui, who uses the term three times in two sentences: "Because Black children represent a disproportionately high number of children in need of homes, they *wait* up to twice as long for permanent homes as white children *wait*. . . . An insufficient number of Black families are available for these *waiting* children." The next sentence speaks of "*delays* in the placement of Black children" (937). At no point does she consider that another name for this "waiting" might be the period in which birth parents, usually mothers, are scrambling to get their children back. Once the conversation is defined in terms of *waiting* or *delay*, the illegitimacy of the claims of birth parents on their own children has already been presumed. See Forde-Mazrui, "Black Identity and Child."

95. Bartholet, *Nobody's Children*.

96. The line is Bill Clinton's; see Berke, "Clinton: Getting People off Welfare." In a campaign ad initially broadcast on September 9, 1992, Clinton said, "I have a plan to end welfare as we know it."

97. Hancock, *The Politics of Disgust*.

98. Specifically, Utah, Washington, and Virginia; see Smith, *Welfare Reform and Sexual Regulation*, 163–67.

99. Perry, "The Transracial Adoption Controversy," 43.

100. Uniform Adoption Act, *Prefatory Note* at 1 (1994).

101. Gilles and Kroll, *Barriers to Same-Race Placement*, 17, 21, 27.

102. Ibid.

103. U.S. Department of Health and Human Services, "Child Maltreatment 2003."

104. Roberts, *Shattered Bonds*, 33–46.

105. U.S. Department of Health and Human Services, "Child Maltreatment 2003"; and Bernstein, "Family Law Collides with Immigration and Welfare Rules."

106. U.S. Department of Health and Human Services, "AFCARS Report, FY 2006."

107. Bartholet, "Where Do Black Children," 1183–88.

108. See Simon and Altstein, *Adoption, Race, and Identity: From Infancy through Adolescence* (1992); Simon and Altstein, *Adoption, Race, and Identity: From Infancy to Young Adulthood* (2001); Simon and Altstein, *Transracial Adoptees*; Simon and Altstein, *Transracial Adoption* (1977); Simon and Altstein, *Transracial Adoption: A Follow Up* (1981); Simon, Altstein, and Melli, *Case for Transracial Adoption*; Bartholet, *Family Bonds*; Bartholet, *Nobody's Children*; Bartholet, "Private Race Preferences"; Bartholet, "Race Separatism"; and Bartholet, "Where Do Black Children Belong?"

109. Roberts, *Shattered Bonds*, 29–46.

110. Quiroz, *Adoption in a Color-Blind Society*.

111. Brown and Bailey-Etta, "An Out-of-Home Care System in Crisis."

112. U.S. Department of Health and Human Services, "AFCARS Report, FY 2003."

113. Wulczyn, Chen, and Hislop, "Foster Care Dynamics."

114. *King v. Smith*; and Golden, *Message in a Bottle*.

115. Armstrong, *Conceiving Risk*, 173.

116. Plantz, *Indian Child Welfare*.

117. Melmer, "Congresswoman Attacks Indian Child Welfare Act"; and Melmer, "Adoption Bill 'Guts' the ICWA."

118. Adamec and Pierce, *Encyclopedia of Adoption*; see "Multiethnic Placement Act (MEPA)," http://encyclopedia.adoption.com/entry/Multiethnic-Placement-Act-MEPA/233/1.html.

119. Schmitt, "Adoption Bill Facing Battle over Measure on Indians."

120. *Mississippi Choctaw Indian Band v. Holyfield* 490 U.S. 30 (1989).

121. Kennedy, *Interracial Intimacies*, 81.

122. Williams, "Spare Parts, Family Values, Old Children, Cheap."

123. Roberts, *Shattered Bonds*, vii.

124. Metzenbaum, "S. 1224."

125. U.S. Congress, "No Place to Call Home," 7.

4. FROM REFUGEES TO MADONNAS

1. Belkin, "Life after Infertility Treatments Fail."

2. Altstein and Simon, *Intercountry Adoptions*; see also Weil, "International Adoption"; Selman, "Intercountry Adoption in the New Millennium"; Selman, "Intercountry Adoption in Europe after the Hague Convention"; Selman, "Intercountry Adoption: Research, Policy and Practice"; and Lovelock, "Intercountry Adoption as a Migratory Practice."

3. "Fotografías desgarradoras en blanco y negro de pequeñines latinoamericanos descalzos, de ojos grandes y mirada triste." All translations mine. See Camil, "Tráfico de inos."

4. See *San Francisco Chronicle*, "Ragged, Hungry, Broke, Harvest Workers Live in Squalor"; and *San Francisco Chronicle*, "What Does the 'New Deal' Mean to This Mother and Her Children?"

5. The digital archive of photos from the Farm Security Administration, Office of War Information is online at the Library of Congress's American Memory website, http://memory.loc.gov/ammem/fsowhome.html. See also Fahlman, "Constructing an Image of the Depression."

6. See Curtis, Mallach, and Milwaukee Art Museum, *Photography and Reform*; and Rosenblum, Hine, and Torosian, *Lewis Hine, Ellis Island*.

7. For a brief history of Save the Children, see http://www.savethechildren.net/alliance/about_us/history.html. Susan Sontag explores both the confidence with which even commentators as sophisticated as Virginia Wolf imagined that photos of war could only work to further antiwar sentiment and the naiveté of such a view (see Sontag, *Regarding the Pain of Others*). However complex the effects of such photos might be, there is no escaping the certainty of their intention.

8. *New York Times*, "U.S. Asks Pictures to Dramatize Food Needs in Germany."

9. Cousins, "Hiroshima—Four Years Later."

10. See *The Fog of War*.

11. Arthur, "Letter."

12. Malis, "Letter."

13. Joseph Adelson, "Is Women's Lib a Passing Fad," *New York Times Magazine* (March 19, 1972), cited in May, *Homeward Bound*, 58.

14. Ibid., 162.

15. Snoddy, "Letter."

16. Gibson and Moore, "Letter."

17. Keller, "Letter."

18. On the importance of domestic spaces in photography for a different time and place, see Armstrong, *Fiction in the Age of Photography.*

19. Clarke, *True Light.*

20. Clarke, "Letter."

21. Cited in Klein, "Family Ties."

22. See UNICEF, "The 1950s: Era of the Mass Disease Campaign," UNICEF, http://www.unicef.org/sowc96/1950s.htm. See also Black, *Children First.*

23. UNICEF United States Fund, "How Trick-or-Treat for UNICEF Began," UNICEF United States Fund, http://youth.unicefusa.org/trickortreat/About/trick-or-treat-for-unicef-60-anniversary.html.

24. *Colliers,* "Ambassador at Large."

25. See *Parents,* "New Style Halloween."

26. See Archival Sources, Center for Creative Photography: United Nations, Korean Reconstruction Agency, "Speech Delivered before the Unkra" (New York: UNKRA, 1953), Josef Breitenbach Papers, Box AG90, November 12, 1953.

27. See Archival Sources, Center for Creative Photography: Thurston, "What about Our Reconstruction of Korea."

28. See Archival Sources, Center for Creative Photography: Breitenbach, *Women of Asia.*

29. See *New York Times,* "Hoover Backs Bill to Waive Quota Act for Reich Children."

30. Wyman, *Paper Walls,* 14–20.

31. Collins, "Monarch as Alternative," 23.

32. Wyman, *Paper Walls,* 4–9.

33. Laqueur, *Generation Exodus.*

34. Wyman, *Paper Walls,* 75–98.

35. Laqueur, *Generation Exodus.* See also *New York Times:* "Legion Group Hits Refugee Measure"; "Landon Endorses Bill for Refugees"; "Hoover Backs Bill to Waive Quota Act for Reich Children"; "Business Women Ask Child Refugee Aid/Jersey Federations Suggests Each Club Support One"; and "Aid to Child Exiles in U.S. Is Mapped/Experts Plan Selection and Placement of 20,000 by Non-Sectarian Group/Quaker Body to Choose/Youngsters Would Be Placed in Homes to Be Picked by Social Agencies."

36. *New York Times,* "Hoover Backs Bill to Waive Quota Act for Reich Children."

37. Wyman, *Paper Walls,* 28.

38. Forbes and Weiss, "Unaccompanied Refugee Children"; and Wyman, *Paper Walls,* 97–98.

39. See Ressler, Boothby, and Steinbeck, *Unaccompanied Children;* and Legarreta, *The Guernica Generation.*

40. Truman, "President Truman's Statement and Directive on Displaced Persons."

41. See Forbes and Weiss, "Unaccompanied Refugee Children."

42. Ibid., 8.

43. See Lovelock, "Intercountry Adoption as a Migratory Practice."

44. Klein, "Family Ties and Political Obligation"; Buck and Harris, *For Spacious Skies;* MacMillan, "Born between East and West"; Buck, "The Children America Forgot"; and Conn, *Pearl S. Buck.*

45. Klein, "Family Ties and Political Obligations."

46. Buck, "The Children America Forgot."

47. Bagdikian, *The Media Monopoly*.

48. See Rogers, *Dearest Debbie*; Holt, Wisner, and Albus, *The Seed from the East and Outstretched Arms*; Holt and Wisner, *Seed from the East*; and Holt, *Created for God's Glory*.

49. Didion, *Miami*, 122.

50. Torres, *The Lost Apple* cites "declassified CIA documents" related to the Taylor report as a source on the CIA's involvement with Radio Swan (note 8, page 290); Ramón Torreira Crespo and José Buajasán Marrawi, *Operación Peter Pan: Un Caso de Guerra Psicológica Contra Cuba* (La Habana: Editora Política, 2000), citing David Atlee Philips, *The Night Watch* (New York: Ballantine, 1997), 303.

51. Torreira Crespo and Buajasán Marrawi, *Operación Peter Pan*, 90.

52. Ibid., 94.

53. Torres, *The Lost Apple*.

54. Ibid.

55. National Public Radio, "Pedro Pan."

56. Hochfeld, "Problems of Intercountry Adoption"; Kim, Hong, and Kim, "Adoption of Korean Children by New York Area Couples"; and Francis M. Koh, *Oriental Children in American Homes: How Do They Adjust?* (Minneapolis, MN: East–West Press, 1981), cited by Weil, "International Adoption."

57. Hübinette, "Comforting an Orphaned Nation."

58. Warren, *Escape from Saigon*; Lipman, "My Lai"; and *Daughter from Danang*.

59. Edward A. Olsen, "Rescuing Amerasians: A Moral Imperative," *Christian Science Monitor* (November 24, 1982), cited in Jana Lipman, " 'The Face Is the Road Map' Romanticism and Remorse," unpublished manuscript.

60. Congressional Record–House, H8352 (October 1, 1982), cited in Lipman.

61. DeBonis, *Children of the Enemy*, 79.

5. UNCIVIL WARS

1. Melani McAlister, "Cultural History of the War Without End."

2. It rose to 7,350, still a small number relative to 2006, when about 20,000 were adopted. See Rule, "Couples Taking Unusual Paths for Adoption."

3. Ibid.; see also Evan B. Donaldson Adoption Institute, "International Adoption Facts."

4. See, e.g., Grandin, *The Last Colonial Massacre*; Stern, *Remembering Pinochet's Chile*; Tate, "Paramilitaries in Colombia"; Cornell and Roberts, "Democracy, Counter-Insurgency, and Human Rights"; Guillermoprieto, "Letter from Lima"; and Amnesty International, *Amnesty International Report 2003: Paraguay*.

5. Grandin, *The Last Colonial Massacre*, 4.

6. Comadres, http://www.comadres.org/main_english.html.

7. Coordinadora Nacional de Viudas de Guatemala, http://www.conavigua.org.gt/; and Grupo de Apoyo Mutuo, http://www.gam.org.gt/.

8. Federación Latinoamerican de Asociaciones de Familiares de Detenidos-Desaparecidos, http://www.desaparecidos.org/fedefam/.

9. The lawyers at the Asociación Pro-Búsqueda de Niñas y Niños Desaparecidos helped me understand why this was so critical; interview by author with Zaira Navas, attorney for Asociación Pro-Búsqueda de Niñas y Niños Desaparecidos, July 19, 2005, San Salvador, El

Salvador. The Mexican magazine *Proceso* has also been covering this unfolding story; see Archival Sources: Dalton, "Ante la corte interamericana"; Dalton, "Cicatrices no cerradas de la guerra"; Dalton, "El Salvador"; Izquierdo, "Abuelas de la Plaza de Mayo."

10. See Proyecto Interdiocesano de Recuperación de la Memoria Histórica (REMHI), *Guatemala: Nunca Más*; Comisión de la Verdad para El Salvador, *De la locura a la esperanza*. As the late Jon Cortina, a Jesuit priest and one of the founders of Pro-Búsqueda, related to me and in countless press interviews, when he was collecting testimony for the truth commission report, a handful of parents came forward with the stories of how the military had disappeared their children; interview by author with Jon Cortina, co-founder of Asociación Pro-Búsqueda de Niñas y Niños Desaparecidos, San Salvador, July 19, 2005, San Salvador, El Salvador.

11. Dalton, "Ante la corte interamericana."

12. See Abuelas de la Plaza de Mayo "Abuelas de la Plaza de Mayo," http://www.abuelas .org.ar/.

13. Krauss, "Ex-Argentine Junta Leader Held in 70's Kidnapping"; Izquierdo, "Detrás del caso Herrera de Noble"; *La Jornada*, "España pedirá a Argentina extraditar a 40 represores."

14. Izquierdo, "Detrás del caso Herrera de Noble"; *La Jornada*, "España pedirá a Argentina extraditar a 40 represores."

15. McKinley, "Mexico Charges Ex-President in '68 Massacre of Students."

16. Liga Guatemalteca de Higiéne Mental, *Corazones en fiesta*, 53. My translation, this and following texts in Spanish.

17. Ibid., 55.

18. I use the word "Castilian" rather than Spanish in order to do justice to the two other Spanish languages suppressed but not eradicated during the Franco years: Catalan and Basque.

19. Comisión para el Esclarecimiento Histórico (CEH), *Guatemala, memoria del silencio* = *Tz'inil Na'tab'al*, capitol de recomendaciones, 66 (my translation).

20. Informe de la Recuperación de la Memoria Histórica, *Guatemala: Nunca Más*, 38.

21. Oficina de Derechos Humanos de Arzobispado de Guatemala (ODHAG), *Hasta encontrarte*, 60.

22. Goldman, *The Art of Political Murder*.

23. Maco Garavito, e-mail correspondence to the author, May 21, 2008.

24. Ibid.

25. See Amnesty International, *Guatemala*; McConahay, "On a Valentine's Day, Iowa Mom Discovers She Is Guatemala Massacre Survivor"; and *Discovering Dominga*.

26. See *Discovering Dominga*.

27. Ibid.

28. Indeed a number of popular titles once published by small presses are still in wide distribution, including Bouvard, *Revolutionizing Motherhood*; Agosín, *Circles of Madness*; and Agosín, *Mothers of Plaza de Mayo*.

29. According to the WorldCat.org database, accessed in October 2009, only Yale owns all three of them. In addition, University of California, Berkeley; the Library of Congress; and Princeton own *De barro y de hierro* (2002); University of Texas, Tulane, University of Kansas, University of Florida, Princeton, and Columbia own *A voz en grito* (2003); and University of Kansas owns *Corazones en fiesta* (2005).

30. Abuelas de Plaza de Mayo, *Niños desaparecidos en la Argentina desde 1976*, 126–27;

Arditti, *Searching for Life*, 51; Asociación Pro-Búsqueda de Niñas y Niños Desaparecidos, *El día mas esperado*, 311–24; Comisión para el Esclarecimiento Histórico (CEH), *Guatemala, memoria del silencio = Tz'inil Na'tab'al*, vol. 5, conclusion note 28, page 28; Oficina de Derechos Humanos de Arzobispado de Guatemala (ODHAG), *Hasta encontrarte*, 140; and Proyecto Interdiocesano de Recuperación de la Memoria Histórica, *Guatemala: Nunca Más*.

31. See Bouvard, *Revolutionizing Motherhood*; Arditti, *Searching for Life*; and Taylor, *Disappearing Acts*.

32. For more on the ideological support for sending the children of so-called subversives to members of the military, see Comisión Nacional sobre la Desaparición de Personas, *Nunca más*, 286.

33. Arditti, *Searching for Life*, 50.

34. Ibid., 57.

35. Ibid., 109–11.

36. Ibid., 70–71.

37. Ibid., 71.

38. Riding, "Argentines Fight for Orphans of a Dirty War"; Rodriguez, *Nacidos en la sombra*.

39. Abuelas de Plaza de Mayo, *Niños desaparecidos en la Argentina desde 1976*; Abuelas de Plaza de Mayo, *Niños desaparecidos en la Argentina entre 1976 y 1983*; Taylor, *Disappearing Acts*; Arditti, *Searching for Life*; Abuelas de Plaza de Mayo, *Filiación, Identidad, Restitución*.

40. Eduardo Nachman, personal communication with author, January 11, 2006.

41. Arditti, *Searching for Life*, 61–63.

42. Second Vatican Council, "Gaudium et Spes."

43. The Peruvian theologian Gustavo Gutiérrez was the person most responsible for spreading the phrase, following the publication of his very influential book; see Gutiérrez, *Teología de la liberación*. For the CELAM (bishop's) documents, see Hennelly, *Liberation Theology*.

44. Hernández Pico, "Child Adoption: Another Form of Violence"; interview by author with Jon Cortina, co-founder of Pro-Búsqueda, San Salvador, El Salvador, July 19, 2005; and Asociación Pro-Búsqueda de Niñas y Niños Desaparecidos, *El día mas esperado*.

45. Arditti, *Searching for Life*, 63.

46. Boler, "The Mothers Committee of El Salvador," 543, 546.

47. Asociación Pro-Búsqueda de Niñas y Niños Desaparecidos, *El día mas esperado*, 39.

48. Dalton, "Cicatrices no cerradas de la guerra"; Coloma, "El Salvador/Guatemala: '¿Dónde están los niños?'"; Buncombe, "El Salvador's War Children Return to Their Roots"; Kahn, "War Child Who 'Disappeared' Finds Her Way Back"; Rohter, "El Salvador's Stolen Children Face a War's Darkest Secret"; Asociación Pro-Búsqueda de Niñas y Niños Desaparecidos, *El día mas esperado*; interview by author with Jon Cortina, co-founder of Pro-Búsqueda.

49. Sprenkels and Asociación Pro-Búsqueda de Niñas y Niños Desaparecidos, *Historias para tener presente*, 56–57.

50. Interview by author with Jon Cortina, cofounder of Pro-Búsqueda; Dalton, "Cicatrices no cerradas de la guerra"; Laínez Vilaherrera, Hasbún Alvarenga, and Asociación Pro-Búsqueda de Niñas y Niños Desaparecidos, *Tejiendo nuestra identidad*.

51. Rohter, "El Salvador's Stolen Children Face a War's Darkest Secret."

52. Interview by author with Zaira Navas, attorney for Pro-Búsqueda; Dalton, "Ante la corte interamericana."

53. Weiner and Dillon, "Shadowy Alliance—A Special Report."

54. Comisión para el Esclarecimiento Histórico (CEH), *Guatemala, memoria del silencio = Tz'inil Na'tab'al.*

55. Francisco Goldman, *Art of Political Murder*; Way, "Mayan in the Mall"; Moreton, *God and Wal-Mart.*

56. Much has been written about this; for the process of the production of the silence, see, e.g., Wilkinson, *Silence on the Mountain*; Trouillot, *Silencing the Past.*

57. Murillo Estrada and Liga Guatemalteca de Higiéne Mental, *A voz en grito*, 9.

58. Liga Guatemalteca de Higiéne Mental, *De barro y de hierro*; *Corazones en fiesta*; and *A voz en grito*; Murillo Estrada and Liga Guatemalteca de Higiéne Mental, *A voz en grito.*

59. Liga Guatemalteca de Higiéne Mental, *Corazones en fiesta*, 45.

60. Ibid., 49.

61. Ibid., 46.

62. Americas Watch, "Civil Patrols in Guatemala."

63. Green, *Fear as a Way of Life.*

64. Grandin, *The Blood of Guatemala.*

65. Or a hybrid version thereof, as when every man in the community wears a baseball cap that replaces the traditional hat, or the striking prevalence of Puma brand T-shirts, adorned, of course, with the traditional jaguar.

66. Liga Guatemalteca de Higiéne Mental, *Corazones en fiesta*, 40–41.

67. Ibid., 43–44.

68. On this point, see especially Green, *Fear as a Way of Life.*

69. Martínez, "Franco y su cacería de los 'ninos rojos.'"

70. Gill, *The School of the Americas.*

71. The interviewees are Javel Davis and Sabrina Harmon; see *Standard Operating Procedure.*

72. Deborah Levenson-Estrada, "Opened Veins: Living Death and Masculinity in Guatemala's Youth Gangs (Maras)," paper delivered at the Congress of the Latin American Studies Association, Puerto Rico, March 15–18, 2006.

73. Martín Medem, *Niños de repuesto.*

74. See Archival Sources: *Prensa Libre*, "Ley de adopción: Proyecto pasó en primera lectura" and *Prensa Libre*, "Ley de adopción: Persisten irregularidades en al proceso de aprobacion."

75. See Nitlápan-Envio Team, "Economic Crisis: A Ticking Time Bomb." See Archival Sources: Hernández, "Adopción de menores, un gran negocio," 12; and *La Hora*, "Trafico de niños."

76. See Casa Alianza and Myrna Mack Survivors Foundation, *Adoptions in Guatemala.*

77. June Weinstock, "The Zapatista Uprising," e-mail to Jose Gutiérrez, Fairbanks, Alaska, reposted to misc.activism.progressive, February 3, 1994, This can now be found at the Google group misc.activism.progressive, http://groups.google.com/group/misc.activism.progressive/topics.

78. Booth, "Babies Are Disappearing."

79. Abigail E. Adams, "Gringas, Ghouls, and Guatemala," 114.

80. See Archival Sources: García, "Florece el mercado negro de órganos humanos."

81. See Archival Sources: Canteo, "Cateos y más detenciones en Santa Lucía Cotzumalguapa"; and Frayssinet, "Guatemala: de los ogros comeninos, a los traficantes de menores."

82. See Archival Sources: Hernández, "Crece preocupación por robo de niños."

83. See Archival Sources: Tulio Trejo, "Policía alerta sobre sicosis pública por robo de menores."

84. Ibid.

85. See Archival Sources: *La Republica*, "Tres acusados de secuestrar niños estuvieron a punto de ser linchados."

86. See Archival Sources: *Prensa Libre*, "Padres temen secuestro de niños"; *La Hora*, "Robaniños causan alarma en zone 18."

87. See *Prensa Libre*, "MP reporta 66 niños robados."

88. See Archival Sources: *La Republica*, "Robo de niños mantiene en vio a población."

89. Ibid.

90. See Archival Sources: *La Hora*, "Crece psicosis por robo de niños"; Ramírez Espada, "Linchan a norteamericana por robar niños."

91. This seems ironic, given that the Italian political theorist Giorgio Agamben uses the term analytically to describe the conditions under which human rights can (always) be violated. See Agamben, *Homo Sacer*.

92. See *Revista Envio*, "The State of Law in a State of Coma"; Arana, "¡Yankees Hippies Go Home!"; Golden, "Guatemala's Counter-Coup"; and Human Rights Watch/Americas, *Human Rights in Guatemala During President de León Carpio's First Year*.

93. See *Revista Envio*, "The State of Law in a State of Coma"; and Lopez, "Dangerous Rumors."

94. See Orlebar, "Child Kidnaping Rumors Fuel Attacks on Americans; Guatemala."

95. See Johnson, "Rumors, Rage, Xenophobia in Guatemala."

96. Jose Gutierrez, "Radio Farabundi Marti in Australia: June Weinstock," post to the Google group misc.activism.progressive, April 18, 1994, http://groups.google.com/group/misc.activism.progressive/browse_thread/thread/d22e04235961fcb2/dcc904beb1d6de2e?hl=en#dcc904beb1d6de2e.

97. See Adams, "Gringas, Ghouls, and Guatemala."

98. See Wilkinson, *Silence on the Mountain*.

99. See Nelson, *A Finger in the Wound*. I know what she means. In the summer of 2006, when I was waiting to meet someone in the town square in Chajul with a group that included two other gringas and two indigenous, Maya-Ixil men, we were taunted by a group of children who accused us of being guerillas. Not much changed in a dozen years, or rather, the apparent invulnerability of gringas had been replaced by a sense that we might legitimately be targets—the simple fact of being in a mixed group, outside the tourist areas, marked us as leftists.

100. Todd Leventhal, "The 'Baby Parts' Myth: Anatomy of a Rumor," http://www.urbanlegends.com/medical/organ.theft/baby.parts/baby_parts_myth.htm.

101. See Scheper-Hughes, "The Global Traffic in Human Organs"; and Briggs, "Adopción transnacional."

102. See Colindres and Morales, "Guatemala."

103. See Lopez, "Dangerous Rumors." See Archival Sources: Lásker, "¿Rodil, traficante?"; Najarro, "Guerra: la casa-cuna patrocinada por Rodil Peralta está legalizada"; J. Avilés, "Desde Guatemala, red internacional de tráfico de niños."

104. See Archival Sources: *La Hora*, "Abogado Rubén Darío Ventura fue capturado por supuesta participación en robo de niños."

105. See Archival Sources: Tulio Trejo, "Rescatan a tres menores de casa cuna clandestina"; *Prensa Libre*, "GH rescata a tres niños en casa cuna clandestina"; *La Hora*, "Fijan fianza de Q.10 mila a dos niñeras implicadas en casa cuna clandestina"; *Siglo XXI*, "PN recupera a tres niños en casa cuna clandestina"; *La Hora*, "Descubren casa cuna en la Zona 7 cinco menores liberados por la P.N."; and Véliz S., "Autoridades Desmantelan Casa Cuna de Traficantes de Niños."

106. See Archival Sources: *Prensa Libre*, "Un código que 'nació muerto'"; and Ortega, "Urge regular las adopciones."

107. Laura Briggs, personal communication with Marcos, July 19, 2005.

108. Much of this is based on personal communications with children, adoptive families, and human rights workers in Guatemala and El Salvador. In Guatemala I interviewed two women kidnapped by the military as children and now reunited with their birth families, Marta López Santiago and Jacinta López Santiago (personal communication, July 10, 2006); extensive conversations with Darcy Alexandra of Pro-Búsqueda over the course of 2005 and 2006; personal communication with Barbara Herbert in 2000; also Pro-Búsqeda's remarkable collection of narratives of "re-encountered" children, *Historias Para Tener Presente* (San Salvador: UCA Editores, 2002).

109. Marenn, *Salvador's Children*, 11.

110. Ibid.

111. Noonan, "Adoption and the Guatemalan Journey to American Parenthood."

6. LATIN AMERICAN FAMILY VALUES

1. *New York Times*, "Guatemala: Stolen Girl Tied to Adoption."

2. Selman, "Intercountry Adoption."

3. Sandoval, "'Soy una sobreviviente'"; and *Prensa Libre*, "Ministerio Público y Fundación Sobrevivientes suscriben convenio de cooperación."

4. Susana Luarca de Umaña, "FAQs: Responses to Questions Raised with ADA on Adoptions in Guatemala" ADA News, June 14, 2008, http://www.adaguatemala.org/English/news/2008/06/faqs_responses_to_questions_ra.html.

5. See U.S. Department of State, Bureau of Consular Affairs, "Immigrant Visas Issues to Orphans Coming to the U.S."

6. U.S. Department of State, Office of Children's Issues, "Intercountry Adoption: Total Adoptions." See also Selman, "The Movement of Children for International Adoption"; Casa Alianza and Myrna Mack Survivors Foundation, "Adoptions in Guatemala: Protection or Business?"; and Garzaro, "Primeros en el mundo."

7. Way, "The Mayan in the Mall."

8. Grann, "A Murder Foretold."

9. See Archival Sources: Corado de López, "Historia de una adopción frustrada"; Corado de López, "Ordenan dos capturas por caso de adopción ilegal"; Tercero, "Huye presunta secuestradora"; Medina, "Rescatan a niños robados," 8; Rodriguez Muñoz, "Adopción criminal."

10. Colindres and Morales, "Guatemala: Babies for Sale," 45.

11. Goldman, *The Art of Political Murder*, 146. See also Kate Doyle and Jesse Franzblau,

"Historical Archives Lead to Arrest of Police Officers in Guatemalan Disappearance: Declassified Documents Show U.S. Embassy Knew That Guatemalan Security Forces Were Behind Wave of Abductions of Students and Labor Leaders," *National Security Archive*, March 17, 2009, http://www.gwu.edu/~nsarchiv/NSAEBB/NSAEBB273/index.htm.

12. Carp, *Adoption Politics*.

13. Goldberg, *The Means of Reproduction*.

14. See Archival Sources: *Prensa Libre*, "Un código que 'nació muerto' "; Ortega, "Urge regular las adopciones."

15. Ortega, "Madres angustiadas contra código de la niñez," 7.

16. *Al Día* "Rechazan código del niño," 5.

17. Linares Beltranena, "¡Cataplum! destrucción de valores familiares," 12.

18. *Al Día*, "Urgen aprobar código del niño," 5.

19. See *They Shoot Children, Don't They?*; *Diario de Centro America*, "Nineth Montenegro"; and Amnesty International, "Guatemala: Disappearances."

20. See *The Body Parts Business*.

21. Martín Medem, *Niños de Repuesto*.

22. Clemetson, "Adoptions from Guatemala Face an Uncertain Future."

23. See Archival Sources: K. Avilés, "Impunes, tratantes de niños en Guatemala"; K. Avilés, "Robo de infante, delito común en ese país"; K. Avilés, "Se utilizó el Hospital de Malacatán, en Guatemala, como expendio de menores"; J. Avilés "Desde Guatemala, red internacional de tráfico de niños."

24. "Todo es legal, entre comillas, es legal. Nosotros vemos con preocupación la cantidad de gente metida aquí en Guatemala que por unos cuantos quetzales logra sustraer al menor." See Archival Sources: K. Avilés, "Desde Guatemala, red internacional de tráfico de niños"; K. Avilés, "En Quetzaltenango, 29 niños en calidad de productos caducos e inservibles"; J. Avilés, "El tonto del pueblo: Benepl'Acito un nuevo Pinochet"; K. Avilés, "Se utilizó el Hospital de Malacatán, en Guatemala, como expendio de menores"; K. Avilés, "Robo de infante, delito común en ese país: Casa Alianza, ONG Internacional"; K. Avilés, "Impunes, tratantes de niños en Guatemala."

25. Escribano de Leon, "Barreras legales fomentan tráfico de ninos."

26. See Archival Sources: Salazar, "Urge regular adopciones," 4; Najarro, "Fiscalía pide a la CSJ suspender adopciones"; and Barrios, "Documentan 440 adopciones ilegales," 4.

27. Warren, *Indigenous Movements and Their Critics*.

28. See Archival Sources: *El Gráfico*, "Declara la legisladora Rosalina Tuyuc."

29. See Archival Sources: *El Gráfico*, "En comunidades indígenas."

30. Larra, "Se desvanece código."

31. UN Commission on Human Rights, *Rights of the Child*, 9.

32. Instituto Latinoamericano para la Educación y Comunicación, "Adoption and the Rights of the Child in Guatemala," 49.

33. Ibid.

34. The Hague Conference on Private International Law, *Report and Conclusions of the Special Commission*, 29–33.

35. See Selman, "Intercountry Adoption."

36. See Archival Sources: *El Periódico*, "Adopciones cuestionadas," 2.

37. Holt International Children's Services, "Building Child Welfare Capacity in Guatemala."

38. U.S. Embassy Guatemala, e-mail communication to U.S. nationals, July 3, 2007. See also Seijo, "Policía abandonó 9 subestaciones este año"; Seijo, "Su único deseo"; Cereser, Paxtor, and Orantes, "Tensión en Chiquimula por secuestro de niños"; and Paxtor and Ruano, "Turba vapulea a tres mujeres."

39. Casa Alianza, Myrna Mack and Survivors Foundation, *Adoptions in Guatemala*. UNICEF's translation can be downloaded at http://www.brandeis.edu/investigate/gender/adoption/GuatemalaSources.html.

40. Goicoechea, *Report of a Fact-Finding Mission to Guatemala in Relation to Intercountry Adoption*.

41. Kevin, "The Battle Heats Up," guatadopt.com, November 25, 2007; *New York Times*, "Rights Group Faults U.S. on Guatemala."

42. Kevin, "UNICEF Calls for a Moratorium," guatadopt.com, October 17, 2004.

43. Melissa Griebel, e-mail, October 2, 2007.

44. Kevin, "Halloween Campaign," guatadopt.com, October 27, 2004.

45. Lisa, "Is Adoption from Guatemala Wrong," Guatemala Adoption, Adoption.com, http://guatemala.adoptionblogs.com/index.php?cat=2191.

46. Goldman, *The Art of Political Murder*, 69.

47. See Archival Sources: López Ovando, "Casa Alianza y PGN denuncian ilegalidad en adopción de niños"; *Siglo XXI*, "MP investigará acusaciones contra abogada de Umaña, anuncia Pérez."

48. MacHarg, "Breaking Covenant."

49. Goldman, *The Art of Political Murder*.

50. Human rights groups like the Lawyers Committee for Human Rights, Amnesty International, and the Grupo de Apoyo Mutuo have championed her case for years. Even the skeptical U.S. State Department termed the account that her disappearance was political "credible." See U.S. Department of State, Bureau of Democracy, Human Rights, and Labor, "Guatemala: Country Reports on Human Rights 2000," 13.

51. Adams, "Campaigner for Children's Rights Is Put on Trial."

52. U.S. Department of State, Adoption Alert, December 28, 2009, http://adoption .state.gov/news/guatemala.html (cited February 17, 2010).

53. Bordon, "Advierten robo de 6 niños al día."

54. Kane, "The Movement of Children for International Adoption"; Selman, "The Movement of Children for International Adoption."

55. Scheper-Hughes, "Theft of Life."

56. Fonseca, "An Unexpected Reversal"; Kane, "The Movement of Children for International Adoption"; Selman, "The Movement of Children for International Adoption."

57. Fonseca, "An Unexpected Reversal," 35–36.

58. Abreu, *No bico da cegonha*; Abreu, "Baby-Bearing Storks."

59. Cobián, "Autoridades involucradas/Adopción ilegal de niños en Jalisco"; Cobián, "Investigan a exagente del MP vinculado a robo de infant"; and Cobián, "Procesan en Jalisco a implicados en adopciones ilegales."

60. Halbfinger, "U.S. Accuses 3 of Smuggling Mexican Babies."

61. Ortiz, "Identifican a traficante de menores."

62. Allen, "Women Accused of Smuggling Used a Friendly Approach"; Cason and Brooks, "Tres detenidos en EU acusados de tráfico de bebés mexicanos"; Halbfinger, "U.S. Accuses 3 of Smuggling Mexican Babies"; and Thompson, "In Mexico, Children, and Promises, Unkept."

63. David Kruchkow, "When You Wish Upon a Star: An Adoption Story," http://www.adoptionagencychecklist.com/page655.html.

64. De Viana, "Presentarán queja."

65. Thompson, "In Mexico, Children, and Promises, Unkept."

66. In 1979 a mother in Tijuana claimed that her daughter was kidnapped from a hospital with a birth certificate in the name of an American couple from California. Most likely this was a prearranged adoption, but the birthmother changed her mind. The Mexican courts found for the birth mother, but the U.S. courts—as would become common—refused to enforce the decision, and the California couple kept the child. Thereafter, documented cases become less personal. In 1990 Eusebio Zavala Milinia was arrested by Mexican security forces for trying to take five children between the ages of five and eleven from Michoacán to sell them in Texas. That same year, Noemí Castellanos Benítez, a nurse at a maternity hospital in Guadalajara, was arrested by the police for trying to kidnap a newborn and accused of being part of a ring that sold children in New Jersey. A lawyer, José Luis Martínez Escanamé, was sentenced to five and a half years in prison for arranging illegal adoptions of Mexican children to Europe and the United States. In June 1992 authorities discovered an illegal adoption ring headed by two lawyers, Jesús Espinoza Mandujano and Arturo Soler Alí, operating out of Tijuana and Tuxtla Gutiérrez, Chiapas, selling children for $10,000 to couples from Canada and the United States. Another network was discovered in Ciudad Juárez, directed by Próspero Arzola, where children between the ages of three months and six years were "exhibited" for U.S. couples at various prices. In 1993 in Mexico City a twelve-year-old girl was returned to her mother ten years after she had been kidnapped from a market where her mother worked as an *ambulante*. She had been sold to a couple in Michoacán for 500,000 pesos. See Campbell and Hernández, "Robo de una niña con ayuda official"; Campbell, "Tráfico de niños a Estados Unidos"; Campbell, "Nuevo obstáculo para que una mujer recupere a su hija"; Moraflores, "Exportaban niños a estados unidos/dos detenidos/descubren federales una red de traficanted de menores"; García, "Acusado de enviar niños a Europa y EU"; Mergier, "El documento misterioso/Ante la ONU el gobierno mexicano denunció el tráfico de órganos de niños: luego dijo que siempre no"; Velediaz, "Recuperan a su hija"; Allen, "Women Accused of Smuggling Used a Friendly Approach"; Cason and Brooks, "Tres detenidos en EU acusados de tráfico de bebés mexicanos"; García, "Asegura cónsul que autoridades sabían de tráfico de menores"; Halbfinger, "U.S. Accuses 3 of Smuggling Mexican Babies"; MacCormack, "Black-Market Babies/Illicit Adoptions Inflame a Sensitive Nerve in Mexico, an Impoverished Country That Cherishes Its Children"; Ortiz, "Identifican a traficante de menores"; Thompson, "In Mexico, Children, and Promises, Unkept"; and David Kruchkow, "When You Wish Upon a Star: An Adoption Story," http://www.adoptionagencychecklist.com/page655.html.

67. MacCormack, "Black Market Babies."

68. Poniatowska, "Los desaparecidos politicos"; and Poniatowska, *La Noche de Tlatelolco*.

69. Stiglitz, *Globalization and Its Discontents*.

70. Watson, "Blood Relations"; Semo, "La negociación inevitable."

71. Kane, "The Movement of Children for International Adoption."

72. *Reforma*, "Protege cancillería a niños adoptados por extranjeros"; Morales, "La OEA, por fin un logro: se reconoce que existe el tráfico de menores"; Martínez, "El comercio de organos de niños mexicanos, por miseria, indiferencia, corrupcion e impunidad: Martin Medem"; Martínez, "Eric Sottas exige a la CNDH investigar a 17 clínicas de trasplantes en

Ciudad Juárez y Tijuana/está confirmado en México el tráfico de órganos infantiles";
Martín Medem, *Niños de repuesto*; Díaz, "La vía, trámites expeditos de adopción"; Vera and
Monge, "El robo de niños desborda la capacidad de la procuradurias para atacarlo, recoonce
la PGR"; and Mergier, "El documento misterios."

73. Vargas, "Adoptan hogar fuera de Mexico."

74. Kane, "The Movement of Children for International Adoption."

75. Selman, "The Movement of Children for International Adoption."

76. U.S. Department of State, Bureau of Consular Affairs, "Immigrant Visas Issued to
Orphans Coming to the U.S.: Top Countries of Origin," http://web.archive.org/web/
19961125141913/http://travel.state.gov/orphan_numbers.html.

77. From the Secretaría Nacional de Adopciónes (SNA) website numbers, it seems that
adoptions peaked for Spain around 2000 (102) after increasing from 2 in 1995 to 144 in 1999.
For Italy the numbers seem to vary more randomly.

78. See Leinaweaver, *The Circulation of Children*; Samper, "Cannibalizing Kids"; Campion-
Vincent, "The Baby-Parts Story"; and Williams, "Death in the Andes."

79. Emery, "Thousands of Peruvian Babies Available for Adoption"; Portillo, "Peru:
Illegal Adoption of Children, a Lucrative Business"; Silva, "Archbishop Says Latin American
Children Killed for Organs."

80. See Robinson, "In Peru, Anxieties over Adoption"; Robinson, "An Arrest for Trafficking Changes Adoption Debate"; Nash, "Lima Journal"; Zambito, "Attorney's Odyssey Ends
with Justice"; Constable, "The Family Man."

81. Maria Galup, personal communication, December 5, 2008. See also Cornell and
Roberts, "Democracy, Counter-Insurgency, and Human Rights"; and Poole and Renique,
"Terror and the Privatized State."

82. Lovelock, "Intercountry Adoption as a Migratory Practice."

83. Cardarello, "The Movement of the Mothers of the Courthouse Square."

84. Yngvesson, *Belonging in an Adopted World*.

85. Claudia Fonseca has made this point most forcefully and persuasively; see Fonseca,
Caminhos da adoção; Fonseca, "Child Circulation in the Brazilian Favelas"; and Fonseca,
"Patterns of Shared Parenthood among the Brazilian Poor." See also Leinaweaver, *The
Circulation of Children*. In my experience everyday conversations in Mexico and Guatemala
confirm this point as well. For Mexico, see Blum, "Public Welfare and Child Circulation";
and Blum, *Domestic Economies*. Where two-parent lesbian and gay adoption is not legally
possible, the second parent is an informal adopter. Stepparents in blended families who do
not go through the expense and hassle of a legal adoption are also informal adopters.

86. See Archival Sources: Casa Alianza and Myrna Mack Survivors Foundation, "Adoptions in Guatemala."

87. See Archival Sources: Pérez, "Tortura ¿Impunidad sin límite?"

88. UNICEF, *State of the World's Children 1994* (New York: Oxford University Press, 1994.

89. Friedsky, "Giuliani's Mexico City Game"; and Gerson, "In Mexico City, Few Cheers
for Giuliani."

90. See Archival Sources: Cobián, "Investigan a exagente del MP vinculado a robo de
infante."

91. See Bar Din, "Trastornos de roles y géneros en familias marginadas"; Scheper-
Hughes, *Death without Weeping*.

92. Zarembo, "A Place to Call Home."

93. Holmes, "Jesse Helms Dies at 86."

94. David Kruchkow, "When You Wish Upon a Star: An Adoption Story," http://www.adoptionagencychecklist.com/page655.html.

95. Although it was never mentioned in the indictment, some believed that the seventeen Long Island children were the tip of the iceberg. Kruchkow cites evidence for believing that Reyes was involved in illegal adoption from Colombia and Peru; the Mexican parents' group FIND charge that he was involved in five hundred illegal adoptions from Mexico. Although neither source is conclusive, they certainly raise interesting questions.

96. David Kruchkow, "When You Wish Upon a Star: An Adoption Story," http://www.adoptionagencychecklist.com/page655.html, ch. 11.

97. Thompson, "Promises and Children Unkept."

98. *Arizona Republic*, "Adoption Suspect Ordered to NY."

99. David Kruchkow, "When You Wish Upon a Star: An Adoption Story," http://www.adoptionagencychecklist.com/page655.html.

100. See, e.g., Smolin, "Child Laundering."

7. GAY AND LESBIAN ADOPTION

1. Nagourney and Cooper, "Transcript: The Times Interviews John McCain."

2. See BBC News, "Belgium Passes Gay Adoption Law"; Yejeda, "Legaliza España los matrimonios entre personas del mismo sexo"; BBC News, "South African Gays Win Adoption Battle"; Crumley, "France Overruled on Gay Adoption."

4. See Archived Sources: Frausto Crotte, "Reportaje hijos homosexuals"; *El Universal*, "Provida adopción homosexuals"; *El Universal*, "Conapred homofobia institucionalizada"; and BBC News, "Two Brazilian Gay Men Adopt Girl."

3. See Archival Sources: *Lesbian Connection*, "Announcing the Start of the Lesbian Mothers National Defense Fund."

4. See *Mom's Apple Pie: The Heart of the Lesbian Mothers' Custody Movement.*

5. Ibid.

6. See Gregg Lange, "Lesbian Mothers National Defense Fund Holds First Benefit Fundraiser on October 19, 1974," *Historylink.org: The Free Online Encyclopedia of Washington State History*, http://www.historylink.org/index.cfm?DisplayPage=pf_output.cfm&file_id=1173.

7. See Lewin, *Lesbian Mothers.*

8. Ibid., 3–4. See *Sandy and Madeleine's Family.*

9. Polikoff, "The Limits of Visibility."

10. Polikoff, *Beyond Straight and Gay.*

11. Ayres, "Judge's Decision in Custody Case Raises Concerns."

12. *Bowers v. Hardwick*, 478 U.S. 186, 106 S. Ct. 2841, 92 L. Ed. 2d 140, at 194.

13. Ayres, "Gay Woman Loses Custody of Her Son to Her Mother."

14. Shiltz, *The Mayor of Castro Street*, 212–13.

15. Talbot, "The Devil in the Nursery."

16. Clendinen, "Curbs Imposed on Homosexuals as Foster Parents."

17. See Cooper, "Placement of Foster Children with Gay Couple Is Revoked"; and Cooper, "Some Oppose Foster Placement with Gay Couple."

18. Lehigh and Miller, "The Damage Done."

19. Ibid.

20. Johnston, "State Pulls Foster Kids from Gay Male Couple"; *Boston Globe*, "Haith Doesn't Represent Neighborhood Group."

21. *Boston Globe*, "A Normal Home Setting."

22. See Archival Sources: Erlin, "GLDC Spring 1986."

23. Anonymous, "Love Me, I'm a Presidential Liberal."

24. Clendinen, "Curbs Imposed on Homosexuals as Foster Parents."

25. Ibid.

26. Phillips and Miga, "Duke on Hot Seat in Gay Foster Issue."

27. See Archival Sources: Erlin, "GLDC Spring 1986." See also Phillips, "Official: Gays Not Barred from Foster Role," 6.

28. Polikoff, "The Limits of Visibility."

29. Phillips and Gulley, "DA Probing Charges of Abuse of Foster Kids"; Pokorny, "Foster Care Controversy Resurfaces"; Margaret Cerullo, "Martin Luther King Day speech."

30. Herman, *The Antigay Agenda*, 32–50.

31. Applebome, "Jerry Falwell, Leading Religious Conservative, Dies." Israel was important to Falwell and other premillennial dispensationalists because their end-times eschatology suggested that Jews needed to be in Palestine before the second coming of Christ could happen.

32. Posner, "What Falwell Never Learned"; Applebome, "Jerry Falwell, Leading Religious Conservative, Dies."

33. LaHaye, *Unhappy Gays*.

34. Posner, "The FundamentaList (No. 58)."

35. Herman, *The Antigay Agenda*, 32–50.

36. Swift, "Gay Revolutionary."

37. Dale Buss, "Homosexual Rights Go to School," *Christianity Today* 37, no. 6 (1993): 70–72, cited in Herman, *The Antigay Agenda*, 57.

38. Herman, *The Antigay Agenda*, 77, 15–16; Focus on the Family, "Historical Timeline: A Look at the First 30 Years of Focus on the Family," http://www.focusonthefamily.com/about_us/news_room/history.aspx.

39. Herman, *The Antigay Agenda*, 137.

40. *Romer v. Evans* 517 U.S. 620 (1996).

41. Ibid. at 632.

42. Colson, "Why Not Gay Marriage."

43. Shiltz, *The Mayor of Castro Street*.

44. Hunter and Polikoff. "Custody Rights of Lesbian Mothers: Legal Theory and Litigations Strategy."

45. Ibid.; Polikoff, "The Limits of Visibility"; Ricketts and Actenberg, "The Adoptive and Foster Gay and Lesbian Parent"; Riley, "The Avowed Lesbian Mother and Her Right to Child Custody"; Rivera, "Our Straight-Laced Judges," 799; Basile, "Lesbian Mothers"; Armanno, "The Lesbian Mother."

46. Pratt, *Crime against Nature*.

47. Mamo, *Queering Reproduction*; Hornstein "Children by Donor Insemination"; Briggs, "Twenty Years of Making a Difference"; Salholz, "The Future of Gay America." *Newsweek*, "The Talk of Television"; and Fleming, "New Frontiers in Conception"; Suplee, "Sex in the '90s."

48. *Mom's Apple Pie, Newsletter,* "Joint Adoption."

49. See Archival Sources: *Mom's Apple Pie,* "Adoption Politics, Economics, and Identity," 8, excerption from *Conceptions* (Winter 1993). Profuse thanks to Elizabeth Clement at the University of Utah, who found this citation at ONE: The National Gay and Lesbian Archive.

50. See Archival Sources: Erlin, "Notes."

51. Nancy Alach, Karen Beetle, Laura Booth, Katherine Diaz, Eileen Hansen, and Jessica Shubow, *Out and Outraged: Nonviolent Civil Disobedience at the Supreme Court, C.D. Hand-book* (self-published, 1987), 4, from author's personal papers.

52. For example, see Nancy Polikoff's transformation from someone at the forefront of crafting lesbian custody and adoption strategies to someone explaining to a broader gay movement why gay marriage is a bad idea. Hunter and Polikoff, "Custody Rights of Lesbian Mothers"; Polikoff, "The Limits of Visibility"; and Polikoff, *Beyond Straight and Gay Marriage.* Or see signatories, like Nan Hunter, to the "Beyond Same-Sex Marriage" statement, July 26, 2006, http://www.beyondmarriage.org/full_statement.html.

53. For a concise summary of these positions, see Fairyington, "Challenging the Marriage Imperative," 5–7.

54. Kelly, "Why You Should Ignore the 'Millennium March'"; Cagan, "Millennial Missteps"; Birch and Perry, "The Response."

55. Goodstein, "Gay Bishop Plans His Civil Union Rite."

56. See Barb Powell, "CBS, NBC Refuse to Air Church's Television Advertisement," Worldwide Faith News Archives, http://www.wfn.org/2004/11/msg00231.html.

57. Lisa de Moraes, "PBS's Buster Gets an Education"; Leslie Wayne, "Under Fire, PBS Leader Will Leave."

58. This fascinating chronology was assembled by Bloodsworth-Lugo and Lugo-Lugo, "The 'War on Terror' and Same-Sex Marriage." They argue that the shift represented the sharpening of the discourse of national security, which was all about being "with us or with the terrorists," in Bush's memorable phrase, which they analogize to the role of homosexuals and the importance of marriage in the Cold War era. See the Gallup Organization, "Six Out of 10 Americans Say Homosexual Relations Should Be Recognized as Legal," http://www.gallup.com; Frank Newport, "Same-Sex Marriage in the News," Gallup News Service, http://www.lmfct.org/news; CBS News, "Poll: Legalize Same-Sex Marriage?"; Wolfe, "Americans Don't Have Faith in Same-Sex Marriages, Poll Find"; and the Gallup Organization, "Gay and Lesbian Marriages," http://www.gallup.com.poll/focus.

59. Thereafter, opposition declined, although it stayed high throughout 2004. Pew Research Center for People and the Press, "Less Opposition to Gay Marriage, Adoption and Military Service," http://people-press.org/report/273/less-opposition-to-gay-marriage-ad option-and-military-service.

60. CBS News, "CBS Poll: Changing Views of Gay Marriage."

61. Dana Bash, "Bush Renews Calls for Same-Sex Marriage Ban."

62. Rose, *Powers of Freedom*; and Rose, "Governing 'Advanced' Liberal Democracies"; Ong, *Neoliberalism as Exception Mutations in Citizenship and Sovereignty.*

63. Duggan and Kim, "Beyond Gay Marriage."

64. Ferguson, "Seeing Like an Oil Company"; Davis, *City of Quartz*; Harvey, *A Brief History of Neoliberalism.*

65. Wen and Phillips, "Bishops to Oppose Adoption by Gays Exemption Bid Seen from Antibias Laws."

66. Wen, "Catholic Charities Stuns State, Ends Adoptions."

67. Winerip, "A Boy, His 2 Mothers and Some Unlikely Support."

68. Savage, "Is No Adoption Really Better Than a Gay Adoption?"

69. *Goodridge v. Department of Public Health*, 798 N. E. 2d 941 (2003).

70. *In re Marriage Cases*, 43 Cal 4th 757, 815 (Cal. 2008).

71. Ibid. at 816–17, citing Glendon, *The Transformation of Family Law*, 306.

72. It is retrospectively funny, in an awful sort of way, that the court here was following the logic of the arguments offered to a lower court by Eliot Spitzer, in his role as attorney general, who may have known something about the "all too often casual or temporary" nature of heterosexual relations. Spitzer of course subsequently resigned as governor of New York after it was revealed that he was a regular client of a high-price prostitution ring. For his role in promulgating this argument, see Yoshino, "Too Good for Marriage."

73. Ibid.

74. Ehrenreich, "Anatomy of a Failed Campaign."

75. See "Beyond Same-Sex Marriage," http://www.beyondmarriage.org/full_statement .html.

76. Brown, "Antipathy toward Obama Seen as Helping Arkansas Limit Adoption."

EPILOGUE

1. According to Mary Day at Tucson Legal Aid (personal communication, March 1, 2010), the Tucson Police Department has agreed in numerous meetings that they would not act in this way because these sorts of efforts to "catch" people confound numerous legitimate routes to legalization. For example, Congress determined that women in domestic violence situations were entitled to make Violence Against Women Act (VAWA) petitions, because otherwise they might have to stay with a batterer in order to secure her situation in this country (even if she had a legal route to regularize her status in this country, like a USC husband, he could readily refuse to participate, leaving her vulnerable). If the police pick up someone awaiting a hearing on a VAWA petition, they would be "undocumented," deported, and allowed neither to stay nor to testify against the batterer. If the Tucson Police Department routinely inquired after people's legal status, they would be far less likely to report crimes, either where they are a victim or a witness, making the whole community less safe.

2. Chaudry et al., "Facing Our Future Children in the Aftermath of Immigration Enforcement," vii.

3. Bernstein, "U.S. to Overhaul Detention Policy for Immigrants"; Swarns, "Study Says Government Has Improperly Detained Foreign Children."

4. Swarns, "Study Says Government has Improperly Detained Foreign Children."

5. Capps et al., "Paying the Price"; Bernstein, "U.S. to Overhaul Detention Policy"; Inter-American Commission on Human Rights, "IAHCR Visits U.S. Immigration Detention Facilities," Press Release 53/09, http://www.cidh.org/Comunicados/English/2009/53–09eng .htm; Talbot, "The Lost Children"; and Heartland Alliance, "Reports of Sexual Assault at Hutto Detention Center Latest Evidence of Need for Immediate Reform."

6. See Thompson, "After Losing Freedom, Some Immigrants Face Loss of Custody of their Children." See Emily Butera, "Are the Children of Immigrants Becoming Needless Statistics in the Child Welfare System?" *Restore Fairness*, November 16, 2007, http://restore

fairness.org/2009/11/are-children-of-immigrants-becoming-needless-statistics-in-the-child-welfare-system/.

7. Ellen S. Katz, executive director of the William E. Morris Institute for Justice, e-mail correspondence, "DES referrals to ICE—In case you have not seen from other sources—Numbers reimplementation of HB2008," December 4, 2009.

8. Thompson, "Court Rules for Deportee on Custody." See Legal Momentum: The Women's Legal Defense and Education Fund, "Legal Momentum Stands up for Immigrant Women and Children in Nebraska Custody Case," April 29, 2009, http://legalmomentum.typepad.com/blog/2009/04/legal-momentum-stands-up-for-immigrant-women-and-children-in-nebraska-custody-case.html.

9. See Chaudry et al., "Facing Our Future Children in the Aftermath of Immigration Enforcement"; and Capps et al., "Paying the Price."

10. Capps et al., "Paying the Price," 16.

11. Stevens, "America's Secret ICE Castles."

12. Stevens, "Thin ICE."

13. New York Times, "Shame of Postville, Iowa," and its link to the statement of Erik Camayd-Freixas, translator for the Postville raid and professor of Spanish at Florida International University.

14. Capps et al., "Paying the Price," 23.

15. David Montgomery, "Poster Child," Washington Post, May 20, 2007, http://www.washingtonpost.com/wp-dyn/content/article/2007/05/19/AR2007051901212.html.

16. See Reynoso and González Arrecis, "Redada deja a 240 niños sin padres."

17. Rutenberg and Lacey, "Bush Meets Anger Over Immigration Issues as He Promotes Free Trade in Guatemala," 12.

18. See Vásquez and Reynoso, "Migrantes, indignados"; and Dinan, "Bush Stresses Immigration."

19. Bazar, "Citizens Sue After Being Detained in Workplace."

20. Chaudry, "Facing Our Future: Children in the Aftermath of Immigration Enforcement."

21. Bernstein, "U.S. to Overhaul Detention Policy for Immigrants."

22. Fernández, "Pregnant Latina Says She Was Forced to Give Birth in Shackles After One of Arpaio's Deputies Racially Profiled Her."

23. Fernández, "Pregnant and Shackled."

24. Inter-American Commission on Human Rights, "IAHCR Visits U.S. Immigration Detention Facilities," Press Release 53/09, http://www.cidh.org/Comunicados/English/2009/53-09eng.htm.

25. Stern, "Buildings, Boundaries and Blood."

26. Ngai, "Strange Career of the Illegal Alien," 88.

27. Luibheid, "Gender, Sexuality, and Mexican Migration."

28. U.S. Congress, Conference Committees, Illegal Immigration Reform and Immigrant Responsibility Act of 1996, conference report to accompany H.R. 2202, 104th Congress, 2nd sess., House Report 104–828 (Washington, D.C.: U.S. Government Printing Office, 1996), 213, cited in Fix and Zimmermann, "All under One Roof," 416.

29. Martínez, Fertile Matters.

30. Rayner, "What Immigration Crisis?"

31. Hochschild, The Second Shift.

32. Women's age at first child has been climbing steadily since 1970, actually increasing almost every year from 20.1 in 1970 to more than 25 in 2002. It has increased more and faster for white women than for black women, with women "of Hispanic origin" in the middle. This would be consistent with it being a strategy for maintaining middle-class status, as more white women than black or "Hispanic" women are middle-class rather than working class. In 2002 the *average* age of first birth for all white women was almost 27—getting surprisingly close to ages at which fertility is difficult. See Chandra et al., "Fertility, Family Planning, and Reproductive Health of U.S. Women."

33. Hochschild, *The Commercialization of Intimate Life*; Hondagneu-Sotelo, *Doméstica*.

34. Hondagneu-Sotelo and Avila, " 'I'm Here, but I'm There' "; Hondagneu-Sotelo, *Doméstica*. The Bureau of Labor Statistics in 2006 counted 37.2 percent Latino or Hispanic "maids or housekeeping workers," and 19.9 percent was African American. It recorded no nannies, but "childcare workers" were 17.3 percent Latina and 17 percent black. See U.S. Department of Labor, Bureau of Labor Statistics, "Employed Persons by Detailed Occupation, Sex, Race and Hispanic Origin," http://www.bls.gov; U.S. Department of Labor, Bureau of Labor Statistics, "A Profile of the Working Poor, 2006," http://www.bls.gov/cps/cpswp2006.pdf.

Bibliography

ARCHIVAL SOURCES

Guatemala: Archivo de Recortajes Centro de Investigaciones Regionales de Mesoamérica (CIRMA), *31.4 Niñez (Guatemala)*

Al Día. "Rechazan código del niño." July 1 1998.

———. "Urgen aprobar código del niño." July 6, 1998.

Arana, Roberto "Tito." "¡Yankees hippies go home!" *La República*, April 12, 1994.

Barrios, Lucy. "Documentan 440 adopciones ilegales." *Prensa Libre*, April 27, 1998.

Canteo, Carlos. "Cateos y más detenciones en Santa Lucía Cotzumalguapa." *Siglo Veintiuno*, March 14, 1994.

Corado de López, Julia. "Historia de una adopción frustrada." *Siglo XXI*, January 17, 2001.

———. "Ordenan dos capturas por caso de adopción ilegal." *Siglo XXI*, February 1, 2001.

Diario de Centro América. "Nineth Montenegro: Código de la niñez y la juventud se pedirá reforma por sustitución total," November 2, 1999.

El Gráfico. "Declara la legisladora Rosalina Tuyuc: Indígenas adoptan a niños desamparados." July 6, 1998.

———. "En comunidades indígenas hay adopciones voluntarias." July 3, 1998.

El Periódico. "Adopciones Cuestionadas." July 27, 2000.

Escribano de Leon, Carmen. "Barreras legales fomentan tráfico de ninos." *El Grafico*, August 2, 1996.

Frayssinet, Fabiana. "Guatemala: De los ogros comeniños, a los traficantes de menores / Historia de la semana." Inter Press Service teletype, March 15, 1994.

García, Mario David. "Florece el mercado negro de órganos humanos; Se ha hecho frecuente la compra de niños para mutilarlos." *Prensa Libre*, March 13, 1994.

Garzaro, Michelle. "Primeros en el mundo: Exportación de niños." *Siglo Veintiuno*, July 11, 2005.

Hernández, Ramón. "Adopción de menores, un gran negocio." *La Hora*, December 27, 1991.

——. "Crece preocupación por robo de niños." *La Republica*, March 18, 1994.

La Hora, "Abogado Rubén Darío Ventura fue capturado por supuesta participación en robo de niños." January 11, 1995.

——. "Crece psicosis por robo de niños." March 30, 1994.

——. "Descubren casa cuna en la Zona 7 cinco menores liberados por la P.N." July 28, 1994.

——. "Fijan fianza de Q.10 mila a dos niñeras implicadas en casa cuna clandestina." 1994.

——. "Robaniños causan alarma en zona 18." March 22, 1994.

——. "Tráfico de niños." November 30, 1991.

La República. "Robo de niños mantiene en vío a población / Familias extranjeras, especialmente turistas estadounidenses, trendrán protección." March 29, 1994.

——. "Tres acusados de secuestrar niños estuvieron a punto de ser linchados." March 20, 1994.

Larra, Myriam. "Se desvanece código." *Prensa Libre*, February 1, 2000.

Lásker, Sebastián. "¿Rodil, traficante?" *Prensa Libre*, April 23, 1994.

Linares Beltranena, Fernando. "¡Cataplum! Destrucción de valores familiares: Nuevo código de menores." *Prensa Libre*, September 12, 1997.

López Ovando, Olga. "Casa alianza y PGN denuncian ilegalidad en adopción de niños." *Prensa Libre*, September 12, 1997.

Medina, Noé. "Rescatan a niños robados." *Al Día*, July 2, 2001.

Moraflores, Alfonso. "Exportaban niños a Estados Unidos / Dos detenidos / Descubren federales una red de traficantes de menores." *Ovaciones*, July 4, 1990.

Najarro, Oneida. "Fiscalía pide a la CSJ suspender adopciones." *Prensa Libre*, April 25, 1998.

——. "Guerra: la casa-cuna patrocinada por Rodil Peralta está legalizada." *Siglo XXI*, May 2, 1994.

Ortega, Catalino. "Madres angustiadas contra código de la niñez." *El Gráfico*, February 26, 1998.

——. "Urge regular las adopciones." *El Gráfico*, September 15, 1997.

Prensa Libre. "Ley de adopción: Persisten irregularidades en al proceso de aprobación." November 16, 1989.

——. "Ley de adopción: Proyecto pasó en primera lectura." November 3, 1989.

——. "Un código que 'nació muerto.'" February 1, 2000.

Ramírez Espada, Alberto. "Linchan a norteamericana por robar niños." *El Gráfico*, March 30, 1994.

Rodríguez Muñoz, Lucía. "Adopción criminal." *Prensa Libre*, August 12, 2001.

Salazar, Elías. "Urge regular adopciones." *Al Día*, February 27, 1998.

Siglo XXI. "MP investigará acusaciones contra abogada de Umaña, anuncia Pérez." September 16, 1997.

——. "PN recupera a tres niños en casa cuna clandestina." May 11, 1994.

Tercero, Domingo. "Huye presunta secuestradora / Según versiones mujer robaba niños para venderlos en el extranjero." *El Día*, February 1, 2001.

Tulio Trejo, Marco. "Policía alerta sobre sicosis pública por robo de menores / Las fuerzas de seguridad investigan denuncias sobre la desaparición de numerosos niños." *Siglo Veintiuno*, March 24, 1994.

——. "Rescatan a tres menores de casa cuna clandestina." *Siglo XXI*, April 9, 1994.

Vásquez, Julio. "Buscan frenar robo y plagio de menores." *Siglo XXI*, December 9, 2000.

Véliz S., Rony Iván. "Autoridades desmantelan casa cuna de traficantesde niños." *La República*, April 9, 1994.

Mexico: Universidad Nacional Autónoma de México, Hemeroteca Nacional (Mexico City, D.F.)

Avilés, Jaime. "Desde Guatemala, red internacional de tráfico de niños." *La Jornada*, September 22, 1997.

——. "El tonto del pueblo: Beneplácito un nuevo Pinochet." *La Jornada*, April 1997.

Avilés, Karina. "Desde Guatemala, red internacional de tráfico de niños." *La Jornada*, September 22, 1997.

——. "En Quetzaltenango, 29 niños en calidad de productos caducos e inservibles." *La Jornada*, September 21, 1997.

——. "Impunes, tratantes de niños en Guatemala." *La Jornada*, September 2, 1997.

——. "Robo de infante, delito común en ese país: Casa Alianza, ONG Internacional." *La Jornada*, September 23, 1997.

——. "Se utilizó el hospital de Malacatán, en Guatemala, como expendio de menores." *La Jornada*, September 24, 1997.

Camil, Jorge. "Tráfico de niños." *La Jornada*, September 23, 1997.

Cason, Jim, and David Brooks, "Tres detenidos en EU acusados de tráfico de bebés mexicanos." *La Jornada*, May 28, 1999.

El Universal. "Conapred homofóbia institucionalizada." December 15, 2004.

——. "Provida adopción homosexuals." May 6, 2005.

Frausto Crotte, Salvador. "Reportaje hijos homosexuales." *El Universal*, November 3, 2004.

García, Clara Guadalupe. "Acusado de enviar niños a Europa y EU." *La Jornada*, August 17, 1990.

——. "Asegura cónsul que autoridades sabían de tráfico de menores." *Reforma*, May 29, 1999.

La Jornada. "España pedirá a Argentina extraditar a 40 represores." February 10, 2007.

Martín Medem, José Manuel. "Niños de repuesto." *Cambio 16*, April 1, 1996.

Ortiz, Christian. "Identifican a traficante de menores." *Reforma*, January 13, 2000.

Pérez, María Luisa. "Tortura ¿Impunidad sin límite?" *Reforma*, November 20, 1993.

Reforma. "Protege cancillería a niños adoptados por extranjeros." July 25, 1994.

Vargas, Inti. "Adoptan hogar fuera de Mexico." *Mural*, June 29, 2003.

Veledíaz, Juan. "Recuperan a su hija." *Reforma*, December 12, 1993.

Yejeda, Armando. "Legaliza España los matrimonios entre personas del mismo sexo." *La Jornada*, July 1, 2005.

Mexico: Proceso Archives (Mexico City, D.F.)

Campbell, Federico. "Nuevo obstáculo para que una mujer recupere a su hija." *Proceso*, March 10, 1980.

——. "Tráfico de niños a Estados Unidos." *Proceso*, January 29, 1979.

Campbell, Federico, and Javier Hernández. "Robo de una niña con ayuda oficial." *Proceso*, January 1, 1979.

Cobián, Felipe R. "Autoridades involucradas/Adopción ilegal de niños en Jalisco." *Proceso*, January 28, 2001.

———. "Investigan a exagente del MP vinculado a robo de infante." *Proceso*, March 8, 2002.

———. "Procesan en Jalisco a implicados en adopciones ilegales." *Proceso*, November 4, 2003.

Dalton, Juan José. "Ante la corte interamericana." *Proceso*, March 22, 2005.

———. "Cicatrices no cerradas de la guerra." *Proceso*, October 25, 2003.

———. "El Salvador: la deuda con los niños desaparecidos." *Proceso*, March 8, 2003.

Díaz, Gloria Leticia. "La vía, trámites expeditos de adopción: Pruebas del tráfico de niños en Guerrero." *Proceso*, April 18, 1994.

Izquierdo, Marcelo. "Abuelas de la Plaza de Mayo: 25 años de búsqueda." *Proceso*, October 25, 2002.

———. "Detrás del caso Herrera de Noble: La lucha entre Menem y Duhalde." *Proceso*, December 28 , 2002.

Martínez, Sanjuana. "El comercio de organos de niños Mexicanos, por miseria, indiferencia, corrupción e impunidad: Martin Medem." *Proceso*, June 6, 1994.

———. "Eric Sottas exige a la CNDH investigar a 17 clínicas de trasplantes en Ciudad Juárez y Tijuana/Está confirmado en México el tráfico de órganos infantiles: Organización Mundial Contra la Tortura." *Proceso*, March 21, 1994.

———. "Franco y su cacería de los 'ninos rojos.' " *Proceso*, September 1, 2002.

Mergier, Anne Marie. "El documento misterioso/Ante la ONU el gobierno mexicano denunció el tráfico de órganos de niños: luego dijo que siempre no." *Proceso*, November 16, 1992.

Morales, Sonia. "La OEA, por fin un logro: Se reconoce que existe el tráfico de menores." *Proceso*, March 21, 1994.

Semo, Enrique. "La negociación inevitable." *Proceso*, October 3, 1994.

Vera, Rodrigo, and Raúl Monge. "El Robo de niños desborda la capacidad de la procuradurias para atacarlo, reconoce la PGR." *Proceso*, November 16, 1992.

United States: Association of American Indian Affairs Archives, Seeley G. Mudd Manuscript Library, Princeton University (Princeton, NJ)

Associate Solicitor. "Memorandum to Justice Department." In *Native America: A Primary Record. Series 3: The Association on American Indian Affairs Archives—Publications, Programs, and Legal and Organizational Files, 1851–1983*. Princeton, NJ: Seeley G. Mudd Manuscript Library [microfilm edition], undated [1977].

Association of American Indian Affairs (AAIA). "Indian Child Welfare Act [1976 Draft]." In *Native America: A Primary Record. Series 3: The Association on American Indian Affairs Archives—Publications, Programs, and Legal and Organizational Files, 1851–1983*. Princeton, NJ: Seeley G. Mudd Manuscript Library [microfilm edition], 1976.

———. "Indian Child Welfare Act [1977 Draft]." In *Native America: A Primary Record. Series 3: The Association on American Indian Affairs Archives—Publications, Programs, and Legal and Organizational Files, 1851–1983*. Princeton, NJ: Seeley G. Mudd Manuscript Library [microfilm edition], 1977.

——. "Testimony of Faye La Pointe, Puyallup Tribe, before the U.S. Congress, House Committee on Indians and Public Lands hearing on the Indian Child Welfare Act, March 9, 1978." *The Association on American Indian Affairs Archives. Series 3: Legislation, Box 305, folder 3, Indian Child Welfare Act, 1975–1979.* Princeton, NJ: Seeley G. Mudd Manuscript Library.

——. "Testimony of Sister Mary Clare Ciulla, Catholic Social Services, Anchorage, to U.S. House Committee on Indians and Public Lands, September 9, 1978." *The Association on American Indian Affairs Archives. Series 3: Legislation, Box 305, folder 3, Indian Child Welfare Act, 1975–1979.* Princeton, NJ: Seeley G. Mudd Manuscript Library.

United States: Center for Creative Photography Archive, the University of Arizona (Tucson, AZ)

Breitenbach, Josef. *Women of Asia.* London: WM Collins, Sons and Co., 1968.

Thurston, John. "What About Our Reconstruction of Korea." Letter to Josef Breitenbach, May 14, 1956. Josef Breitenbach Papers, Box AG90: 25, Writing and Photography Projects: 1948–1956.

United Nations. Korean Reconstruction Agency. "Speech Delivered before the Unkra." New York: UNKRA, 1953. Josef Breitenbach Papers, Box AG90, Writing and Photography Projects: 1948–1956.

United States: Gay and Lesbian Defense Committee Papers (Boston, MA)

Boston Globe. "Haith Doesn't Represent Neighborhood Group." May 27, 1985.

——. "A Normal Home Setting." Editorial, May 13, 1985.

——. "More U.S. Children Using Foster Care." December 12, 1989.

Cerullo, Margaret. "Martin Luther King Day speech," January 20, 1986. Gay and Lesbian Defense Committee Papers, file, "GLDC Spring 1986."

Cooper, Kenneth J. "Placement of Foster Children with Gay Couple Is Revoked." *Boston Globe,* May 9, 1985.

——. "Some Oppose Foster Placement with Gay Couple." *Boston Globe,* May 8, 1985.

Erlin, Marla. "Notes." Gay and Lesbian Defense Committee Papers, file, "GLDC Spring 1986."

Johnston, Mark. "State Pulls Foster Kids from Gay Male Couple." *Bay Windows,* May 17, 1985.

Lehigh, Scott, and Neil Miller. "The Damage Done." *Boston Phoenix,* May 21, 1985.

Phillips, Frank. "Official: Gays Not Barred from Foster Role." *Boston Herald,* June 17, 1987.

Phillips, Frank, and Andrew Gulley. "DA Probing Charges of Abuse of Foster Kids." *Boston Herald,* January 18, 1986.

Phillips, Frank, and Andrew Miga. "Duke on Hot Seat in Gay Foster Issue." *Boston Herald,* June 19, 1987.

Pokorny, Brad. "Foster Care Controversy Resurfaces: Boys Taken from Gay Couple Allegedly Abused in New Bedford Home." *Boston Globe,* January 19, 1986.

United States: One: National Gay and Lesbian Archive (Los Angeles)

Lesbian Connection. "Announcing the Start of the Lesbian Mothers National Defense Fund," October 1974.

Mom's Apple Pie: A Newsletter of the Lesbian Mothers' Defense Fund. "Adoption Politics, Economics, and Identity," Summer 1983.

——. "Joint Adoption: A Major Victory for LRP," Fall 1987.

PUBLISHED SOURCES

Abreu, Domingos. "Baby-Bearing Storks: An Analysis of Brazilian Intermediaries in the Adoption Proccess." In *International Adoptions: Global Inequalities and the Circulation of Children*, edited by Diana Marre and Laura Briggs, 138–52. New York: NYU Press, 2009.

——. *No bico da cegonha: Histórias de adoção e da adoção internacional no Brasil*. Rio de Janeiro: Relume Dumará, 2002.

Abuelas de Plaza de Mayo. *Filiación, Identidad, Restitución: 15 años de lucha de Abuelas de Plaza de Mayo*. Buenos Aires: El Bloque Editorial, 1995.

——. *Niños desaparecidos en la Argentina desde 1976*. Buenos Aires: Abuelas de la Plaza de Mayo, 1987.

——. *Niños desaparecidos en la Argentina entre 1976 y 1983*. Buenos Aires: Paz Producciones y Abuelas de Plaza de Mayo, 1990.

Accornero, V. H., C. E. Morrow, E. S. Bandstra, A. L. Johnson, and J. C. Anthony. "Behavioral Outcome of Preschoolers Exposed Prenatally to Cocaine: Role of Maternal Behavioral Health." *Journal of Pediatric Psychology* 27, no. 3 (2002): 259–69.

Adamec, Christine, and William Pierce. *The Encyclopedia of Adoption*. 2nd ed. New York: Facts on File, 2000. http://www.encyclopedia.adoption.com.

Adams, Abigail E. "Gringas, Ghouls, and Guatemala: The 1994 Attacks on North American Women Accuse of Body Organ Trafficking." *Journal of Latin American Anthropology* 4, no. 1 (1998): 112–33.

Adams, David Wallace. "Fundamental Considerations: The Deep Meaning of Native American Schooling, 1880–1900." *Harvard Educational Review* 58, no. 1 (1988): 1–28.

Adoption.com. "Why the Federal Government Must Regulate Adoption." Adoption.com, http://library.adoption.com/articles/why-the-federal-government-must-regulate-adoption.html (accessed February 15, 2010).

Agamben, Giorgio. *Homo Sacer: Sovereign Power and Bare Life*. Stanford: Stanford University Press, 1998.

Agosín, Marjorie. *Circles of Madness: Mothers of the Plaza de Mayo* [*Círculos de locura: Madres de la Plaza de Mayo*]. Photographs by Alicia D'Amico and Alicia Sanguinetti. Translated by Celeste Kostopulos-Cooperman. Fredonia, NY: White Pine Press, 1992.

——. *Mothers of Plaza de Mayo: The Story of Renée Epelbaum, 1976–1985*. Trenton, NJ: Red Sea Press, 1990.

Akwesasne Notes. "An Editorial Comment on Indian Children Who Need Homes," January/February 1972.

——. "'Far from the Reservation' Title of Study of Indian/White Adoptions," January/ February 1972.

——. "Good Intentions Are Not Enough!" Early Summer 1974.

——. "Latest in the 'Social Genocide' Field: Adoption of Indian Children by White Families," September 1972.

——. "Michigan Indian Groups Searching for Homes to Avoid Losing Children," May 1972.

——. "Potawatomis Assert Jurisdiction over Children: Win Landmark Decision," Early Summer 1974.

——. "Prairie Native Groups Try to Keep Children with Their People," Early Summer 1974.

——. "Rift in N.W.T. Council over Native Adoption Practices and Priorities," January/ February 1972.

——. "Saskatchewan Native People Ask for Control of Adoption and Group Care of Indian, Metis Children," January/February 1972.

——. "Social Genocide: Challenge the Cycle of Adoption," Early Summer 1974.

——. "Social Genocide: Someone Else Is Caring for Our Children—Abusive Practices," Early Summer 1974.

——. "We Cannot Be Critical Unless We Ourselves Are Willing to Take Action," May 1972.

Allen, Mike. "Women Accused of Smuggling Used a Friendly Approach." *New York Times,* May 31, 1999.

Altstein, Howard, and Ruth G. McRoy. *Does Family Preservation Serve a Child's Best Interests?* Washington, D.C.: Georgetown University Press, 2002.

Altstein, Howard, and Rita J. Simon, eds. *Intercountry Adoption: A Multinational Perspective.* New York: Praeger Publishers, 1991.

Americas Watch Committee. *Civil Patrols in Guatemala.* New York: Americas Watch Committee, 1986.

Amnesty International. *Amnesty International Report 2003: Paraguay.* London: Amnesty International, 2003. http://www.unhcr.org/refworld/docid/3edb47de6.html.

——. *Guatemala: "Disappearances": Briefing to the UN Committee Against Torture.* London: Amnesty International, 2000. http://www.amnesty.org/en/library/info/AMR34/04 4/2000/en.

Applebome, Peter. "Jerry Falwell, Leading Religious Conservative, Dies." *New York Times,* May 15, 2007.

Archuleta, Margaret, Brenda Child, K. Tsianina Lomawaima, and Heard Museum. *Away from Home: American Indian Boarding School Experiences, 1879–2000.* Phoenix; Santa Fe: Heard Museum; Distributed by Museum of New Mexico Press, 2000.

Arditti, Rita. *Searching for Life: The Grandmothers of the Plaza de Mayo and the Disappeared Children of Argentina.* Berkeley: University of California Press, 1999.

Arizona Republic. "Adoption Suspect Ordered to NY; Douglas Man Had Good Intentions, Lawyer Says." June 1, 1999: B1.

Armanno, Benna F. "The Lesbian Mother: Her Right to Child Custody." *Golden Gate Law Review* 4, no. 1 (1973): 1–18.

Armstrong, Elizabeth M. *Conceiving Risk, Bearing Responsibility: Fetal Alcohol Syndrome and the Diagnosis of Moral Disorder.* Baltimore: The Johns Hopkins University Press, 2003.

Armstrong, Nancy. *Fiction in the Age of Photography: The Legacy of British Realism.* Cambridge, MA: Harvard University Press, 1999.

Arthur, Helen S. "Letter." *Saturday Review*, October 22, 1949.

Askin, D. F., and B. Diehl-Jones. "Cocaine: Effects of In Utero Exposure on the Fetus and Neonate." *Journal of Perinatal and Neonatal Nursing* 14, no. 4 (March 2001): 83–102.

Asociación Pro-Búsqueda de Niñas y Niños Desaparecidos. *El día más esperado*. San Salvador: UCA Editores, 2001.

——. *Historias para tener presente*. San Salvador: UCA Editores, 2002.

Associated Press. "None of 33 kids taken by US Baptists is an orphan." *Arizona Daily Star*, February 21, 2010.

Atkinson Trading Co. v. Shirley, 532 U.S. 645 (2001).

Austin, Linda Tollett. *Babies for Sale: The Tennessee Children's Home Adoption Scandal*. Westport, CT: Praeger, 1993.

Austin, Mary. "The Folly of the Officials." *Forum*, March 1924.

Ayres, B. Drummond. "Gay Woman Loses Custody of Her Son to Her Mother." *New York Times*, September 8, 1993.

——. "Judge's Decision in Custody Case Raises Concerns." *New York Times*, September 9, 1993.

Azuma, Scott D., and Ira J. Chasnoff. "Outcome of Children Prenatally Exposed to Cocaine and Other Drugs: A Path Analysis of Three-Year Data." *Pediatrics* 92, no. 3 (September 1993): 396–402.

Babb, L. Ann. *Ethics in American Adoption*. Westport, CT: Bergin and Garvey, 1999.

Bagdikian, Ben. *The Media Monopoly*. 5th ed. Boston: Beacon Press, 1997.

Bailey, Beth L. *From Front Porch to Back Seat: Courtship in Twentieth-Century America*. Baltimore: The Johns Hopkins University Press, 1988.

Bainbridge, Bill. "U.S. Adoption Agent Guilty of Visa Fraud." *Phnom Penh Post*, December 19, 2003.

Balcolm, Karen. "The Logic of Exchange: The Child Welfare League of America, The Adoption Resource Exchange Movement and the Indian Adoption Project, 1958–1967." *Adoption and Culture* 1, no. 1 (2008): 1–65.

Bar Din, Anne. "Trastornos de roles y géneros en familias marginadas." *Debate Feminista* 4, no. 7 (1993): 201–11.

Barsh, Russel Lawrence. "The Indian Child Welfare Act of 1978: A Critical Analysis." *Hastings Law Journal* 31 (1980): 1287–336.

Bartholet, Elizabeth. *Family Bonds: Adoption and the Politics of Parenting*. Boston: Houghton Mifflin, 1993.

——. "International Adoption: Thoughts on the Human Rights Issue." *Buffalo Human Rights Law Review* 13 (2007): 151–203.

——. *Nobody's Children: Abuse and Neglect, Foster Drift, and the Adoption Alternative*. Boston: Beacon Press, 1999.

——. "Private Race Preferences in Family Formation." *Yale Law Journal* 107, no. 7 (1998): 2351–56.

——. "Race Separatism in the Family: More on the Transracial Adoption Debate." *Duke Journal of Gender Law and Policy* 2, no. 1 (Spring 1995): 99–105.

——. "Where Do Black Children Belong? The Politics of Race Matching in Adoption." *University of Pennsylvania Law Review* 139 (1991): 1163–256.

Bash, Dana. "Bush Renews Call for Same-Sex Marriage Ban." CNN, May 17, 2004.

Basile, R. A. "Lesbian Mothers." *Women's Rights Law Reporter* 2, no. 2 (1974): 3–18.

Bazar, Emily. "Citizens Sue after Being Detained in Workplace; An Inconvenience or a Violation of Rights?" *USA Today*, June 25, 2008.

BBC News. "Adopted Guatemalan Baby 'Stolen.' " July 24, 2008.

———. "Belgium Passes Gay Adoption Law." April 21, 2006. http://news.bbc.co.uk/2/hi/europe/4929604.stm.

———. "South African Gays Win Adoption Battle." September 28, 2001. http://news.bbc.co.uk/2/hi/africa/1569061.stm.

———. "Two Brazilian Gay Men Adopt Girl." November 22, 2006. http://news.bbc.co.uk/2/hi/americas/6174438.stm.

Beiser, Morton. "A Hazard to Mental Health: Indian Boarding Schools." *American Journal of Psychiatry* 131, no. 3 (1974): 305–6.

Belkin, Lisa. "Life after Infertility Treatments Fail." Motherlode, *New York Times*, September 10, 2010. http://parenting.blogs.nytimes.com/2009/09/10/life-after-infertility-treatments-fail/.

Bensen, Robert. *Children of the Dragonfly: Native American Voices on Child Custody and Education*. Tucson: University of Arizona Press, 2001.

Berebitsky, Julie. *Like Our Very Own: Adoption and the Changing Culture of Motherhood, 1851–1950*. Lawrence: University Press of Kansas, 2000.

Berke, Richard L. "Clinton: Getting People Off Welfare." *New York Times*, September 10, 1992.

Berlant, Lauren Gail. *The Queen of America Goes to Washington City: Essays on Sex and Citizenship*. Series Q. Durham: Duke University Press, 1997.

Berlin, Ira, and Leslie S. Rowland. *Families and Freedom: A Documentary History of African-American Kinship in the Civil War Era*. New York: New Press, 1997.

Bernstein, Nina. "Family Law Collides with Immigration and Welfare Rules." *New York Times*, November 20, 2000.

———. "U.S. to Overhaul Detention Policy for Immigrants." *New York Times*, August 6, 2009.

Berrick, Duerr. *Faces of Poverty: Portraits of Women and Children on Welfare*. New York: Oxford University Press, 1995.

Besharov, Douglas. "The Worst Threat Is Mom Herself." *Washington Post*, August 6, 1989, B1.

Billingsley, Andrew. "Elements of a Comprehensive Program for the Welfare of Black Children." In *Nation Building Time, Proceedings of the Fifth Annual Conference of NABSW*. New York, April 18–21, 1973. Detroit: Multitech, 1974.

Billingsley, Andrew, and Jeanne M. Giovannoni. *Children of the Storm: Black Children and American Child Welfare*. New York: Harcourt, Brace, Jovanovich, 1972.

Birch, Elizabeth, and Troy Perry. "The Defense." *Gay Community News* 23, no. 4 (Spring 1998): 22–23.

Black, Maggie. *Children First: The Story of UNICEF, Past and Present*. New York: Oxford University Press, 1996.

Blanchard, Evelyn. "The Question of Best Interest." In *The Destruction of American Indian Families*, edited by Steven Unger, 57–60. New York: Association on American Indian Affairs, 1977.

Bloodsworth-Lugo, Mary K., and Carmen R. Lugo-Lugo. "The 'War on Terror' and Same-Sex Marriage: Narratives of Containment and the Shaping of U.S. Public Opinion." *Peace and Change* 30, no. 4 (2005): 469–88.

Blum, Ann S. *Domestic Economies: Family, Work, and Welfare in Mexico City, 1884–1943.* Lincoln: University of Nebraska Press, 2009.

———. "Public Welfare and Child Circulation, 1877–1925." *Journal of Family History* 23, no. 3 (1998): 240–71.

The Body Parts Business. Directed by Judy Jackson. Montreal, Canada: National Film Board of Canada, 1993. Video recording.

Boehm, Bernice. "An Assessment of Family Advocacy in Protective Cases." *Child Welfare* 41, no. 1 (1962): 10–16.

Boler, Jean. "The Mothers Committee of El Salvador: National Human Rights Activists." *Human Rights Quarterly* 7, no. 4 (1985): 541–56.

Bonnin, Gertrude, Charles H. Fabens, and Matthew Sniffen. *Oklahoma's Poor Rich Indians: An Orgy of Graft and Exploitation of the Five Civilized Tribes, Legalized Robbery.* Philadelphia: Indian Rights Association, 1924.

Booth, William. "Babies Are Disappearing; Ugly Rumors Abound, and a Tourist's Life Is at Stake." *Washington Post*, May 17, 1994: C1.

Bordon, Alejandro. "Advierten robo de 6 niños al día." *La Reforma*, April 24, 2002.

Bouvard, Marguerite Guzman. *Revolutionizing Motherhood: The Mothers of the Plaza de Mayo*, Latin American Silhouettes. Wilmington, DE: Scholarly Resources Inc., 1994.

Bowers v. Hardwick, 478 U.S. 186, 106 S. Ct. 2841, 92 L. Ed. 2d 140.

Briggs, Laura. "Adopción transnacional: Robo de criaturas, familias homoparentales y el neoliberalismo." *Debate Feminista* 17, no. 33 (2006): 46–68.

———. "Twenty Years of Making a Difference: A History of the Fenway Community Health Center." *Opening New Doors.* Publication of the Fenway Community Health Center, 1991.

Brissett-Chapman, Sheryl, and Mareasa Issacs-Shockley. *Children in Social Peril: A Community Vision for Preserving Family Care of African American Children and Youths.* Washington, D.C.: Child Welfare League of America, 1997.

Brookings Institution. Institute for Government Research. *The Problem of Indian Administration: A Report of a Survey Made at the Request of Honorable Hubert Work, Secretary of the Interior, and Submitted to Him, February 21, 1928.* Baltimore: The Johns Hopkins University Press, 1928.

Brown, Annie Woodley, and Barbara Bailey-Etta. "An Out-of-Home Care System in Crisis: Implications for African American Children in the Child Welfare System." *Child Welfare* 76, no. 1 (1997): 65–83.

Brown, Robbie. "Antipathy toward Obama Seen as Helping Arkansas Limit Adoption." *New York Times*, November 8, 2008.

Buck, Pearl S. "The Children America Forgot." *Readers Digest*, September 1967.

Buck, Pearl S., and Theodore F. Harris. *For Spacious Skies: Journey in Dialogue.* New York: John Day Company, 1966.

Buncombe, Andrew. "El Salvador's War Children Return to Their Roots." *Independent*, July 17, 2006.

Byler, William. "The Destruction of American Indian Families." In *The Destruction of American Indian Families*, edited by Steven Unger, 1–11. New York: Association on American Indian Affairs, 1977.

Byler, William, Sam P. Deloria, and A. Gurwitt. "Another Chapter in the Destruction of American Indian Families." *Yale Reports* no. 654 (1973). Radio program.

Cagan, Leslie. "Millennial Missteps: Eclipsing a Grassroots Movement." *Gay Community News* 24, no. 1 (1998): 18–23.

Campion-Vincent, Veronique. "The Baby-Parts Story: A New Latin American Legend." *Western Folklore* 49, no. 1 (1990): 9–25.

Canby, William C., Jr. *American Indian Law in a Nutshell.* 4th ed. Nutshell Series. St. Paul, MN: West, 2004.

Capps, Randy, Rosa Maria Castañeda, Ajay Chaudry, and Robert Santos. *Paying the Price: The Impact of Immigration Raids on America's Children.* A Report by the Urban Institute for the National Council of La Raza. Washington, D.C.: National Council of La Raza, 2007.

Cardarello, Andréa. "The Movement of the Mothers of the Courthouse Square: 'Legal Child Trafficking,' Adoption and Poverty in Brazil." *Journal of Latin American and Carribean Anthropology* 14, no. 1 (2009): 140–61.

Carp, E. Wayne. *Adoption Politics: Bastard Nation and Ballot Initiative 58.* Lawrence: University Press of Kansas, 2004.

Casa Alianza and Myrna Mack Survivors Foundation. *Adoptions in Guatemala: Protection or Business?* With support from the Social Movement for the Right of Children and Adolescents, Human Rights Office of the Archbishop of Guatemala (ODHAG), and Guatemalan Social Welfare Secretariat. Translation by UNICEF. Guatemala: Guatemala, 2007. http://www.brandeis.edu/investigate/gender/adoption/GuatemalaSources.html.

CBS News. "CBS Poll: Changing Views of Gay Marriage," June 15, 2008. http://www.cbsnews .com/stories/2008/06/13/opinion/polls/main4180335.shtml?source=RSS&attr=_4 180335.

———. "Poll: Legalize Same-Sex Marriage?" July 30, 2003. http://www.cbsnews.com/sto ries/2003/07/30/opinion/polls/main565918.shtml?tag=mncol;lst;4.

Centers for Disease Control and Prevention. National Vital Statistics System. "Birth Data." http://www.cdc.gov/nchs/births.htm.

Cereser, Leonardo, Edwin Paxtor, and Coralia Orantes. "Tensión en Chiquimula por secuestro de niños." *Prensa Libre,* June 19, 2007.

Chandra, Anjani, Gladys M. Martinez, William D. Mosher, Joyce C. Abma, and Jo Jones. *Fertility, Family Planning, and Reproductive Health of U.S. Women: Data from the 2002 National Survey of Family Growth.* Vital Health Statistics. Series 23: Data from the National Survey of Family Growth, no. 25. Hyattville, MD: U.S. Department of Health and Social Services, Centers for Disease Control, National Center for Health Statistics, 2005. http://www.cdc.gov/nchs/data/series/sr_23/sr23_025.pdf.

Chaudry, Ajay, Randy Capps, Juan Manuel Pedroza, Rosa Maria Castañeda, Robert Santos, and Molly M. Scott. *Facing Our Future Children in the Aftermath of Immigration Enforcement.* Washington, D.C.: Urban Institute, 2010. http://www.urban.org/url.cfm?ID=41 2020.

Chavkin, Wendy. "Cocaine and Pregnancy—Time to Look at the Evidence." *Journal of the American Medical Association* 285, no. 12 (2001): 1626–27.

Cheever, Susan. "The Nanny Track." *New Yorker,* March 6, 1995.

Cherokee Nation v. Georgia, 30 U.S. 1 (1831).

Chicago Defender. "Adoptive Parents." May 26, 1973.

———. "Black Renaissance." March 5, 1969.

Chicago Tribune. "Pregnant Drug User Glad for Jail." December 16, 1989.

Child Advocacy Clinic. The University of Arizona. *Child Advocacy Handbook*. Tucson, AZ: Child Advocacy Clinic, 2000. http://www.law.arizona.edu/depts/clinics/cac/index2.html.

Clarke, J. Calvitt. *Letter to A Colleague*. October 27, 1950. http://wwww.christianchildrens fund.org/content.aspx?id=299.

——. *The True Light*. New York: Arcadia House, 1934.

Clemetson, Lynette. "Adoptions from Guatemala Face an Uncertain Future." *New York Times*, May 16, 2007.

Clemetson, Lynette, and Ron Nixon. "Breaking through Adoption's Racial Barriers." *New York Times*, August 17, 2006.

Clendinen, Dudley. "Curbs Imposed on Homosexuals as Foster Parents." *New York Times*, May 25, 1985.

Clines, Francis X. "Group Will Seek Militants' Fund." *New York Times*, May 28, 1969.

Cloward, Richard, and Frances Fox Piven. "A Strategy to End Poverty." *Nation*, May 2, 1965.

Cohen, Felix S. *Handbook of Federal Indian Law with Reference Tables and Index*. U.S. Department of the Interior. Office of the Solicitor. Washington, D.C.: U.S. Government Printing Office, 1942.

Cohen, Richard. "Dealing with Illegitimacy." *Washington Post*, November 23, 1993: A21.

Cohen, Stanley. *Folk Devils and Moral Panics: The Creation of the Mods and Rockers*. Sociology and the Modern World. London: MacGibbon and Kee, 1972.

Cohen, Wilbur J. "Public Assistance Provisions for Navajo and Hopi Indians: Public Law 474." *Social Security Bulletin* (June 1950): 8–10.

Colindres, F., and C. Morales. "Guatemala: Babies for Sale." *World Press Review* (from *La Crónica*), May 1994.

Collier, John. "American Congo." *Survey*, August 1, 1923.

——. "America's Treatment of Her Indians." *Current History* (August 1923): 771–78.

——. "No Trespassing." *Sunset* (May 1923): 14–15.

——. "Our Indian Policy." *Sunset* (March 1923): 13–15.

——. "Plundering the Pueblos." *Sunset* (January 1923): 21–25.

——. "The Pueblos' Land Problem." *Sunset* (November 1923): 15.

——. "The Pueblos' Last Stand." *Sunset* (February 1923): 19–20.

——. "Red Atlantis." *Survey* (October 1922): 15–16.

Colliers. "Ambassador-at-Large." November 9, 1956.

Collins, Seward. "Monarch as Alternative." In *Conservatism in America since 1930*, edited by Gregory Schneider. New York: NYU Press, 2003.

Coloma, Dina. "El Salvador/Guatemala: '¿Dónde Están Los Niños?' ('Where Are the Children?')." Amnesty International, November 18, 2004. http://www.amnesty.org/en/library/info/AMR02/001/2004/en.

Colson, Charles. "Why Not Gay Marriage." *Christianity Today*, October 28, 1996.

Comisión de la Verdad para El Salvador. *De la locura a la esperanza: la guerra de los doce años en El Salvador*. San Salvador: Editorial Universitaria, Universidad de El Salvador, 1993.

Comisión Nacional sobre la Desaparición de Personas. Argentina. *Nunca más: Informe de la Comisión Nacional sobre la Desaparición de Personas*. Buenos Aires: EUDEBA, 1984.

Comisión para el Esclarecimiento Histórico (CEH). *Guatemala, memoria del silencio* = *Tz'inil Na'tab'al*. v. 12. Guatemala City: CEH, 1998.

Conn, Peter J. *Pearl S. Buck: A Cultural Biography*. New York: Cambridge University Press, 1996.

Constable, Pamela. "The Family Man; Some Say James Gagel Is an Adoption Angel; Others, Especially in Peru, Disagree." *Washington Post*, January 12, 1997, F01.

Cornell, Angela, and Kenneth Roberts. "Democracy, Counter-Insurgency, and Human Rights: The Case of Peru." *Human Rights Quarterly* 12 (1990): 529–53.

Correy, Hebert. "He Carries the White Man's Burden." *Colliers*, May 12, 1923.

Cousins, Norman. "Hiroshima—Four Years Later." *Saturday Review*, September 17, 1949.

Cowger, Thomas W. *The National Congress of American Indians: The Founding Years*. Lincoln: University of Nebraska Press, 1999.

Crumley, Bruce. "France Overruled on Gay Adoption." *Time*, January 24, 2006.

Curtis, Verna Posever, Stanley Mallach, and Milwaukee Art Museum. *Photography and Reform: Lewis Hine and the National Child Labor Committee*. Milwaukee: Milwaukee Art Museum, 1984.

Daily, David W. *Battle for the BIA: G. E. E. Lindquist and the Missionary Crusade against John Collier*. Tucson: University of Arizona Press, 2004.

Daughter from Danang. Directed by Gail Dolgin and Vicente Franco. In *American Experience*. Public Broadcasting System. Waltham, MA: Balcony Releasing, 2002. Film.

Davis, Angela. *Are Prisons Obsolete?* New York: Seven Stories Press, 2003.

——. *Women, Race, and Class*. New York: Vintage, 1983.

Davis, Mike. *City of Quartz: Excavating the Future in Los Angeles*. New York: Verso, 1990.

Day, Dawn. *The Adoption of Black Children: Counteracting Institutional Discrimination*. Lexington, MA: Lexington Books, 1979.

DeBonis, Steven. *Children of the Enemy: Oral Histories of Vietnamese Amerasians and Their Mothers*. Jefferson, NC: McFarland Co., 1995.

Deloria, Vine, Jr. *Custer Died for Your Sins: An Indian Manifesto*. 1969. Norman: University of Oklahoma Press, 1988.

Denning, Michael. *The Cultural Front: The Laboring of American Culture in the Twentieth Century*. New York: Verso, 1996.

de Moraes, Lisa. "PBS's 'Buster' Gets an Education." *Washington Post*, January 27, 2005.

de Viana, Virginia. "Presentarán queja: la secretaría de relaciones exteriores no ha respondido a la Fundación Nacional de Investigaciones de Niños Robados." *El Imparcial.com*, August 31, 1999.

Didion, Joan. *Miami*. 1987. New York: Vintage, 1998.

Dinan, Stephen. "Bush Stresses Immigration; Guatemala Pushes for an End to All Deportations." *Washington Times*, March 13, 2007.

Discovering Dominga. Directed by Patricia Flynn and Mary Jo McConahay. Jaguar House Films, Independent Television Service, and KQED-TV. Berkeley: University of California Extension Center for Media and Independent Learning, 2002. Video recording.

Dollard, John. *Caste and Class in a Southern Town*. New Haven, CT: Yale University Press, 1937.

Dorow, Sara K. *Transnational Adoption: A Cultural Economy of Race, Gender, and Kinship*. New York: NYU Press, 2006.

Dorris, Michael. *The Broken Cord*. New York: Harper, 1990.

Duberman, Martin. "Documents in Hopi Indian Sexuality." *Radical History Review* 20 (1979): 99–130.

Dubinsky, Karen. "Babies without Borders: Rescue, Kidnap, and the Symbolic Child." *Journal of Women's History* 19, no. 1 (2007): 142–50.

Du Bois, W. E. B., ed. *Some Efforts for Social Betterment among American Negroes*. Atlanta: Atlanta University, 1898.

———. *The Negro American Family*. Atlanta: Atlanta University, 1908.

Duggan, Lisa. *The Twilight of Equality? Neoliberalism, Cultural Politics, and the Attack on Democracy*. Boston: Beacon Press, 2003.

Duggan, Lisa, and Richard Kim. "Beyond Gay Marriage." *Nation* 281, no. 3 (2005): 24–27.

Duke, Lynn. "Crack Abuser's Baby Is Born, Doctors Don't Yet Know Cocaine's Effect On Infant." *Washington Post*, December 29, 1989.

———. "D.C. Revises Infant Death Figures; Rate for 6 Months Remains More Than Twice National Average." *Washington Post*, December 16, 1989: B3.

———. "For Pregnant Addict, Crack Comes First/Drug Use Blamed for D.C. Infant Deaths." *Washington Post*, December 18, 1989, A1.

Ebony. "The Fight for Black Babies." September 1973.

Edwards, Laura F. *Gendered Strife and Confusion: The Political Culture of Reconstruction*. Urbana: University of Illinois Press, 1997.

Egan, Timothy. "The Missionary Impulse." *New York Times*, Opinionator, February 24, 2010.

Ehrenreich, Ben. "Anatomy of a Failed Campaign." *Advocate* (2008): 34–37.

Elkins, Stanley M. *Slavery: A Problem in American Institutional and Intellectual Life*. Chicago: University of Chicago Press, 1959.

Elmer-DeWitt, Phillip. "Scandals the Cruelest Kind of Fraud." *Time*, December 2, 1991.

Emery, Alex. "Thousands of Peruvian Babies Available for Adoption." Associated Press, December 14, 1990.

Equipo Maíz. *El neoliberalismo*. San Salvador: Imprenta Criterion, 1992.

Erikson, Jane. "Doctors Mislabel Defects: Fetal Alcohol Misdiagnosed." *Arizona Daily Star*, November 27, 1995: 1A.

Evan B. Donaldson Adoption Institute. "International Adoption Facts." http://www.adopt ioninstitute.org/FactOverview/international.html (accessed September 10, 2010).

Fahlman, Betsy. "Constructing an Image of the Depression: New Deal Photography in Arizona." In *Visions in the Dust: Photographing Depression-Era Arizona*. Tucson: University of Arizona, forthcoming.

Fairyington, Stephanie. "Challenging the Marriage Imperative." *Gay and Lesbian Review Worldwide*, January/February 2007.

Faludi, Susan. *Backlash: The Undeclared War against American Women*. New York: Crown, 1991.

Fanshel, David. *Far from the Reservation: The Transracial Adoption of American Indian Children*. Metuchen, NJ: Scarecrow Press, 1972.

Ferguson v. City of Charleston, 532 U.S. 67 (2001).

Ferguson, James. "Seeing Like an Oil Company: Space, Security, and Global Capitalism in Neoliberal Africa." *American Anthropologist* 107, no. 3 (2005): 377–82.

Ferguson, Roderick A. *Aberrations in Black: Toward a Queer of Color Critique*. Minneapolis: University of Minnesota Press, 2004.

Fergusson, Erna. "Crusade from Santa Fe." *North American Review* (Winter 1936): 378–79.

Fernández, Valeria. "Pregnant and Shackled: Hard Labor for Arizona's Immigrants." *New American Media*, January 26, 2010.

———. "Pregnant Latina Says She Was Forced to Give Birth in Shackles after One of Arpaio's Deputies Racially Profiled Her." *Phoenix New Times*, October 20, 2009.

Fessler, Ann. *The Girls Who Went Away: The Hidden History of Women Who Surrendered Children for Adoption in the Decades before Roe v. Wade*. New York: Penguin Press, 2006.

Fisher v. District Court, 424 U.S. 382 (1976).

Fix, Michael, and Wendy Zimmermann. "All under One Roof: Mixed-Status Families in an Era of Reform." *International Migration Review* 35, no. 2 (Summer 2001): 397–419.

Fleming, Anne Taylor. "New Frontiers in Conception." *New York Times*, July 20, 1980.

Fog of War: Eleven Lessons from the Life of Robert S. McNamara. Directed by Errol Morris. Sony Picture Classics, 2003. Film.

Foley, Neil. *The White Scourge: Mexicans, Blacks, and Poor Whites in Texas Cotton Culture*. Berkeley: University of California Press, 1997.

Fonseca, Claudia. *Caminhos da adoção*. São Paulo, SP: Cortez Editora, 1995.

——. "Child Circulation in the Brazilian Favelas: A Local Practice in a Globalized World." *Anthropologie et Societes* 24, no. 3 (2000).

——. "Patterns of Shared Parenthood among the Brazilian Poor." In *Cultures of Transnational Adoption*, edited by Toby Alice Volkman. Durham: Duke University Press, 2005.

——. "An Unexpected Reversal; Charting the Course of International Adoption in Brazil." *Adoption and Fostering* 26, no. 3 (2002): 27–40.

Forbes, Susan S., and Patricia Fagan Weiss. "Unaccompanied Refugee Children: The Evolution of U.S. Policies." *Migration News* 3 (1985): 3–36.

Forde-Mazrui, Kim. "Black Identity and Child Placement: The Best Interests of Black and Biracial Children." *Michigan Law Review* 92 (1993–1994): 925–67.

Frank, Deborah, M. Augustyn, and W. G. Knight. "Growth, Development and Behavior in Early Childhood Following Prenatal Cocaine Exposure: A Systematic Review." *Journal of the American Medical Association* 285, no. 12 (2001): 1613–25.

Franklin, Sarah. *Embodied Progress: A Cultural Account of Assisted Conception*. New York: Routledge, 1997.

Fraser, C. Gerald. "Blacks Condemn Mixed Adoptions." *New York Times*, April 10, 1972.

——. "Black Social Workers Assail Agencies." *New York Times*, November 7, 1971.

Frazier, Edward Franklin. *The Negro Family in the United States*. Chicago: University of Chicago Press, 1939.

Freundlich, Madelyn. *The Market Forces in Adoption*. Adoption and Ethics, vol. 2. New York: Child Welfare League of America, 2000.

Friedsky, Noah. "Giuliani's Mexico City Game: A Story of Fear, Power, and Money." *Narco News Bulletin*, September 11, 2003.

Fullilove, Mindy Thompson, Anne Lown, and Robert Fullilove. "Crack 'Hos and Skeezers: Traumatic Experiences of Women Crack Users." *Journal of Sex Research* 29, no. 2 (1992): 275–87.

Gailey, Christine Ward. "Ideologies of Motherhood and Kinship in U.S. Adoption." In *Ideologies and Technologies of Motherhood: Race, Class, Sexuality, Nationalism*, edited by Heléna and France Winddance Twine Ragoné, 11–55. New York: Routledge, 2000.

Gans, Herbert J. *The War Against the Poor: The Underclass and Antipoverty Policy*. New York: Basic Books, 1995.

García Canclini, Néstor. *Hybrid Cultures: Strategies for Entering and Leaving Modernity*. Minneapolis: University of Minnesota Press, 1995.

Garrett, Laurie. *Betrayal of Trust: The Collapse of Global Public Health*. New York: Hyperion, 2000.

Gearino, Dan. "Hope and Risk: Money, Hope Lost in Failed Adoptions." *Des Moines Courier*, February 20, 2006.

Gerson, Daniela. "In Mexico City, Few Cheers for Giuliani." *New York Sun*, April 11, 2005.

Gibbs, Nancy. "With Her Malawi Adoption, Did Madonna Save a Life or Buy a Baby?" *Time*, October 22, 2006.

Gibson, Etta, and Myrtle Moore. "Letter." *Saturday Review*, October 29, 1949.

Gilbert, Olive, ed. *Narrative of Sojourner Truth, a Bondswoman of Olden Time*. Reprint of 1878 ed. New York: Arno Press, 1968.

Gill, Lesley. *The School of the Americas: Military Training and Political Violence in the Americas*. Durham: Duke University Press, 2004.

Gilles, Tom, and Joe Kroll. *Barriers to Same-Race Placement*. St. Paul, MN: North American Council on Adoptable Children, 1991.

Gilmore, Ruth. *Golden Gulag: Prisons, Surplus, Crisis, and Opposition in Globalizing California*. Berkeley: University of Californa Press, 2007.

Glendon, Mary Ann. *The Transformation of Family Law: State, Law, and Family in the United States and Western Europe*. Chicago: University of Chicago Press, 1989.

Goicoechea, Ignacio. *Report of a Fact-Finding Mission to Guatemala in Relation to Intercountry Adoption*. The Hague, Netherlands: Hague Conference on Private International Law, 2007. http://hcch.e-vision.nl/upload/wop/mission_gt33e.pdf.

Goldberg, Carole. "Descent into Race." UCLA *Law Review* 49 (2002): 1373–94.

Goldberg, Michelle. *The Means of Reproduction: Sex, Power, and the Future of the World*. New York: Penguin Press, 2009.

Golden, Janet. " 'An Argument That Goes Back to the Womb': The Demedicalization of Fetal Alcohol Syndrome, 1973–1992." *Journal of Social History* 33, no. 2 (1999): 269–98.

———. *Message in a Bottle: The Making of Fetal Alcohol Syndrome*. Cambridge, MA: Harvard University Press, 2005.

Golden, Tim. "Guatemala's Counter-Coup: A Military About-Face." *New York Times*, June 3, 1993.

Goldman, Francisco. *The Art of Political Murder: Who Killed the Bishop?* New York: Grove Press, 2007.

Goldstein, Joseph, Anna Freud, and Albert J. Solnit. *Beyond the Best Interests of the Child*. New York: Free Press, 1973.

Goodridge v. Department of Public Health, 798 N. E. 2d 941 (2003).

Goodstein, Laurie. "Gay Bishop Plans His Civil Union Rite." *New York Times*, April 25, 2008.

Gordon, Linda. *Heroes of Their Own Lives: The Politics and History of Family Violence*. New York: Viking, 1988.

Graff, E. J. "The Lie We Love." *Foreign Policy*, November/December 2008.

Graham, Ruth, and Sara Dormon. *I'm Pregnant . . . Now What?* Ventura, CA: Regal Books, 2002.

Grandin, Greg. *The Blood of Guatemala: A History of Race and Nation*. Durham: Duke University Press, 2000.

———. *Empire's Workshop: Latin America, the United States, and the Rise of the New Imperialism*. New York: Metropolitan Books, 2006.

———. *The Last Colonial Massacre: Latin America in the Cold War*. Chicago: University of Chicago Press, 2004.

Grann, David. "A Murder Foretold." *New Yorker*. April 4, 2011.

Grant, L. Trevor. *The Politicization of Foster Care in New York City*. Trinidad: Yacos Press, 1996.

Green, Linda. *Fear as a Way of Life: Mayan Widows in Rural Guatemala*. New York: Columbia University Press, 1999.

Greene, Donna. "Move toward Adoptions." *New York Times,* March 7, 1999.

Grow, Lucille J. *A New Look at Supply and Demand in Adoption.* New York: Child Welfare League of America, 1970.

Grow, Lucille J., and Deborah Shapiro. *Black Children, White Parents: A Study of Transracial Adoption.* New York: Child Welfare League of America, 1974.

———. *Transracial Adoption Today: Views of Adoptive Parents and Social Workers.* New York: Child Welfare League of America, 1975.

Guillermoprieto, Alma. "Letter from Lima." *New Yorker,* October 29, 1990.

Gutiérrez, Gustavo. *Teología de la liberación.* Lima: CEP, 1971.

Gutiérrez, Elena. *Fertile Matters: The Politics of Mexican-Origin Women's Reproduction.* Austin: University of Texas Press, 2008.

Gutman, Herbert. *The Black Family in Slavery and Freedom, 1750–1925.* New York: Pantheon Books, 1976.

Hager, C. Steven, and Tina Law. *Handbook on the Indian Child Welfare Act.* Oklahoma City: Oklahoma Indian Legal Services, 1997.

The Hague Conference on Private International Law. *Report and Conclusions of the Special Commission on the Practical Operation of the Hague Convention of 29 May 1993 on Protection of Children and Co-operation in Respect of Intercountry Adoption, 28 November– 1 December 2000.* The Hague, the Netherlands: The Hague Conference, 2001. http:// www.hcch.net/index_en.php?act=publications.details&pid=2273&dtid=2.

Halbfinger, David. "U.S. Accuses 3 of Smuggling Mexican Babies." *New York Times,* May 28, 1999.

Hall, Sarah. "Zahara's Biological Mom Speaks Up." *E! Online,* November 20, 2007. http:// www.eonline.com/uberblog/b56790_Zaharas_Biological_Mom_Speaks_Up.htm.

Hall, Stuart, Chas Critcher, Tony Jefferson, John N. Clarke, and Brian Roberts. *Policing the Crisis: Mugging, the State and Law and Order.* New York: Palgrave MacMillan, 1978.

Hancock, Ange-Marie. *The Politics of Disgust: The Public Identity of the Welfare Queen.* New York: NYU Press, 2004.

Hansen, Mary Eschelbach, and Daniel Pollack. "Transracial Adoption of Black Children: An Economic Analysis." Working paper series, Department of Economics, American University, 2007. http://w.american.edu/cas/economics/repec/amu/workingpapers/20 07–01.pdf.

Harvey, David. *A Brief History of Neoliberalism.* New York: Oxford, 2005.

Hawkins-Leon, Cynthia. "The Indian Child Welfare Act and the African American Tribe: Facing the Adoption Crisis." *Brandeis Journal of Family Law* 36, no. 2 (1997): 201–18.

Heartland Alliance. "Reports of Sexual Assault at Hutto Detention Center Latest Evidence of Need for Immediate Reform." Heartland Alliance, National Immigrant Justice Center, June 1, 2010. http://www.immigrantjustice.org/press/detention/huttoassault.html.

Heffelfinger, A., S. Craft, D. White, and J. Shyken. "Visual Attention in Preschool Children Prenatally Exposed to Cocaine: Implications for Behavioral Regulation." *Journal of the International Neuropsychological Society* 8, no. 1 (2002): 12–21.

Henderson, Alice Corbin. "Death of the Pueblos." *New Republic,* November 29, 1922.

Hennelly, Alfred T., ed. *Liberation Theology: A Documentary History.* Maryknoll, NY: Orbis, 1990.

Herman, Didi. *The Antigay Agenda: Orthodox Vision and the Christian Right.* Chicago: University of Chicago Press, 1997.

Herman, Ellen. "The Adoption History Project." http://darkwing.uoregon.edu/adoption (accessed September 1, 2010).

————. *Kinship by Design: A History of Adoption in the Modern United States*. Chicago: University of Chicago Press, 2008.

Hernández Pico, Juan. "Child Adoption: Another Form of Violence." *Revista Envío*, November 2008.

Hochfeld, E. "Problems of Intercountry Adoption." *Children* 1 (1954): 143–47.

Hochschild, Arlie Russell. *The Commercialization of Intimate Life: Notes from Work and Home*. Berkeley: University of California Press, 2003.

————. *The Second Shift: Working Parents and the Revolution at Home*. New York: Viking, 1989.

Hollinger, Joan H., and National Resource Center on Legal and Court Issues (ABA Center on Children and the Law). *A Guide to the Multiethnic Placement Act of 1994: As Amended by the Interethnic Adoption Provisions of 1996*. Washington, D.C.: National Resource Center on Legal and Court Issues, 1998. http://www.acf.hhs.gov/programs/cb/pubs/mepa94/index.htm.

Holmes, Steven A. "Jesse Helms Dies at 86; Conservative Force in the Senate." *New York Times*, July 5, 2008.

Holt, Bertha (and as told to Dorothy Kaltenbach). *Created for God's Glory*. Eugene, OR: Holt International Children's Services, 1982.

Holt, Bertha, and David Wisner. *Seed from the East*. Los Angeles: Oxford University Press, 1956.

Holt, Bertha, David Wisner, and Harry Albus. *The Seed from the East and Outstretched Arms*. Eugene, OR: Holt International Children's Services, 1992.

Holt International Children's Services. "Building Child Welfare Capacity in Guatemala." Eugene, OR: Holt International Children's Services, October 2006.

Hondagneu-Sotelo, Pierrette. *Doméstica: Immigrant Workers Cleaning and Caring in the Shadows of Affluence*. Berkeley: University of California Press, 2001.

Hondagneu-Sotelo, Pierrette, and Ernestine Avila. " 'I'm Here, But I'm There': The Meanings of Latina Transnational Motherhood." *Gender and Society* 11 (1997): 548–71.

Hornstein, Francie. "Children by Donor Insemination: A New Choice for Lesbians." In *Test-Tube Women: What Future for Motherhood*, edited by Rita Arditti, Renate Duelli Klein, and Shelley Minden, 373–81. London: Pandora, 1984.

Howard, Margaret. "Transracial Adoption: Analysis of the Best Interest Standard." *Notre Dame Law Review* 59, no. 3 (1984): 503–55.

Howell, Signe. *The Kinning of Foreigners: Transnational Adoption in a Global Perspective*. London: Berghahn Books, 2007.

————. "Return Journeys and the Search for Roots: Contradictory Values Concerning Identity." In *International Adoption: Global Inequalities and the Circulation of Children*, edited by Diana Marre and Laura Briggs, 256–70. New York: NYU Press, 2009.

Hübinette, Tobias. "Comforting an Orphaned Nation: Representations of International Adoption and Adopted Koreans in Korean Popular Culture." PhD dissertation, Stockholm University, 2005.

Human Rights Watch/Americas. *Human Rights in Guatemala During President de León Carpio's First Year*. New York: Human Rights Watch, 1994.

Humphries, Drew. *Crack Mothers: Pregnancy, Drugs, and the Media*. Women and Health. Columbus: Ohio State University Press, 1999.

Hunter, Nan, and Nancy Polikoff. "Custody Rights of Lesbian Mothers: Legal Theory and Litigations Strategy." *Buffalo Law Review* 25 (1976): 691–732.

Hutchings, Donald E. "The Puzzle of Cocaine's Effects Following Maternal Use during Pregnancy: Are There Reconcilable Differences?" *Neurotoxicology and Teratology* 15, no. 5 (September–October 1993): 281–86.

Incident at Oglala. Directed by Michael Apted. New York: Miramax/Spanish Fork Motion Picture Company, 1991. DVD.

Indian Affairs. "AAIA and Devils Lake Sioux Protest Child Welfare Abuses." June–August 1968.

——. "AAIA Reunites Five Indian Families." April–May 1975.

——. "Boarding Schools Assailed." April–May 1972.

——. "The Destruction of Indian Families." January 1973.

——. "HEW to Study Child Welfare Abuses." September–November 1968.

——. "Indian Child Welfare and the Schools." September–November 1968.

Indian Family Defense. "The Abduction of Benita Rowland." Winter 1974.

——. "Book Review." July 1976.

——. "Court Actions." Winter 1974.

——. "Devil's Lake Sioux Resistance." Winter 1974.

——. "Historic School Victory." December 1976.

——. "NACA Report." May 1975.

——. "Senate Probes Child Welfare Crisis." May 1974.

Instituto Latinoamericano para la Educación y Comunicación, for UNICEF. "Adoption and the Rights of the Child in Guatemala." Guatemala, 2000. http://poundpuplegacy.org/files/Guatemala-UNICEFILPECENG.pdf.

Jackson, Derrick Z. "America's Shameful Little Secret." *Boston Globe*, December 24, 1989: A20.

Jacobs, Harriet A., Lydia Maria Francis Child, and Jean Fagan Yellin. *Incidents in the Life of a Slave Girl: Written by Herself.* Cambridge, MA: Harvard University Press, 1987.

Jacobs, Margaret. "The Eastmans and the Luhans: Interracial Marriage between White Women and Native American Men, 1875–1935." *Frontiers: A Journal of Women Studies* 23, no. 3 (2002): 29–54.

——. *Engendered Encounters: Feminism and Pueblo Cultures, 1879–1934.* Lincoln: University of Nebraska Press, 1999.

——. "Making Savages of Us All: White Women, Pueblo Indians, and the Controversy over Indian Dances in the 1920s." *Frontiers: A Journal of Women Studies* 17, no. 3 (1996): 178–209.

Jacobson, J. L., and S. W. Jacobson. "Prenatal Alcohol Exposure and Neurobehavioral Development: Where Is the Threshold?" *Alcohol Health and Research World* 18 (1994): 30–36.

Johnson, Patrick. *Native Children and the Child Welfare System.* Toronto: Canadian Council on Social Development in Association with James Lorimer and Co., 1983.

Johnson, Rudy. "Group to Battle 'Anti-Blackism.'" *New York Times*, February 23, 1969.

Johnson, Tim. "Rumors, Rage, Xenophobia in Guatemala." *Miami Herald*, March 28, 1994.

Johnson, Troy R. "List of Federally Non-Recognized Tribes." California State University, Long Beach. http://www.csulb.edu/~gcampus/libarts/am-indian/tribes/ (accessed September 11, 2010).

Jones, Jacqueline. *Labor of Love, Labor of Sorrow: Black Women, Work, and the Family from Slavery to the Present.* New York: Basic Books, 1985.

Jones, Sondra. " 'Redeeming' The Indian: The Enslavement of Indian Children in New Mexico and Utah." *Utah Historical Quarterly* 67 (1999): 220–41.

Juno. Directed by Jason Reitman. Los Angeles: 20th Century Fox, 2007. DVD.

Kahn, Joseph. "War Child Who 'Disappeared' Finds Her Way Back: Mass. Woman Sees El Salvador Family." *Boston Globe*, April 5, 2007.

Kaltenbach, Karol. "The Effects of Maternal Cocaine Abuse on Mothers and Newborns." *Current Psychiatry Reports* 2, no. 6 (2000): 514–18.

Kane, Saralee. "The Movement of Children for International Adoption: An Epidemiologic Perspective." *Social Science Journal* 30, no. 4 (1993): 323–39.

Keller, Helen. "Letter." *Saturday Review of Literature*, June 3, 1950: 24.

Kelley, Robin D. G. *Hammer and Hoe: Alabama Communists During the Great Depression.* Chapel Hill: University of North Carolina Press, 1990.

——. *Race Rebels: Culture, Politics, and the Black Working Class.* New York: Free Press, 1994.

——. *Yo' Mama's Disfunktional! Fighting the Culture Wars in Urban America.* Boston: Beacon Press, 1997.

Kelly, Janis. "Why You Should Ignore the 'Millennium March.' " *Off Our Backs*, October 1998.

Kelly, Lawrence C. *The Assault on Assimilation: John Collier and the Origins of Indian Policy Reform.* Albuquerque: University of New Mexico Press, 1983.

Kempe, C. Henry, Brandt Steele, William Doregmueller, and Henry Silver. "The Battered Child Syndrome." *Journal of the American Medical Association* 181 (1962): 17–24.

Kennedy, Randall. *Interracial Intimacies: Sex, Marriage, Identity, and Adoption.* New York: Pantheon, 2003.

Kim, Eleana. *Adopted Territory: Transnational Korean Adoptees and the Politics of Belonging.* Durham: Duke University Press, 2010.

Kim, S. P., S. Hong, and B. S. Kim. "Adoption of Korean Children by New York Area Couples: A Preliminary Study." *Child Welfare* 58, no. 7 (1979): 419–27.

King, Commissioner, Department of Pensions and Security, State of Alabama, et. al. v. Smith et. al. Appeal from the United States District Court for the Middle District of Alabama, 392 U.S. 309 (1968).

Klein, Christina. "Family Ties and Political Obligation: The Discourse of Adoption and the Cold War Commitment to Asia." In *Cold War Constructions: The Political Culture of United States Imperialism, 1945–1966*, edited by Christina Appy, 35–66. Amherst: University of Massachusetts, 2000.

Klein, Naomi. *The Shock Doctrine: The Rise of Disaster Capitalism.* New York: Metropolitan Books / Henry Holt, 2007.

Koren, Gideon, Daphne Chan, Julia Klein, and Tatiana Karaskov. "Estimation of Fetal Exposure to Drugs of Abuse, Environmental Tobacco Smoke, and Ethanol." *Therapeutic Drug Monitoring* 1, no. 1 (2002): 23–25.

Koren, Gideon, Heather Shear, Karen Graham, and Tom Einarson. "Bias against the Null Hypotheses: The Reproductive Hazards of Cocaine." *Lancet* 2, no. 8677 (1989): 1440–42.

Kornbluh, Felicia Ann. *The Battle for Welfare Rights: Politics and Poverty in Modern America.* Philadelphia: University of Pennsylvania Press, 2007.

Krauss, Clifford. "Ex-Argentine Junta Leader Held in 70's Kidnapping." *New York Times*, June 10, 1998, A3.

Krauss, Elissa, and American Civil Liberties Union. *Hospital Survey on Sterilization Policies.* New York: American Civil Liberties Union, 1975.

Krauthammer, Charles. "Crack Babies Forming Biological Underclass." *St. Louis Post-Dispatch*, July 30, 1989.

——. "Put Cocaine Babies in Protective Custody." *St. Louis Post-Dispatch*, August 6, 1989.

LaHaye, Tim. *Unhappy Gays: What Everyone Should Know About Homosexuality.* Wheaton, IL: Tyndale House, 1978.

Laínez Vilaherrera, Rosa América, Gianina Hasbún Alvarenga, and Asociación Pro-Búsqueda de Niñas y Niños Desaparecidos. *Tejiendo nuestra identidad: Sistematización de la experiencia del equipo de psicología de Pro-Búsqueda.* San Salvador: UCA Editores, 2004.

Laqueur, Walter. *Generation Exodus: The Fate of Young Jewish Refugees from Nazi Germany.* Hanover, NH: University Press of New England for Brandeis University Press, 2001.

Lawrence, D. H. "Letter." *New York Times*, December 24, 1922.

Lawrence-Webb, Claudia. "African American Children in the Modern Child Welfare System: A Legacy of the Flemming Rule." In *Serving African American Children: Child Welfare Perspectives*, edited by Sondra Jackson and Sheryl Brissett-Chapman, 9–30. New York: Transaction Publishers, 1998.

Leavitt, Steven D., and Stephen J. Dubner. *Freakonomics: A Rogue Economist Explores the Hidden Side of Everything.* New York: William Morrow, 2005.

Leavy, Walter. "Should Whites Adopt Black Children." *Ebony*, September 1987.

Lee, Chana Kai. *For Freedom's Sake: The Life of Fannie Lou Hamer.* Urbana: University of Illinois Press, 1999.

Legarreta, Dorothy. *The Guernica Generation—Basque Refugee Children of the Spanish Civil War.* Reno: University of Nevada Press, 1984.

Lehigh, Scott, and Neil Miller. "The Damage Done." *Boston Phoenix*, May 21, 1985.

Leinaweaver, Jessaca. *The Circulation of Children: Kinship, Adoption, and Morality in Andean Peru.* Durham: Duke University Press, 2008.

In re Lelah-Puc-Ka-Chee, 98 F. 429, 431 (N.D. Iowa 1899).

Lemonick, Michael D. "Trying to Fool the Infertile." *Time*, March 13, 1989.

Lewin, Ellen. *Lesbian Mothers: Accounts of Gender in American Culture.* Anthropology of Contemporary Issues. Ithaca, NY: Cornell University Press, 1993.

Liga Guatemalteca de Higiéne Mental. *A voz en grito: Testimonios de familiares de niñez desaparecida durante el conflicto armado interno en Guatemala.* Guatemala: Magna Terra Editoriales, 2003.

——. *Corazones en fiesta: historias de familias reunidas después del conflicto armado.* Guatemala: Magna Terra Editoriales, 2005.

——. *De barro y de hierro: Familiares de niñez desaparecida en el conflicto armado interno en Guatemala.* Guatemala: Liga Guatemalteca de Higiéne Mental, 2002.

Lipman, Jana. "My Lai: Amerasians in Vietnam and the United States." Honors thesis, Brown University, 1996.

Littlewood, Thomas. *The Politics of Population Control.* Notre Dame, IN: University of Notre Dame Press, 1977.

Lomawaima, K. Tsianina. "Domesticity in the Federal Indian Schools: The Power of Authority of Mind and Body." *American Ethnologist* 20, no. 2 (1993): 227–40.

——. *They Called It Prairie Light: The Story of Chilocco Indian School.* Lincoln: University of Nebraska Press, 1994.

Long, Delores. "Bennett: Take Infant If Mother Is on Drugs." *Boston Globe*, December 12, 1989.

Lopez, Laura. "Dangerous Rumors." *Time*, April 18, 1994.

Lovelock, Kirsten. "Intercountry Adoption as a Migratory Practice: A Comparative Analysis of Intercountry Adoption and Immigration Policy and Practice in the United States, Canada and New Zealand in the Post W.W. II Period." *International Migration Review* 34, no. 3 (Fall 2000): 907–49.

Luibheid, Eithine, and Robert Buffington. "Gender, Sexuality, and Mexican Migration." In *Beyond the Border: The History of Mexico-U.S. Migration*, edited by Mark Overmyer-Velázquez. New York: Oxford University Press, 2011.

Lyslo, Arnold. "Background on Indian Adoption Project." In Fanshel, *Far from the Reservation*, 33–49.

Lyter, Deanna. "No Citizenship, No Welfare: American Indians and Arizona's Aid to Dependent Children Program." Paper presented at the annual meeting of the American Sociological Association, Atlanta Hilton Hotel, Atlanta, August 16, 2003. http://www.allacademic.com/meta/p107497_index.html (accessed January 3, 2010).

Maas, Henry S., and Richard E. Engler. *Children in Need of Parents*. New York: Columbia University Press, 1959.

Macauley, Jacqueline, and Steward Macauley. "Adoption for Black Children: A Case Study of Expert Discretion." *Research in Law and Sociology* 1 (1978): 265–318.

MacCormack, John. "Black-Market Babies/Illicit Adoptions Inflame a Sensitive Nerve in Mexico, an Impoverished Country that Cherishes Its Children." *San Antonio Express-News*, April 19, 2000.

MacHarg, Kenneth. "Breaking Covenant." *Christianity Today: A Magazine of Evangelical Conviction*, November 1, 2004.

MacMillan, Mary. "Born between East and West." *Saturday Review*, July 23, 1966.

Malis, Lawrence. "Letter." *Saturday Review*, October 22, 1949.

Mamo, Laura. *Queering Reproduction: Achieving Pregnancy in the Age of Technoscience*. Durham: Duke University Press, 2007.

Mankiller, Wilma, and Michael Wallace. *Mankiller: A Chief and Her People*. New York: St. Martin's Press, 1999.

Mannes, Marc. "Factors and Events Leading to the Passage of the Indian Child Welfare Act." *Child Welfare* 74, no. 1 (1995): 264–82.

Mansnerus, Laura. "Market Puts Price Tags on the Priceless." *New York Times*, October 26, 1998, A1.

Marenn, Lea. *Salvador's Children: A Song for Survival*. Columbus: Ohio State University Press, 1993.

In re Marriage Cases, 183 P.3d 384. (2008).

Martín Medem, José Manuel. *Niños de repuesto: Tráfico de menores y comercio de órganos*. Madrid, Spain: Editorial Complutense, 1994.

Martínez, Elena. *Fertile Matters: The Politics of Mexican-Origin Women's Reproduction*. Austin: University of Texas Press, 2008.

Matthiessen, Peter. *In the Spirit of Crazy Horse: The Story of Leonard Peltier and the FBI's War on the American Indian Movement*. New York: Viking Press, 1983.

May, Elaine Tyler. *Homeward Bound: American Families in the Cold War Era*. New York: Basic Books, 1988.

McAlister, Melani. "A Cultural History of the War Without End." *Journal of American History* 89 (2002): 439–55.

McConahay, Mary Jo. "On a Valentine's Day, Iowa Mom Discovers She Is Guatemala Massacre Survivor." *La Prensa*, July 21, 2000.

McGirr, Lisa. *Suburban Warriors: The Origins of the New American Right*. Princeton, NJ: Princeton University Press, 2001.

McGrory, Mary. "Orphanage Idea Has Many Parents." *Washington Post*, December 13, 1994, A2.

McKenzie, Richard. "Revive the Orphanage." *American Enterprise* 7, no. 3 (1996): 59–62.

McKinley, James. "Mexico Charges Ex-President in '68 Massacre of Students." *New York Times*, July 1, 2006.

Melmer, David. "Adoption Bill 'Guts' the ICWA." *Indian Country Today*, May 21, 1996.

———. "Congresswoman Attacks Indian Child Welfare Act." *Indian Country Today*, May 4, 1995: A2.

Melosh, Barbara. *Strangers and Kin: The American Way of Adoption*. Cambridge, MA: Harvard University Press, 2002.

Metzenbaum, Sen. Howard. "Commentary: S. 1224—in Support of the Multiethnic Placement Act." *Duke Journal of Gender Law and Policy* 2 (1995): 165–68.

Mills, Kay. *This Little Light of Mine: The Life of Fannie Lou Hamer*. New York: Dutton, 1993.

Mink, Gwendolyn. *The Wages of Motherhood: Inequality in the Welfare State, 1917–1942*. Ithaca, NY: Cornell University Press, 1995.

Mink, Gwendolyn, and Rickie Solinger, eds. *Welfare: A Documentary History of Politics and Policy*. New York: NYU Press, 2003.

Mississippi Choctaw Indian Band v. Holyfield, 490 U.S. 30 (1989).

Modell, Judith Schachter. *A Sealed and Secret Kinship: The Culture of Policies and Practices in American Adoption*. New York: Berghahn Books, 2002.

Mom's Apple Pie: The Heart of the Lesbian Mothers' Custody Movement. Directed by Jody Laine, Shan Ottey, and Shad Reinstein. San Francisco: Frameline, 2006. Video recording.

Moody, Anne. *Coming of Age in Mississippi*. New York: Dial Press, 1968.

Moore's Weekly. "Love Me, I'm a Presidential Liberal." March 7, 1988.

Moreton, Bethany. *Between God and Wal-Mart*. Cambridge, MA: Harvard University Press, 2009.

Morgan, Lynn M., and Elizabeth F. S. Roberts. "Rights and Reproduction in Latin America." *Anthropology News* 50, no. 3 (2009): 12–16.

Morton v. Mancari, 417 U.S. 535 (1974).

Muncy, Robyn. *Creating a Female Dominion in American Reform, 1890–1935*. New York: Oxford University Press, 1991.

Murillo Estrada, Nora, and Liga Guatemalteca de Higiéne Mental. *A Voz en grito: Contra el olvido y el silencio*. Guatemala: Liga Guatemalteca de Higiéne Mental, 2003.

Murray, Charles. "Coming White Underclass." *Wall Street Journal*, October 29, 1993.

Myers, Joseph A. *They Are Young Once but Indian Forever: A Summary and Analysis of Investigative Hearings on Indian Child Welfare, April 1980*. Oakland, CA: American Indian Lawyer Training Program, 1981.

Nagourney, Adam, and Michael Cooper. "Transcript: The Times Interviews John McCain." *New York Times*, July 13, 2008.

Nash, Nathaniel. "Lima Journal; Ordeal in Peru: Cuddling a Baby, Clinging to Hope." *New York Times*, June 9, 1992.

National Association of Black Social Workers. "National Association of Black Social Workers—Their Position on Interracial Adoptions." *Black Caucus* 5, no. 3 (1973): 9–10.

——. *Preserving Families of African Ancestry.* http://www.nabsw.org/mserver/Preserving
Families.aspx.

National Public Radio. "Pedro Pan." *All Things Considered,* May 3, 2000.

Navajo Tribal Council. "Tribal Policy on Adoption of Navajo Orphans and Abandoned or
Neglected Children." In *The Destruction of American Indian Families,* edited by Steven
Unger, 85–86. New York: Association on American Indian Affairs, 1977.

Neal, Leora. "The Case against Transracial Adoption." *Focal Point* 10, no. 1 (1996): 18–28.
http://www.rtc.pdx.edu/PDF/fpS96.pdf.

Nelson, Barbara J. *Making an Issue of Child Abuse: Political Agenda Setting for Social Problems.* Chicago: University of Chicago Press, 1984.

Nelson, Diane M. *A Finger in the Wound: Body Politics in Quincentennial Guatemala.* Berkeley: University of California Press, 1999.

Neufeld, John. *Edgar Allen.* New York: S. G. Phillips, 1968.

New York Times. "Aid to Child Exiles in U.S. Is Mapped/Experts Plan Selection and
Placement of 20,000 by Non-Sectarian Group/Quaker Body to Choose/Youngsters
Would Be Placed in Homes to Be Picked by Social Agencies." March 31, 1939.

——. "Anti-Gay, Anti-Family." November 11, 2008.

——. "Business Women Ask Child Refugee Aid/Jersey Federations Suggests Each Club
Support One." May 22, 1939.

——. "Drip, Drip, Drip: Adopted Mulatto Infant." April 4, 1966.

——. "Drive to Push Seat Belt Use by Children." November 23, 1999.

——. "Guatemala: Stolen Girl Tied to Adoption." July 24, 2008.

——. "Hoover Backs Bill to Waive Quota Act for Reich Children." April 23, 1939.

——. "Landon Endorses Bill for Refugees," *New York Times,* April 25, 1939.

——. "Legion Group Hits Refugee Measure." *New York Times,* May 5, 1939.

——. "The 1994 Election: In Their Own Words; The Republican Promises." November 11, 1994.

——. "Rights Group Faults U.S. on Guatemala." September 24, 1985.

——. "The Shame of Postville, Iowa." Opinion, July 13, 2008. http://www.nytimes.com/
2008/07/13/opinion/13sun2.html.

——. "U.S. Asks Pictures to Dramatize Food Needs in Germany, Japan." October 14, 1947.

Newsweek, "Adopting Black Babies," November 3, 1969.

——. "The Talk of Television." October 29, 1979.

Ngai, Mae M. "The Strange Career of the Illegal Alien: Immigration Restriction and
Deportation Policy in the United States, 1921–1965." *Law and History Review* 21, no. 1
(Spring 2003). http://www.historycooperative.org/journals/lhr/21.1/ngai.html.

Nicaragua Solidarity Network of Greater New York. "Guatemala: Mob Hysteria Leaves US
Woman in Coma." *Nicaragua Solidarity Network of Greater New York Weekly News
Update on the Americas,* April 10, 1994.

Nitlápan-Envio Team. "Economic Crisis: A Ticking Time Bomb." *Revista Envio* 69 (March
1986).

Noonan, Emily. "Adoption and the Guatemalan Journey to American Parenthood." *Childhood* 14, no. 3 (2007): 301–91.

In re N.S., 474 N.W. 2d 96, 100 (S.D. 1991).

Officer, James E. "Termination as Federal Policy: An Overview." In *Indian Self-Rule: First-
Hand Accounts of Indian-White Relations from Roosevelt to Reagan,* edited by Kenneth R.
Philp, 114–28. 1986. Logan, UT: Utah State University Press, 1995.

Oficina de Derechos Humanos de Arzobispado de Guatemala (ODHAG). *Hasta encontrarte: Niñez desaparecida por el conflicto armado interno en Guatemala*. 2000. 3rd ed. Guatemala: ODHAG, 2005.

Omi, Michael, and Howard Winant. *Racial Formation in the United States: From the 1960s to the 1990s*. 2nd ed. New York: Routledge, 1994.

O'Neill Murray, Kasia, and Sarah Gesiriech. "A Brief Legislative History of the Child Welfare System." Background Paper. Washington, D.C.: Pew Commission on Children in Foster Care. http://pewfostercare.org/research/docs/Legislative.pdf.

Ong, Aihwa. *Neoliberalism as Exception Mutations in Citizenship and Sovereignty*. Durham: Duke University Press, 2006.

Oreskovic, Johanna, and Trish Maskew. "Red Thread or Slender Reed: Deconstructing Prof. Bartholet's Mythology of International Adoption." *Buffalo Human Rights Law Review* 14 (2008): 71–128.

Orlebar, Edward. "Child Kidnaping Rumors Fuel Attacks on Americans; Guatemala: Military May Be Fomenting Fear of Foreigners. Hysteria May Invite Hard-Liner Backlash." *Los Angeles Times*, April 2, 1994.

Orleck, Annelise. *Storming Caesar's Palace: How Black Mothers Fought Their Own War on Poverty*. Boston: Beacon Press, 2005.

Paltrow, Lynn, D. Cohen, and C. A. Carey. *Year 2000 Overview: Governmental Responses to Pregnant Women Who Use Alcohol or Other Drugs*. Philadelphia, PA: National Advocates for Pregnant Women of the Women's Law Project, 2000.

Parents. "New Style Halloween." October 1955.

Parlin, Charles. "Women Versus the Kremlin." *Ladies' Home Journal*, 1967.

Patton, Sandra. *Birthmarks: Transracial Adoption in Contemporary America*. New York: NYU Press, 2001.

Paul, Julius. "The Return of Punitive Sterilization Proposals: Current Attacks on Illegitimacy and the AFDC Program." *Law and Society Review* 3 (1968): 77–106.

Pavlik, Steve. "Of Saints and Lamanites: An Analysis of Navajo Mormonism." *Wicazo Sa Review* 8, no. 1 (1992): 21–30.

Paxtor, Edwin, and Wendy Ruano. "Turba vapulea a tres mujeres una muere, otra resultó quemada y la tercera no aparece." *Prensa Libre*, June 16, 2007.

Peretti, Jacques. "Madonna, Mercy and Malawi: Her Fight to Adopt a Second African Child." *Guardian.co.uk*, June 12, 2009. http://www.guardian.co.uk/music/2009/jun/12/madonna-mercy-malawi.

Perry, Twila L. "The Transracial Adoption Controversy: An Analysis of Discourse and Subordination." *NYU Review of Law and Social Change* 33 (1994).

Philp, Kenneth R. *John Collier's Crusade for Indian Reform, 1920–1954*. Tucson: University of Arizona Press, 1977.

Plantz, Margaret. *Indian Child Welfare: A Status Report: Final Report of the Survey of Indian Child Welfare and Implementation of the Indian Child Welfare Act and Section 428 of the Adoption Assistance and Child Welfare Act of 1980*. Washington, D.C.: U.S. Department of the Interior, 1988.

Pleck, Elizabeth Hafkin. *Domestic Tyranny: The Making of Social Policy against Family Violence from Colonial Times to the Present*. New York: Oxford University Press, 1987.

Polikoff, Nancy D. *Beyond Straight and Gay Marriage: Valuing All Families under the Law*. Boston: Beacon Press, 2007.

———. "The Limits of Visibility: Queer Parenting under Fire: A History of Legal Battles." *Gay Community News* 24, no. 3–4 (1999): 38–48.

Poniatowska, Elena. *La noche de Tlatelolco: Testimonios de historia oral.* México: Ediciones Era, 1971.

———. "Los desaparecidos políticos." In *Fuerte es el silencio*, edited by Elena Poniatowska, 138–80. Mexico City: Ediciones Era, 1983.

Poole, Deborah, and Gerardo Renique. "Terror and the Privatized State: A Peruvian Parable." *Radical History Review* 85 (Winter 2003): 150–63.

Portillo, Zoraida. "Peru: Illegal Adoption of Children, a Lucrative Business." Inter Press Service, January 23, 1992.

Posner, Sarah. "The FundamentaList (No. 58)." *American Prospect*, November 19, 2008.

———. "What Falwell Never Learned." *American Prospect*, May 17, 2007.

Pratt, Minnie Bruce. *Crime against Nature.* Ithaca, NY: Firebrand, 1990.

Prensa Libre. "Ministerio Público y Fundación Sobrevivientes suscriben convenio de cooperación." February 12, 2008.

———. "MP reporta 66 niños robados." March 30, 1994.

———. "Padres temen secuestro de niños en Zona 18." March 23, 1994.

———. "Una muere, otra resultó quemada y la tercera no aparece." June 16, 2007.

Proyecto Interdiocesano de Recuperación de la Memoria Histórica (REMHI). *Guatemala: Nunca Más.* 12 vols. Guatemala City: Gako, 1998. http://www.fundacionpdh.org/lesa humanidad/informes/guatemala/informeREMHI.htm.

Prucha, Francis Paul, ed. *Documents of United States Indian Policy.* 2nd ed. Lincoln: University of Nebraska Press, 1990.

Quadagno, Jill S. *The Color of Welfare: How Racism Undermined the War on Poverty.* New York: Oxford University Press, 1994.

Quiroz, Pamela Anne. *Adoption in a Color-Blind Society.* Lanham, MD: Rowman and Littlefield, 2007.

Rainwater, Lee, and William L. Yancey. *The Moynihan Report and the Politics of Controversy.* Cambridge, MA: MIT Press, 1967.

Raspberry, William. "Addicts and Babies." *Washington Post*, December 20, 1989.

Raymond, Barbara Bisantz. *The Baby Thief: The Untold Story of Georgia Tann, the Baby Seller Who Corrupted Adoption.* New York: Caroll and Graff, 2007.

Rayner, Richard. "What Immigration Crisis?" *New York Times*, magazine, January 7, 1996.

Recovery of Historical Memory Project. *Guatemala: Never Again. The Official Report of the Human Rights Office, Archdiocese of Guatemala.* Abridged English edition. Maryknoll, NY: Orbis, 1999.

Relf v. Weinberger 565 F.2d 722 (1977).

Rembis, Michael A. "I Ain't Been Reading While on Parole: Experts, Mental Tests, and Eugenic Commitment Law in Illinois, 1890–1940." *History of Psychology* 7, no. 4 (2004): 225–47.

Ressler, Everett M., Neil Boothby, and Daniels Steinbeck. *Unaccompanied Children: Care and Protection in Wars, Natural Disasters, and Refugee Movements.* New York: Oxford University, 1988.

Revista Envio. "The State of Law in a State of Coma." May 1994.

Reynoso, Conié, and Francisco González Arrecis. "Redada deja a 240 niños sin padres." *Prensa Libre*, March 9, 2007.

Riben, Mirah. *The Stork Market: America's Multi-Billion Dollar Unregulated Adoption Industry*. Dayton, NJ: Advocate Publications, 2007.

Ricketts, Wendell, and Roberta Actenberg. "The Adoptive and Foster Gay and Lesbian Parent." In *Gay and Lesbian Parents*, edited by Frederick W. Bozett, 89–111. New York: Praeger, 1987.

Riding, Alan. "Argentines Fight for Orphans of a Dirty War." *New York Times*, December 30, 1987.

Riley, Marilyn. "The Avowed Lesbian Mother and Her Right to Child Custody: A Constitutional Challenge That Can No Longer Be Denied." *San Diego Law Review* 12 (1975): 799–864.

Rivera, Rhonda R. "Our Straight-Laced Judges: The Legal Position of Homosexual Persons in the United States." *Hastings Law Journal* 30 (1979): 799–955.

Roberts, Dorothy E. *Killing the Black Body: Race, Reproduction, and the Meaning of Liberty*. New York: Vintage, 1997.

——. *Shattered Bonds: The Color of Child Welfare*. New York: Basic Civitas Books, 2002.

Robinson, Eugene. "An Arrest for Trafficking Changes Adoption Debate." *Chicago Sun-Times*, March 15, 1992.

——. "In Peru, Anxieties over Adoption; Some Accused of 'Baby Selling' to Exploit American Market." *Washington Post*, March 8, 1992.

Rodríguez, Andrea. *Nacidos en la sombra: La historia secreta de los mellizos Reggiardo Tolosa y el subcomisario Miara*. Buenos Aires: Editorial Sudamericana, 1996.

Rogers, Dale Evans. *Dearest Debbie (In Ai Lee)*. Westwood, NJ: Revell, 1965.

Rohter, Larry. "El Salvador's Stolen Children Face a War's Darkest Secret." *New York Times*, August 5, 1996.

Romer v. Evans, 517 U.S. 620 (1996).

Rose, Nikolas. "Governing 'Advanced' Liberal Democracies." In *Foucault and Political Reason: Liberalism, Neo-Liberalism and Rationalities of Government*, edited by Andrew Barry, Thomas Osborne, and Nikolas Rose, 37–64. Chicago: University of Chicago Press, 1996.

——. *Powers of Freedom: Reframing Political Thought*. New York: Cambridge University Press, 1999.

Rosenblum, Walter, Lewis Wickes Hine, and Michael Torosian. *Lewis Hine, Ellis Island: Memories and Meditations of Walter Rosenblum on the Life and Work of an American Artist*. Homage. Toronto: Lumiere Press, 1995.

Rosenthal, Abe M. "How Much Is a Baby Worth?" *New York Times*, December 15, 1989.

Rothman, Barbara Katz. *The Tentative Pregnancy: Prenatal Diagnosis and the Future of Motherhood*. New York: Viking, 1986.

Rule, Sheila. "Couples Taking Unusual Paths for Adoption." *New York Times*, July 26, 1984.

Rutenberg, Jim, and Marc Lacey. "Bush Meets Anger over Immigration Issues as He Promotes Free Trade in Guatemala." *New York Times*, March 12, 2009.

Salholz, Eloise. "The Future of Gay America." *Newsweek*, March 12, 1990.

Samper, David. "Cannibalizing Kids: Rumor and Resistance in Latin America." *Journal of Folklore Research* 39, no. 1 (2002): 1–32.

San Diego Union-Tribune. "Unwed Mom Fighting to Keep Infant." March 15, 1984.

San Francisco Chronicle. "Ragged, Hungry, Broke, Harvest Workers Live in Squaller." March 10, 1936.

——. "What Does the 'New Deal' Mean to This Mother and Her Children?" March 11, 1936.

Sandoval, Julieta. " 'Soy una sobreviviente.' " *Prensa Libre*, April 20, 2008.

Sandy and Madeleine's Family. Directed by Sherrie Farrell, John Gordon Hill, and Peter M. Bruce. San Francisco: Multi Media Resource Center, 1973. Film.

Sargeant, Elizabeth Shepley. "Big Powwow of Pueblos." *New York Times*, November 26, 1922.

———. "Last First Americans." *Nation*, November 29, 1922.

———. "The Red Man's Burden." *New Republic*, January 16, 1924.

Sargent, James D., Magda G. Peck, and Michael Weitzman. "Bicycle-Mounted Child Seats: Injury Risk and Prevention." *American Journal of Diseases of Children* 142 (July 1988): 765–7.

Savage, Dan. "Anti-Gay, Anti-Family." *New York Times*, November 11, 2008.

———. "Is No Adoption Really Better Than a Gay Adoption?" *New York Times*, September 8, 2001.

Schene, P. A. "Past, Present, and Future Roles of Child Protective Services." *Future of Children* 8 (1998): 23–38.

Scheper-Hughes, Nancy. *Death without Weeping: The Violence of Everyday Life in Brazil*. Berkeley: University of California Press, 1992.

———. "The Global Traffic in Human Organs." *Current Anthropology* 41, no. 2 (2000): 191–224.

———. "Theft of Life: The Globalization of Organ Stealing Rumors." *Anthropology Today* 12, no. 3 (1996): 3–11.

Schmitt, Eric. "Adoption Bill Facing Battle over Measure on Indians." *New York Times*, May 8, 1996.

Schoen, Johanna. *Choice and Coercion: Birth Control, Sterilization, and Abortion in Public Health and Welfare*. Chapel Hill: University of North Carolina Press, 2005.

Schwalm, Leslie A. *A Hard Fight for We: Women's Transition from Slavery to Freedom in South Carolina*. Urbana: University of Illinois Press, 1997.

Scott, Daryl Michael. *Contempt and Pity: Social Policy and the Image of the Damaged Black Psyche, 1880–1996*. Chapel Hill: University of North Carolina Press, 1997.

Sealander, Judith. *The Failed Century of the Child: Governing America's Young in the Twentieth Century*. Cambridge: Cambridge University Press, 2003.

Second Vatican Council. "Gaudium et Spes: Pastoral Constitution on the Church in the Modern World." Promulgated by His Holiness, Pope Paul VI on December 7, 1965. http://www.vatican.va/archive/hist_councils/ii_vatican_council/documents/vat-ii_cons_19651207_gaudium-et-spes_en.html.

Seijo, Loreno. "Policía abandonó 9 subestaciones este año: Turbas descargaron su ira contra agentes e inmuebles." *Prensa Libre*, July 20, 2007.

———. "Su único deseo: Tener su familia propia." *Prensa Libre*, April 15, 2007.

Selman, Peter. "Intercountry Adoption: Research, Policy and Practice." In *The Child Placement Handbook: Research, Policy and Practice*, edited by Gillian Schofield and John Simmonds. London: BAAF, 2009.

———. "Intercountry Adoption in Europe after the Hague Convention." In *Developments in European Social Policy: Convergence and Diversity*, edited by R. Sykes and P. Alcock. Bristol: Policy Press, 1998.

———. "Intercountry Adoption in the New Millennium; the 'Quiet Migration' Revisited." *Population Research and Policy Review* 21, no. 3 (2002): 205–25.

———. "The Movement of Children for International Adoption; Developments and Trends in Receiving States and States of Origin, 1998–2004." In *International Adoption: Global Inequalities and the Circulation of Children*, edited by Diana Marre and Laura Briggs, 32–51. New York: NYU Press, 2009.

Sevilla, Graciela, and Kathleen Ingley. "Adoption Suspect Ordered to NY; Douglas Man Had Good Intentions, Attorney Says." *Arizona Republic*, June 2, 1999.

Shepherd, Elisabeth. "Adopting Negro Children: White Families Find It Can Be Done." *New Republic* 150, no. 25 (1964): 10–12.

Shiltz, Randy. *The Mayor of Castro Street: The Life and Times of Harvey Milk*. New York: St. Martin's Press, 1982.

Shirk, Martha. "Foster Parents Struggle with Babies in Pain." *St. Louis Post Dispatch*, November 19, 1989.

Silva, Vidal. "Archbishop Says Latin American Children Killed for Organs." *United Press International*, May 2, 1991.

Silverman, Stephen. "Angelina Jolie: We Should Support Madonna." *People*, January 8, 2007.

Simon, Rita James. "An Assessment of Racial Awareness, Preference, and Self-Identity among White and Adopted Non-White Children." *Social Problems* 22 (1974): 43, 45.

Simon, Rita James, and Howard Altstein. *Adoption, Race, and Identity: From Infancy through Adolescence*. New York: Praeger, 1992.

——. *Adoption, Race, and Identity: From Infancy to Young Adulthood*. 2nd ed. New Brunswick, NJ: Transaction Publishers, 2001.

——. *Transracial Adoptees and Their Families: A Study of Identity and Commitment*. New York: Greenwood Publishing, 1987.

——. *Transracial Adoption*. New York: Wiley, 1977.

——. *Transracial Adoption: A Follow Up*. Lexington, Mass.: Lexington Books, 1981.

Simon, Rita James, Howard Altstein, and Marygold Shire Melli. *The Case for Transracial Adoption*. Washington, D.C.: American University Press, 1994.

Singer, L. T., R. Arendt, and S. Minnes. "Cognitive and Motor Outcomes of Cocaine-Exposed Infants." *Journal of the American Medical Association* 287, no. 15 (2002): 1952–60.

Smith, Andrea. *Conquest: Sexual Violence and American Indian Genocide*. Cambridge, MA: South End Press, 2005.

Smith, Anna Marie. *Welfare Reform and Sexual Regulation*. New York: Cambridge University Press, 2007.

Smolin, David M. "Child Laundering: How the Intercountry Adoption System Legitimizes and Incentivizes the Practices of Buying, Trafficking, Kidnapping, and Stealing Children." *Wayne Law Review* 52 (2006): 113–200.

Snoddy, Mrs. John H. "Letter." *Saturday Review*, October 8, 1949.

Solinger, Rickie. *Beggars and Choosers: How the Politics of Choice Shapes Adoption, Abortion, and Welfare in the United States*. New York: Hill and Wang, 2001.

——. *Pregnancy and Power: A Short History of Reproductive Politics in America*. New York: NYU Press, 2007.

——. *Wake Up Little Susie: Single Pregnancy and Race Before Roe v. Wade*. New York: Routledge, 1992.

Sontag, Susan. *Regarding the Pain of Others*. New York: Farrar, Strauss, Giroux, 2003.

Spar, Debora L. *The Baby Business: How Money, Science, and Politics Drive the Commerce of Conception*. Boston: Harvard Business School Press, 2006.

Sprenkels, Ralph, and Asociación Pro-Búsqueda de Niñas y Niños Desaparecidos, eds. *Historias para tener presente: Los relatos extraordinários de cinco jóvenes que perdieron a sus familias y que, luego de la guerra, las volvieron a encontrar.* San Salvador: UCA Editores, 2002.

Standard Operating Procedure. Directed by Errol Morris. New York: Sony Pictures Classics, 2008. Film.

Starker, Steven. *Oracle at the Supermarket.* New Brunswick, NJ: Transaction Publishers, 1989.

Stearns, Peter N. *Anxious Parents: A History of Modern Childrearing in America.* New York: NYU Press, 2003.

Stern, Alexandra Minna. "Buildings, Boundaries and Blood: Medicalization and Nation-Building on the Mexican Border, 1900–1930." *Hispanic American Historical Review* 79, no. 1 (Spring 1999): 41–81.

———. *Eugenic Nation: Faults and Frontiers of Better Breeding in America.* Berkeley: University of California Press, 2005.

Stern, Steve. *Remembering Pinochet's Chile: On the Eve of London 1998.* The Memory Box of Pinochet's Chile. Durham: Duke University Press, 2004.

Stevens, Jacqueline. "America's Secret ICE Castles." *Nation,* December 16, 2009.

———. "Thin ICE." *Nation,* June 5, 2008.

Stiglitz, Joseph. *Globalization and Its Discontents.* New York: Norton, 2002.

Stolley, Kathy S. "Statistics on Adoption in the United States." *Adoption* 3, no. 1 (1993): 26–42.

Strong, Pauline Turner. "What Is an Indian Family? The Indian Child Welfare Act and the Renascence of Tribal Sovereignty." *American Studies* 46, no. 3–4 (2005): 205–31.

Sudbury, Julia, ed. *Global Lockdown: Race, Gender, and the Prison-Industrial Complex.* New York: Routledge, 2005.

Suplee, Curt. "Sex in the '90s." *Washington Post,* January 8, 1989.

Swarns, Rachel. "Study Says Government Has Improperly Detained Foreign Children." *New York Times,* June 19, 2009.

Swift, Michael. "Gay Revolutionary." *Gay Community News,* February 15–21, 1987.

Talbot, Margaret. "The Devil in the Nursery." *New York Times,* January 7, 2001.

———. "The Lost Children: What Do Tougher Detention Policies Mean for Illegal Immigrant Families." *New Yorker,* March 3, 2008.

Tate, Winifred. "Paramilitaries in Colombia." *Brown Journal of World Affairs* 8, no. 1 (2001): 163–75.

Tauber, Michelle, and Jennifer Wulff. "Angelina Adopts a Girl: And Baby Makes Three." *People,* July 18, 2005.

Taylor, Diana. *Disappearing Acts: Spectacles of Gender and Nationalism in Argentina's "Dirty War."* Durham: Duke University Press, 1997.

They Shoot Children, Don't They? Directed by Judy Jackson. London: Casa Alianza, 1991. DVD.

Thompson, Ginger. "After Losing Freedom, Some Immigrants Face Loss of Custody of their Children." *New York Times,* April 23, 2009.

———. "Court Rules for Deportee on Custody." *New York Times,* June 28, 2009.

———. "In Mexico, Children, and Promises, Unkept." *New York Times,* June 2, 1999.

Time. "Dan Quayle vs. Murphy Brown." June 1, 1992.

———. "The Saddest Epidemic." September 10, 1984.

Torpy, Sally J. "Endangered Species: Native American Women's Struggle for Their Reproductive Rights and Racial Identity." Masters thesis, University of Nebraska, 1998.

Torreira Crespo, Ramón, and José Buajasán Marrawi. *Operación Peter Pan: Un caso de guerra psicológica contra cuba*. La Habana: Editora Política, 2000.

Torres, María de los Angeles. *The Lost Apple: Operation Pedro Pan, Cuban Children in the U.S., and the Promise of a Better Future*. Boston: Beacon Press, 2003.

Trombley, Stephen. *The Right to Reproduce: A History of Coercive Sterilization*. London: Weidenfeld and Nicholson, 1988.

Trouillot, Michel Rolph. *Silencing the Past: Power and the Production of History*. Boston: Beacon Press, 1997.

Truman, Harry S. "President Truman's Statement and Directive on Displaced Persons." *New York Times*, December 23, 1945.

Unger, Steven. *The Destruction of American Indian Families*. New York: Association on American Indian Affairs, 1977.

UNICEF United States Fund. "How Trick-or-Treat for UNICEF Began." UNICEF United States Fund. http://youth.unicefusa.org/trickortreat/About/trick-or-treat-for-unicef-60-anniversary.html (accessed September 24, 2010).

Uniform Adoption Act. http://www.law.upenn.edu/bll/archives/ulc/fnact99/1990s/uaa94.htm (accessed September 24, 2010).

United Nations Children's Fund (UNICEF). "The 1950s: Era of the Mass Disease Campaign." New York: UNICEF. http://www.unicef.org/sowc96/1950s.htm.

United Nations Commission on Human Rights. *Rights of the Child: Report of the Special Rapporteur on the Sale of Children, Child Prostitution and Child Pornography, Ms. Ofelia Calcetas-Santos*. Addendum, Report on the Mission to Guatemala, January 27, 2000. E/CN.4/2000/73/Add.2. http://daccess-ods.un.org/access.nsf/Get?Open&DS=E/CN.4/2000/73/Add.2&Lang=E.

U.S. Bureau of the Census. "Statistical Brief: Housing of American Indians on Reservations—Plumbing." Washington, D.C.: Government Printing Office, 1995.

U.S. Congress. House. Committee on Ways and Means. *The Green Book: Overview of Entitlement Programs*. Washington, D.C.: U.S. Government Printing Office, 1992.

———. House. Select Committee on Children Youth and Families. *No Place to Call Home: Discarded Children in America: A Report Together with Additional and Dissenting Views*. 101st Congress, 1st sess. Washington, D.C.: U.S. Government Printing Office, 1990.

U.S. Congress. Senate. Judiciary Committee. *Hearing Before the Subcommittee to Investigate Juvenile Delinquency, Interstate Adoption Practices*. 84th Congress, 1st sess., July 15–16, 1955. Washington, D.C.: U.S. Government Printing Office, 1955.

———. Senate. Judiciary Committee. *Revolutionary Activities with the United States: The American Indian Movement: Report of the Subcommittee to Investigate the Administration of the Internal Security Act and Other Internal Security Laws*. Washington, D.C.: U.S. Government Printing Office, 1976.

———. Senate. Select Committee on Indian Affairs. *Indian Child Welfare Act of 1977: Hearing, on S. 1214, To Establish Standards for the Placement of Indian Children in Foster or Adoptive Homes, To Prevent the Breakup of Indian Families, and For Other Purposes*. 95th Congress, 1st sess., August 4, 1977. Washington, D.C.: U.S. Government Printing Office, 1977.

———. Senate. Select Committee on Indian Affairs. "Indian Child Welfare Statistical Survey, July 1976, Appendix G." *Indian Child Welfare Act of 1977: Hearing, on S. 1214, To Establish*

Standards for the Placement of Indian Children in Foster or Adoptive Homes, To Prevent the Breakup of Indian Families, and For Other Purposes. 95th Congress, 1st sess., August 4, 1977. Washington, D.C.: U.S. Government Printing Office, 1977.

———. Senate. Select Committee on Indian Affairs. "Statement of Beatrice Gentry, Chairman, Commission on Indian Affairs, Commonwealth of Massachusetts." *Indian Child Welfare Act of 1977: Hearing, on S. 1214, To Establish Standards for the Placement of Indian Children in Foster or Adoptive Homes, To Prevent the Breakup of Indian Families, and For Other Purposes.* 95th Congress, 1st sess., August 4, 1977. Washington, D.C.: U.S. Government Printing Office, 1977.

———. Senate. Select Committee on Indian Affairs. "Statement of Eric Eberhard, Navajo Nation." *Indian Child Welfare Act of 1977: Hearing, on S. 1214, To Establish Standards for the Placement of Indian Children in Foster or Adoptive Homes, To Prevent the Breakup of Indian Families, and For Other Purposes.* 95th Congress, 1st sess., August 4, 1977. Washington, D.C.: U.S. Government Printing Office, 1977.

———. Senate. Select Committee on Indian Affairs. "Statement of Raymond Butler, Acting Deputy Commissioner, Bureau of Indian Affairs." *Indian Child Welfare Act of 1977: Hearing, on S. 1214, To Establish Standards for the Placement of Indian Children in Foster or Adoptive Homes, To Prevent the Breakup of Indian Families, and For Other Purposes.* 95th Congress, 1st sess., August 4, 1977. Washington, D.C.: U.S. Government Printing Office, 1977.

———. Senate. Select Committee on Indian Affairs. "Testimony of Harold C. Brown, Commissioner of LDS Social Services / Director of Personal Welfare Services, Church of Jesus Christ of Latter-day Saints, Accompanied by Robert Barker, Council." *Indian Child Welfare Act of 1977: Hearing, on S. 1214, To Establish Standards for the Placement of Indian Children in Foster or Adoptive Homes, To Prevent the Breakup of Indian Families, and For Other Purposes.* 95th Congress, 1st sess., August 4, 1977. Washington, D.C.: U.S. Government Printing Office, 1977.

U.S. Department of Health and Human Services. Administration on Children Youth and Families. "The AFCARS Report: Interim FY 2003 Estimates as of June 2006." http://www.acf.hhs.gov/programs/cb/stats_research/afcars/tar/report10.htm (accessed September 10, 2010).

———. Administration on Children Youth and Families. "The AFCARS Report: Preliminary FY 2006 Estimates as of January 2008." http://www.acf.hhs.gov/programs/cb/stats_re search/afcars/tar/report14.htm (accessed September 10, 2010).

———. Administration for Children, Youth and Families. "Child Maltreatment 2003." http://www.acf.hhs.gov/programs/cb/pubs/cm03/index.htm (accessed September 10, 2010).

U.S. Department of Health, Education, and Welfare. Office of Human Development. *Indian Child Welfare: A State-of-the-Field Study.* Washington, D.C.: U.S. Department of Health, Education, and Welfare, 1976.

U.S. Department of Labor. Office of Policy Planning and Research. *The Negro Family: The Case for National Action.* Edited by Daniel Patrick Moynihan. Washington, D.C.: U.S. Government Printing Office, 1965.

U.S. Department of State. Bureau of Consular Affairs. "Immigrant Visas Issues to Orphans Coming to the U.S." http://web.archive.org/web/20060201023322/http://travel.state .gov/family/adoption/stats/stats_451.html (accessed Jan. 19, 2006).

———. Bureau of Consular Affairs. "Significant Source Countries of Immigrant Orphans." http://www.travel.state.gov/pdf/MultiYearTableXIII.pdf (accessed September 10, 2010).

———. Bureau of Democracy, Human Rights, and Labor. "Guatemala: Country Reports on Human Rights 2000." Washington, D.C.: State Department, 2001.

———. Office of Children's Issues. "Intercountry Adoption: Cambodia." http://adoption.sta te.gov/country/cambodia.html (accessed September 1, 2010).

———. Office of Children's Issues. "Intercountry Adoption: Total Adoptions." http://adopti on.state.gov/news/total_chart.html. (accessed September 27, 2010).

U.S. Department of Transportation. National Highway Transportation and Safety Administration. "Bicycle Helmet Use Laws." http://www.nhtsa.dot.gov/people/injury/New-fact-sheet03/BicycleHelmetUse.pdf (accessed September 24, 2010).

U.S. General Accounting Office. *Foster Care: Recent Legislation Helps States Focus on Finding Permanent Homes for Children, but Long-Standing Barriers Remain.* GAO–02–585. Washington, D.C.: U.S. Government Printing Office, 2002. http://www.gao.gov/new.items/d02585.pdf.

Uziel, Anna Paula. "Homosexuality and Adoption in Brazil." *Reproductive Health Matters* 9, no. 18 (2001): 34–42.

Van Biema, David. "The Storm over Orphanages." *Time*, December 12, 1994.

Vásquez, Claudia, and Conié Reynoso. "Migrantes, indignados." *Prensa Libre*, March 14, 2007.

Vizenor, Gerald, ed. *Survivance: Narratives of Native Presence.* Lincoln: University of Nebraska Press, 2008.

Wallace, David. "Campaigner for Children's Rights Is Put on Trial." *Times*, January 23, 2003.

Wander, Jonathan. "Love and Haiti." *Pittsburgh Magazine*, January 2009.

Warren, Andrea. *Escape from Saigon: A Vietnam War Orphan Becomes an American Boy.* New York: Farrar, Straus and Giroux, 2004.

Warren, Kay B. *Indigenous Movements and Their Critics: Pan-Maya Activism in Guatemala.* Princeton, N.J.: Princeton University Press, 1998.

Watson, Russell. "Blood Relations." *Newsweek*, March 13, 1995.

Way, John T. "The Mayan in the Mall: Development, Culture and Globalization in Guatemala, 1920–2003." PhD dissertation, Yale University, 2006.

Wayne, Leslie. "Under Fire, PBS Leader Will Leave When Contract Ends in '06." *New York Times*, February 16, 2005.

Weaver, Audrey. "From the Weaver." *Chicago Defender*, May 6, 1972.

———. "From the Weaver." *Chicago Defender*, January 20, 1973.

Weil, Richard H. "International Adoption: The Quiet Migration." *International Migration Review* 18, no. 2 (1984): 275–93.

Weiner, Tim, and Sam Dillon. "Shadowy Alliance—A Special Report; In Guatemala's Dark Heart, C.I.A. Lent Succor to Death." *New York Times*, April 2, 1995.

Wen, Patricia. "Catholic Charities Stuns State, Ends Adoptions—Gay Issue Stirred Move by Agency." *Boston Globe*, March 11, 2006.

Wen, Patricia, and Frank Phillips. "Bishops to Oppose Adoption by Gays Exemption Bid Seen from Antibias Laws." *Boston Globe*, February 16, 2006.

Westermeyer, Joseph. "The Ravage of Indian Families in Crisis." In *The Destruction of American Indian Families*, edited by Steven Unger, 47–56. New York: Association on American Indian Affairs, 1977.

In re Whiteshead. 124 N.W. 2d 694 (N.D. 1963).

Wilkerson, Isabel. "Michigan Couple Is Ordered to Return Girl, 2, to Biological Parents." *New York Times*, March 31, 1993.

Wilkinson, Daniel. *Silence on the Mountain: Stories of Terror, Betrayal, and Forgetting in Guatemala*. Boston: Houghton Mifflin, 2002.

Williams, Gareth. "Death in the Andes: Ungovernability and the Birth of Tragedy in Peru." In *Latin American Subaltern Studies Reader*, edited by Ileana Rodriguez, 260–84. Durham: Duke University Press, 2001.

Williams, Patricia. "Spare Parts, Family Values, Old Children, Cheap." In *Critical Race Feminism: A Reader*, edited by Adrien Katherine Wing, 151–58. New York: NYU Press, 1997.

Wilson, James. *The Earth Shall Weep: A History of Native America*. New York: Grove Press, 1998.

Winerip, Michael. "A Boy, His 2 Mothers and Some Unlikely Support." *New York Times*, April 19, 2006.

Wolfe, Alan. "Americans Don't Have Faith in Same-Sex Marriages, Poll Finds." *Washington Post*, August 14, 2003.

Woodley Brown, Annie, and Barbara Bailey-Etta. "An Out-of-Home Care System in Crisis: Implications for African American Children in the Child Welfare System." *Child Welfare* 46 (1997): 65–84.

Working Life. "Wages and Benefits: Real Wages (1964–2004)." http://www.workinglife .org/wiki/index.php?page=Wages+and+Benefits%3A+Real+Wages+%281964– 2004%29 (accessed September 19, 2010).

Wulczyn, F., L. Chen, and K. Hislop. *Foster Care Dynamics 2000–2005: A Report for the Multistate Foster Care Data Archive*. Chicago: Chapin Hall Center for Children, 2007.

Wunder, John. "Review: Kenneth R. Philp, *Termination Revisited: American Indians on the Trail to Self-Determination, 1933–1953*; Thomas Cowger, *the National Congress of American Indians: The Founding Years*." *American Historical Review* 106, no. 2 (2001): 600–601.

Wyman, David S. *Paper Walls: America and the Refugee Crisis, 1938–1941*. Amherst: University of Massachusetts Press, 1968.

Yellin, Jean Fagan. *Women and Sisters: The Antislavery Feminists in American Culture*. New Haven, CT: Yale University Press, 1989.

Yngvesson, Barbara. *Belonging in an Adopted World: Race, Identity, and Transnational Adoption*. Chicago: University of Chicago Press, 2010.

Yoshino, Kenji. "Too Good for Marriage." *New York Times*, July 14, 2006.

Young, Leontine. *Out of Wedlock: A Study of the Problems of the Unmarried Mother and Her Child*. New York: McGraw-Hill, 1954.

Zambito, Thomas. "Attorney's Odyssey Ends with Justice." *Record*, December 14, 1996.

Zarembo, Alan. "A Place to Call Home: The Anger, Tears and Frustrating Runarounds of a Guatemalan Adoption Case." *Newsweek*, July 15, 2002.

Zuckerman, Barry. "Effects on Parents and Children." In *When Drug Addicts Have Children*, edited by Douglas Besharov and Kristina W. Hanson, 49–63. Washington, D.C.: Child Welfare League of America/American Enterprise Institute, 1994.

Zuckerman, B., D. A. Frank, and L. Mayes. "Cocaine-Exposed Infants and Developmental Outcomes: 'Crack Kids' Revisited." Letter; Comment. *Journal of the American Medical Association* 287, no. 15 (2002): 1990–91.

Index

Laura Briggs is professor and chair of the Department
of Women, Gender, and Sexuality Studies at the
University of Massachusetts, Amherst.

Library of Congress Cataloging-in-Publication Data
Briggs, Laura, 1964–
Somebody's children : the politics of transracial and
transnational adoption / Laura Briggs.
p. cm.
Includes bibliographical references and index.
ISBN 978-0-8223-5147-4 (cloth : alk. paper)
ISBN 978-0-8223-5161-0 (pbk. : alk. paper)
1. Adoption—United States. 2. Interracial adoption—
United States. 3. Intercountry adoption—United
States. 4. Child welfare—United States. I. Title.
HV875.55.B75 2012
362.7340973—dc23
2011035893